Building Modern Active Directory

Engineering, Building, and Running Active Directory for the Next 25 Years

Evgenij Smirnov

Apress®

Building Modern Active Directory: Engineering, Building, and Running Active Directory for the Next 25 Years

Evgenij Smirnov
Berlin, Berlin, Germany

ISBN-13 (pbk): 979-8-8688-0940-8
ISBN-13 (electronic): 979-8-8688-0941-5
https://doi.org/10.1007/979-8-8688-0941-5

Copyright © 2024 by Evgenij Smirnov

This work is subject to copyright. All rights are reserved by the Publisher, whether the whole or part of the material is concerned, specifically the rights of translation, reprinting, reuse of illustrations, recitation, broadcasting, reproduction on microfilms or in any other physical way, and transmission or information storage and retrieval, electronic adaptation, computer software, or by similar or dissimilar methodology now known or hereafter developed.

Trademarked names, logos, and images may appear in this book. Rather than use a trademark symbol with every occurrence of a trademarked name, logo, or image we use the names, logos, and images only in an editorial fashion and to the benefit of the trademark owner, with no intention of infringement of the trademark.

The use in this publication of trade names, trademarks, service marks, and similar terms, even if they are not identified as such, is not to be taken as an expression of opinion as to whether or not they are subject to proprietary rights.

While the advice and information in this book are believed to be true and accurate at the date of publication, neither the authors nor the editors nor the publisher can accept any legal responsibility for any errors or omissions that may be made. The publisher makes no warranty, express or implied, with respect to the material contained herein.

Managing Director, Apress Media LLC: Welmoed Spahr
Acquisitions Editor: Smriti Srivastava
Development Editor: Laura Berendson
Editorial Assistant: Kripa Joseph

Cover designed by eStudioCalamar

Cover image designed by Freepik (www.freepik.com)

Distributed to the book trade worldwide by Springer Science+Business Media New York, 1 New York Plaza, Suite 4600, New York, NY 10004-1562, USA. Phone 1-800-SPRINGER, fax (201) 348-4505, e-mail orders-ny@springer-sbm.com, or visit www.springeronline.com. Apress Media, LLC is a California LLC and the sole member (owner) is Springer Science + Business Media Finance Inc (SSBM Finance Inc). SSBM Finance Inc is a **Delaware** corporation.

For information on translations, please e-mail booktranslations@springernature.com; for reprint, paperback, or audio rights, please e-mail bookpermissions@springernature.com.

Apress titles may be purchased in bulk for academic, corporate, or promotional use. eBook versions and licenses are also available for most titles. For more information, reference our Print and eBook Bulk Sales web page at http://www.apress.com/bulk-sales.

Any source code or other supplementary material referenced by the author in this book is available to readers on GitHub. For more detailed information, please visit https://www.apress.com/gp/services/source-code.

If disposing of this product, please recycle the paper

Table of Contents

About the Author xv
About the Technical Reviewer xvii
Acknowledgments xix
Introduction xxi

Chapter 1: Problems with AD 1
    1.1 Structural Challenges 3
        1.1.1 A Domain Controller Does More Than "Control" the Domain 3
        1.1.2 AD Is Self-managed 3
        1.1.3 AD Is Always a Snapshot 4
        1.1.4 No Tracking of AD's Own Activity 5
        1.1.5 AD Has Lots of Hardcoded Behaviors 6
    1.2 Questionable Defaults 6
    1.3 The Misunderstood AD 9
        1.3.1 AD Is Not IAM 11
        1.3.2 AD Is Not Configuration Management 12
        1.3.3 AD Is Probably Not Your Enterprise Directory Either 13
        1.3.4 The Misunderstood Demand for Flexibility 14
    1.4 Patterns and Anti-patterns 15
    1.5 Summary 18

TABLE OF CONTENTS

Chapter 2: A Modern AD 21
2.1 Modern Work Requirements 22
2.2 Directory Security 24
2.3 Modern AD Tenets 26
2.3.1 Security First 27
2.3.2 Automate All the Way...27
2.3.3 Stick to the Policies 28
2.3.4 Prepare for Exceptions 29
2.3.5 Prepare for Change...30
2.3.6 Prepare for Disaster 31
2.4 Lookup, Authentication, Authorization, and Configuration 33
2.5 A Modern AD Is Hybrid – Cloud Integration 34
2.6 Summary...37

Chapter 3: Engineering Topology 39
3.1 Site Autonomy – If a WAN Link Goes Down..............................40
3.2 Forest and Domain Topologies 44
3.2.1 Anatomy of a Multi-domain Forest 45
3.2.2 Motivation for the Multi-domain Anti-pattern................46
3.2.3 Multi-domain Forest: Extreme Anti-patterns 50
3.2.4 Motivation of the Multi-forest Pattern 52
3.2.5 Challenges of a Multi-forest User Base 53
3.3 Naming Conventions for Domains...55
3.3.1 Externally Resolvable AD Domains 58
3.3.2 Disjoint DNS Namespaces 58
3.3.3 Other Naming Conventions Involved in AD Topology 59
3.4 Sites and Subnets 60
3.4.1 Change Convergence Time 63
3.4.2 RID Master Visibility..63

TABLE OF CONTENTS

- 3.4.3 PDC Emulator Visibility 64
- 3.4.4 Old and New Defaults 65
- 3.4.5 The Guiding Principles for Site Topology Engineering 66
- 3.4.6 Site Name and Location Attribute 68
- 3.4.7 Sites and Subnets in a Multi-forest Organization 69

3.5 AD Distribution and Placement 71
- 3.5.1 Domain Controller Distribution 71
- 3.5.2 Global Catalog Placement 72
- 3.5.3 Application Partitions 74
- 3.5.4 FSMO Role Distribution 76

3.6 Read-Only Domain Controllers 79
- 3.6.1 If RODCs Are Justified 80

3.7 Administration (Red) Forest 81

3.8 Modern Design Defaults 82
- 3.8.1 From the Inside Out 83
- 3.8.2 First Sanity Check: Spoke-hub Connectivity 86
- 3.8.3 Risky Sites 88
- 3.8.4 Satellite Sites 88
- 3.8.5 Site Links and Bridges 89
- 3.8.6 A Word on Firewalls 91
- 3.8.7 Populating the Location Attribute 91

3.9 Summary 92

Chapter 4: Engineering Lookup 93

4.1 Disclosing Information vs. Preventing Reconnaissance 94
- 4.1.1 Starting from Scratch 95
- 4.1.2 AD As an Enterprise Address Book 97

TABLE OF CONTENTS

- 4.2 Structures, Permissions, and Defaults 98
  - 4.2.1 How Many OUs Does a Domain Need? 99
  - 4.2.2 Permissions on AD Objects 103
  - 4.2.3 The Case of Replication Rights 105
  - 4.2.4 Everyone Can See Everything in AD? 106
- 4.3 Defining Visibility and Hiding the Crown Jewels in Plain Sight 109
  - 4.3.1 Can't Abuse What They Can't See 110
  - 4.3.2 Hiding Objects from View – List Mode 112
  - 4.3.3 Removing Pre-Windows 2000 Compatible Access 113
  - 4.3.4 Invisible Privileged Identities – the Evil and the Good 115
  - 4.3.5 Changing Schema Permissions and Default SDs – Worth the Hassle? 119
- 4.4 Name Resolution and Service Location 121
  - 4.4.1 There's More to Life Than Just DNS 121
  - 4.4.2 DNS and Reconnaissance 123
  - 4.4.3 Other Ways to Bulk Access DNS Data 125
  - 4.4.4 External DNS and Its Abuse 126
  - 4.4.5 DNS Record Creation 127
  - 4.4.6 DNS Security Enhancements 130
- 4.5 Lookup in Perimeter Networks 131
  - 4.5.1 DNS Lookup from the Edge 131
  - 4.5.2 LDAP Querying and Binding 132
- 4.6 Modern Defaults 133
  - 4.6.1 Restrict Read Permissions 134
  - 4.6.2 Provide Visibility to Non-privileged Users 135
  - 4.6.3 Provide Visibility to Computers 136
  - 4.6.4 What Other Objects Have to Be Visible? 137
  - 4.6.5 Restrict Users' Own Visibility 137

TABLE OF CONTENTS

    4.6.6 Restrict DNS Access 138

    4.6.7 Provide DMZ Access If Needed 139

  4.7 Summary 140

Chapter 5: Engineering Authentication 141

  5.1 Authentication Protocols in AD 143

    5.1.1 NTLM: "Prove Who You Are" 144

    5.1.2 Kerberos: "Here's Who I Am" 147

  5.2 Engineering Kerberos for Security and Usability 151

    5.2.1 AD Authentication the Engineer's Way 152

    5.2.2 Protecting from Credential Harvesting 155

    5.2.3 Implementing a Basic Authentication Policy for Tier 0 157

    5.2.4 Next-Level Harvesting Protection: Credential Guard 161

    5.2.5 Protecting Against Service Ticket Abuse 162

    5.2.6 Strengthening Kerberos Encryption 166

    5.2.7 Protecting Against Stealing Valid Service Tickets 169

    5.2.8 Strong Protection for Interactive Administrator Sessions 171

  5.3 Getting Rid of NTLM 173

    5.3.1 An NTLM-less AD Environment 173

    5.3.2 First Things First: Fix What You Know 177

    5.3.3 Start Logging Where It's Easiest 180

    5.3.4 Down the Rabbit Hole 183

    5.3.5 When You're Done with NTLM… 184

  5.4 Service and Task Accounts 184

    5.4.1 Service Account Typology 185

    5.4.2 Making Sense of "Service Account Sprawl" 188

    5.4.3 Identifying Service Accounts 193

    5.4.4 Minimizing the Risk of Kerberoasting 195

TABLE OF CONTENTS

- 5.5 Computer Accounts 196
- 5.6 From Domain Join to Domain Takeover 198
  - 5.6.1 The Default Behavior 198
  - 5.6.2 Let an Admin Do the Work – but Be on Your Toes 201
  - 5.6.3 The Joy of Ownership 201
  - 5.6.4 The Modern Domain Join Process 202
  - 5.6.5 More Local Magic 204
- 5.7 Tickets from the Cloud 205
- 5.8 Certificate-Based Authentication 207
  - 5.8.1 Next-Level Privileged Access 209
- 5.9 Engineering Trusts 211
  - 5.9.1 Dimensions of a Trust 212
  - 5.9.2 Trust Anti-patterns 214
  - 5.9.3 Fortifying a One-Way Trust 214
- 5.10 Authentication in Perimeter Networks 215
  - 5.10.1 Logon from the Perimeter 216
  - 5.10.2 User Access from the Wild Wide World 217
- 5.11 Modern Defaults 219
  - 5.11.1 Password Policy Defaults 219
  - 5.11.2 Kerberos Defaults 220
  - 5.11.3 Privileged Access Defaults 221
  - 5.11.4 Session Protection Defaults 221
  - 5.11.5 Service Account Defaults 221
  - 5.11.6 Trust Defaults 222
  - 5.11.7 PKI Defaults 222
- 5.12 Summary 222

TABLE OF CONTENTS

Chapter 6: Engineering Authorization 225

6.1 Working with Groups and Object Hierarchies...226
6.1.1 Nested Groups vs. Propagated Permissions...227
6.1.2 The Much-Dreaded Token Bloat..231
6.1.3 Enumerating Group Memberships...233

6.2 Role-Based Access Control (RBAC) Models 235
6.2.1 AGDLP – Lots and Lots of Groups 237
6.2.2 AGDLP, AGUDLP, or AUDLP?...240
6.2.3 Leveraging Distribution Groups 240

6.3 Delegating Administrative Tasks 241
6.3.1 Delegating AD Administration: Tier 0 243
6.3.2 Delegating AD Administration: Lower Tiers.....................................244
6.3.3 Delegating Group Policy Administration 244
6.3.4 Delegating DNS Administration 245
6.3.5 Delegating Server Administration...246
6.3.6 Delegating Client Administration 246

6.4 Modern Defaults...247
6.4.1 RBAC Is Not Always the Answer 247
6.4.2 Ask Where They Get Authorization Info From.....................................248
6.4.3 File Servers Are Still at the Core of Most Authorization Frameworks...248
6.4.4 Administration Is Different..249

6.5 Summary...250

Chapter 7: Engineering Configuration 251

7.1 AD and Configuration Management 251
7.1.1 Configuration Delivery – What's in the Box? 252

7.2 Engineering Group Policy..255
7.2.1 Factors Influencing Group Policy Engineering...................................256

ix

TABLE OF CONTENTS

- 7.2.2 Group Policy Security Considerations 259
- 7.2.3 The Right Tools for the Job 260
- 7.2.4 Creating the Framework 261
- 7.3 Advanced Group Policy Techniques 266
  - 7.3.1 Do Not Use the Central Store 266
  - 7.3.2 Leverage Starter GPOs 267
  - 7.3.3 Only Link GPOs to Sites If Absolutely Necessary 267
  - 7.3.4 Use Loopback Correctly 268
  - 7.3.5 Policy Caching and Wait for Network 269
- 7.4 Engineering Domain Controllers 270
  - 7.4.1 Domain Controller Sizing 271
  - 7.4.2 Domain Controller Networking 272
  - 7.4.3 PDC Emulator 273
  - 7.4.4 All Other Writeable DCs 275
  - 7.4.5 RODCs 278
- 7.5 Securing Domain Controllers 278
  - 7.5.1 SYSVOL Share Hardening 279
  - 7.5.2 LSA Protection 280
  - 7.5.3 BitLocker on DCs 281
- 7.6 Domain Join as Priority One Design Area 282
  - 7.6.1 Know Your Provisioning Scenarios 282
  - 7.6.2 Administrator Entering Credentials 284
  - 7.6.3 Automated Domain Join of a VM by a Third-Party System 286
  - 7.6.4 Automated Domain Join You Can Influence Directly 286
  - 7.6.5 Monitoring and Cleanup 288
  - 7.6.6 Removal of Default Local Group Nestings 289

TABLE OF CONTENTS

7.7 Default Containers 290

    7.7.1 "Intended Accidental" Object Creation 291

7.8 Summary 292

Chapter 8: Engineering Administration 293

8.1 Privileged Access 295

    8.1.1 Interactive Administration 296

    8.1.2 Remoting Protocols 300

    8.1.3 Remote but Interactive 303

    8.1.4 Break-Glass Accounts 306

    8.1.5 Workstations and Jumphosts 307

    8.1.6 A PAW Needs Its Claws 311

    8.1.7 A Word on "Cloud PAW" 313

8.2 Delegation of Privileges While Reducing the Attack Surface 314

    8.2.1 Granular Permissions, Red Forest, and Task Recurrence ... 315

    8.2.2 Delegating AD Administration 317

    8.2.3 Delegating GPO Administration 319

    8.2.4 Delegating DNS Administration 322

    8.2.5 Delegating PKI Administration and Certificate Issuance 323

8.3 Using Automation 325

    8.3.1 On Schedule and on Demand 325

    8.3.2 Storing and retrieving credentials 328

    8.3.3 Do Not Compete with Your Own Automation 331

    8.3.4 Prevent Automation Sprawl 331

    8.3.5 Sign Your Scripts 332

8.4 Using Desired State 332

8.5 Summary 334

TABLE OF CONTENTS

Chapter 9: Building a Modern AD **335**

9.1 Fast-Tracking Design 336
9.1.1 Gather Only the Most Significant Requirements 336
9.1.2 Create a Design Proposal 339

9.2 Secure from the Beginning 340
9.2.1 Deal with Insecure Applications You Know About 341
9.2.2 Start with Proper Delegation Early 342
9.2.3 When to Introduce the Red Forest 345

9.3 Creating Prerequisites 345
9.3.1 Prepare and Maintain a Test Environment 346
9.3.2 Storage and Backup 347
9.3.3 Permanent and Temporary Networks 349
9.3.4 Time Source 350

9.4 Preparing for Change 351
9.4.1 Changes in Requirements vs. Changes in Infrastructure ... 352
9.4.2 New Technology 353

9.5 Preparing for Disaster 356
9.5.1 Disaster-Resilient Design Options 356
9.5.2 A Special Kind of Disaster 358

9.6 Deploying a Modern AD in a Secure Manner 359
9.6.1 Remote Seeding Cells 360
9.6.2 Red Forest and PKI 361

9.7 Putting AD into Production 363
9.7.1 Onboarding Applications 363
9.7.2 Onboarding Users 365

9.8 Summary 366

TABLE OF CONTENTS

Chapter 10: Operating a Modern AD 369

10.1 Day-to-Day Operations 369
10.1.1 Battling Configuration Drift 370
10.1.2 Implementing Changes in Topology 373

10.2 Incorporating New Technology 374
10.2.1 Changes in Platform Technology Foundational to AD 374
10.2.2 Exceptional Application Requirements 375
10.2.3 At the End of the Lifecycle 378

10.3 Security Operations 379
10.3.1 Ongoing Systems Hardening 380
10.3.2 Supporting Security Scans and Pentests 380

10.4 Backup and Restore 382
10.4.1 Anti-patterns Galore 382
10.4.2 The Case of AD Restore 385
10.4.3 Not Everything Is Stored in the Database 387
10.4.4 A Restore Is the Only Proof That a Backup Exists 389
10.4.5 How Many DCs Should You Back Up? 390
10.4.6 Is There Operational Value in WSB Backups? 392

10.5 Disaster Recovery 393
10.5.1 AD Disaster Typology 101 394
10.5.2 AD Disaster Recovery Anti-patterns 396
10.5.3 AD Disaster Recovery as Part of a Global DR Effort 398
10.5.4 Disaster Recovery in a Hybrid AD 399

10.6 Functional Monitoring 403
10.6.1 Monitoring AD Health 404
10.6.2 Designing Tier 0 Monitoring 405

xiii

TABLE OF CONTENTS

10.7 Security Monitoring..408
    10.7.1 Attack Surface Monitoring...408
    10.7.2 Attack Path Analysis 409
    10.7.3 Using Functional Monitoring for Security Monitoring 410
    10.7.4 Tapping into Your SOC's Behavior-Based Monitoring........410
10.8 Summary..411

Chapter 11: Transitioning to a Modern AD................................413

11.1 In Situ Modernization vs. Migration 415
    11.1.1 Coexistence Is the Real Challenge 416
    11.1.2 What Is "Migrated"?...418
    11.1.3 User First or Application First?...420
    11.1.4 Application Is King 423
11.2 In Situ Modernization 425
    11.2.1 The Case of Intraforest Restructuring..............................427
11.3 "Rejuvenation Migration"..428
11.4 Mergers and Acquisitions – Migrating into Existing Infrastructure...........429
    11.4.1 Anatomy of an (AD) Merger 429
    11.4.2 Divestment from the Previous Owners' Point of View 432
11.5 Migrating People and Processes Along with Systems 435
11.6 Summary..436

Chapter 12: Conclusion..439

Appendix A: Glossary..443

Appendix B: Ten Immutable Laws of Security 471

Appendix C: Ten Immutable Laws of Security Administration..........473

Appendix D: Internet Sources 475

Index..479

About the Author

Evgenij Smirnov has 30 years of experience in IT and IT security consulting. Besides directory services and groupware, he has been and is still active in the virtualization and platform management space. One of his greatest passions is PowerShell, where he is a regular community contributor and Microsoft Most Valuable Professional (MVP). After leaving consulting to assume a position with Semperis, joining a team of the industry's foremost Active Directory experts, he decided to share his AD-related experience, valued by so many customers over the years, and author this book. You can reach him via @cj_berlin on Twitter (X), @cj-berlin.bsky.social on BlueSky, and evgenijsmirnov on LinkedIn.

About the Technical Reviewer

Sourabh Mishra is an entrepreneur, developer, speaker, author, corporate trainer, and animator. He is a Microsoft guy; he is very passionate about Microsoft technologies and a true .Net Warrior. Sourabh started his career when he was just 15 years old. He's loved computers from childhood. His programming experience includes C/C++, Asp.Net, C#, Vb.net, WCF, Sqlserver, Entity Framework, MVC, Web API, Azure, Jquery, Highcharts, and Angular. He is actively involved in Devops activities and provides solutions for different teams. Sourabh has been awarded a Most Valuable Professional (MVP) status. He has the zeal to learn new technologies, sharing his knowledge on several online community forums.

He is the author of *Practical Highcharts with Angular*, a book by Apress.

He is the founder of "IECE Digital" and "Sourabh Mishra Notes," an online knowledge-sharing platform where one can learn new technologies very easily and comfortably.

You can reach him on YouTube (`https://www.youtube.com/c/sourabhmishranotes`) and Twitter (X) (`https://twitter.com/sourabh_mishra1`).

Acknowledgments

Sharing knowledge is one of the greatest perks of our profession. The path that led me to writing this book began in the 1990s, and its beginnings have been rather rocky – the budding German IT community was a pretty rough patch back in the day if you did not know certain people personally (which, at that time, I didn't). It was not until the early 2000s that I discovered a "home away from home" on the Minasi R&D Technical Forum. My first and biggest thanks go to Mark Minasi for being the cornerstone and the glue, along with all the wonderful people who were the main contributors to that community. Willem Kasdorp, whose bottomless Active Directory knowledge always drove me to learn more about the subject and who demonstrated the engineer's approach to AD problems time and time again. Joe McGlynn and Tim Bolton, who both made the community the warm and welcoming place that it was and who remain good friends to this day. I cannot list everybody here, but if you were active on the Minasi Forum around 2009, know you are not forgotten.

The European PowerShell conference (PSConfEU) got me into public speaking and introduced me to the PowerShell community at large, for which my eternal gratitude goes to Dr. Tobias Weltner, Jeffrey Snover, Rob Sewell, Gael Colas, and Aleksandar Nikolic. Rubbing shoulders with the PowerShell folks helps keep my thinking critical, flexible, and outside the box. Instant problem solvers like Mathias Jessen and Friedrich Weinmann have always been an example in finding practical approaches to a new problem – something that resonates deeply with my own background as a physicist.

ACKNOWLEDGMENTS

When writing about a 25-year-old technology, the author inevitably ends up standing on the shoulders of giants. Books published early in the Active Directory lifecycle by Sakari Kouti, Mika Seitsonen, Jeremy Moskowitz, Guido Grillenmeier, Joe Richards, Brian Desmond, Joe Kaplan, Ryan Dunn, Brian Komar, and many others still are valuable sources of knowledge and will remain so as long as AD is around.

Countless experts have provided little tidbits of knowledge over the years in the form of online publications, blog posts, videos, or conference talks. Jorge de Almeida Pinto, Andrea Pierini, Elad Shamir, Sean Metcalf, Jens Künzler, Will Schroeder, Lee Christensen, Uwe Gradenegger, Sapir Federovsky, and many, many others I cannot list here contributed to our collective pool of Active Directory and security knowledge we can now all dip into, and this book is no exception. Many of these original concepts became "accepted wisdom" over the years, and since the Internet has already started forgetting and keeps doing so at an alarming pace, tracing the original source of a particular bit of knowledge is not always possible.

Last but not least, I thank my wife, Walerija Weiser, for her unyielding support and seemingly endless patience. A special "thank you" and a big scratch behind the ears belong to Lumi and Dina for reminding me every day that IT is not as important as we may sometimes think it is and that the simple things in life keep us healthy and happy. I hope this book will give you some quality time back, dear reader, by providing answers it took me 25 years to find on my own.

Introduction

A "modern" Active Directory? Aren't we talking about the decades-old and inherently insecure Microsoft identity technology that is always mentioned when there has been a spectacular data breach? The one that Microsoft itself is trying to put out to pasture and replace by the "truly modern" and much more secure Entra ID (formerly known as "Azure Active Directory")? The one Windows Server role that arguably got the least developer love of all the major features of the product in recent years?

That's the one. And if the experience of the last 25 years is anything to go by, we'll still have Active Directory power on-premises identity landscapes 25 years from now. Some of the peculiarities of AD will probably be amended by Microsoft in the years and decades to come; some have been fixed already or are being actively worked on as I write these lines. But the bad reputation AD has acquired since its release is only partly Microsoft's fault. It's always been a "team effort" that led to unstable, insecure or otherwise undesired configurations. The most important members of this "team" are, besides Microsoft itself,

- Architects who designed the environment, in some cases 20 or 25 years ago. These designs have often not been revisited since their inception, while both the product and its usage in the organization have evolved.
- Administrators who maintain the directory landscape, often using decades-old management paradigms and tooling, which, by the way, is not always a bad thing.

- Third parties who provide hardware and software products that integrate with AD. These are often overlooked in the early stages of AD design or redesign; however, these systems are of extreme importance, and we will talk about them constantly throughout the book. The designation "third party" includes Microsoft product groups outside of Windows Server.

- End users who adopted certain behaviors when dealing with identity, authentication, and authorization in their daily jobs. I am being deliberately vague here about what those undesired behaviors are, since both "too modern" approaches, like expecting identity to be secure by design, and "too old-fashioned" ones, like reusing one's passwords for every service, can be detrimental to security.

To survive the next 25 years without a major disaster, cyber or otherwise, we need all parts of our team to work towards the common goal of combining modern approaches to AD architecture and administration with modern paradigms in user behavior and third party integration. So yes, there **is** such a thing as a "modern AD," but achieving this state is a people challenge as much as it is a technological one. This is what this book is about.

Design vs. Engineering

The notion of "AD design" invokes mixed feelings in many IT professionals who have gone through this process – either on the customer side of the table or as consultants doing the design, or maybe even both in the course of their career. Enormous amounts of time have been spent in design sessions throughout the industry – more often than not with very little output to show for it except some paperwork. And even the paperwork that is generated does not always survive the first encounter with reality, which leads to tossing the paperwork overboard and just building the system the way implementers intended it to be built from the beginning, based on their experience and preferences, design be damned.

This has been my experience in many AD architecture and transformation projects as well. I have seen this happen in small businesses with a couple of hundred seats, and also in complex, large organizations spread all over the globe. My friend and mentor Mark Minasi said in a conference talk around 2008: *"Part of it is my fault, people like me. Part of it is Microsoft's fault, because Microsoft is focussed on big clients, and they're saying 'design, design, design, design.'"* However, in all but the smallest implementations, the chaotic approach to implementing Active Directory usually results in an environment that is not future-proof, unmanageable, and, in some cases, not performant or resilient enough to serve the needs of the organization. How, then, can we find a middle way between "design for design's sake" and the "creative chaos"?

One part of the problem is that, while there usually is a "driver" for an AD design or transformation initiative, organizations are often incapable of translating this "driver" (a merger with another company, a recent security incident, ongoing problems with mission-critical systems where AD has been identified as the culprit, the list can go on forever!) into a set of requirements that are actually implementable using the technology at hand. Professional requirements engineers, in the rare cases such expertise ends up being called upon to assist an AD project, may find themselves in an unusual situation: instead of providing a framework for selecting a technology to fulfill organizational requirements, they have to work within the confines of a technology already pre-selected and not necessarily familiar to them. To make things even worse, some of the requirements come from within the technology itself, making them invisible to everyone but the AD experts participating in the project.

INTRODUCTION

In this book, we will be making a clear distinction between "Design" and "Engineering" and focussing on the latter. Design is about formulating requirements, while engineering is about fulfilling them. Design is about naming conventions, number of users, and the geographical distribution of both consumers of directory services and the teams tasked with managing them – in short, things that neither architects nor implementation consultants can do anything about. Engineering, on the other hand, is about security, reliability, usability, and performance. Very few of the requirements we'll have to engineer solutions for come from design. Most of them are either intrinsic or imposed by the third parties we mentioned in the last section.

We will talk about how much design a modern AD really needs in Chapter 9, "Building a Modern AD."

What Is This Book?

Dozens of books have been written about Active Directory and related topics like Group Policy or Certificate Services in the course of the last 25 years. Most of them grace my bookshelf today, more than a meter of compressed knowledge, most of it still valid. Yet there remains a gap that I believe deserves to be filled, and this book is an attempt to do so.

Most of the specialized books on AD fall into one of two categories:

- "Cookbooks" that provide "The How" – ready-to-run recipes for concrete tasks, usually without explaining what it is that led to these tasks landing on your desk because it is expected that you know the rationale already

- "Internals" books that explain in great detail "The What" – the inner workings of particular AD features (or even Windows Server features that are utilized by AD, like file sharing or VSS)

Then there are numerous non-specialized Windows Server books that will cover AD as a subset of the functionality of the product, much like they cover File Services or Hyper-V. They will tell you what AD is and what the main components are that comprise it. Last but not least, there are several excellent programming references for developers out there. These are mostly rather dated but, since Active Directory has not changed all that much, by no means outdated. If you understand C# and crave more detailed knowledge, one of these could be a nice complement for your "internals" type book.

What none of those books will teach you is "The Why" of engineering and operating an enterprise directory service within the requirements both of the organization (including 3rd party systems the organization may insist on running) and the generally accepted security standards and practices. It is expected that you can somehow correlate all those different requirements and translate them into well-defined technical tasks. It is then with these tasks that the "internals" books will help you optimize and refine your implementation, while the "cookbooks" will provide screenshots and script code to expedite the execution. The book you're now holding in your hands takes you a step back and helps you make the engineering decisions that bridge the gap between the high-level design and fine-grained implementational guidance.

This is not to say that this book will leave you with a full whiteboard but an empty datacenter. You may fully expect to see screenshots and PowerShell code snippets strewn across the length of the book. You will also find entire scripts linked in the References section, crafted both by the author and various knowledgeable third parties out there.

You probably already noticed that there is no chapter in this book dedicated to security. This is because security and identity are inseparably interwoven, so that every part of our engineering effort includes a security aspect by default. When we speak about modern AD being able to support your identity infrastructure for 25 years to come, its ability to withstand more and more sophisticated attacks we are seeing evolve every day plays

INTRODUCTION

a major part. You are probably getting AD hardening recommendations every day in your inbox or on social media. The problem with hardening against a single attack vector is that it's usually a "small" measure, both in terms of the amount of work needed and its positive effect on the attack surface. However, these "small" actions tend to have big consequences if deployed into live environments, which causes administrators to chalk the attack vector up as a risk rather than implement the hardening measure. The "engineering" approach of this book introduces implementation paradigms rather than separate measures so that 1:1 mapping of our suggestions to, say, MITRE ATT&CK TTPs will rarely be possible.

Who Is This Book For?

The ideal reader of this book, the one peer group that I believe will potentially benefit from it the most, is an Active Directory administrator with several years of experience who is currently pivoting into consulting, architecture, or security. But an enterprise architect or a security architect may also find inspiration in these pages if on-premises or hybrid identity systems fall under their purview. A staff AD manager who has to work with system integrators, security vendors, and consultants will probably find this book useful for cross-checking both design and implementation advice from these third parties. In many AD implementations and migrations I have been part of over the last decades, I would have wished that my counterparts on the customer side had read this book before engaging with me. In a way, this book is my belated gift to my former clients' AD staff.

Most of this book is deliberately written assuming a "greenfield" implementation. I appreciate that most projects are not done in a sterile environment but rather in a live situation where there are real-world constraints both on the technical and on the people side. However, the greenfield assumption allows us to tune out the two sentences that will certainly kill any constructive discussion in its cradle, the ones that played a significant part in my decision to leave consulting: **"it can't be done"** and **"it can't be done in our organization."** On a green field, everything that is possible technically and makes sense from the security and usability standpoint is doable, so let's engineer a modern AD in a best possible way and then convince the skeptics that it can be done, even in our organization. We will cover transitioning to a modern AD and integrating its concepts into an existing environment in Chapter 11.

If you are not working for a large multinational corporation or a government organization, some of the suggestions in this book might strike you as "oversized" or even as "overkill." I appreciate that there is a sweet spot where the complexity necessary to provide secure and reliable identity infrastructure equals the complexity of the environment being managed, and every bit of added complexity beyond that point is uneconomical. To accommodate these reservations, in this book we will differentiate between "a small business" and an "enterprise." However, this distinction will not be based purely on size or the number of "seats" but rather on the complexity of the management organization itself. To place your particular organization correctly, try to imagine your ideal IT management infrastructure and ask yourself these questions:

- Can more than two persons within your IT be trusted with Tier 0 administration, both from the trustworthiness and knowledge standpoint?

- Must, for whatever reason, there be more than two persons *permanently* trusted with Tier 0 administration?

- Will there have to be more than one physical location where both Tier 0 systems and Tier 0 administrators are found?

If you had to answer "yes" at least once, you qualify as "enterprise," as far as this book is concerned!

INTRODUCTION

A Word on "Best Practice"

This book is about providing technological solutions for problems that are only in part of technical nature. Many questions you will be asked when engineering an AD organization are political, commercial, or behavioral ones. There will always be many possible, formally correct answers to each of these questions, several answers that can claim to be technically feasible, and usually even more than one "good" answer. Therefore, you should not expect this book to provide "definitive" answers or "best practices," nor is the author a "guru" or "the world's foremost expert" on those matters.

What you can expect, however, are solutions that

- Will work under the described circumstances
- Ensure optimal security and good availability of the overall environment
- Have proven to be actionable in multiple real-world settings

If a particular approach outlined here differs from how you've been taught to do it, it does not mean that you, your mentors, or the author are "wrong." There probably just are multiple solutions to the same problem. If you're ready to accept the tenets of "modern AD," all I ask is that you do not reject this book's suggestions outright just because you've never done it this way before!

The Five "Active Directories"

This book is about "Active Directory." However, this moniker does not belong to a single product but rather to a large family of identity and security technologies found in Windows Server. As I write these words in late 2023, Microsoft is finalizing the process of renaming its cloud-based identity service known as "Azure Active Directory" to "Entra ID," so that from 2024 onwards, everything "AD" is only to be found on-premises again. These overarching names are a part of Microsoft's naming tradition. Right now, new "Copilots" are popping up like mushrooms after a summer rain; a couple of years ago, it was all "Defenders." Old timers may recall the "Forefront" era of Microsoft security products, and even the "System Center" suite lost its first member, the Configuration Manager, to Intune two years ago.

Compared to these, "Active Directory" has been a fixture for over 20 years. Apart from "Azure AD" that came and went, there are five roles comprising the suite:

Feature	Description
AD Directory Services	ADDS was the first "Active Directory" technology consisting of an LDAP-conformant directory service, Kerberos authentication facility, and Windows DNS integration. It is the main topic of this book.
AD Lightweight Directory Services	Originally known as "Active Directory Application Mode" (ADAM) and being delivered as a separate download rather than a Windows Server role, ADLDS provides the LDAP part of AD, including the extensible schema and multimaster replication ability, without the Kerberos part or DNS integration. We will see several uses of ADLDS throughout this book, mostly for providing AD lookups to untrustworthy systems.
AD Certificate Services	Although parts of Microsoft's PKI implementation predate AD (there was a Certificate Server in the Option Pack of Windows NT), it's with ADCS that Windows Server can provide a wide spectrum of Enterprise PKI services to a variety of systems, including smart card authentication in Active Directory itself! It is mainly the smart card authentication in Kerberos that earned ADCS its place in this book.

(*continued*)

INTRODUCTION

Feature	Description
AD Federation Services	A later addition to the family, ADFS provides federated (claim-based) authentication to almost any application designed to consume it.
AD Rights Management Services	The ability to easily share information and documents via email or portable media, thus circumventing any permissions that may have been in place for those documents within their home organization, called for providing a Digital Rights Management facility within the documents themselves, and ADRMS is Microsoft's answer to that requirement. We will not be talking about it in this book, because it does not really enhance or augment AD, although it does integrate with ADCS. RMS is still part of Windows Server, but in the real world out there it has been all but replaced, rather successfully, by "Microsoft Purview Information Protection."

There have been several pivotal moments in the development history of AD, which is why in this book we will measure the passage of time not in years but rather in Windows Server versions that brought these changes with them, like Kerberos AES encryption in 2008R2 or Authentication Policies in 2012R2. The calendar year in which these changes materialized in a particular organization may vary, in some cases rather significantly. In 2024, I could name several companies that are still living in the Server 2003 world.

AD and "The Cloud"

How can we be so sure that Active Directory will remain relevant for years and decades to come? The answer is twofold. First, Active Directory will be *available* for many years still: Windows Server 2025 is going to be released in late 2024 or early 2025; it will most probably have the usual ten-year support lifecycle, and all five ADs are part of the package, Directory

Services even receiving new features for the first time since 2016! There has been zero communication about deprecating any of these features, so if Windows Server release history is anything to go by, the earliest AD that can be put on notice is 2028, and if Microsoft decides to really go through with it, it will be removed from Server 2031. This, however, is very unlikely to happen.

The second part of the answer is even more important: If you ask anybody who advocates getting rid of AD what should ultimately replace it, the answer is never "MicroFocus eDirectory" or "openLDAP + Shibboleth," although all three products are being used with great success in private and public organizations. No, the answer is always "The Cloud," which, since we are looking at the Microsoft ecosystem, ultimately means Azure AD, which became Entra ID in 2023. And, if 100% of your applications are in the cloud or at least support cloud-based authentication and authorization (i.e., SAML), you absolutely should join your workstations directly to Azure AD, break synchronization, and shut down your AD. However, there will always be IT environments where having the most basic services like name resolution and authentication off-premises is not an option:

- Facilities that have to continue functioning if or when their Internet uplinks should go offline: hospitals, other critical infrastructure, manufacturing plants, and the like.

- Organizations or their divisions not allowed to have any digital contact with the outside world. Handling classified and sensitive information can fall into this category, despite all attempts at establishing cloud services considered "secure enough" even for these use cases.

INTRODUCTION

- Organizations whose economic survival depends on applications or systems that do not support cloud-native authentication protocols. In an ideal world, these mission-critical systems would be declared "technical debt" and cleaned out as soon as possible. In reality, it is these very systems that probably have the longest lifecycle in the entire environment!

No one can predict what the IT landscape in your organization is going to look like 25 years from now. We will probably see some sort of "hybrid" deployment in most cases. Now, in 2024, Microsoft is working on providing deployment alternatives where the cloud part of a hybrid identity will be the leading one. At the end of the day, this may even be a good thing for the on-premises part, because by using technologies like password writeback, password quality control, and self-service password reset in Entra ID, hybrid customers already get functionality Microsoft failed to provide (or chose not to provide) natively for on-premises AD.

Like all tight integrations, hybrid identity has risks of its own, risks that you, as the maintainer of a modern AD infrastructure, are going to have to minimize by good engineering and mitigate by good management.

AD and Third-Party Systems

Active Directory, being the foundation of identity and security in most organizations at the time of writing, does not exist in a vacuum. Every AD forest has lots of third-party systems more or less closely attached to it. Some of them "consume" AD functionality, that is, rely on AD for authentication, authorization, or maybe even configuration and data storage. These systems are a main source of functional requirements we have to deal with when engineering and maintaining AD. Many of the implementational deficiencies we'll be discussing in the next chapter are due to third-party requirements rather than lack of knowledge or diligence on the administrators' part. The typical problems one has to overcome or, more often still, work around are

- Legacy protocols like SMBv1, NTLM, or DES encryption hardcoded into the software
- Explicit check for privileges by checking the membership in certain groups rather than effective access to the required resources
- Inability to properly locate Domain Controllers leading to them having to be configured within the solution, sometimes even by IP address rather than FQDN
- Requirement to have overprivileged legacy service accounts
- Excessive data queries, usually carried over from the Windows NT era where every account was able to read all readable properties of any object in the entire domain.

The list can go on *ad infinitum*. More often than not, these systems are not selected by IT for their exceptional security and compatibility with the modern requirements, but rather procured by other departments for their functionality, or even "because the CFO's previous company used that" (true story). You have to be prepared to accommodate new requirements that may be below your accepted standard without compromising the overall security posture.

On the other hand, there are third-party tools and solutions that enhance the native capabilities of AD and help administrators maintain its reliability, availability, and security while minimizing the necessary effort – which is not to say that these solutions do not introduce their own requirements that may be detrimental to the overall security of the

INTRODUCTION

organization, like the requirement that Protected Application mode be disabled for LSASS on Domain Controllers or Credential Guard deactivated on member machines.

Skills Most Needed in a Modern AD

What skills should an IT professional working with a modern AD implementation possess today? In the past, there used to be lots of AD administrators who managed to get by just clicking around in the MMC consoles or some third-party tools. In the modern world, even working with legacy systems like Active Directory, you're going to need a deeper understanding of the underlying technology and a more readily available skill set in managing and troubleshooting this technology than may have been necessary 15 years ago:

- You should have a very good grasp of how LDAP works, know how to bind to a directory, and execute a search. Being able to create a complex LDAP filter is a bonus; knowing the limitations is a must.

- Understanding how DNS works in Windows and the ability to quickly pinpoint a source of DNS malfunction is a very important skill to have. It will save you hours of troubleshooting one day.

- It surprises me every time how many AD-related issues arise due to replication errors and misconfigurations. If your environment sports more than one physical site, knowing how DC locator, site coverage, and DFS-R replication work is paramount.

- When it comes to security, permissions are the lifeblood of both attack scenarios and systems hardening. Knowing how Windows permissions management works is extremely important.

- AD is all about authentication. Nobody expects you to decrypt Kerberos tickets in your head, but a solid understanding of how Kerberos and NTLM work and what factors influence their behavior can and will help you harden and protect your network going forward.

- Knowing how things work is great, but being able to put that knowledge to practical use is what makes all the difference. This is especially true in situations where your environment is in a degraded state, either due to a cyber incident or to a different kind of disaster. Learning and practicing PowerShell can be a lifesaver in these situations. But even at peacetime, scripts and automation are codified, condensed knowledge. The more you automate, the less you need to document, and the less friction there will be when onboarding a new team member!

Windows Security in general and known attack vectors in particular are very important to keep in mind as an Active Directory professional, since AD is foundational to the security posture of your entire organization.

Understanding how Group Policy works is a very useful skill, but depending on your particular implementation, you could absolutely succeed in the AD field without having in-depth knowledge about GPO.

INTRODUCTION

Conventions in This book

Wherever "Active Directory" is referenced in this book, ADDS is implied. "ADLDS" and "LDS" are always used interchangeably; ADCS may sometimes find itself called "Enterprise PKI," and if "SAML authentication" is mentioned, ADFS is probably what's providing it.

Since an optimal topology for a specific AD implementation may – and often will – include several forests, all managed by one Red forest and trusting each other in varying directions and scopes, we will refer to the entirety of these as the "AD Organization." This is not to be confused with the terminology of Microsoft Exchange or Azure DevOps that also use the term "organization." A fun fact about forests: for the German translation of Windows, Microsoft chose to call an AD "forest" a *Gesamtstruktur*, which roughly translates to an "overall structure." A name that would indeed be more fitting to describe several forests under common management! In any other language that I was able to check, Microsoft simply went with the local equivalent of "forest."

For the requirement level indication, we will adhere to the definitions laid out in RFC 2119, as long as the key words specified in the RFC are capitalized as clarified by RFC 7841.

We will be talking about "Tier Zero" objects and systems, both within and outside AD. Unless specified explicitly, this book and the concept of a modern AD are **not** assuming that your organization has implemented any kind of codified administrative tiering, either by following Microsoft's ESAE model or otherwise. For determining what assets belong to Tier Zero, this book assumes the SpecterOps definition from June 2023:

> Tier Zero is a set of assets in control of enterprise identities and their security dependencies.

This amends the original Microsoft definition that contained the implicit assumption that all Tier Zero assets control each other. However, a hypervisor driving a domain controller VM is clearly a Tier Zero system while not being controlled by any AD security principals – some of which are undoubtedly Tier Zero!

PowerShell is our tool of choice for managing Microsoft infrastructure. Wherever there is a mention of "PowerShell" in this book, Windows PowerShell that is part of Windows up to and including the upcoming Windows Server 2025 is assumed. While the modules and namespaces referenced in this book will mostly work in open-source PowerShell on Windows, this interoperability does not, at the time of writing, extend to other platforms such as Linux and MacOS for which PowerShell is available.

PowerShell one-liners and code snippets used in this book will be formatted like this:

```
Get-ADUser -LDAPFilter "(sAMAccountName=freddy)"
```

Wherever there is a mention of object classes, attributes, CMDshell, or PowerShell commands or other immutable values, they will be formatted like this: **sAMAccountName**.

Summary

In this introduction, we have established the need for an engineering approach to Active Directory. After two and a half decades of doing design for design's sake, sticking to the vendor defaults, and misusing AD for functions it has never been intended to fulfill in the enterprise, both security and usability requirements dictate that we change the approach to building and operating AD to a more requirements-oriented one. This sets the scene for the rest of this book.

Most importantly, we introduced the term "AD Organization" as a sum of multiple AD forests bound together by trust relationships.

We have looked at the five Windows Server roles that comprise the "Active Directory" suite, of which we will mostly discuss Active Directory

INTRODUCTION

Domain Services (which we will call "AD" going forward), with a bit of Lightweight Directory Services (ADLDS) and Certificate Services (ADCS). Then we have defined the book's target audience and discussed the merits of "best practices" and this book's relationship to them. We finished off with the tools and skills required to operate a modern AD, with a word of warning that third-party tools may not share Active Directory's exceptional longevity.

Last but not least, we have defined conventions that will be used throughout the book.

CHAPTER 1

Problems with AD

Active Directory, while still foundational for most organizations' identity and security, has got a miserable reputation – first and foremost, for its security. A very well-respected IT security professional and a fellow Microsoft MVP recently described AD as "a cybersecurity cancer" and called for abandoning it as quickly as possible in favor of SAML-based authentication systems and, ultimately, cloud. This may or may not be feasible middle-term in your particular organization, and the fact that you're reading this book indicates that you probably fall into the second category, which means that you, like a big portion of the IT world, are stuck with AD for the foreseeable future, making it not a "cancer that can only be attacked by chemo and radiation" but rather a "problem that needs a solution." And since acknowledging the problem is the necessary first step to solving it, we will devote this chapter to looking at why AD actually appears to be so incredibly bad at what it's been designed to do and what organizations are trying to have it do (*there is a difference between the two; we'll get to that in a bit*).

Another frequently cited "deficiency" of AD is the tooling that Microsoft provides to manage it as a part of Windows or, more precisely, of the Remote Server Administration Toolkit (RSAT). Surprisingly enough, in my experience, IT teams that have been given a third-party AD management toolkit that served their needs stopped complaining about the inadequacy of the inbox tooling almost immediately, even though it caused them to have to implement a new tool with its own learning curve, lifecycle management, and set of idiosyncrasies. So maybe it's just Microsoft leaving the tooling to partners to provide, as was its wont for a very long time.

CHAPTER 1 PROBLEMS WITH AD

The problems with and around AD are to be found in one of the five categories:

- Foundational design decisions made by Microsoft, some of them as far back as the mid-1990s. We can do nothing about them but rather have to work with (or around) them until we're ready to let AD go.

- Default settings AD comes with that may or may not be a good fit for our particular implementation and absolutely deserve to be changed where they aren't. However, there often is a strong pushback against doing so, mostly because of the interdependencies being too complex to fully understand the consequences of every particular measure.

- Unmanaged expectations about what AD actually is and miscommunication about what it is not. This is partly Microsoft's fault, but the bulk of the blame should be placed on IT managers and architects who would sometimes prefer to let sleeping dogs lie rather than have their project questioned and postponed yet again.

- Implementational decisions and configurations we make in and around AD along the way.

- Management processes regarding both AD itself and applications that make use of it. And even if your organization does not have formalized processes for managing its IT (as it should!), you still have processes in place, the sole difference being the inability to gauge your adherence to these processes.

CHAPTER 1   PROBLEMS WITH AD

1.1 Structural Challenges

We will not recapitulate the history of Active Directory and technologies that preceded it, nor does the author have enough inside knowledge to classify Microsoft's design decisions by whether each particular one "seemed a good idea at the time." There are, however, several of these design and engineering cornerstones that ultimately lead to the security mess an unhardened AD is today. Much of how AD works is taken for granted nowadays, but the fact that these things cannot be changed does not make seeing them as the result of a conscious choice any less valuable for an AD (security) professional like you.

1.1.1 A Domain Controller Does More Than "Control" the Domain

The name "Domain Controller" suggests an entity external to the domain controlling it and the objects within, much as a traffic controller usually does not participate in said traffic while on duty. This perception could not be further from the truth, though. Not only a Domain Controller can itself be controlled by objects inside the domain, there is, in fact, no other entity capable of controlling the DC since it does not have a local security accounts database! In a manner of speaking, a **Domain Controller is the domain**.

Is it the only way to design this? Of course not. But this is how it was designed even before AD, in Windows NT's domain model, which leads us directly to the next item.

1.1.2 AD Is Self-managed

Since each DC "is" the domain, there are no "superusers" outside of the domain to manage its contents and security. This means that any entity capable of managing AD is itself an AD entity. With Windows NT, it had to be an account from the same domain; the first iteration of Active Directory that was part of Windows 2000 Server would require an account from the same forest, which, as security boundaries go, is equivalent. It was not before forest trusts were introduced in Server 2003 that concepts like that of a Red Forest became possible, allowing for effective separation of privileges.

Yet even if we choose not to manage our production AD using principals from the directory itself, it does not render such management impossible. A user with administrator privileges is just a user. Making it an administrator is literally just an act of elevating its privileges.

Could this have been designed differently? Absolutely. One could create a separate partition for administrative users and hardcode it so that only these users are able to change the security descriptor of objects in all the other partitions. Make the administrative users unable to log on interactively except to Domain Controllers, and some of the most prolific attack scenarios known today would not have been possible to execute.

1.1.3 AD Is Always a Snapshot

Active Directory has greatly matured in terms of stability and resilience over the decades. It almost magically keeps object data in a synchronized state across datacenters and geographical regions, in some cases around the globe. In today's largest domains, change convergence is still something to keep an eye out for, but it's nowhere as big a challenge as it was in the early 2000s. However, even today AD will only ever produce the current state of each object while not disclosing very much about how the object got in that state:

- It is not known what security principal created the object. Sometimes the creator of an object remains its owner, but that can be easily changed by an administrator after the fact and it's not always the case to begin with.

- It is not easily known what property of an object changed to which value and when, nor is the previous value easily obtained. Replication metadata can provide some limited insights here, but it's not reliable and may require looking at all Domain Controllers hosting the partition where the object in question is located.

- It is not known who made which change to an object. While this information may be available from the audit logs short-term, it would require a complete, gap-free transfer of these logs to some sort of long-term storage (usually dubbed "SIEM," although this is not always technically correct).

Long story short, the only data that is reliably available in AD using only out-of-box tooling is the current state of all the objects.

1.1.4 No Tracking of AD's Own Activity

Several well-known attack paths against Active Directory are based on the fact that a Domain Controller, when asked to validate a ticket and to proceed accordingly, doesn't know, nor care, whether that ticket was actually issued by a DC in the specified domain. It only validates whether the ticket *looks like it was issued by a valid DC*. Given the hardware specifications at the time of AD's inception, this was the only sane decision to make. Still, it would be nice if AD could keep track of every TGT and TGS it issues for the duration of their lifetime and require reauthentication every time an apparently valid but unknown ticket is presented.

1.1.5 AD Has Lots of Hardcoded Behaviors

To be completely fair, hardcoded behaviors are not necessarily always a bad thing. As mentioned earlier, having administrator privileges hardcoded rather than granted by another administrator would probably have saved us some headaches, security-wise. Active Directory has lots of these hardcoded behaviors: the list of the "privileged groups" (or at least one half of it), the function of the "Protected Users" group, or the N-2 lockout protection feature, just to name a few. Some of the infamous "Microsoft's 15 minutes" timeouts are hardcoded into the product as well.

For an AD engineer, it's important to know these features, because these constitute the unmovable limits of what our engineering effort is going to be able to achieve.

1.2 Questionable Defaults

Some of the design decisions that ultimately gave Active Directory such a bad reputation, security-wise, are, in fact, not foundational or hardcoded but rather stem from the default settings Microsoft decided to grace us with. Every computer program has to come with *some* defaults, but in the case of AD, it's both the "program" itself and the data in it that come with default values. Normally, building out a new system starts with an empty shell to be filled with your individual content, much like a building that you have to paint inside and fill with furniture so that you can live and work there. However, if you install a new forest by promoting a pristine Windows Server 2022 to a Domain Controller, it comes with 238 objects (not counting the obvious ones: the schema, the domain itself, the newly promoted Domain Controller hosting it, and the default Administrator account you are using for accessing the directory for the first time) and 1166 explicit permissions, not counting the inherited ones – and this is just in the domain partition! It is at this point that many admins, architects, and implementation consultants abandon the engineering approach and just accept the defaults because "they're probably there for a reason" and "things will probably break if we change them." This is supported by a variety of assessment tools that warn not about insecure or less-than-optimal configurations but rather about non-default ones. Ironically, some of these products call themselves "best practice analyzers," yet again suggesting that the defaults Microsoft put in there are, in fact, optimal for this particular implementation (which, of course, Microsoft knows nothing about).

A comprehensive list of highly questionable Active Directory defaults could fill this entire chapter and still be far from complete, but here are some highlights that have to be dealt with in every implementation:

- Domain Admins are local admins on every member, server and client alike. Although this is not a "setting that has received an unhelpful default value" but is, in fact, hardwired in the domain join process in Windows, it can easily be corrected immediately after the join by applying a Group Policy or by automation. Organizations that put administrative tiering in place have mitigated this effect, but the amount of pushback these tiering initiatives have received from administrators in the past is an indicator of how attractive working in "God mode" can be for us humans, even for those who should, in theory, know better.

- Promoting a member server to a Domain Controller does not change the owner of its computer object in AD. We will talk about it in more detail in Chapter 7, but many enterprise deployment products can leave you with Domain Controller computer objects owned by an account whose password is stored in clear text in a configuration file readable by anyone!

- Every user can join up to ten machines to a domain. This is a combination of an AD attribute value

    ms-DS-MachineAccountQuota=10

    a Group Policy setting (Add Workstations to Domain=Authenticated Users), and a hardwired behavior connecting the two. The irony: The expected user behavior that led to this "feature" never materialized, because it is not how people use Windows in organizations. At the time of writing, with cloud-joined workstations on the rise, this actually became "a thing," and we will see in a couple of years what Entra ID and Intune administrators will ultimately end up doing about it. But legitimate work computers added to an on-premises AD by a legitimate non-admin user I have yet to see in the field. Computers added to AD in malicious intent by abusing this configuration are a completely different story...

- Authenticated users are able to view any security principal in any domain of the forest and large parts of the Configuration partition. This led to the saying "in AD, everybody can see everything," which, while not exactly true, does reflect the easiness of reconnaissance that AD offers an attacker after they were able to make authenticated contact. "Authenticated users" include domain-joined computers from the own forest and also from all trusted forests, so that this level of reconnaissance does not require hijacking a user session – computer-level access like what the Log4j vulnerability provided is as powerful.

- The infamous "Pre-Windows 2000 Compatible Access" group gives authenticated users even more privileges. "Pre-Windows 2000" means Windows NT, an operating system that went out of support in 2004. That is 20 years before this book comes off the press, 18 years before the release of Server 2022, and nesting of Authenticated Users into "Pre-Win2K" is still the default. We will talk about it more in Chapter 4.

- Everybody can create a DNS record. Well, not quite everybody and not just any record. But by default, Authenticated Users can create not only host and service records but also subdomains, delegations, and other object types, opening the door to a plethora of attack paths.

The list can go on. Other "Active Directories" add their own questionable defaults to the already explosive mix, Certificate Services being by far the worst-behaving sibling, security-wise.

In this book, we will not try to engineer our way around these default values and behaviors. Instead, we will pretend that the defaults are not there and provide sensible values that satisfy modern AD requirements. In Chapter 11, we will look at introducing our "modern defaults" into existing AD organizations.

1.3 The Misunderstood AD

To successfully engineer, implement, and maintain Active Directory for the foreseeable future, it is extremely important to understand what AD is – i.e., what Microsoft intended it to do – and, even more importantly, what it is not. It is ignoring these most basic facts that leads to unstable, less-than-performant, and insecure AD implementations. I have seen more of

CHAPTER 1   PROBLEMS WITH AD

these over the years than I care to remember, but each one left a feeling of sadness about wasted chances and avoidable frustration. In a nutshell, AD (we specifically mean "Domain Services" by this, remember?) provides you with four types of functionality:

- Directory data store with the ability to perform authenticated LDAP lookups of objects in that directory.

- Authentication facility offering Kerberos and NTLM as authentication protocols. You can extend it to SAML by adding ADFS to your identity solution, but the authentication between ADFS and AD will still be restricted to Kerberos or NTLM.

- Authorization claim provider. The claims can be issued in the form of group memberships added to the authentication token or, starting with Server 2012R2, as a part of Kerberos claim-based authentication extension. All information required to provide authorization claims to clients is stored in the directory.

- Configuration information (Group Policy) store, offering SMB shares for authenticated download of Group Policy payloads and GPO configuration in the directory for determining the correct set and order of policies.

All AD does is offer other systems access to information stored in it. It does **not**, however, even begin to fulfill the following very important functions:

- Verify or ensure the validity and consistency of the information stored in the directory **with regard to the business intent behind it**.

- Maintain the lifecycle of the objects stored in the directory, including the file shares serving Group Policies.

In short, Active Directory is not a management system for anything, nor was it ever intended to be. It's a very robust, performant, geo-redundant, multi-master *delivery* system for several types of information and data.

1.3.1 AD Is Not IAM

We talked about AD lacking the most basic change tracking and attribution features earlier in this chapter. Add the lack of any kind of policy-based or rule-based provisioning or lifecycle management, and it becomes obvious that AD is not, by any standards, an identity management system. Same goes for access management – while AD is capable of storing and serving claims that will be used for authorization, it does not hold any knowledge of the applications processing these claims nor about the business intent behind the claims. Nor does AD have any way of provisioning authorization rules in any application except in Active Directory itself – an ability that, if misused, leads to privilege escalation and ultimately to "domain dominance."

This does not prevent organizations from declaring AD to be their "identity management" or at least their "source of truth for identity" – until the day Active Directory data gets compromised, either by an attacker or by an administrative error, without any practical way to track or revert these changes.

My favorite example of an anti-pattern that stems from this misunderstanding is the requirement (found both internally and externally, especially in critical infrastructure) to preserve user accounts far beyond the date of the user leaving the organization, in some cases even so long as for ten years. I've never been able to elicit a solid

CHAPTER 1   PROBLEMS WITH AD

justification for this requirement, but a user account lying dormant and stripped of all its significant attributes and group memberships will not yield any information beyond the fact that this user has existed at some point in time. After you have rotated all DCs due to an operating system upgrade, replication metadata will not even reveal when the user got moved to the Leavers OU and deactivated! If your business has intrinsic or regulatory requirements of this nature, you need a proper lifecycle management for identity and access.

Microsoft does provide enterprise-grade identity management tooling by means of "Microsoft Identity Manager" (MIM), which offers a powerful metadirectory, connectors to several identity stores beyond AD and Entra ID, and a certificate lifecycle management facility. In terms of access management, no first-party tooling will help you achieve the complete access management lifecycle, even for Microsoft products. While Central Access Policies (one of the less frequently used AD features) allow administrators to provision and keep their claim-based access policies in one place, deploying these policies is still done strictly within the application itself. Support for Central Access Policies is currently limited to file services, and there is no indication that other products will implement it anytime soon.

Entra ID and Azure, on the other hand, provide both identity and access management capabilities, which increases the perceived pressure to abandon on-premises AD in favor of the cloud-based offerings.

1.3.2 AD Is Not Configuration Management

Active Directory delivers configuration data to its member machines in two ways: values stored in directory objects and their attributes (Exchange makes the most extensive use of it) and Group Policy. Neither facility offers even the most basic management capabilities:

- Version and change control
- Change history
- Comparison between the current and the desired state of the affected systems

In a small organization with limited IT resources, having a robust configuration delivery mechanism may be sufficient. But even in those scenarios where rolling out extensive configurations by means of Group Policy, including software installations, scripts, etc., makes economical sense, IT managers should keep in mind that the configuration **management** happens in the administrators' heads.

The lack of management capabilities that AD exhibits in regard to member systems fully extends to the systems that constitute AD itself, i.e., Domain Controllers. While it is possible to apply a partial desired state to DCs by using Group Policy and AD attributes, the management of this configuration information happens outside of AD – more often than not in the heads of the IT staff or in Excel spreadsheets.

1.3.3 AD Is Probably Not Your Enterprise Directory Either

This may come as a surprise, but exposing LDAP directories to the end user never became a very common practice in the Windows world. You might still find it in use at a research facility or at a university where there is a need to access directories from partner organizations; many backend services are provided by UNIX or Linux machines and clients are often loosely managed. But in a Microsoft-centric environment, even if your organization does provide a searchable employee directory, it is usually not a direct connection against the identity store but some sort of application that will cache and prepare this information for searching and viewing. Microsoft Exchange is a great example of this functionality.

It provides address book views to its clients (Outlook or Outlook Web Access), where administrators have the ability to restrict which mailboxes, distribution lists, or contacts each employee is permitted to see. However, neither the filtering of the allowed recipients nor the representation of their data towards the client application is achieved by means of Active Directory and LDAP. We will talk about internal lookup in more detail in Chapter 4.

1.3.4 The Misunderstood Demand for Flexibility

The value proposition of a directory service always includes a promise of flexibility. You can store objects of many kinds, extend their property sets by extending the directory schema, and even provide applications with robust and geo-redundant data storage facilities by creating separate application partitions just for the purpose. In spite of many hardcoded behaviors we spoke about earlier in this chapter, Active Directory is an excellent example for this sort of flexibility. Things, however, tend to get complicated when AD organizations start pushing the limits of extensibility just because it's possible. Custom application partitions may end up being ignored by a directory management solution you are looking to put in place. Organization-specific schema extensions have been known to both collide with third-party extensions, make integrations with IAM solutions and migration products very cumbersome or even impossible, and – especially in large organizations – blow up the database size by storing data that could be better stored elsewhere. LDAP directories are a good fit for certain kinds of data, but not for every sort of structured data an application might want to store. But even if a directory-type store is what the application in question is optimized for, there is always the possibility of using an ADLDS instance rather than putting application data into AD directly.

In the case of AD, the expectation of unlimited flexibility extends from the directory and lookup part to its other important function – the authentication. Administrators expect to be able to incorporate any third-party technology into AD as long as it supports either NTLM or Kerberos in some kind of implementation. And, while there is nothing wrong with this requirement (if it indeed is one from the business point of view), more often than not it leads to leaving AD forests largely unhardened and as close to the factory defaults as possible, for fear that one of these customizations might break compatibility to some hypothetical application going forward.

Common misunderstandings about what AD is and how it is intended to be used lead to a variety of common anti-patterns that we have to deal with on our journey towards modern AD.

1.4 Patterns and Anti-patterns

All aspects of Active Directory that have not been hardcoded by Microsoft are managed by humans. Architects, consultants, and administrators all leave their footprints in every AD forest they design, build, and manage. Everybody has their life experience, their lessons, both "soft-learned" (in a classroom or from books like this one) and hard-learned ones. These, along with "we have always done it this way" and "this will not work in this company," lead to repeating patterns in AD designs and implementations. Some of these patterns are good for creating clear, manageable, and secure directory designs and providing guidance on administering these directories that is both secure and user-friendly. Some examples of such patterns that are found in the field are

- New objects are redirected to custom containers to apply both ACLs and Group Policies to them right from the moment of creation.

- Default Domain Policy only contains the default settings (but with non-default values). All other settings are managed by dedicated Group Policy objects.

- Admin users are put into "Protected Users." Some organizations even go so far as to put default privileged groups like Domain Admins into Protected Users.

- At least Tier 0 (Domain Admin-level access) is enforced. The usual way to do it is by Group Policy; however, this can be hardened even further by using Authentication Policies.

- Exchange is deployed with Split Permissions or, better still, in a resource forest.

- Granular service accounts separation that allows to reliably locate service accounts and manage their password lifecycle – or, when the time comes, replace them by Group Managed Service Accounts (gMSA) or, starting with the upcoming Windows Server 2025, Delegated Managed Service Accounts (dMSA).

- Default privileged groups are empty, Schema Admins membership only gets assigned if there are planned changes to the schema.

They are worth including in your modern AD toolkit. Others, however, will take you on a bumpy journey that will result in overly complicated, barely manageable, and still not very secure infrastructure. These are the anti-patterns you want to avoid, yet many of them are likely to be observed in almost every AD organization:

- Complex domain structures without justification (e.g., "empty forest root domain as a matter of routine"). We will talk about it in Chapter 3.

- OU structures not reflecting their purpose (e.g., OUs reflect the org chart while only used for GPO application).

- Site links do not reflect physical WAN topology, which has a negative impact on both locating DCs and the replication itself.

- Default privileged groups are used to only achieve parts of their functionality (Print Operators, for instance, allow interactive logon to Domain Controllers, which is not what this group is mostly used for). The remaining permissions these groups provide are "open attack surface."

- Group Policies not aligned with their purpose impacting both performance and manageability.

- GPOs linked to sites without proper justification. This is not a problem per se, as long as everybody remembers this linkage is in place.

- Logon/Logoff scripts linked in AD, reducing the accounts' flexibility and providing an attacker with valuable information about the attack vectors for the particular user.

- Password policies not reflecting the actual attack surface. We will talk about it in detail in Chapter 5.

- User creation by copying existing users (the fact that Small Business Server even had a wizard for that does not make it good practice). There are hardly more convenient ways to introduce configuration drift than this management practice.

- Windows Server backups of DCs to widely readable file shares. We will cover this in Chapter 10.

- DHCP server or Certificate Authorities co-located on Domain Controllers. This affects both security and manageability of your Active Directory in a decidedly negative way!

- Entra ID Connect deployed with Express settings, opening a whole collection of well-known attack paths that lead directly to cloud dominance and, combined with other popular misconfigurations, can also provide an attacker with a very short path to domain dominance!

- Read-only Domain Controllers (RODC) in DMZ networks. We will talk about it in depth in Chapter 5.

These and many other anti-patterns need to be unclipped from your tool belt and thrown overboard as soon as possible if you want your AD organization to survive the next 25 years!

1.5 Summary

In this chapter, we analyzed the problems that led to Active Directory's bad reputation. Some of them are due to architectural decisions made by Microsoft even before AD materialized. Unmanaged expectation and attempt to misuse AD for functionality it has never been intended to provide add to that. A slew of problems are rooted in default settings and permissions that are theoretically changeable but in practice are defined at installation time and cemented by third-party applications that assume these settings are in place.

And then there are problems caused by the design, implementation, and management of concrete AD environments. To deal with AD-related problems, both real and perceived, architects, consultants, and administrators have developed a wide collection of patterns – and anti-patterns! – some of which have not been revisited for 25 years.

We will take care of all these problem areas in the course of the following chapters.

CHAPTER 2

A Modern AD

To properly engineer a modern AD, including all the management processes that ensure its continual operation, we have to understand the requirements an enterprise identity store needs to fulfill. These requirements typically come from multiple sources:

- The requirements of modern work, including user mobility over a multitude of geographical locations, networks, and endpoint devices
- The requirements of identity, application, and infrastructure security
- The requirements of resilience and recoverability in case of a wide-scale disruption, be it a cyberattack or a massive outage of public networks or services

Pitting these requirements against each other and "letting the market decide the outcome" has not worked very well for IT organizations in the past, although many an IT veteran may regard this as "the way of the world." A modern AD architecture, on the other hand, will try to emphasize the areas where the engineering implications of the various requirements amplify each other. The Laws #7 and #8 of the "10 Immutable Laws of Security Administration" give an example of this by declaring a well-administered and clearly structured network easiest to defend. These principles work against both ever-present cyberattacks and unreasonable demands from other parts of the business!

CHAPTER 2   A MODERN AD

2.1 Modern Work Requirements

Back when AD was introduced to the world, enterprise IT looked quite differently to what we are used to today. An endpoint device would usually weigh upwards of 20 lbs, rest under the user's desk, and be firmly wired into the rest of the IT infrastructure by a network cable. Moving a client device to a different network segment was a result of a larger change like internal restructuring or an employee moving to a different department. Users would come into the office in the morning and leave in the afternoon (whether they would shut their PC down or leave it running is an entirely different question). Several employees sharing the same endpoint was fairly common in certain industries, whereas an employee moving between endpoints on a regular basis was an exception rather than the rule. A mere Windows generation later, laptop computers and workstation pools became much more common and so did employee mobility – both between endpoints and between networks or even geographical locations. NOKIA Communicator, BlackBerry, and iPhone introduced new working paradigms for both knowledge workers and frontline staff, while vendors like Citrix and VMware helped bring even legacy applications to these new, ultra-mobile device form factors. The COVID pandemic of 2020–2022 established inherently insecure home Wi-Fi as a legitimate network location for corporate devices; privately owned and largely unmanaged computers have become legitimate clients for business applications. Both are a permanent fixture in today's enterprise IT.

The applications landscape has become far more volatile as well – new business processes require new applications, and those require authentication and authorization. This is where Active Directory becomes involved and provides the glue that holds the application zoo together by offering a common identity platform.

Today, an IT organization has to satisfy multiple "new work"-related requirements, in addition to those imposed by the business anyway, like security and reliability. These new requirements are mostly those of flexibility:

- Geographical locations and networks. The macro-geography is getting more diverse by the day due to globalization, pandemic-imposed "work from abroad" locations, and a wider geographical distribution of the skilled workforce. But micro-geographical conditions have become more varying as well – working from a Starbucks rather than from home or at the office is quite common among knowledge workers.

- New applications that require authentication, authorization, and user profiles of some kind get onboarded regularly, and more often than not, IT and IT security are not involved in the purchasing decisions.

- While the operating systems market has stabilized both for large form factor endpoints (desktops and laptops) and for mobile devices (smartphones and tablets), endpoint integration with enterprise IT is still in flux. Vendors are experimenting with platform and OS hardening to make their endpoints less likely to be taken over by a drive-by download or a zero-touch messaging attack. Cloud operators introduce new approaches to authentication, device management, and data handling. Governments require better data protection and easier discoverability by law enforcement – both at the same time! Completely new classes of devices like smart watches and equally smart TV sets slowly but steadily establish their market share in the enterprise endpoint landscape.

CHAPTER 2   A MODERN AD

As an enterprise identity and security architect or administrator, you have to contend with this ever-changing playing field. Unfortunately, the hardest task you are facing is not even that of finding a technical solution to each new set of requirements. Being informed about impending changes and ideally involved in the purchasing decisions before contracts are signed and the implementation deadlines announced is much harder to achieve in many businesses. I've had to deal with enterprises where talking to IT before starting negotiations with a third-party vendor amounted to a culture change the business wasn't interested in and IT never had enough influence to demand. This book cannot give you actionable advice on how to deal with people; however, having your answers ready and being able to estimate business risks of a certain technology definitely helps being taken more seriously by management.

2.2 Directory Security

One of the biggest challenges when working in identity is ensuring its security. If your identity is not secure, nothing is. Modern Windows Server versions and Active Directory running on them offer numerous security controls, but the compatibility-bound default settings and 20-year-old design anti-patterns that govern these controls tend to yield less-than-optimal results in practical implementations. This is something we need to take care of by engineering.

Windows does not bring much to the table in terms of reactive security. Audit logs can offer some insights into what is going on in the environment – provided auditing was enabled during the time span we are interested in and had not been tampered with. We will look at what is logged where in certain authentication scenarios because knowing what's normal is key to successful troubleshooting. But collecting, correlating, and searching audit logs at scale to produce actionable intelligence is something you are definitely going to need a third-party product for. In this book, we are not going to recommend a particular product nor offer implementation advice, but search for "SIEM" and you will be presented with a wide selection of choices.

Therefore, proactive security will be this book's primary focus. In the "modern AD" engineering paradigm, we will embrace the fact that IT security of any kind is not about risk avoidance but rather about risk management. Instead of trying to harden AD and all the systems around it until they become unusable, only to discover that there is a novel attack vector circumventing all that hardening, we will engineer our Active Directory in a way that makes every phase of an attack as expensive as possible while still providing required functionality to legitimate users and applications.

Permissions are the lifeblood of every security architecture. Assigning permissions in a targeted manner will help us achieve least privilege and harden our modern Active Directory both against attacks and unintended behavior by legitimate administrators. However, AD comes with tons of permissions already assigned to pre-defined groups. And while it's natural for a Windows administrator to leave the default groups' permissions in place and just ensure that they are normally empty, this approach introduces several problems:

- Some of the default groups, like "Everyone" or, most notably, "Authenticated Users," are not actually real groups that are populated explicitly; their associations are achieved by virtue of a successful authentication. Therefore, permissions assigned to these default principals will always be granted unless revoked or denied.

- If a group is given permissions that a malicious actor would like to exploit, they might be able to perform a token injection or, should they acquire replication rights, a sidHistory or primaryGroupID injection. This, of course, applies to custom principals as well as to the default ones, but the custom principals' identities have to be determined first, usually by evaluating directory permissions at scale, whereas the default principals' SIDs are well known, even if the attacker may not have read access to them at the current stage of the attack!

Protecting against elevation of access is a hard requirement these days; therefore, in our "modern AD" security framework, we will have to introduce appropriate measures for this.

2.3 Modern AD Tenets

To satisfy all the different requirements, including long-term manageability, flexibility, and resilience, our engineering effort of building and operating a modern AD will adhere to the following six guiding principles that will help us reconcile business needs, security, and cost of operation:

- Security first
- Automate all the way
- Stick to the policies
- Prepare for exceptions
- Prepare for change
- Prepare for disaster

Let's look at them in more detail and translate them to actual actions a technical team knows how to take.

2.3.1 Security First

Most complaints about Active Directory have always been about its lack of "security by default"; we have looked into that in the last chapter. Security needs to come first – this is true both for engineering and operating your Active Directory! This does not necessarily mean building a Fort Knox out of your directory service and rendering it unusable for anything except being secure. But the approach should be "start from a most secure state and relax towards the business requirements" rather than "start at defaults and harden until the hardened state clashes with the business requirements."

There must be some red lines, too, for the cases where security requirements are in contradiction with those of business flexibility. If, for instance, at some point you have achieved disabling NTLM authentication for all AD accounts, reenabling it because a new application requires NTLM cannot be a routine decision made in operations – this needs to go all the way up, with a risk assessment prepared in a management-ready manner. Another red line should always be relaxing any security-related configuration *beyond the Windows defaults* – those are not deemed secure enough as it is!

2.3.2 Automate All the Way

Maintaining a complex enterprise environment always entails doing the same thing in a lot of different places – applying the same permissions to many folders on different levels, setting the same registry settings or firewall rules on a multitude of devices, and so on. The modern AD paradigm is not going to ease this burden – quite on the contrary, new cases will pop up where you need to deploy the same change to many instances. In the past, many administrators and consultants have chosen less-than-optimal solutions for fear of spending hours or even days doing the same repetitive task and making mistakes or overlooking things in the process.

One of the goals of our modern AD approach is to overcome the simplified, yet still very complex, defaults to achieve better security and sometimes even better manageability of the overall environment. This means that the more granular way will become the "right way" more often. However, the modern AD cannot be managed by repetitive efforts and manual labor. In fact, even the conventional AD should not be managed that way. In the UNIX world, there is a decades-old saying: "whenever you have to do something more than once, script it." To survive the next 25 years in directory services administration, you'll have to adopt this guiding principle.

Do not let the argument of perceived complexity fool you into making wrong architectural or operational decisions. Repeating the same operation a thousand times is not *complexity*; it's *lack of automation*. If you embrace automation, the prospect of having to add thousands of identical permission entries or firewall rules is just a question of providing the target objects to the automation engine.

In this book, we cannot assume that any commercial tooling available today will stay on the market for decades. This is why we will concentrate on the capabilities present in the product itself and enhanced by open-source software, the latter having better chances of long-term survival, even if some of the previous users end up becoming maintainers! That being said, while building your own toolset and developing skills around it, do keep in mind that a true "modern AD" will probably not be very manageable by graphical tools provided by Microsoft out of the box. At least *some* scripting and automation capabilities will have to be available even in a degraded state!

2.3.3 Stick to the Policies

Mark Minasi once put "knowing what is normal" on the list of 24 rules that helped him survive in IT. This is one of the most fundamental principles of systems management to this day. Comparing the current state to the "observed good" (i.e., "normal") instead of the "known good" (i.e., "desired") state is becoming more and more common and even serves as the technological basis for security products such as VMware NSX Distributed Firewall Threat Prevention and several others like it.

With the "modern AD," you will be taking this one step further and not only knowing but defining what is "normal" in your particular environment. This is not to say that *all* vendor defaults have to be replaced by different values or *all* default behaviors augmented by explicit configurations. In many instances, default values and behaviors are acceptable, but to become "known good" configurations, they have to be enforced in exactly the same way deviations from defaults are enforced. If you look at CIS hardening guides or even at Microsoft SCT recommendations, you will find that the recommended values are often the default ones, at least for the more modern versions of the products. The difference between a CIS-compliant environment and a "loosely hardened" one is, therefore, that all configurations and not just the non-default ones are enforced by policy.

The "people" side of the modern AD paradigm also calls for adherence to the accepted policy. Many established practices like administrative tiering only reinforce by technical means what security-conscious administrators should be doing anyway – use different accounts for systems of different security levels and do not reuse passwords for different applications.

Create your set of policies, draw your red lines, educate your admins and users, and your AD will serve you faithfully for decades to come.

2.3.4 Prepare for Exceptions

After the previous section, this may sound like a contradiction, but the real world is going to force you to break your own rules from time to time. There is, however, one thing that is worse than deviating from a well-architected policy: A deviation from a policy that has been hastily improvised because there wasn't time for good planning and careful execution. A big portion of overpermissioned service accounts, disabled firewall rules, and exposed administrator credentials found in security audits falls into this category.

For every hardening measure or, more generally, for every change in configuration that deviates from the defaults, the process of creating the exception for this measure must be engineered and documented up front. This requires at least as much effort as engineering the change itself, in some cases even more. But this effort will pay off one day! First, if an exception MUST be created, you already have a plan in place and do not need to improvise, which carries the risk of creating a security loophole. Second, if a department in your organization wants to implement something that needs an exception from hardening, you can put a price tag and a risk estimate on it right away – which may well lead to management overruling this decision!

It is not very often, however, that an application vendor – especially one whose product requires legacy configurations – will be able to tell you exactly what needs to be relaxed or reverted to Microsoft defaults and for what parts of the lifecycle (sometimes relaxed configurations are only needed for installation and you can get back to your accepted standard afterwards). For these cases, and you will probably experience them regularly, a test environment will prove invaluable. Your test lab does not have to reflect all the aspects of your production AD, but it needs to be built using the same engineering and hardening principles you use for production.

2.3.5 Prepare for Change

I have seen AD forests that had been created by a migration from Windows NT and did not change much ever since, nor did the management processes around Active Directory in those organizations evolve over time. However, time brings change even for the most stagnant of organizations.

Companies merge with each other, get renamed, restructure internally, or carve out parts of the business to be sold to investors. And the identity infrastructure must be able to keep up with these changes.

By engineering your AD in a way that does not introduce any unnecessary but irreversible dependencies, you are prepared for at least those changes that you can anticipate. This way your team can assist the business in any transformations that will undoubtedly come its way without compromising security, reliability, and usability of your most important services.

Not all decisions that have to be made on the way to a "change-friendly" AD are of technical nature. Be prepared to have discussions that belong in the "design" area rather than "engineering" and also to hear a lot of "this will never work in our organization." If you can explain what happens in the course of a major structural change if your architecture is used and also if the "we have always done it this way" design is followed, your chances of winning most of these arguments will improve dramatically. Having managers on the change advisory board who already went through this sort of transformation in their previous roles can help a lot here, too.

2.3.6 Prepare for Disaster

Active Directory has become extremely resilient against your typical day-to-day computer and networking maladies – a failed hard drive, a misbehaving network card, or even a loss of a domain controller. This has lulled many IT teams into a false sense of AD being somehow "indestructible," even though the threat landscape has evolved. In the early 2000s, if we were talking about a disaster that affected AD, it was always about a *natural* disaster. These days, however, a flood or a lightning strike is not likely to take out your basic IT services (the 2022 fire in OVHCloud's Strasbourg datacenter may be one of those exceptions that prove the rule). On the other hand, a professionally executed ransomware attack from a state-sponsored hacker group, or even from an independent one, is definitely going to put your emergency recovery procedures to the test.

CHAPTER 2   A MODERN AD

Since AD is foundational for both security and functionality of your enterprise IT, you will probably do whatever is necessary to prevent a true disaster from happening in the first place. Still, having an action plan in case your directory service has been put out of commission is paramount. There are two schools of thought in regard to that action plan, and each of them has its merits and comes with its own risks: "restore" and "rebuild." We will cover the individual benefits in more detail in Chapter 10, but the risks are spread over many different categories, and we'll point them out as we go. Whichever path you end up following, do not keep your emergency procedures handbook (exclusively) in a location whose function depends on AD. If someone insists that it *must be* that SharePoint Wiki because all standard procedures are kept there, print it out, export it to a portable format like HTML or PDF, and put it on a thumb drive. Make sure that there are no cleartext passwords stored in that documentation!

There is one last piece of advice that I would like to share here. In case of a disaster, especially if you are facing a cyber attack at a later stage, your organization will need a communications channel to its staff that is completely independent from the existing data and application infrastructure. When MAERSK got hit by NotPetya in 2017, employees at the container terminals set up WhatsApp chats and other instant messaging groups to coordinate their work. We should learn from these spectacular cases and provide a fallback channel ahead of time. This is more of a political challenge than a technical one, and in countries where the workers' right to privacy and self-determination is being protected by the law, the employer will probably not be able to just direct the staff to use their private mobile phones for work. But even if they could, the challenges of providing a reasonably secure public communications platform to use, designing onboarding and offboarding processes, and determining the amount of business-related information that can be shared there, still remain. Better have the departments responsible for crisis management figure out these things in advance than ad-lib them when the disaster has actually struck!

2.4 Lookup, Authentication, Authorization, and Configuration

What do we expect from a "modern Active Directory"? It has to provide the four functions AD has been designed to offer, but security, data protection, and resilience considerations demand that the scope of each function be restricted compared to the out-of-box offering:

- **Lookup:** Every authenticated computer and user MUST be able to obtain directory information (objects and their attributes) necessary for performing its business-related tasks. Additionally, every computer and user SHOULD be able to locate a suitable domain controller for authentication by using DNS; every user and computer MUST be able to locate servers and services necessary for performing their business-related tasks. Ideally, no information beyond that will be disclosed by the directory.

- **Authentication:** Every legitimate user and computer MUST be able to perform Kerberos authentication using the strongest cryptography supported by Active Directory at the time, either by a combination of User Principal Name and password or by a certificate. Encryption downgrade to a weaker AES dialect SHOULD be considered a tolerable exception, a downgrade to RC4 MUST be considered a severe exception. Protocol downgrade to NTLM MUST be considered a severe exception and be authorized at the highest level the organization reserves for security-related changes.

- **Authorization:** Every authenticated user and computer MUST be provided a set of claims suitable by performing authorization in any application that consumes Active Directory. These CAN be either group memberships, Kerberos claims, or a combination of both.

- **Configuration:** Every member computer and authenticated user MUST be served a set of configuration parameters to be consumed both by the operating system and applications running on top of it. These configuration parameters CAN be delivered in the form of Group Policy settings and preferences, attributes of own AD object (e.g., **mail** attribute of a user that enables Outlook to perform its autoconfiguration), attributes of other AD objects (e.g., Exchange service connection points in the configuration partition that point Outlook to a suitable Autodiscover webservice), or a combination of the above. All security-related configuration parameters SHOULD be consumed by the members in a way that directory-provided configurations override local ones but not the other way around.

In Chapters 4 through 7, we will engineer our AD functions according to these requirements.

2.5 A Modern AD Is Hybrid – Cloud Integration

Unless yours is one of these organizations that are buried in a disused missile silo under a mountain, you are probably looking at running a hybrid infrastructure of some kind. And it's a fairly safe bet that your first – or only – cloud identity component ends up being Microsoft Entra ID,

CHAPTER 2   A MODERN AD

formerly known as Azure AD. It is supported as the cloud identity provider for the absolute majority of cloud-native business applications. It also provides several controls and facilities that allow for truly enhancing the security posture even of your on-premises infrastructure. In fact, in the current (at the time of writing) Microsoft Privileged Access architecture, the cloud part is the component providing the secure management plane, the separation of duties, and the zero-trust access to the most privileged components. Microsoft's current EDR/XDR offerings, such as "Microsoft Defender for Identity," and their SIEM proposition ("Microsoft Sentinel") are all based in the cloud and only ever connect to on-premises components through dedicated agents.

However, the single greatest benefit both in terms of security and overall experience you can *really* derive from "the Cloud," and something you should start talking about early within your IT organization, is getting client endpoints out of your Active Directory. Despite all progress we have made on attack detection and prevention, the endpoint remains the uncontested champion in the "First point of entry for attackers" category. The human operating it is viewed by many security experts as the weakest link in the entire security architecture of organizations such as yours, which, by the way, means that you absolutely should continue investing in security awareness training and user education – well-trained end users not only help keep your infrastructure secure, they also produce less support tickets!

By removing your endpoint devices from the Kerberos realm of your AD and joining them directly to the cloud-based directory, you achieve instant benefits in multiple areas:

- Provisioning of new devices or reprovisioning of existing ones (e.g., after a major repair involving a hard disk replacement) does not include a domain join, which is a threat vector that is very hard to truly mitigate. You are still going to have to join your

35

- **servers** to AD, but those are usually restricted to very well-defined networks, so it is easy to isolate both by network segmentation and security boundaries. We will cover this in more detail in Chapter 7.

- You can still provide Kerberos authentication towards on-premises resources, but NTLM is not possible from a cloud-joined endpoint. This means you do not need to worry about regular users utilizing NTLM anymore. It also means that you will have to find an exception if you *do* have legacy applications that require NTLM to work, but those exceptions (terminal servers, authentication proxies, etc.) will be confined to your datacenter so not quite as easy to reach and exploit from a compromised cloud endpoint.

- Cloud is moving towards passwordless authentication much faster than on-premises infrastructures will ever be able to. This means that while user provisioning will still fall under your remit, other rather labor-intensive parts of the user account lifecycle, such as diagnosing account lockouts and resetting forgotten passwords, will not have to be handled by the Active Directory team anymore – an overall more satisfying experience both for the affected users and administrators tasked with managing their accounts.

A major hindrance in transitioning to purely cloud-joined clients is the very widespread practice of misunderstanding and misusing AD as a configuration management facility. Using a combination of Group Policies, Windows Deployment Services (sometimes enhanced by Microsoft Deployment Toolkit, MDT), and very sophisticated VBS and PowerShell scripting, some companies have achieved very efficient and flexible client management… that is firmly chained to the on-premises Active Directory! For these organizations, migrating their clients to the cloud means rebuilding their client management from the very foundations up. Ideally, this would involve rethinking the enterprise endpoint and its relationship to the user. Sadly, however, it is not what ends up happening in many scenarios. Administrators try to recreate all the peculiarities of their bespoke client management in the new environment, without the latter offering the required degree of flexibility. In the best case, it's "only a chance wasted in IT"; in the worst case, this leads to business disruption and a lack of acceptance both on the end-user and management level. You must avoid this on your cloud journey, and the best way to achieve it is by starting early and involving everybody who has a say in it in the new client design without creating undue pressure by setting deadlines. Testing until everybody is at least 80% satisfied – this is a far better objective than having 80% of stakeholders completely satisfied and also one that's easier to achieve.

2.6 Summary

In this chapter, we investigated the requirements our engineering effort will have to fulfill, along with the functionality – lookup, authentication, authorization, and configuration – we need to take into account when creating and maintaining our Active Directory organization. Functional requirements introduced by systems and applications that consume AD have to be reconciled with three further sets of requirements, both of which have implications for the topology, internal structure, and management processes of our AD:

- Employee mobility
- Site autonomy
- Directory security

CHAPTER 2 A MODERN AD

To accommodate all these different requirements, our "Modern AD" engineering paradigm will follow a set of six guiding principles, from "Security First" to "Prepare for Disaster." And since a modern AD is most probably going to be hybrid, we highlighted cloud-joined clients as the easiest and most rewarding way to take advantage of the cloud part of hybrid identity.

CHAPTER 3

Engineering Topology

Active Directory presents us with a wide selection of topology choices – forests that trust each other (or not) and domains that make them up, geographical distribution to sites with site links following the physical layout of the corporate WAN (sometimes they don't, leading to less-than-optimal function of the directory environment and interesting troubleshooting sessions), custom DNS and application partitions with their own replication scopes, read-only domain controllers thrown into the mix, and thousands of individual settings that govern the replication and site coverage behavior of our AD organization. Topology is the one area of the entire engineering effort that probably has the smallest security implications, apart from the fact that the forest and not the domain is the true security boundary in AD. Yet topology is important – for the overall resilience and manageability of our identity infrastructure, and good manageability tends to go hand in hand with good security. It is also important in case of recovery from a catastrophic failure, be it due to a cyber incident or to more mundane causes.

Before we start discussing replication scopes, security boundaries, RID pools, sites, and services, let me get one thing out of the way: If, by the terminology of this book (as laid out in the Introduction), your organization qualifies as "enterprise," you absolutely need a Red Forest. The concept of a Red (or Management, or Bastion) forest is not new. It had been practiced by security-conscious organizations at least since 2008R2, and it was codified by Microsoft around 2012 as a part of its ESAE ("Enhanced Security Admin Environment") administration model. ESAE was deprecated in early 2021 after receiving a somewhat limited adoption over the years, to be replaced by a more generalized, zero-trust-based cloud-first security model, which, at the time of writing, has yet to prove its merit. With the release of Server 2025, forest trusts will get an additional hardening implemented by default, thus making the concept of a Red Forest even more attractive. The opponents of the Red Forest model often cite added complexity and limited benefits. In reality, however, the added complexity is negligible. In terms of required infrastructure, we are looking at a really small number of domain controllers, ideally in their own network segment, in order to take advantage of the existing datacenter firewall. Any other systems that help establish secure management of your privileged infrastructure have to be deployed and maintained anyway, whichever forest they end up being joined to. For the very small price of maintaining a handful of additional DCs, you get the benefit of keeping all active Tier 0 security principals out of your production directory! This makes both initial reconnaissance and privilege escalation so much more difficult for a malicious actor.

3.1 Site Autonomy – If a WAN Link Goes Down

Before you can leave design behind and start engineering your directory service, there is one very important question that needs to be answered by the business:

> For each geographical location within the enterprise, what functionality MUST be available to the users if the location's network becomes isolated from other locations, especially from central hub sites and, potentially, from the Internet?

CHAPTER 3   ENGINEERING TOPOLOGY

Getting answers to this is a design exercise that can prove much more involved than you would have anticipated at first. To successfully coax the required information out of the business, you will probably have to rephrase the question several times, depending on whom you are talking to. Translating the answers back into technical requirements concerning AD and its associated services also requires knowledge of the applications and their underlying infrastructure.

For example, if the business expects that ERP application XYZ be available in case of a site isolation, this requirement exists on several layers:

1. The users must be able to boot up their computers and obtain network connectivity in the first place. This means local physical workstations (as opposed to VDI served from another location to thin clients) and network infrastructure services like DHCP and possibly Network Access Control (NAC), both of which have to be provided on site.

2. The users must be able to authenticate to their computers to get to the desktop environment. This may involve authenticating to Active Directory, using cached AD credentials, using local accounts, or using a cloud-based authentication provider like Entra ID (in which case we have to assume that the cloud connectivity will be there even if the WAN to HQ is down).

3. After the users start the XYZ client component (which can be a web browser or an application-specific executable), it must be able to connect to the application's back-end, be it a web-based

middleware, a central database server, or a file-based database in a file share. In each case, this resource must be available locally on site, and some sort of name resolution and authentication will be necessary to locate and access the resource. Some applications provide offline working capabilities, which may or may not be sufficient to tide the site over until the WAN outage has been fixed.

4. There may be even more to this – for instance, if the application involves printing on a remote printer or transferring data to a different geographical location for it to take further action like shipping items out of a warehouse or uploading a production job to a machine control module. These processes may also require AD to be available at certain sites.

Sometimes this kind of dependency analysis will reveal sites that, if isolated, cannot do any meaningful work regardless of Active Directory being present locally or not. These are usually good candidates for not having a local replica of any AD partitions belonging to a wider domain or forest:

- If the bandwidth to a hub site or to neighboring sites is sufficient for running remote applications, transferring data, and replicating AD on top of all this, then there is probably enough bandwidth for lookup and authentication against DCs in a neighboring (hub or spoke) site.

- If the bandwidth to any other site is too low even for AD replication (and it needs a lot less bandwidth today than it did back in 2000!), it's probably too low for application access as well.

If a site absolutely needs local authentication even in an isolated state (usually because there are mission-critical applications that are local to the site), providing a separate AD forest for that site can be a viable alternative. This path leads to a multitude of site-local forests, which at first seems counterintuitive because it requires more management. However, this additional management is of the kind that can be easily taken care of by automation, and the administration of all site-local forests can (and should) be carried out from the single central Red Forest. If a site becomes isolated, no changes in its local forest can, therefore, be made, but this is true for other topology choices as well – changes made in a central location will not replicate to the local site until the WAN link is reestablished.

In the modern world, you may be faced with an additional requirement that, unfortunately, makes site-local forests far less viable: that of employee mobility between the different sites, which would mean that an employee normally working at HQ in Seattle might be ordered to do some work at the Nairobi plant and would expect to access the usual central services plus applications local to that site using their AD login. This is not an unsolvable problem, even using multiple site-local forests (accounts can be provisioned in multiple forests, passwords can be kept in sync using the password reset facility of your IAM, role and permission groups can contain accounts from multiple forests belonging to the same user), but the extra complexity it introduces will become transparent to the end user at some point, and you end up getting more, not less, trouble tickets – which of course means this topology choice was wrong in light of the requirements!

If the mobility and site autonomy requirements do become mutually exclusive, you will probably have to accept that today's WAN links are usually pretty reliable and chalk site isolation up as an "acceptable risk." You should not, however, accept this risk blindly, but rather be aware of what a prolonged outage of an Active Directory site really entails. Present it to the business prior to finalizing your AD organization's topology and have the business' risk managers sign off on that. It's not IT's place, nor its job, to decide about the business impact of a WAN outage after all.

3.2 Forest and Domain Topologies

Your AD's forest and domain structure is something that is very important to "get right," because changing it after the fact usually constitutes a full-scale migration (we will talk about that in greater detail in Chapter 11). The anti-pattern you are absolutely going to want to avoid here is a multi-domain forest – a topology that was considered an accepted best practice in the early days of AD design and one that is encountered fairly often even today. This is not to say that a multi-domain forest has no justification at all as a topology option, but it should definitely not be your default choice when implementing forests and domains for your organization. The other obvious alternatives that present themselves are

- A global single-domain forest encompassing the entire geographical distribution of the enterprise, its different applications (inasmuch as they are related to AD), and security zones

- A multitude of single-domain forests dedicated to either geographical sites (we discussed this in the previous section) or certain applications with their specific AD integrations and security concerns (Exchange deployed in a resource forest model is a classic example)

In short, every time you are about to add a new domain to a forest that, until now, only had one domain, I urge you to halt and ask yourself if an additional forest would not constitute a better alternative.

3.2.1 Anatomy of a Multi-domain Forest

The objects that all domains in a forest share are

- Schema partition
- Configuration partition
- Forest-wide security groups like "Enterprise Admins" (those are only allowed to exist in the forest root domain but have extremely high privileges in all domains by default)
- UPN suffix list (it's stored in the configuration partition)
- Trust relationships provided by forest trusts (they are created in the forest root domain)
- DNS zones that are set to replicate forest-wide (ForestDnsZones being yet another shared partition)
- Forest-wide FSMO roles: Domain Naming Master and Schema Master
- Universal groups which, although possibly spread throughout the forest's domains, can have members from different domains and also permissions assigned to them in domains different from the one they belong to
- Somewhat misleadingly, Domain Local groups which can have members from everywhere, including trusted domains or forests
- The Global Catalog

The dependency on the Global Catalog is also something that a single-domain forest presents an elegant solution for, both in terms of replication and the (in)significance of the Infrastructure Master FSMO role.

Given that domains within a forest do not constitute a security boundary, you could also say that all domains in the same forest share a common attack surface! With default permissions assigned to standard privileged groups, elevation from Domain Admin to Enterprise Admin (or to Domain Admin in a different domain of the same forest) only takes one step: using replication, a malicious actor is able to put the SIDs of the desired admin groups into sidHistory of an account in the domain they control!

In contrast, the following objects that truly belong to a single domain within a forest are

- NetBIOS name of the domain
- Domain partition
- DNS zones that are set to replicate domain-wide
- Global groups, although the name seemingly suggests otherwise
- Domain-wide FSMO roles: PDC Emulator (PDCe), RID Master, and Infrastructure Master

3.2.2 Motivation for the Multi-domain Anti-pattern

How, and why, did generations of directory architects arrive at the popular multi-domain forest design? Early Microsoft documentation definitely left an impression that multiple domains are necessary in a forest above a certain size. Apart from that and the universal "because we can" justification, the following factors usually played a significant role in considering this topology option:

CHAPTER 3　ENGINEERING TOPOLOGY

- **Logon domain user experience:** This is due to Windows prepopulating the NetBIOS name of the domain the computer is a member of (or a different one, configured by Group Policy) on the logon screen. In a single-domain forest encompassing multiple business entities within one enterprise, some of the users may be upset because they are shown the "wrong business unit" as "their" domain at logon! Not using company branding in NetBIOS names helps avoid this; we will discuss it later in this chapter. Had we started educating users to log on using their UPN early on, this would never have become an issue since UPN suffixes are valid forest-wide, making the domain part of the UPN independent of the domain the account actually belongs to!

- **Local distribution:** The classic design example for this are "continental domains" that are subordinated to a central company domain, i.e., "company.com," "na.company.com," "eu.company.com," "au.company.com," and so on. This sort of subdivision implies that underwater cables and satellite uplinks may go down one day (they do sometimes!). In this case, the domain remains fully manageable within its own locality. This sort of geographical distribution is often motivated by replication; however, many of the changes that occur within a domain are reflected in the Global Catalog, which is replicated forest-wide. In case of unreliable or slow WAN links, this leads to the practice of not providing the Global Catalog in certain sites. This can be made to work (unless there is an application that specifically requires the GC to be available) but has other implications as well. A further motivator for separating regional domains is the placement of FSMO roles such as PDC emulator and RID master, which we will discuss further in this chapter.

- **Misinterpreted separation of concerns:** The two arguments above are often combined in order to give locally operated business units within the enterprise a degree of "self-determination" in how they manage "their" AD. In reality, this just makes managing the entire forest more cumbersome without adding any tangible value. If central IT decides to deploy an Exchange cumulative update, they must ensure that all domain controllers in all domains and sites are operational – Exchange CUs always contain schema and configuration updates and will not continue until the changes to these objects have replicated to all DCs forest-wide. And, while Exchange certainly is an extreme example of this sort of dependency, reliance on forest-wide replication for operational changes is by no means a trait unique to Exchange.

If you would like to delegate the management of objects belonging to a certain business unit to that unit's IT, the only way to actually achieve it within a common forest is by assigning permissions. The amount of effort necessary to do so in a separate domain is identical to deploying the same set of permissions to an OU. But you should absolutely avoid taking a shortcut and giving the business unit's IT Domain Admin rights in "their" domain; otherwise, you will end up having lots of de facto Enterprise Admins, most of whom have no business managing anything outside of their own little fiefdom.

CHAPTER 3   ENGINEERING TOPOLOGY

Some management processes do, in fact, benefit from having separate domains managed by separate IT teams:

- Domain join into the default container (i.e., without specifying the OU path at join time). Separate domains mean separate default containers, which may be desirable. However, an account doing this sort of join usually ends up being overpermissioned anyway, so the AD topology might be the last stimulus you need to finally revisit this process and enforce specifying the target OU as a part of domain join. All modern OS deployment systems, including even the free ones like MDT, offer this capability. We will talk about domain join at length in Chapters 5 and 7.

- Domain local groups isolation. If the RBAC model adopted by the organization uses lots of authorization groups spread across multiple resources, placing these resources in different domains helps reduce the number of groups every user has in their security token; so does spreading the resources across multiple forests. We will discuss this in detail in Chapter 6.

- If the business unit's admins are given permissions to create a Group Policy object, that object will usually be visible to all other business units sharing the same domain as well since one domain's GPOs all reside in the same container. This can be amended by either using a third-party tool for managing GPO or by providing GPO templates with edit permissions assigned to the respective IT team. We will visit this topic in Chapter 7.

- If a certain business unit exhibits a considerably higher churn rate than others within the same organization (e.g., student accounts as compared to faculty), this will lead to RIDs having gaps in their sequence. Separating high-privilege, low-churn objects out into a "permanent staff domain" can help keep an eye on continuity within that domain. On the other hand, relying on RIDs always being continuous as a foundation for an identity management process will usually leave you disappointed anyway.

If you encounter such processes within your organization, you now have arguments in your quiver that will help you optimize these processes or have management order the responsible IT teams to do so.

3.2.3 Multi-domain Forest: Extreme Anti-patterns

We already stated that a multi-domain forest is a topology choice you would usually want to avoid for a multitude of reasons but might be compelled to use if the physical network topology makes a flat single-domain forest untenable. However, even if you find yourself in multi-domain land, there is still a more severe anti-pattern you should avoid at all costs: having more than two levels of domain hierarchy as shown, for example, in Figure 3-1.

CHAPTER 3 ENGINEERING TOPOLOGY

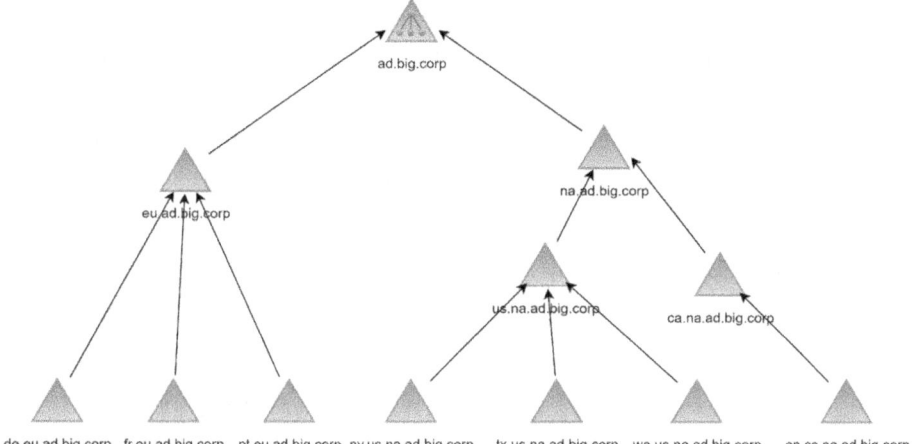

Figure 3-1. *This multilayer topology is a waste of resources and your time*

In this forest, only the domains at the bottom, i.e., individual states, provide any value to the business. The root domain is, strictly speaking, not needed but could save you some CPU cycles and network bandwidth if you decide to deploy the root domain to all locations since there will hardly be any replication going on within the root domain if it's effectively empty. But the layers in between are a waste of energy, rack space, and – last but not least – your troubleshooting effort if things were to go awry one day. Cross-domain authentication within such a forest is also slower and less reliable than in a more compact topology; however, if users from Ontario (on.ca.na.big.corp) end up working in France (fr.eu.big.corp) on a semi-permanent basis, you will probably put a shortcut trust in place and provision domain controllers in the requisite geolocations anyway.

Another design option that deserves a warning is not actually per se bad *if you are required to run a multi-domain forest*: multiple trees in a forest. In the above example, this would let the architect eliminate the root domain and just put eu and na domains on top of their individual trees. One of them would still be the root domain in terms of containing enterprise-wide objects and being the point of forest trust, but you could maintain contiguous namespaces without NA being "visually" a child of EU or vice versa. Why have we put it under "extreme anti-patterns" though? The answer is to be found not so much in AD itself but in people and tools managing it. There are countless applications that are, in theory, multi-domain capable but, in practice, will not work in a multiple-tree model. Usually, these applications will also break in any but strictly hierarchical namespace, including disjoint DNS namespace designs.

3.2.4 Motivation of the Multi-forest Pattern

Splitting the identity landscape into multiple forests by applications is usually quite straightforward, Exchange being the most popular example by far. This allows for a very simple yet reliable separation of

- Administrative privileges
- Schema and configuration extensions
- Attack surfaces
- Replication scopes (an application provisioned only in HQ is completely unaffected by a peripheral site going down or becoming isolated)

Mergers and Acquisitions, which have become commonplace in many industries, can also benefit immensely from having business units reside in separate forests. Adding a new forest can be reverted easily and without leaving a trace in case of a later divestment, whereas domains and partitions in the corporate forest are not nearly as easy to split. A very dangerous scenario, security-wise, is a split of an existing forest where the receiving organization receives copies of domain controllers with the objects belonging to the remaining parts of the organization cleaned out (*but still present as tombstones or even in the Recycle Bin*).

When talking about forest trusts as security boundaries, remember that even a one-way trust is not 100% impenetrable, at least at the time of writing (Server 2022 being the most recent generally available version). The Trusted Domain object (in the trusting forest) is has a matching computer object in the trusted forest with a password synchronized between the two so a domain takeover in the trusting forest *does* provide you with a valid "authenticated user" in the trusted forest. This will change with Server 2025 in that this object class will not be allowed to authenticate going forward but will still provide a synchronized shared secret necessary to facilitate the trust.

3.2.5 Challenges of a Multi-forest User Base

In comparison, splitting *users* belonging to the same overarching organization into multiple forests, be it by business unit or by locality, introduces two major challenges:

1. **Global Catalog:** Objects from a different, even trusted, forest will not be part of the GC. If this is only needed for lookup, e.g., populating an organization-wide address book, this is usually solvable by either providing a metadirectory that contains objects from all forests, or by creating contacts in every forest for the users from the other forests, or by having the application serving the address book query multiple sources. In most cases, this challenge can be overcome by automation, sometimes even by utilizing your existing identity management.

2. **UPN suffix routing:** A typical usability technique, and one that should always be encouraged, is setting the users' UPN to their email address and having them authenticate using this value rather than by

NETBIOS name or a UPN derived from the DNS name of their domain. Several years ago, we used to call this logon experience "Facebook-type logon." In a multi-user-forest scenario with a common SMTP namespace, this means that multiple forests end up having to authenticate UPNs with the same suffix. This is not supported by suffix routing in Active Directory if the forests are to share any trust relationship. Figure 3-2 shows the very verbose error message you are going to get if you try to set this up.

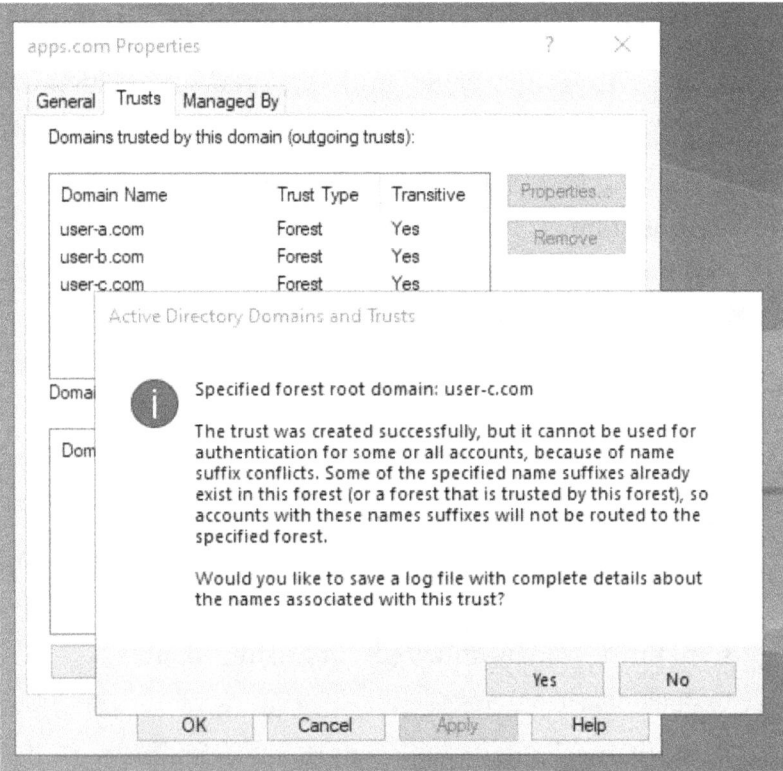

Figure 3-2. *Suffix routing does not support multiple routing targets for the same suffix*

CHAPTER 3   ENGINEERING TOPOLOGY

For pure LDAP bind operations, an ADLDS instance with proxy authentication can take care of the suffix routing dilemma (we will look at this in more detail in Chapter 5). For all other authentication scenarios like interactive logon or Kerberos pass-through, including Exchange installed in a resource forest, "Facebook logon" using one global SMTP namespace (i.e., UPN suffix) will not work across multiple user forests.

> **Note**   Exchange Online or Entra ID in general does not have this restriction since no actual Kerberos trusts are being used. If you do provide Kerberos authentication towards on-premises resources for cloud accounts, suffix routing *will* be an issue in this scenario as well.

3.3 Naming Conventions for Domains

Unlike in Goethe's Faust, not all names are "noise and smoke" in Active Directory. They have the potential of influencing functionality, usability, and sometimes even security of the environment (e.g., when they overlap with other names not controlled by your organization). The most important names you'll have to decide upon are

- Domain NetBIOS names
- Domain DNS names (FQDNs)
- UPN suffixes
- SPN suffixes (FQDNs of service endpoints)

Upon initialization of an AD domain, its FQDN is the default UPN and SPN suffix for all identities in that domain.

CHAPTER 3   ENGINEERING TOPOLOGY

Technically, you can assign whatever UPNs you like to your user accounts without "officially" adding their suffixes to the forest's configuration, as long as they are unique forest-wide. Those UPNs will be perfectly valid for authentication within the forest. However, suffix routing will not kick in unless you explicitly add the suffix to the forest, so cross-forest authentication is not going to work with such UPNs.

The requirements we presented in the previous chapter offer a good basis for domain naming decisions. The main guiding principle should be acknowledging that a domain rename always constitutes a full-scale migration and has to be avoided at all costs. This means you should choose domain names using rules that will not force you to change those names in the future:

- Do not use company names (BIGFIRM/ad.bigfirm.com) because companies sometimes get renamed, and if that happens, using the previous name might end up being the least politically correct thing one can do.

- Do not use the FQDN of your company's website for AD domains. First, those tend to change even faster than company names. And second, domain members will not be able to resolve that FQDN to its external address if you do. You could work around this by using a proxy, but then the proxy server cannot use the same DNS server AD uses for name resolution. This is not ideal and adds complexity.

- Do not use years (AD2024/ad2024.local) because... well, time passes, and no one will ever give much thought to the question of which year your forest was established in.

- Avoid long names because your users will have to type them at some point. However, when using short names, you should also avoid choosing ones that are overly generic like **CORP.DOM** because this will pose problems in case of a merger if the other company happens to choose the same name.

- If you design a large and complex organization with multiple domains and forests containing users, you are most probably dealing with a user population that will have absolutely no problem logging on to D093575 every morning. Having domains numbered in this manner is a good protection against overlapping names in the future. But do not use postcodes, phone routing prefixes, or other universally assigned numbers in this case. Talk to HR; they may have their own codes for business units, in which case it is a very good idea to reflect these in your domain structure.

- Avoid overlapping names. It's perfectly okay to have **na.company.com** and **eu.company.com** as separate forests in your AD organization, but if you do, do NOT introduce **company.com** into the mix – this will cause all sorts of problems!

- If you do operate multi-domain forests in your Active Directory, avoid "reverse hierarchies." It is possible to create **company.com** as a subdomain of **it.ad.company.com**, but you will be surprised how many applications will refuse to perform cross-domain lookup or authentication in this scenario.

3.3.1 Externally Resolvable AD Domains

The question of whether or not to use externally resolvable domain names for Active Directory domains is as old as AD itself. Since March 2013, the decision in favor of non-resolvable domains became slightly less final, because virtually any domain suffix can, in theory, get registered as a TLD, but not many of previously not universally resolvable suffixes have achieved any real traction on the public Internet. Proponents of using externally resolvable names for AD domains cite the ability to obtain externally validated TLS certificates for internal servers. However, it is very easy – and in some cases, tremendously beneficial – to publish **SRV4711.DOMAIN.INT** as **crm.our-company.com**. This works for both name resolution (the term "Split-Brain DNS" having wrongly acquired a bad reputation, the author prefers the term "Split-Horizon DNS") and Kerberos authentication, because SPNs are not tied to a particular list of domain suffixes and can be chosen to match the FQDN used by the clients to reach the service.

However, if you decide to use an externally resolvable domain name, make sure your organization actually owns it. Otherwise, you could be opening several paths for attacking your infrastructure. An attacker could try to lure your users to a server looking exactly as if it came from your domain and even protected by a certificate that their browsers will successfully validate. This is the best possible foundation for harvesting your users' credentials, thus gaining a foothold in your directory.

3.3.2 Disjoint DNS Namespaces

When planning your AD domain namespaces, give some thought to DNS (we will discuss this further in the next chapter). The anti-pattern you have to avoid here is "disjoint namespaces," i.e., domain member computers having their primary DNS suffix set to a different DNS domain than the

FQDN of the AD domain they are a member in. The motivation for using disjoint namespaces often lies in the separation of computers' FQDNs (by geography or business unit) while keeping their AD memberships consolidated to one domain. For client computers where DNS records are refreshed frequently due to the clients having dynamic IP addresses, this can help conserve network bandwidth by restricting the replication scope of regional DNS zones to DNS servers in their respective region. If that is your main concern, a disjoint namespace can help. But for servers whose DNS records do not change on a constant basis, causing replication, you should always keep their primary DNS suffix set to the FQDN of their AD domains. Otherwise, Kerberos authentication towards these servers will become unwieldy, and for some applications it will even fail, in spite of you having added all requisite SPNs to the computer object!

3.3.3 Other Naming Conventions Involved in AD Topology

There are other types of topology objects that you have to provide a consistent naming convention for, like AD sites, site links, and bridges, but their naming usually does not affect functionality or security, nor is it normally of any concern to the end users. However, in a multi-forest AD organization where users from one forest routinely log on to machines belonging to a different, but trusting, forest, you will benefit immensely from having identical site names and subnet assignments across all the forests. This will allow the DC Locator process for the user logon and GPO application to take a shortcut and just use the name of the site the computer belongs to, instead of going through the user forest topology and determining the correct site for the DC lookup. This brings us directly to the next section.

CHAPTER 3   ENGINEERING TOPOLOGY

3.4 Sites and Subnets

Sites and subnets describe the geographical (i.e., physical) distribution of your environment, to be used both by Active Directory itself (to calculate the required replication pathways) and by "AD-aware" systems and applications (mostly to determine which Domain Controllers and DNS servers to use for lookup and authentication). The closer this description aligns with the reality of your organization's IP addressing and routing, the less troubleshooting you can expect to have to be involved in going forward. You want to avoid authentication or lookup requests going to a domain controller at the other end of the world while there are DCs available in closer proximity, network-wise. To achieve this, you must exercise very good care in linking sites with each other, regardless of whether they contain domain controllers or not.

> In this book, we will only be considering IP-based AD replication. SMTP-based replication is a fascinating topic and served us well in the past in scenarios where only public – and rather unreliable – networks were available between AD sites (seagoing ships are one classic example), but it is safe to say that at the time of writing, the age of SMTP replication has passed. It has already been deprecated – but not yet removed – from Windows.

Note   An additional setting on your domain members is required to have them honor the replication cost for locating the DC in case that no DC is found in the member's own site. This setting, named **Try Next Closest Site**, is governed by Group Policy and found under **Computer Configuration\Policies\Administrative Templates\System\Net Logon\DC Locator DNS Records**.

CHAPTER 3 ENGINEERING TOPOLOGY

Not every physical WAN topology lends itself equally well to operating Active Directory on top of it. An ideal WAN is fully meshed so that there are no limitations to which site can access systems in which other site, and the purpose of reflecting the available bandwidth and latency in AD is mainly to contain as much AD traffic as possible within local networks and prefer high-bandwidth, low-latency links over the slower ones. However, more often than not, you will find some sort of hub and spoke topology that you have to reflect in the AD design.

Figure 3-3. *A typical enterprise WAN is not always designed with AD in mind*

For successful topology engineering, you should spend some time with the network team to understand the principles and restrictions their WAN design has to adhere to. This will also allow you to understand where that team could, in fact, introduce changes like additional routes or transfer networks that would make your life easier and the resulting AD organization more resilient and performant. In any case, draw a network map like the one in Figure 3-3 and keep it up-to-date.

CHAPTER 3   ENGINEERING TOPOLOGY

For describing topologies, we will be using the following terminology throughout this book:

- A **hub site** is a site where a number of IT infrastructure services are being run and managed, including Active Directory, DNS, and other fundamental network services. A hub site typically features well-equipped datacenter rooms, backup and monitoring facilities, and direct links to the locations where operators administering the infrastructure are situated.

- A **hub** represents a collection of hub sites connected with each other by very fast links, each of these sites having identical connectivity to any other locations. Two datacenter tracts within one building complex can work as a hub.

- A **spoke** or **spoke site** is a site that contains domain controllers from one or more relevant domains but is not directly managed. Administrative changes are usually made in a hub site and replicated out to the spokes. A spoke has a direct link to a single hub site or to multiple sites of the same hub. Sometimes shortcut site links between spokes of the same hub are introduced if supported by the underlying physical network.

- A **satellite site** is a site that has site links to one or more spoke, or even hub, sites but *no domain controllers* so that all AD-related services – lookup, authentication, and configuration – are provided from the neighboring site using site coverage mechanisms.

When engineering an Active Directory on top of a multi-hub, multi-spoke WAN, there are usually three concerns that have to be addressed.

3.4.1 Change Convergence Time

"Convergence time" means the maximum time that it takes for a change of an AD object made in one site to be propagated to every other site in the forest. Depending on your WAN, you may end up having long convergence between spoke sites attached to different hubs. This performance indicator, however, is often misinterpreted, not to say overrated, especially if you are able to propagate changes between hub sites very quickly by using notification-based replication. In this case, changes significant for a particular spoke site's operation either originate within that same site (like computer changing its password or a user updating their lastLogonTimestamp attribute) and propagate instantly or are made in a central hub (administrative changes) and propagate within one hop – again, assuming that replication between hubs is instant.

3.4.2 RID Master Visibility

Every time a domain controller exhausts its RID pool (500 RIDs by default) or when a new DC is being promoted and must obtain its initial RID pool, the DC in question must have line of sight connectivity to the DC holding the RID master role. Looking at Figure 3-3, to promote a DC in one of the South American spoke sites, the RID master role must be transferred into the South America hub site, at least temporarily. If your AD is managed in a centralized fashion, the RID pool in the spokes will usually last a long time because very few objects that have a SID (users, computers, or groups) are normally created in those sites. The most frequent operation requiring a RID from the local pool is joining a computer to a domain. We will show in Chapters 5 and 7 that creating a computer object *by performing a join operation* introduces multiple problems so that this process, again, should be automated – which can well happen in a central site so that by the time the new computer is ready to join the domain in a spoke site, its computer object is already replicated to that site without consuming a local RID there. An extreme example of local RID exhaustion is a non-persistent VDI configured to not reuse computer objects but discard and recreate them. If you are required to place this sort of resource in a spoke site, a separate domain or even forest for these ephemeral computers would definitely be an engineering decision worth considering.

3.4.3 PDC Emulator Visibility

In terms of Active Directory's own behavior, line of sight to PDCe is required to push password changes made against another DC to PDCe in a prioritized manner. This behavior resonates with the functionality of a Windows NT domain, where any changes could only be written to the domain database by the PDC. The corresponding behavior of *verifying* logons against the PDCe in case of a local logon failure was also hardwired in Windows NT, and a setting to disable it in Active Directory was introduced with Server 2003.

While AD itself is perfectly capable of handling PDCe not being accessible from every site, you may encounter applications that insist on talking to the PDCe. While this indicates that the directory service integration behavior of such an application hasn't been revisited since 1999, it may not be up to you to have this particular application modernized or replaced by a better-behaving competing product. Before you start building a complex multi-domain or multi-forest topology around a legacy application, however, you should

- Point out the added cost, complexity, and risk to the business and have them sign off on those
- Talk to the WAN team about adding some routes providing PDCe visibility (you can promise them to avoid clogging up those links by deprioritizing them in your site link topology)

- Have the offending application provisioned only in sites with PDCe visibility if accessing it from other sites by means of terminal servers or VDI is a viable alternative

3.4.4 Old and New Defaults

Active Directory comes with topology defaults that do not make much sense in any real environment: On one hand, a replication schedule of 180 minutes between sites lets dial-up connections come to mind; on the other hand, all site links are bridged by default, suggesting a fully meshed network that most organizations did not have at the time these defaults were defined and many do not have even today. This means that site topology will have to be engineered according to your organization's specific layout.

Today's WAN links usually allow for notification-based replication, making change propagation in your Active Directory faster and convergence time shorter. The overall amount of data transferred over WAN due to AD replication is also largely independent of notification-based vs. schedule-based replication being used – the only scenario where scheduled replication will end up transferring less data involves multiple changes made to the same object and attribute within one replication cycle. It is thus a good idea to make notification-based replication the new default and only use schedules where absolutely necessary. If in doubt, have the WAN team record the data transfer and bandwidth consumption between replication partners and test notification-based replication for a couple of days.

If you absolutely have to use schedules for replication, be aware that they can affect site link transitivity, especially if your schedule requirements not only include the frequency but also the time coverage. If schedules of two site links connecting a site with its neighboring sites do not overlap, the site links will not be transitive, and you might want

CHAPTER 3   ENGINEERING TOPOLOGY

to bridge them to ensure replication. By default, all site links are bridged without a dedicated site link bridge being in place, but this setting is often disabled early when building complex AD topologies (as it should be, we will talk about it later in this chapter).

Regardless of whether you have to use replication schedules or not, you absolutely must consider the cost of replication links. Every new site link you create in the Sites and Services MMC console comes with the cost of 100 assigned to it. So, if you are building a hub and spoke topology but create a site link between two spoke sites (without changing the cost factor for any of the links), it will end up getting used for replication since its cost (100) is lower than the total cost of two spoke links (100 + 100 = 200). Conversely, if you assign the spoke links the cost factor of 10, then the replication through the hub sites will be used.

All these considerations are, of course, only applicable if you let the Knowledge Consistency Checker create the replication links for you and do not alter the replication topology manually, which is what you should always aim for, because it will make your directory so much easier to manage.

3.4.5 The Guiding Principles for Site Topology Engineering

For maintaining sites and subnets, you should stick to the following guiding principles to achieve the best results:

- Define all subnets exactly the same way they are defined in DHCP and/or IP routing. Do not take shortcuts and create "supernets" or "superscopes" – even if you know that all subnets from 10.0.0.0/24 to 10.0.15.0/24 belong to the same physical location, resist the urge to just drop 10.0.0.0/20 into the configuration.

- If you happen to have IP subnets that are not routable by design, you don't need to include them. In fact, you shouldn't include them in your configuration as long as you are sure to get notified by the network team in case they do become connected to the rest of your IP address space one day.

- Each site must be contained entirely within one physical location (more precisely, a subset of your assets where the physical network is 100% under your organization's control). A physical location, on the other hand, can contain multiple AD sites. This will be beneficial in many cases and inevitable in some.

- There must be no site links encompassing sites that have no IP route between them.

- Prefer USE_NOTIFY to replication schedules; in fact, make it your default.

- Always set the cost of replication in a way that reflects your topology.

- Apply the "Try Next Closest Site" Group Policy setting to your domain members as widely as possible.

- There can be sites that do not contain domain controllers but contain member servers or clients. Make sure that such sites always have a direct link to a neighboring site that has domain controllers in it.

- Disable the "All site links are bridged" setting if you do not have a fully meshed network.

CHAPTER 3   ENGINEERING TOPOLOGY

- Do not rely on schedules always overlapping, especially if you have to resort to schedules due to special circumstances like ships only connected to the rest of the infrastructure while in port. If you have to work with replication schedules, define link bridges explicitly.

3.4.6 Site Name and Location Attribute

While site names do not have any real technical implications, having a good naming convention is important for the ease of management (which often translates to improved security posture of the environment). Because most humans are visual, a good naming convention will translate physical proximity to visual proximity when sorted alphabetically. In an organization that is spread geographically, this will usually lead to continents and countries being part of site names, as shown in Figure 3-4.

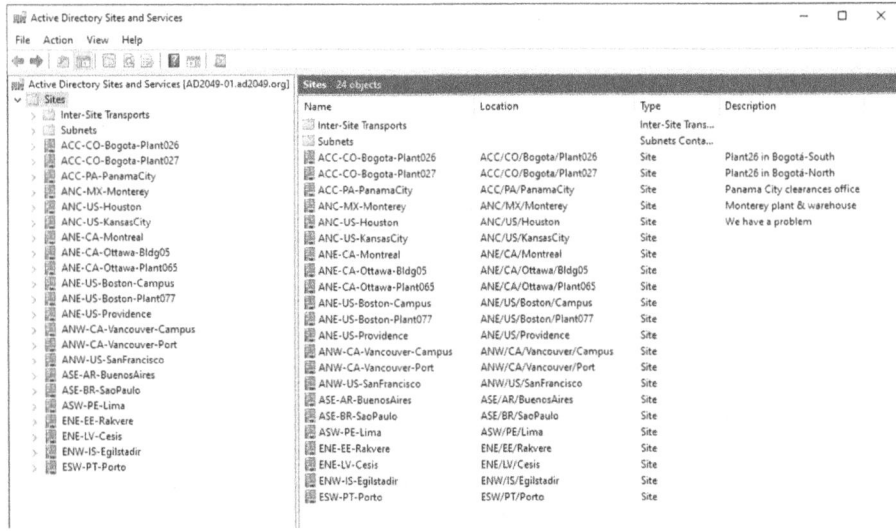

Figure 3-4. *Sites close to each other on the list are also close to each other physically*

Beside name and description that are essential for the ease of (manual) administration but have no functional implications otherwise, topology elements also have an additional text attribute named **location** that can be used to reflect the real-world geography in a slightly different manner. This attribute is available for sites, subnets, computers, and printer queues, along with the rather seldom-used **room** object class. The idea behind it was to enable applications to select an object, specifically a shared printer queue, that is geographically closest to the computer requesting that object. To achieve this goal, the **location** attribute contains a series of strings describing the geographical location, separated by the forward slash character (/) and beginning with the widest subdivision. For example, to describe a printer location in the west wing of the 7th floor of a particular office building, you might put something like "USA/MA/Boston/Campus/Bldg003/Flr07/West" in the **location** attribute of a printer queue. If your sites and subnets also have the location information following the same convention, then a computer from a subnet "USA/MA/Boston/Campus/Bldg003/Flr07" would offer printers from the above location as the most convenient choice to the user trying to map a shared printer from the directory.

If you fill the **location** attribute with any values at all, please make sure you conform to the syntax defined by Microsoft – slash-separated chain of location descriptors, widest to narrowest. Do not put arbitrary notes in there; use the **description** attribute for it.

3.4.7 Sites and Subnets in a Multi-forest Organization

As mentioned in the previous section, in a multi-forest AD organization, it is highly beneficial to have the sites (and to some extent, subnets) defined across all the forests in an identical manner to help streamline the DCLocator processing in cross-forest access scenarios. While this is quite a daunting task if done manually, automation takes care of this easily. Some DDI (DNS + DHCP + IP) management systems even allow for deploying this information into AD forests integrated into them. Whether you want this to be possible in your Red Forest as well is a different question because that would make your external DDI a "Tier Subzero" system or at least require a very specific permissioning within your Configuration partition. But even if your organization only consists of a single forest, spending some time automating sites and subnets will save you lots of time in the future as the physical layout of your organization evolves!

However, the technique of replicating the site topology across forests must not be applied blindly in large and/or complex organizations. Not every forest in your AD organization will have the same distribution of domain controllers across sites, which is why the **linking** of the sites and especially the cost values between sites having a DC and those without one does not have to be identical across all the forests. It's just the site names that you have to "get right" to ensure faster location of logon servers in user forests. In large organizations with hundreds or thousands of sites and thousands or even tens of thousands of subnets, the processing of the topology data introduces a measurable performance hit on every domain controller. Some of this load is avoidable, and you can reduce it by omitting the following components from the site topology:

- Any subnets, no DCs, or member computers from a particular forest will ever belong to. This has no bearing on cross-forest authentication because every machine will have determined its site in its own forest using the subnet information found in that forest. For the DC location in the user forest, it is sufficient that a site by the same name exists in that forest. An example of this could be a resource forest where all DCs and member servers are located in a central datacenter.

- Any sites where no authentication traffic will ever originate from. Red Forest authentication will usually only occur from central sites where Tier 0 IT staff is located.

3.5 AD Distribution and Placement

Once you have figured out what your organization's geographical distribution and WAN topology look like, you have enough information to decide upon the placement of DCs, Global Catalog instances, and FSMO roles.

3.5.1 Domain Controller Distribution

Placing domain controllers in a particular site increases the operational cost of that site while providing site autonomy and usually helping conserve WAN bandwidth at the same time. Trying to keep the number of DCs in your forest at a minimum is a very good engineering objective; however, it should not come at the cost of *reducing* maintainability and resilience. Keeping these factors in mind, we arrive at the following methodology for DC placement:

- Hub sites (central datacenter locations and/or offices containing lots of domain members and users) always get at least two domain controllers from each domain in each forest. Having more than two domain controllers within one site usually does not provide much operational benefit. The only exception here is the PDCe, which you might want to exclude from authentication and lookup while still maintaining resilience and performance.

- If a site requires a read/write domain controller because of site autonomy requirements (or because it serves as a bridge site between a central hub and a subregion), place two of them within that site. The added operational cost is minimal, but two DCs within one site offer better resilience and manageability.

- If your design includes placing read-only domain controllers (RODCs) in a site and the domain members in that site are allowed to connect to the next site, one RODC may be sufficient to tide the site over a WAN outage. If the site's RODCs are the only DCs the members can connect to, place two of them within the site for resilience but take utmost care to configure them in an identical manner. We will discuss this in the next section.

Note Server 2025 introduces several performance enhancements for domain controllers, making scaling them up instead of out a viable approach even in large AD organizations.

3.5.2 Global Catalog Placement

If your organization's business and network requirements allow you to follow our recommendations from the previous chapter and stick to the single-domain forest model, you have nothing to consider for GC or Infrastructure Master role placement because any and all data in the Global Catalog is already contained in the domain partition. In this model, you can safely enable GC on all domain controllers and colocate the Infrastructure Master with your PDCe – it won't put any additional load on that DC because it ultimately has nothing to do!

CHAPTER 3   ENGINEERING TOPOLOGY

If you are forced to consider a multi-domain forest deployment but your network can absorb additional replication traffic, enable GC on every DC and place the Infrastructure Master wherever you like – it doesn't even have to be *accessible* from anywhere, but placing this FSMO role in a well-connected hub site helps ensure up-to-date GC information.

Global Catalog placement only gets tricky if you are forced into a multi-domain forest pattern, **and** replication traffic presents a challenge for some of the site links. This is usually due to geographically constrained domains with very weak network links between the geographical regions. To decide whether you need a GC instance in a particular site, you have to understand *why* you would require cross-domain data in the first place:

- If you have to support an application that is widely used in a poorly connected site and that application *specifically* requires access to Global Catalog, you are probably better off placing a GC in that site and dealing with bandwidth issues for replication than dealing with bandwidth issues for lookup by said application.

- If the only information actually required from the Global Catalog are cross-domain universal group memberships for building the security token, enable Universal Group membership caching (introduced with Server 2003) on the NTDS Site Settings object and do not place a full copy of the Global Catalog in that site. The cache is refreshed every eight hours by default. An instant refresh from the next-hop GC instance can be requested by submitting an **updateCachedMemberships** LDAP operation to the DC.

- If you do have an application that requires GC access from a poorly connected site but it's not very widely used, you can probably get by with UGMC plus providing a copy of the Global Catalog in the next-hop site, e.g., the regional hub site. DNS SRV records registered by the hub site's DCs will point the application to the right place to connect to a GC instance.

3.5.3 Application Partitions

If replication traffic is a concern in your organization's WAN, you'll definitely want to give some thought to replicating DNS changes throughout your AD if AD-integrated DNS is being used. All DNS records are not created equal:

- You definitely want up-to-date information about domain controllers and services they offer delivered to every site in a timely manner. This is usually not a problem because these records, contained in the forest-wide replicated DNS zone `_msdcs.<root-domain>`, are not very dynamic.

- Host (A/AAAA), PTR, and SRV records of application servers are important, but those, too, do not change very often. In a WAN that is not fully routed, a spoke site is usually only concerned about servers located either in the same site or in the next-hop hub site (e.g., regional hub). These changes usually replicate quickly within the region, even if they can take longer to become active in other regions.

- Host records of clients can generate a large amount of updates, especially if DHCP takes care of updating the A record every time a client device changes its network between LAN, WLAN, and VPN.

CHAPTER 3 ENGINEERING TOPOLOGY

The first two classes of DNS updates do not usually lead to problems. For the client's very dynamic DNS records, the first question to ask is whether this information is actually consumed at all (*and while you're at it, you can as well ask if reverse name resolution is needed for client devices – or, in fact, for any services and devices on the network*). Restricting a malicious actor's lateral movement by severely limiting inbound connectivity to clients has become a standard hardening measure in recent years, which in turn decreases the usefulness of up-to-date name resolution.

If you do need clients' FQDNs resolvable to their currently active IP addresses, these FQDNs will have to come from zones with restricted replication scopes. In a multi-domain forest, you can usually achieve good results by just using the respective domain FQDN (*remember, it was your WAN that ultimately forced the multi-domain topology on you!*). If DNS replication becomes a matter of concern within a single-domain forest, you may consider the following design options:

- Reduction of the DNS records' up-to-dateness. Sometimes this information is needed, but it's not vital that DNS is updated within seconds of an IP address change. Sometimes the current address is only useful if it's a LAN IP as opposed to WLAN or VPN. In such cases, configure DHCP servers responsible for WLAN and VPN to not update DNS.

- Custom application partitions with limited replication scopes. Keep them restricted to clients only and be prepared to lose this content in a disaster recovery scenario (it is dynamic anyway, so it's probably not such a great loss).

- Not integrating client-specific DNS namespaces in AD but rather providing standalone DNS servers for them and using DNS replication rather than AD replication to propagate those changes. This way you can configure DNS replication pathways in a completely different manner than those for AD replication.

3.5.4 FSMO Role Distribution

If your network is either fully meshed or built in a hub/spoke design with a **single** hub location, there is a lot to be said for placing all FSMO roles on the same domain controller in a central site (a hub may consist of more than one site as long as every spoke has a site link to every site making up a hub). In a multi-domain forest, place the forest-wide roles (Schema Master and Domain Naming Master) on the PDCe of the forest root domain. The forest-wide roles do not do any work as such so will not add to the resource consumption of the PDCe role. If you perform schema updates or add domains, partitions, or UPN suffixes to the forests, these tasks will be carried out on the machine bearing the respective role, but this additional workload is limited in duration.

Infrastructure Master in a multi-domain forest does have a workload of its own, regardless of the underlying WAN topology. It should be placed in a central location (in regard to the replication scope of its respective domain). However, **if your WAN prevents you from enabling GC on every DC in the domain and you do not have Recycle Bin enabled, you have to place the Infrastructure Master role on a DC that is not hosting a Global Catalog instance** but is nonetheless as well connected as possible. A short outage of this role, on the other hand, will not cause you any discomfort, so there is no need to artificially add multiple non-GC DCs to a central location and move the Infrastructure Master around if you take its previous owner down for maintenance for a short period of time.

RID Master does not have a continuous workload but must be reachable when a DC tries to obtain a new RID pool. AD has a mechanism by which a DC will start requesting a new RID pool once 50% of the current pool capacity has been consumed *but continue issuing RIDs from the previous pool until it is completely exhausted*. Thanks to this behavior, a short interruption of RID Master availability will not cause any significant disruption (*unless, of course, someone chooses to provision a pool of 2000 VDI workstations in a site with 2 DCs while RID Master is not contactable*).

In a more complex WAN topology sporting multiple hubs and numerous spokes not routed to one another, the placement of PDCe and RID Master roles becomes more challenging, so let's look at these two in more detail.

Moving RID Master around to enable DCs in remote spokes to request a new pool is, while automatable, a multi-stage task that requires continuous monitoring and should be avoided if possible. Instead, you should design management processes in your AD in a way that prevents using RIDs for local pools, i.e., all new objects featuring the SID attribute must be created on domain controllers with a line of sight to the RID Master. You can combine this with the **RID Block Size** registry value found in **HKEY_LOCAL_MACHINE\SYSTEM\CurrentControlSet\Services\ NTDS\RID Values** (preset to 0 which corresponds to the default of 500), allocating a larger block of RIDs to DCs in sites without continuous RID Master visibility – but also to all the other DCs, since this value has to be set on the RID Master itself. However, with slightly over a billion RIDs ($2^{30} - 1 = 1{,}073{,}741{,}823$) available per domain, this seeming wastefulness is not going to have you run out of RIDs any time soon.

PDCe role placement is more critical in that most of its functions require constant connectivity from other DCs and potentially even member machines:

- First off, check for applications that specifically require access to PDC(e). We talked about this requirement in Section 3.4.3. If you encounter it in a way that does not yield a successful PDCe placement, delegate it back to the application owner and/or networking team to either create additional network routes or revisit the application's provisioning mechanism.

- If you do not have to contend with legacy applications requiring PDCe visibility from member servers or even clients, you have to take care of AD's own PDCe-related functions: preferential password change replication and account lockout processing. If your organization does not have account lockout configured, you don't have to worry about every DC being able to reach the PDCe in order to have the lockout replicated domain-wide in an urgent manner. If users in remote sites only work with systems located in those sites or in neighboring hub sites, preferential replication of password changes may not be of value either. In this case, you should disable it for those sites to save some CPU cycles on your remote DCs.

- An additional functionality introduced in 2022 to prevent the exploitation of CVE-2022-21857 requires the PDC Emulator of the forest root domain to communicate periodically to all the forests trusting its forest and enumerate all domains in each of the trusting forests.

If the PDCe is not accessible from every other domain controller in its domain, you can save DCs in remote sites some work by disabling the password push and logon verification. The former is done by adding a Netlogon service parameter:

Windows Registry Editor Version 5.00

[HKEY_LOCAL_MACHINE\SYSTEM\CurrentControlSet\Services\Netlogon\ Parameters]
"AvoidPdcOnWan"=dword:00000001

whereas for the latter, a Group Policy **Contact PDC on logon failure** exists under **Computer Configuration\Policies\Administrative Templates\System\Net Logon**. We will look at how to automate these settings in Chapter 7.

3.6 Read-Only Domain Controllers

Read-Only Domain Controllers (RODC) take a special place in the pandemonium of Active Directory anti-patterns. There is hardly another feature in AD that has been misinterpreted and misused as often as RODC has. Many administrators and AD architects still seem to assume that they can magically reduce their organization's attack surface by placing RODCs in DMZs, client subnets, and other parts of the infrastructure where local authentication is required. The thinking is that RODC somehow acts as an "AD firewall," shielding the precious writable DCs from potential mischief. Nothing could be further from the truth.

RODC was developed to protect against one scenario and one scenario only

> A threat actor gains physical control over a domain controller and reads password hashes from its NTDS database, including administrators, domain controller machines, and the **krbtgt** account, the latter leading to a Golden Ticket situation.

Protection from this threat scenario is achieved by not storing password hashes for privileged accounts on the RODC. The underlying assumption is (RODC was developed for the military) that the compromised DC is not able to connect to the rest of its AD forest while being accessed on the physical, i.e., hardware, level by the attacker. An RODC placed online in a physically secure datacenter but on a digitally insecure network segment (DMZ) is quite the opposite of the intended usage of that feature, which is why an "always-connected" RODC does not offer any protection worth the hassle.

3.6.1 If RODCs Are Justified

If your threat model for remote locations is similar to that of the military, i.e., very bad physical security paired with the requirement for local authentication for a clearly defined subset of users and computers in case of site isolation, RODC may well be a valid engineering option for these remote sites. There are some topology considerations that will help you get the most value out of your RODCs:

1. Limit the number of RODCs to one per site, if possible. If the site is large and/or busy enough to warrant a second RODC from the same domain, take utmost care to configure their password caching policies in an identical manner and make all RODCs of that site part of the same password pre-population process.

2. If your "risky site" belongs to a multi-domain forest, limit the number of domains required for offline operation, preferably to just one, even if it goes against your organization's object placement policies.

3. An "RODC site" should only have one replication neighbor.

4. Always enable universal group membership caching on RODC sites in a multi-domain forest. If none of the applications local to the site specifically requires a Global Catalog, not hosting a GC in a risky site is a good choice. In a single-domain forest, attackers will not gain any additional benefit from the GC, so you might as well enable it to accommodate any future application requirements.

Note The **managedBy** attribute of an RODC object actually grants local administrator permissions on the RODC machine. RODCs are unique in this regard – the attribute is of purely organizational value for any other object class that contains it.

3.7 Administration (Red) Forest

From the topology perspective, a Red Forest is no different from any other forest within your AD organization. However, this particular forest has to be especially well protected. Should it one day become compromised, then the best you can do is break trusts from the production (Golden) forests and use break-glass accounts from those forests to regain control.

When engineering the Red Forests' topology and distribution, it is always best to contain it to one central hub or, if every hub only consists of one site, to a pair of hub sites with full visibility and fast replication between them. Adopt the single-domain forest model for your Red Forest, keep the number of domain controllers to a minimum, and colocate all FSMO roles on one DC. That DC should be hosted on the site that provides the best possible connectivity to the Golden Forests.

If we project this supercompact topology onto a vast, multi-hub/multi-spoke multi-forest AD organization the Red Forest is meant to provide administrative principals for, it soon becomes clear that those principals lend themselves well to managing Tier 0 objects in the Golden forest(s) and, depending on the geographical distribution of Tier 1 assets, parts of that tier as well. For Tier 2 management within a particular Golden forest, you'll probably have to provision administrative identities from that forest. Of course, if your network is fully meshed or your site structure is not very complex, you might be able to serve the entire privileged administration needs of your organization from the Red Forest.

Since cross-forest authentication and authorization is crucial to Red Forest operation, you will benefit from reflecting your sites and subnets to the Red Forest as well. You don't need to create all the spoke and satellite sites in the Red Forest, but rather only those where authentication requests might possibly come from. But do use identical naming and optimized linking to speed up DC location. If your Red Forest's DCs are confined to one site, just link all the other sites directly to it by creating a global site link (or keeping the default one).

3.8 Modern Design Defaults

To create the topology in a "modern AD" approach, start with a flat single-domain production forest (and add the single-domain Red Forest if you qualify as "enterprise" or just prefer having a Red Forest in your deployment). If you have known reasons to utilize multiple production forests (e.g., resource forest for Exchange, expected future buy-outs of parts of the organization, etc.), make note of those as well, including applications being provided from every single forest. Map out the physical network with all its geographical sites and regions.

CHAPTER 3   ENGINEERING TOPOLOGY

For the remainder of this chapter, we will assume that you have already got office politics (logon domain display on member devices), misinterpreted separation of concerns (subdomain admins instead of OU delegation), and misguided infatuation with read-only domain controllers (leaving only the cases where those actually make sense) out of the way. Therefore, your forest and domain topology will be defined by three factors:

- Separation of business units for a possible divestment (multiple forests)

- Separation of applications for the reduction of blast radii (multiple forests, e.g., Exchange in a resource forest)

- Geographical distribution of the infrastructure (multiple forests or a multi-domain forest, in case of global UPN namespaces)

3.8.1 From the Inside Out

Start with the site topology. For each physical location, make note of the following:

- Number of users normally working from that site, including VPN connections terminating there. The higher the number of users local to the site, the higher the motivation for putting a domain controller into that site. If AD is used for VPN authentication, VPN concentrators may even require a local DC to be present.

CHAPTER 3　ENGINEERING TOPOLOGY

- Site autonomy requirements and applications expected by the business to be still available in the event of a site isolation. This will help you define which forests and domains have to be available in isolation at which location.

- Physical datacenter infrastructure available at the site. This is important for identifying potential hub sites.

With this information, try building a topology consisting of

- Single hub (remember, a hub can contain multiple hub sites if they are all interchangeable, connectivity-wise)

- Spokes (each spoke being one hop away from the hub)

- Satellites (connected to either hub or spoke and not requiring domain controllers in the site)

- "Risky sites" (sites warranting an RODC for reasons described in Section 3.6)

CHAPTER 3   ENGINEERING TOPOLOGY

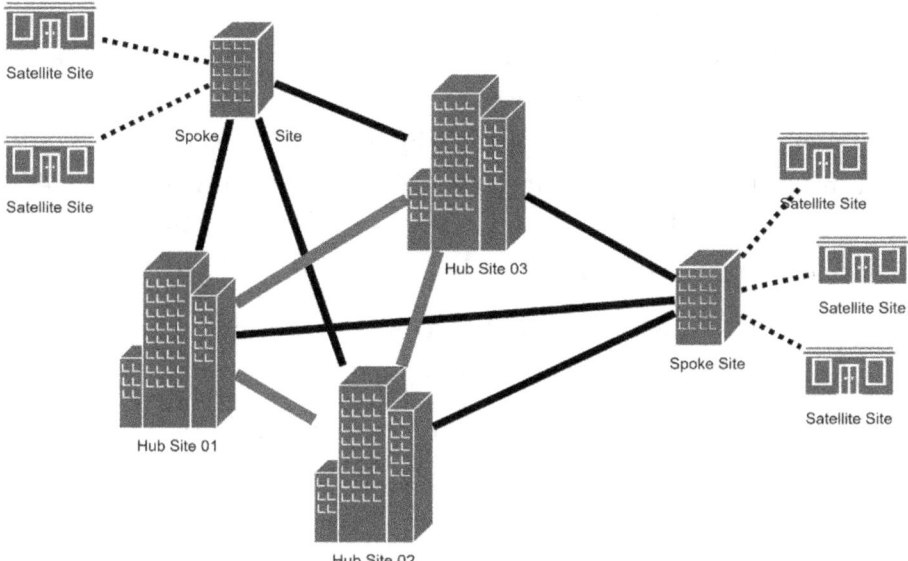

Figure 3-5. *The three hub sites are interchangeable because each is connected to all the spokes*

Mark all candidates for hub sites on the network map like the one shown in Figure 3-5. Those are the sites equipped with datacenter infrastructure, backup facilities, and experienced IT personnel. If you identify more than one hub site, verify that network links between these sites are

- Direct (single-hop)
- Reliable
- Fast

as these sites will host the core of your AD. A good thought experiment in hub site designation is disaster recovery in case of a complete destruction of your AD due to a ransomware or wiperware attack. If you end up dealing with hub sites connected by direct links that are either not fast or not reliable, you may be looking at a multi-forest topology or, less preferably,

85

a multi-domain forest. Talk to the network team to see if there is room for improvement on the infrastructure side or if these improvements are already planned and have maybe even been scheduled!

Knowing your hubs and hub sites is important because FSMO roles requiring interaction (PDCe and RID Master) can wind up in any of them!

Now mark all "obvious" candidates for spoke sites. These are sites that satisfy the following criteria:

- A direct, high-quality link to a hub site or to multiple hub sites if you are designing a multi-site hub

- Good enough datacenter equipment and physical security to allow for placing read/write domain controllers in the site

- Motivation for placing domain controllers in the site: this can be due to site isolation requirements, or satellite sites that otherwise would have no direct links to a hub or to a different spoke site, or a combination of both

3.8.2 First Sanity Check: Spoke-hub Connectivity

In case you have more than one hub, regardless of how many hub sites each hub consists of, verify that every spoke site has an IP route (but not necessarily a direct or exceedingly fast one; going from spoke through its next-hop hub to get to a different hub is perfectly fine) to every hub site in each hub. If only a couple of routes are missing, talk to the network team about establishing them, because this level of reachability allows you to stick with the single-domain forest pattern! Figure 3-6 shows a case of a missing network link between hub sites severely affecting directory services function in the spokes.

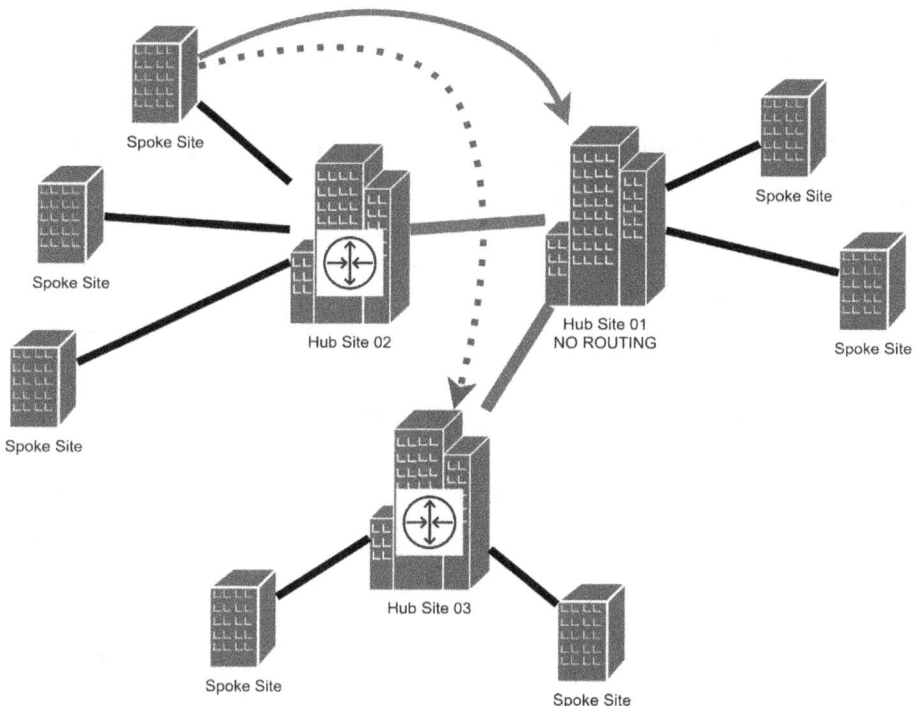

Figure 3-6. *If PDCe or RID master are placed in Hub Site 02 or 03, overall functionality will be affected*

If you have limited connectivity between spokes and hubs, verify if multiple forests for users, clients, and/or applications are a viable design option from the UPN suffix namespace standpoint. A multiple-forest pattern is still preferable to a multi-domain forest both from the security and resilience perspectives. Each of the forests must have full reachability between any spoke site and any hub site in which domain controllers from that forest will be placed.

> **Note** For site coverage, this level of connectivity is not required, a connection from a satellite site to a single spoke or hub site, i.e., to a site hosting a domain controller, is all that is needed. Before you turn to the multi-domain anti-pattern, check if turning the spokes that have limited hub reachability into satellites is something the business would tolerate.

3.8.3 Risky Sites

In case your organization has to employ "risky sites," now is the time to earmark those sites for placing read-only domain controllers (RODC) in them. This will not influence your forest and domain topology, because from the FSMO reachability perspective, these can be treated as satellite sites. RODCs still need contact to the RID Master at the time of DC promotion, but once a RODC has been issued a RID pool, that pool can last forever because no new objects that would need a SID are ever created on an RODC. However, you will probably not promote the RODCs in situ anyway but prepare them in a well-connected site, then change the IP address and site allocation and ship the machines out to the risky sites.

3.8.4 Satellite Sites

All remaining physical network locations are satellite sites. If your network team uses separate IP subnets for VPN clients, you should give some thought to declaring those subnets as satellite sites of the hub or spoke site where the respective VPN concentrator is located. However, keep in mind that this will only provide any real value if your clients are AD members and you actually use the clients' site affinity in Group Policies, configuration management, or login scripts. In case of clients being joined exclusively to Entra ID or not being joined to any directory at all, these "VPN satellites" will just make your site topology more complicated without adding any value.

3.8.5 Site Links and Bridges

Now that you have designated all physical (and maybe even some virtual) locations as hub, spoke, and satellite sites and determined whether this network topology translates to a single-forest, multi-forest, or multi-domain forest design, it's time to turn connections between sites into site links and possibly site link bridges.

Unless your network is fully meshed, disable the global setting "All Site Links Are Bridged." You will still be able to add explicit site link bridges where it's warranted by the physical routing topology.

Create a site link from every direct connection between two physical network locations that you mapped out. For hubs consisting of more than one hub site, create a hub link encompassing all hub sites in a hub, enable USE_NOTIFY, and give it the lowest possible cost value of 1.

Enable USE_NOTIFY on every other site link where this is feasible. When assessing the feasibility of notification-based AD replication for a certain network link, keep in mind that the total amount of replication data transferred over the link does not change very much unless the replication interval is very long and there are multiple changes to the same object and attribute occurring within that interval. For example, if a computer in a remote site is changing networks on a constant basis and its DNS host record gets updated by DHCP every time the IP address changes, every change would replicate out of the site if you use notification-based replication, but only one change would be replicated per interval. For objects in domain and configuration partitions, it is even harder to devise a situation where scheduled replication would result in a significant reduction of the data transfer volume.

CHAPTER 3 ENGINEERING TOPOLOGY

Interval-based replication, therefore, is most useful in scenarios where a connection between two sites cannot or should not be utilized constantly, i.e., *in conjunction with replication schedules*. I really hope that you are able to avoid using schedules on links between hubs so it's just one hop (spoke to hub) that is affected by scheduled replication. If you have "risky sites" attached to spokes, you may potentially get into a situation where both the risky site to spoke site link and the one connecting the spoke to its hub are on schedule. In this case, try to at least keep these two schedules overlapping; otherwise, you will get very long change convergence to the risky sites.

Note If you use replication schedules, make sure the global parameter "Ignore Schedules" is not set!

Once you define the site links, your physical topology becomes functional. In a strict hub and spoke design, where each spoke only has connection to one hub (which can mean multiple connections if the hub consists of multiple hub sites) and each satellite only has connection to one spoke, there is nothing left to do than to deploy domain controllers into hub and spoke sites and wait for the KCC to establish replication connections between them. Same goes for a fully meshed network where all WAN connections are of similar quality. If your network is more complex *and you would like to take advantage of this additional complexity*, you'll have to create additional site links, assign costs to them, and maybe even add site link bridges to your design. When working with costs, map out all possible chains of site links connecting each pair of sites.

If you managed to stick to the single-domain forest model and you are not creating any application partitions with limited replication scopes, you do not need to worry about site link bridges at all because every partition has a replica on every DC and there is no value in having replication connections transiting multiple sites. If you do have multiple domains in one of your forests, or if an application partition is only needed in select sites of your organization (and its size and/or change frequency preclude you from just replicating it forest-wide), site link bridges help translate your transitive network routes into far-reaching replication connections for those domains or partitions.

3.8.6 A Word on Firewalls

Throughout this chapter, we spoke about "routing" and "reachability" and used them almost interchangeably. However, not every network connection that is routable will automatically allow for AD communication due to datacenter firewalls between the subnets and geographical locations. If you talk to the network team about WAN links and IP routes, don't forget to mention that AD will also need certain ports open. Much to the network folks' chagrin, it will include dynamic RPC ports, which the firewalls must be able to handle properly to avoid opening up the TCP port range 49152-65535 on a permanent basis. Do not let them talk you into setting fixed RPC ports (there are separate settings for NTDS and NetLogon) on your DCs before you are able to assess the performance implications of this change.

3.8.7 Populating the Location Attribute

If you plan on using the **location** attribute functionality we described in Section 3.3, populate the attribute in all your sites and subnets. Location paths assigned to subnets must start with the location path of the site containing that subnet and then continue with a subnet moniker, all parts joined by a forward slash character. Because the location is evaluated left to right, the subnet moniker value need not be globally unique. It is perfectly OK and makes managing this functionality easier to have the same names for subnets of the same designation in each site: **SA/BR/RIO/Floor1** and **NA/WA/SEA/Floor1** will not get mixed up because the site part is evaluated first!

3.9 Summary

In this chapter, we analyzed various topology options for your AD organization. "Topology" in this context means both the physical topology of your organization's network (reflected in AD in the form of subnets, sites, and site links) and the logical topology of domains, forests, and trusts. These two aspects of topology cannot be viewed independently of each other because replication and site coverage concerns can lead to multi-forest or multi-domain designs. A multi-domain forest is the least desirable option both from the manageability and security perspective but can be necessary if the UPN suffix namespace must be shared between all parts of the organization while maintaining the Global Catalog and fulfilling site isolation requirements.

We also provided a walk-through for creating both aspects of AD topology from

- Physical network layout
- Site autonomy requirements, including risky sites containing RODCs
- Authentication and authorization requirements

CHAPTER 4

Engineering Lookup

In the previous chapter, we spoke about topology which, while not being a "function" of AD, causes domain controllers and AD members to behave in certain ways. Let us now turn to the first "real" AD function: the "lookup." When we talk about lookup in the context of this book, we will distinguish between two functionalities:

- Finding and viewing objects stored in Active Directory. In most cases, systems and applications will use LDAP to achieve this.

- Finding services, both provided directly by Active Directory like LDAP, Global Catalog, or Kerberos authentication and supported by Active Directory, e.g., any service running on a member server machine and accepting Kerberos authentication from clients. In this case, DNS will be the protocol we'll be mostly looking at; however, even Windows versions supported today experience legacy behaviors when it comes to locating other systems on the network, so we will touch on that as well.

Having proper DNS name resolution is very important, because both TLS (if used for establishing a connection) and Kerberos (if used for authenticating that connection) require that the name supplied by the client to access the service is known to the service – be it as a subject name in a TLS certificate or as the name part of a Kerberos SPN. If you talk to AD

CHAPTER 4 ENGINEERING LOOKUP

old-timers, you are bound to hear them mention at some point that "most AD problems are DNS problems." In environments where basic network services like DNS have historically been designed, implemented, and managed separately from authentication and service provisioning, this is true even to this day. The "modern AD" acknowledges that DNS is crucial to its proper function and offers guidance on integrating name resolution in all AD-related management processes.

4.1 Disclosing Information vs. Preventing Reconnaissance

When enabling other systems and applications to look up information stored in a different system, e.g., in a directory, there is always a balance to be found between disclosing required information and preventing an unauthorized actor from performing reconnaissance using that information. Active Directory defaults have earned it such a bad reputation in terms of finding this balance that many, if not most, IT professionals do not even look beyond the defaults and simply declare that "AD lets everyone see everything." In this book, we will take a different approach and engineer our lookup according to our organization's needs, information protection being one of them.

In this section, we will be mostly talking about directory data and pivot to DNS lookup towards the end. In AD, exposing directory objects to the outside world has been heavily influenced by the notion of a directory service being used as a "phone book." Windows 2000 and XP even had a "Search Directory…" widget in the start menu by default. We cannot really blame Microsoft for designing it that way in the 1990s, because that was the role of an X.500- or LDAP-based directory service ever since directories became a thing a decade or two earlier. However, none of those early directories granted its objects ownership over systems or administrative entities like Active Directory does, hence the need for restricting

CHAPTER 4   ENGINEERING LOOKUP

reconnaissance! And even with the search widget gone from the modern operating systems' start menu, a logged-on user still has lots of out-of-the-box possibilities to perform a directory search: PowerShell, VBS, or – in case Office is installed and macros are not disabled – even VBA!

When looking at permissions to retrieve specific objects and attributes and trying to prevent reconnaissance, remember that in an LDAP search, attributes that are part of the search filter do not have to be part of the search result. So, for example, even if you do not allow a certain user to read the servicePrincipalName property of user objects, that user can still list the accounts where the property is populated by supplying the search filter of **(servicePrincipalName=*)**.

4.1.1 Starting from Scratch

If we were to start with a blank permission set with only AD administrators being able to view and read any of the objects, what permissions would an AD user logging on to a member machine (for the sake of this discussion, we are assuming a domain-joined client – it works differently for cloud-joined devices) and using some of the applications provided by the organization really need? And what permissions does the machine account need to properly support this workflow?

> **Note** Authentication does not require *any* permissions on directory objects for the account being authenticated because those permissions cannot be granted *until authentication was successful*! The domain controller performing the authentication must, of course, be able to view and read the directory object, including its password hash, in order to verify the account and decide whether it receives its logon token or not (after all, the account could be disabled, locked out, or require a password change on the next logon).

95

When a member machine is booting up, its first order of business after authenticating its machine account is determining the site it belongs to in order to properly direct all subsequent communications. To accomplish that, it has to be able to read the topology information found in the Configuration partition of the forest the machine is a member in (**CN=Sites,CN=Configuration,DC=forest,DC=root,DC=domain**). More precisely, the computer object needs read permissions on the subnet its current IP address belongs to and the site containing that subnet. To locate an appropriate domain controller, it will then use SRV records in DNS (they are found in the zone **_msdcs.forest.root.domain**), where Domain Controllers register their records for Kerberos, LDAP, and Global Catalog based on site coverage.

> A machine moving across a subset of sites does not actually require being able to view any of the other sites.

Then the machine will calculate the Resultant Set of Policy (RSoP) for the machine part. For that, it needs to read the **gpLink** and **gpOptions** attributes of its own site, of the domain the computer object belongs to and of each OU between the domain root and the computer object. For each policy linked there, provided that the link is enabled, its AD object located in **CN=Policies,CN=System,DC=one,DC=of,DC=domains** must also be read. These policies may come from different domains in the forest if the forest has multiple domains! In case one or multiple group policies have WMI filters attached to them, these also have to be read from the directory.

In the simplest of scenarios, that's all the access a machine account needs. Up to this point, the machine technically didn't even need read access to its own computer object, let alone any other computers, users, or groups in the directory. In reality, however, some Windows subsystems will need access to their own computer object, but no further than that.

When a user logs on to the machine, their account has to read some of its object's properties: display name, logon script, profile path, and other attributes necessary to create and maintain the user profile. Applications may require access to further directory data. For example, Outlook will need the **mail** attribute in order to perform MAPI autoconfiguration. Logon scripts have been known to make use of attributes like department, job description, or employee ID. There may be other requirements of similar nature due to other applications; however, it's very hard to imagine a scenario where an application would require access to *other* user objects in the directory in order to just do its job.

Defining the visibility of groups is not quite as straightforward. For the purpose of gaining access to resources and privileges on the local system, Windows only needs the group SIDs that are part of the user's logon token. However, the names of the groups, at least those from the user's own domain, are resolved by other means than a simple LDAP lookup so that you will not be able to prevent a user from knowing the names of the groups they are a member of. But this is usually not disclosing much as long as you do not allow access to other attributes like **description**, **managedBy**, or **member**! And, of course, for Windows and most applications to work properly, a user account doesn't have to be able to view and read anything about any groups it is not a member of!

If you look at permissions Active Directory is installed with, you will notice that they are way more relaxed than the bare minimum described above. This is because the original purpose of a directory service is to provide information to users in a searchable, filterable, and sortable way, not to restrict access to it. Let's look at this use case in light of today's business requirements.

4.1.2 AD As an Enterprise Address Book

To decide on allowing a certain user or machine account access to a large number of objects in the directory, always look at the use case. What application will be used to access the data, in what form will directory information be surfaced to the end user, and what shall the end user do with it? The primary use case for directory lookup is most certainly email. However, not every email system requires access to the address information by individual users. Exchange, for example, not only uses the Exchange servers' machine accounts to pull the requisite AD information but also provides a proprietary address book protocol that has nothing to do with LDAP. But even if LDAP is indeed being used, it may not be the account making practical use of the directory data that needs access to it. This is typical for multifunction printers/scanners offering scan to email. These devices often use an LDAP bind account for directory access, and it's this account that technically needs read access to mail-enabled users and groups. Conversely, if email is the intended use case, the account performing an LDAP lookup does not need any access to users or groups that do not have their **mail** attribute populated – the search filter will most probably include a **(mail=*)** clause, so, from the application's point of view, the objects without email may just as well not be present at all!

4.2 Structures, Permissions, and Defaults

Working with a directory service usually makes you think about the data stored in it in a two-dimensional way because that's how the directory's hierarchical structure is presented in the console. However, for the accessing user or client, the view may well be one-dimensional if they only perform searches against the directory and do not care what container subtree a particular object is in as long as it has been found and all the attribute values the application needs are part of the search result.

For defining the objects' visibility, on the other hand, container (Organizational Unit) structures are crucial because that's where you should apply permissions that would then propagate to the objects within the OU. OUs are also your possible entry points (Base DNs) for searching, which, while not *enforcing* any visibility restrictions for an unconstrained search, can help restrict visibility *within a particular application*. However, applications using LDAP searches seldom offer the ability to perform a search against *multiple* base DNs, making this sort of "security by obscurity" less practicable and way less effective than it potentially could have been. This is why in this book we will assume that every application searches the entire directory and craft our OU and permission structures based on that assumption.

4.2.1 How Many OUs Does a Domain Need?

Before you start designing the OU structure of your organization's domains, understand what functionality OUs actually offer and what you will be using them for specifically. Contrary to a long-standing belief and despite the name suggesting otherwise, OUs are **not** intended for reflecting your organizational hierarchy. That's what the **managedBy** attribute is for, and the Hierarchical Address Book feature in Microsoft Exchange 2010 and later is a great example of how it's done.

In contrast, OUs in Active Directory can serve these four use cases:

1. Application of permissions (*The same wisdom that dictates to not apply permissions to individual files on a file server but rather to folders and have them propagate to subfolders and files also applies here.*)

2. Application of Group Policies (*There are WMI filter and security filtering, but not having a GPO linked anywhere between an object and the domain root is the best way of ensuring that this policy will not be applied to that object. We will revisit this in Chapter 7.*)

CHAPTER 4   ENGINEERING LOOKUP

3. Visual – not organizational! – grouping of objects for those administrators who use the built-in MMC consoles or LDAP browser tools as opposed to searching for the desired object throughout the entire directory

4. Base DN for searches as described above

You should define the purpose of OUs in your particular AD organization early in the design process and stick to this framework going forward. However, even if you define that certain OUs may only contain certain object classes, you should not rely on it being adhered to, both for permissioning and GPO application. For example, if you decide to provision OU structures like the one depicted in Figure 4-1

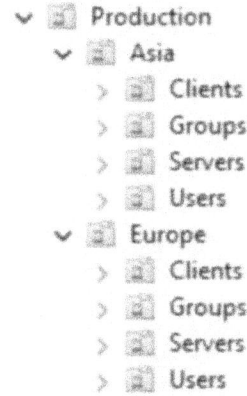

Figure 4-1. *OUs for specific object classes*

and the Asian administrators should have the permission to create and manage group objects in the Asia OU subtree, you should grant permissions on "descendant group objects" on "OU=Asia" level, not on "OU=Groups,OU=Asia" level – dropping a group object into a wrong OU would result in it not being manageable otherwise. The permission to *create* group objects, on the other hand, should only be granted at the "OU=Groups,OU=Asia" level to prevent Asian admins from creating groups in a wrong container!

In the above example, the main purpose of the OU structure seems to be delegating the management of regional AD objects to regional IT teams and possibly providing base OUs for region-based LDAP searches. There are other OU schemes that work well for the respective organizations. Generally, use cases 1 and 2 above are stronger motivators for a particular OU structure than 3 and/or 4. Whatever your organization's motivation ends up being, avoid the anti-pattern of introducing too many OU levels. A good starting point is the following structure (the names of non-default OUs can vary according to your naming conventions):

Path (from domain root)	Default	Purpose
Privileged	No	A top-level OU to cancel out access to privileged objects by unprivileged identities. Your tiering groups, Tier 0 systems such as Certification Authorities, local admin groups, and other privileged objects go into this OU. Its contents MUST not be visible or findable by unprivileged users; however, certain scenarios, like configuration by GPO, might require you to make an exception.
Domain Controllers	Yes	This is a "well-known object" in your domain; you should leave it in place and not move your DCs out of it. It is theoretically possible to change the well-known name of this container, but there is no benefit of doing so since well-known objects are listed in the domain root, so chances are that they can be viewed by any authenticated user anyway.

(continued)

CHAPTER 4　ENGINEERING LOOKUP

Path (from domain root)	Default	Purpose
New Objects	No	Redirect your default users and computers container here. This OU should remain empty 100% of the time because your user provisioning processes will always specify the correct target container and so will your highly regulated domain-joined procedure. To reinforce that, apply a group policy to this OU denying logon rights to everyone and closing the Windows Firewall inbound completely. This OU SHOULD not be visible or findable by unprivileged users. There is very little benefit in providing separate custom OUs for "new users" and "new computers."
Applications	No	This is where you put (in appropriate sub-OUs) your application servers, service accounts, and application-specific groups, i.e., what is usually defined as Tier 1 objects. Permissions on these OUs and their substructures will vary depending on how your application landscape is structured. We will talk about tiering and zoning in the next chapter.
Production	No	All non-privileged objects are put into a substructure of this OU. This may include users, groups, client computers, and sometimes even servers, especially if a particular server's computer object needs to be visible to clients and/or users.

After creating such a structure, you then proceed to move the privileged groups and users from the default "Users" container to an OU underneath the "Privileged." Some objects located there by default, like the disabled Guest account and the "Guests" and "Domain Guests" groups, are not privileged per se, but they also do not need to be seen by anybody except AD administrators. Do not delete the default containers, even though you redirected the default paths for new users and computers to the "New Objects" OU. Some applications may disregard the redirection and just use "Users" and "Computers" for application-specific new objects (if your AD was instantiated using a non-English OS, these applications may also fail in your environment even if you don't change anything). There is also no supported way of redirecting the "Builtin" container so leave that in place, too. Objects located within the "Builtin" container have a **systemFlags** bit set that prohibits them from being moved. To preserve compatibility, leave those objects in place. You can still restrict visibility of the Builtin objects by editing the ACL of the container.

A good start for the substructure of the "Privileged" OU is separating out those privileged groups that have to be visible to unprivileged objects. For example, if you choose to remove "Domain Admins" from the local admin group on member computers by using Group Policy Preferences, the group must be visible to those computer objects.

4.2.2 Permissions on AD Objects

Active Directory introduced very granular access control to information stored within it as compared to a Windows NT domain. It reaches all the way down to attribute level and even has, in addition to "write," a "validated write" permission to attributes like **servicePrincipalName** or **dnsHostName** where writing a certain value to an attribute is conditional upon the value satisfying certain constraints. Sadly, after implementing these control mechanisms, Microsoft then chose the path of focussing on compatibility rather than security in granting permissions to objects and structures created by default upon instantiation of an AD forest.

This makes it your job to define the necessary permissions on all the different object types in order to expose the information your applications need for functioning while concealing data that might be abused by a malicious actor if it is revealed to them early in their attack cycle.

CHAPTER 4   ENGINEERING LOOKUP

To be able to properly engineer your AD permissions structure, you need to know some ground rules about how permissions are granted and how AD evaluates them:

- Every object class has a default security descriptor stored in the schema, which constitutes the explicit access control list (ACL) that an object of that class has assigned upon creation.

- The explicit ACL can then be amended by editing the access control entries (ACE), either as a part of the provisioning process for the object or at a later time.

- Then the explicit ACL is overlaid with ACEs inherited from the container the object has been placed into, its parents, and ultimately from the root of the tree, the Naming Context (domain or partition).

- Inheritance can be broken both at container and at object level – after all, containers are also valid AD objects, and objects of other classes can serve as parent objects for other objects.

- In case of a conflict, explicit permissions override inherited ones; an explicit Allow will override an inherited Deny. This is true not only at the object (leaf) level but at any level of the inheritance hierarchy.

- Granted at the same level, Deny permissions override Allow ones.

An old admin wisdom dictates that having Deny permissions in the mix makes it harder to visually evaluate the effective access. You should respect this wisdom regardless of the amount of automation you are ready to bring to bear for permission management in your AD. If you should find yourself in a troubleshooting situation one day, you might end up analyzing effective permissions manually, and not having Deny ACEs helps preserve your sanity. On the other hand, if forgoing a single Deny entry would result in dozens of Allow entries on different OU levels and additional authorizing groups needed to correctly model permissions, simplicity and brevity should prevail:

> If forced to work with out-of-box tooling in Windows, you should familiarize yourself with the oldest tool in the kit – LDP.EXE. It is highly superior to the MMC-based tools in more than one regard and even surfaces one particular permission (Write SACL) those newer tools will not allow you to view or set.

4.2.3 The Case of Replication Rights

Beside permissions granting direct read/write access to objects and their attributes or enabling advanced functions such as object creation, deletion, setting or resetting a password, or unexpiring a password, there is one particular set of permissions that deserves a special mention: replication rights. There are six distinct permissions related to replication, five of which are actively used by AD itself and thus present in the default ACLs.

It is important to remember that, once you assign a security principal one of the "Replicate Directory Changes" rights (there are three of them) on a naming context head, you cannot limit what objects from that NC the assignee is allowed to request replication for – it will ultimately be able to see all of them! And the specific right or rights that you assign govern which attribute values the assignee will be able to replicate, "Replicate Directory Changes All," providing access to all attributes, including the secret ones like password hashes that are not readable via LDAP. By default, these rights are assigned to Domain Controllers (who obviously need them since they are involved in replication) and, rather surprisingly, to the "Domain Admins" group. It goes without saying that members of that group can normally be trusted with everybody's password hashes and Golden Tickets; still having this permission pre-provisioned by default is a design decision that bears revising.

4.2.4 Everyone Can See Everything in AD?

Before we dive into defining visibility of AD objects, we should spend a moment looking at what ACLs a typical AD domain gets instantiated with, because those are the permissions a poorly designed application (or simply an older one, hailing from Windows NT times) might assume are always in place. Such applications may refuse to work correctly until they are able to retrieve all the information exposed by the defaults.

In terms of revealing more information than we would like to expose, we can limit ourselves to looking at unprivileged identities. Permissions granted to those by default are often described, in layman's terms, as "everyone can see everything in AD." Assuming that the first contact of an attacker to Active Directory is either a user that clicked on a malicious link or a workstation that got hit by a drive-by download or the likes of the Log4j vulnerability, we have to examine the following permission levels:

- Permissions granted to literally everyone, i.e., to the Everyone virtual group which includes guests and service accounts; prior to Server 2003, it also included anonymous access but that has changed

- Permissions granted to the "Authenticated Users" virtual group

- Permissions granted to the "Pre-Windows 2000 Compatible Access" group which, by default, includes "Authenticated Users" as member

- Permissions granted to "Domain Users" and "Domain Computers"
- Permissions granted to the SELF security principal

There is one major difference in dealing with permissions granted to virtual groups such as "Authenticated Users" and real groups such as "Domain Users." A security principal's membership in a real group can be removed, so you have the option to leave the default ACEs in place and just remove the unprivileged object from the respective group. A "membership" in a virtual group represents a hardcoded behavior of the operating system, so the only way to revoke permissions granted to a virtual group is by actually removing the ACEs. While removing default ACEs does make it harder to make an exception or roll back a hardening change, I recommend you take the engineering approach and do not leave ACEs in place that should not normally be used.

The following permissions are granted by default on user objects:

Granted to	Granted by	Permission
Everyone	Default SD	Change password
Pre-Win2K	Domain Root	Read "Account Restrictions" property set
Pre-Win2K	Domain Root	Read "Logon Information" property set
Pre-Win2K	Domain Root	Read "Group Membership" property set
Pre-Win2K	Domain Root	Read "General Information" property set
Pre-Win2K	Domain Root	Read "Remote Access Information" property set
Pre-Win2K	Domain Root	Read all properties
Pre-Win2K	Domain Root	Read permissions
Pre-Win2K	Domain Root	List contents

(continued)

CHAPTER 4   ENGINEERING LOOKUP

Granted to	Granted by	Permission
Authenticated Users	Default SD	Read "General Information" property set
Authenticated Users	Default SD	Read "Public Information" property set
Authenticated Users	Default SD	Read "Personal Information" property set
Authenticated Users	Default SD	Read "Web Information" property set
Authenticated Users	Default SD	Read permissions
SELF	Default SD	Read all properties
SELF	Default SD	Read permissions
SELF	Default SD	Change password
SELF	Default SD	Send-As, Receive-As
SELF	Default SD	Read/Write "Personal Information" property set
SELF	Default SD	Read/Write "Email Information" property set
SELF	Default SD	Read/Write "Web Information" property set
SELF	Domain Root	Read/Write "Private Information" property set
SELF	Domain Root	Read/Write msDS-AllowedToActOnBehalfOfOtherIdentity

Apart from the "Read permissions" entry found in the default SD, all attributes directly related to security are readable by "Pre-Windows 2000 Compatible Access" group rather than "Authenticated Users" or "Everyone" which means that removing that legacy group from the picture will already take you a long way towards a more secure and less talkative AD!

For computers and groups, the effect of the legacy access group on information disclosure is not as big since in Windows NT domains (which is what "Pre-Windows 2000" actually means), those object classes were not as rich on attributes and additional functionality as user objects.

4.3 Defining Visibility and Hiding the Crown Jewels in Plain Sight

In a better world, there wouldn't be anything inherently wrong with disclosing all sorts of directory information to authenticated users, except for retrieving and transferring more data than actually necessary. The threat landscape being what it is at the time of writing (and there is no indication that the situation should improve in the future) careful engineering of a directory service requires imposing severe limitations on what information is being surfaced to whom.

However carefully engineered, there will always be a requirement to have "God mode" security principals, or at least principals that are capable of *reading* all non-secret attributes of all objects in all domains and partitions. It is only using such accounts that audit and documentation tools can provide a complete view, attack path, and/or attack surface analysis since all of these tools have been developed with the notion of the default permissions we described in the previous section being in place.

It is extremely seldom, however, that a highly privileged identity becomes the first point of contact for an attacker. Usually, it's a non-privileged user or a member computer (workstation or server) whose identity serves as the security context for first reconnaissance. Our first order of business will therefore include protecting important security-related information from these generic identities.

4.3.1 Can't Abuse What They Can't See

Many organizations embarking on the journey of restricting visibility in their directory services are hesitant to hide parts of the directory data from everyone's view for fear that some important applications might break if permissions get changed from the Microsoft defaults. Keep in mind that the application developer has never seen your (or any customer's) Active Directory so all they can safely assume is that there are the following objects:

- Basic structures like schema, site topology, and NC roots
- Default containers and groups (well-known objects)
- The built-in Administrator account (the one with the RID 500)
- The built-in Guest account (the one with the RID 501)
- The user starting the application on a client machine (or running a service on an application server)
- The client machine the client piece is started on
- The server machine the service is running on
- Authorization groups required by the application, if any

That's mostly it! The application does not know, or care, about your privileged identities, groups, or machines. Ideally, it should not care about the RID-500 Administrator and the "Domain Admins" group either, but it's a well-known fact that these objects are always present. This means that if you completely blank out the privileged objects from the regular users' and computers' read access, the probability that something breaks is very low. After all, no matter what the sales rep told you, your business applications are not capable of clairvoyance, so it can't possibly know that the other

CHAPTER 4 ENGINEERING LOOKUP

objects you created exist in the first place! The same goes for objects you create in the directory after the application was put into production: it worked without them; why should it suddenly stop working if you add them and then hide them from view?

Every now and then you will encounter a particularly nosy application that expects to be able to read certain properties from every object it is able to see. To avoid costly troubleshooting, just stick to this rule:

Note If you want to completely remove read access to certain objects for non-privileged identities, make sure that those objects cannot be enumerated by listing child objects in their parent containers.

Whether the client piece or the service account should be able to see all the non-privileged accounts authorized to use the application depends on what the application actually does. It may well be the case if the application allows one user to assign tasks to another user, or book their calendar, or search for documents created by them. That's OK, although you should analyze the required access very carefully and only allow those identities to be found that are actually required. And maybe it's not the end user but only the service account that needs to see them all, like in the case of a network scanner we discussed earlier in this chapter!

Note There is another aspect to "can't abuse what they can't see." Generations of identity admins have been putting all sorts of information available in the primary identity sources into AD without even knowing whether any application can use and/or surface that data. An **employeeID** can be abused for phishing or other kinds of social engineering and is still widely readable. It becomes even worse if a piece of information *is* needed for an application but doesn't

111

have to be surfaced to the user, e.g., an RFID token for door locks and follow-me printers matched to the employee number. Always consider not putting information into AD in the first place, and if it is needed but not going to be surfaced, restrict visibility of the attributes involved as severely as possible!

4.3.2 Hiding Objects from View – List Mode

How do we hide Active Directory objects from view? The simplest way to achieve it is by putting objects we don't want our regular users and computers to see into a container and remove any "Read" and "List contents" rights on that container. This can absolutely work for hiding privileged objects (that's why we introduced the "Privileged" OU in the previous section), but once you start limiting visibility among non-privileged objects, things can get complicated very fast. Since you can only "truly hide" a complete OU but not a single object in it

- If you deny all read permissions on an object but leave "List contents" permissions in place on the parent OU, the object will still be visible but have an "unknown" type since the objectClass property cannot be retrieved.

- If you deny "List contents" on an OU, none of the objects in it can be retrieved by searching or browsing, regardless of the rights on a particular object itself.

To help remediate this, a special "List Object mode" can be activated by setting the third digit of the forest-wide **dsHeuristics** attribute to "1" (if nothing else is configured there, this is done by setting the value to "001"). In this mode, if you deny "List content" on parent but grant "List object" both on parent and child, the child object will be visible. If you decide to go down that route, keep in mind that in the "List Object mode," the "List object" permission is the one ultimately controlling the objects' visibility, regardless of any other permissions granted or denied to them.

Microsoft warns us that "List Object mode" is likely to come with a performance penalty if used at scale because domain controllers end up querying and evaluating more permissions to determine the result set of each query. This should not deter you from using the "List Object mode" if it makes sense otherwise – just take the potential performance hit into account when right-sizing your DCs and determining which of them other systems will be connecting to in order to perform LDAP searches.

4.3.3 Removing Pre-Windows 2000 Compatible Access

In the previous section, we looked at permissions that the "Pre-Windows 2000 Compatible Access" group grants by virtue of "Authenticated Users" being nested into that group by default. These permissions do not disclose any objects that otherwise would stay hidden, nor do they grant access to attributes a well-behaved application would have any business reading. Its only purpose is accommodating legacy applications that may require that for any user or group object that is visible *at all*, all attributes that were part of the object in a Windows NT domain are readable and return sensible values.

In some environments, you might encounter one or several computer accounts being direct members of the legacy access group. These will most probably turn out to be computers hosting an Enterprise CA (the instantiation process of an Enterprise CA includes adding its computer as a member of the group for every domain in the forest). This facility is needed for one specific use case that not every organization has implemented – Certificate Manager restrictions. An example of this feature being utilized with an enterprise CA is shown in Figure 4-2:

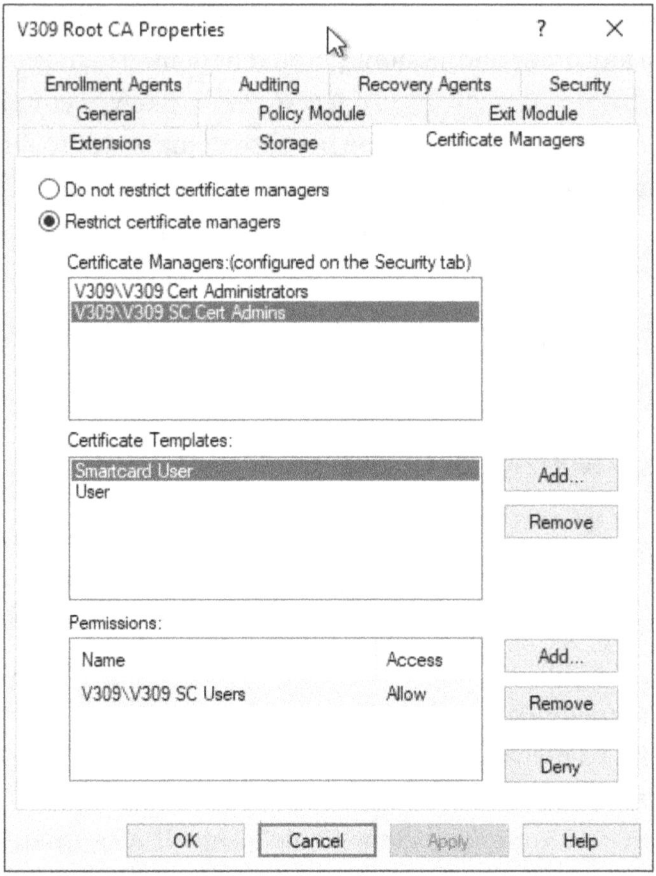

Figure 4-2. *If Certificate Managers are used, CA computer needs access to tokenGroups*

To process this feature, a CA needs to access the group memberships of each user requesting a certificate from a published and managed template. More precisely, access to the **tokenGroupsGlobalAndUniversal** computed attribute is required. "Pre-Windows 2000 Compatible Access" provides this access but reveals much more information along the way. To access this attribute in a more targeted manner, Active Directory provides a well-known group "Windows Authorization Access Group" with the SID **S-1-5-32-560**. By default, this group has "Enterprise Domain Controllers" as a member, but adding your CA computers to that group allows you to remove them from legacy access and keep the Certificate Manager restriction functional.

Thus, removing legacy access from your AD forest is a four-step process:

1. Remove "Authenticated Users" from "Pre-Windows 2000 Compatible Access" and verify that all applications work as expected.

2. Remove your CA computers from "Pre-Windows 2000 Compatible Access" (the group should now be empty).

3. If Certificate Manager restrictions are being used, add your CA computers to "Windows Authorization Access Group."

4. If everything is working as expected, remove permissions granted to the "Pre-Windows 2000 Compatible Access" group on the root of each domain in your forest.

When building out new certification authorities within the forest, you must add them to "Windows Authorization Access Group" if Certificate Manager restrictions are to be used with the particular CA.

4.3.4 Invisible Privileged Identities – the Evil and the Good

Hiding entire objects or containers from view leads to a very important question: What implications will hidden objects have if they are also hidden from administrators' view, not only from unprivileged identities? The answer, of course, depends on who is doing the hiding and how it is accomplished.

CHAPTER 4   ENGINEERING LOOKUP

Threat actors have known for a long time that denying read access to a user account for everyone does not prevent that account from authenticating. This allows for a persistence technique of creating a "God" account and then conveniently hiding it from being viewed by anybody. To give the account godlike privileges, adding it to a privileged group as an explicit member is obviously not a very good idea, nor will explicit permission entries for that account stay hidden for long (some admins routinely remove ACEs containing non-resolvable SIDs, which is what a hidden admin would look like in the tools). If, however, the cybercriminal has attained enough permissions to perform a DCShadow-style attack, they can inject SIDs of privileged groups into the hidden admin's **sidHistory** attribute so that they will automatically become part of its logon token!

Detecting these hidden administrators is not an easy task since they cannot be retrieved by any LDAP searches. Administrators actively looking for hidden objects must replicate every single object from the directory and either analyze its ACL or check whether it is retrievable by LDAP using a highly privileged account. Sometimes attackers neglect to deny SYSTEM access to their hidden accounts so that they can be discovered by running LDAP searches in the security context of a Domain Controller. More often, however, these hidden deities are detected accidentally by someone analyzing logs and trying to resolve – unsuccessfully, in the case of these hidden accounts – the SIDs found in the events.

In addition to not being easily detectable, privileged identities hidden by ACLs are also not very manageable (a typical "hidden God" introduced by a malicious actor is only manageable by itself). This technique, therefore, does not lend itself very well to providing administrator accounts that would not be visible by a threat actor who managed to move further along their attack chain – past initial reconnaissance but not yet far enough to be able to perform DCSync and DCShadow with impunity.

Luckily for us, Server 2016 and later provide us with a mechanism much more sophisticated and way better manageable. With the optional feature "Privileged Access Management," we get two powerful techniques which allow us to effectively hide the most important parts of our privileged access framework – the identities that are assigned permissions to perform administrative tasks in our directory. All we need to use these techniques is a Red Forest, assuming all forests involved in our organization are on the forest functional level of 2016 anyway. Server 2016 introduced a new class, **msDS-ShadowPrincipal**, into Active Directory schema. Objects of this class are located in a special container within the Red Forest's Configuration partition and can be mapped to security principals from the "golden" forest. For the shadow principals to work, the unidirectional forest trust between golden and Red forests must be defined as a PIMTrust (governed by two bits in the **trustAttributes** attribute of the **trustedDomain** object) and be set to be "Forest transitive" in both forests, regardless of their domain topology. After that, it's pretty straightforward:

- A security principal (user/group/computer) from the "golden" forest is granted permissions in that forest to perform administrative tasks; groups are best suited to be used with shadow principals.

- A shadow principal is created in the Red Forest and linked to the privileged group from the golden forest by assigning that group's SID to the **msDS-ShadowPrincipalSid** attribute of the shadow principal.

- A user from the Red Forest is added to the **member** attribute of the shadow principal.

If the user from the Red Forest attempts to access resources in the "golden" forest through the PIM trust, the SID of the privileged group is added to the Kerberos token of that user, along with all permissions that have been granted to that group. On the other hand, an attacker moving around in the "golden" forest and trying to enumerate the members of

CHAPTER 4   ENGINEERING LOOKUP

the privileged group will find the group empty at all times since all the memberships are shadowed and thus can only be found within the Red Forest. Setting up a PIM trust is a straightforward and well-documented procedure. The only part of it that is not self-explanatory is making the trust transitive on both sides (shown for the Red Forest side in Figure 4-3) even if there are only two single-domain forests involved in PIM.

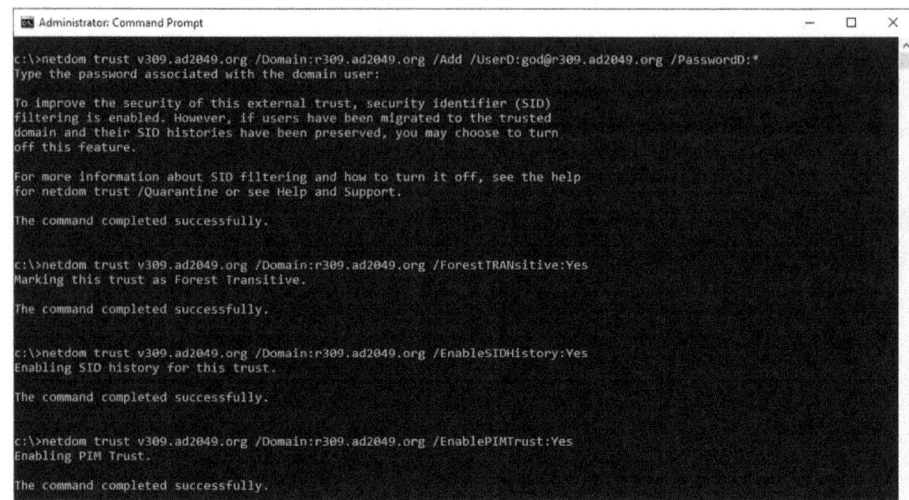

Figure 4-3.   *Setting up a PIM trust is straightforward*

To harden this even further, you can use the second technique from the "Privileged Access Management" optional feature – time-based group memberships. These can be used for both conventional group memberships and **member** attribute assignments of shadow principals. Time-based group memberships of any nature lead to Kerberos ticket lifetime being limited to the shortest membership's time-to-live (TTL). Once the TTL is up, the Kerberos ticket must be renewed and does not contain the temporarily assigned SID anymore!

Note At the time of writing, a one-way trust can be penetrated if the attacker attains DCSync capability. They will only get normal computer object's permissions in the trusted forest, but this may be enough to obtain critical information from the Red Forest. To mitigate this, you can use Authentication Policies in the Red Forest (we will look at those in the next chapter) and also hide identities from view within that forest using techniques discussed here.

4.3.5 Changing Schema Permissions and Default SDs – Worth the Hassle?

Editing the schema outside of Microsoft's own schema updates is not for the faint of heart, so let's look at what benefits we can expect from adjusting either schema permissions, default security descriptors for certain object classes, or both. Before we do that, however, keep in mind that permissions for Microsoft-defined classes and attributes will probably be rectified by the next schema update which is likely to occur when you introduce a new operating system version as a Domain Controller, and so will the **defaultSecurityDescriptor** attribute. So, whatever you undertake in the schema, you'll have to automate it and reapply your customizations after each schema update.

There is not much in the schema that you would want to hide from someone doing reconnaissance in your environment, since most of the standard AD schema is well known and not specific to your environment. If you start customizing for security reasons, then it's your customizations that bear restricting visibility. By default, "Authenticated Users" are granted a generic Read permission, which includes reading all properties and also reading permissions. You should usually be able to revoke the "read permissions" right from "Authenticated Users" without any issues by removing a check mark from the respective ACE on the Schema NC. If you modify **defaultSecurityDescriptor** of any classes, you might want to remove the permission to read that property as well, so as to not reveal the default permission set to the potential attacker. There is, however, a caveat there: if non-privileged users are allowed to create any class of objects in AD (by default, for example, everyone can create a DNS record), they have to be able to read the **defaultSecurityDescriptor** of that class!

All things considered, it's usually not worth the effort to restrict schema visibility, but removing excessive permissions from the **defaultSecurityDescriptor** can help harden the directory against reconnaissance. At the very least, you could remove the "read permissions" right granted to "Authenticated Users" by removing the **(A;;RC;;;AU)** ACE bracket from the **defaultSecurityDescriptor** of the **User** and **inetOrgPerson** classes. Privileged identities and groups are given that right by other means, and unprivileged ones usually do not need it nor care about it. A further step towards limiting visibility would be removing "Authenticated Users" from the **defaultSecurityDescriptor** altogether – SELF already has "read all properties" granted to it, so any application requiring directory information about the user running it would be satisfied, and other unprivileged identities would have to be given necessary read permissions by other means.

Instead of modifying the defaults, you can always use provisioning automation to remove undesired ACEs from new objects. Whichever way you choose to go depends on how big the potential of "accidentally created objects" is in your organization. While you're working on reducing that, you might as well limit the blast radius by restricting the default ACEs on new objects.

CHAPTER 4   ENGINEERING LOOKUP

4.4 Name Resolution and Service Location

A different kind of "lookup" that can also result in unwanted information disclosure is Domain Name System (DNS). DNS is crucially important for Active Directory's function since it provides information about the AD services like LDAP, Global Catalog, or PDC Emulator, depending on the AD site the querying computer is on. But it also holds information about computers in your environments, services they provide, and other data that could be valuable for malicious reconnaissance.

4.4.1 There's More to Life Than Just DNS

Contrary to popular belief, DNS is not the only name resolution protocol active by default on a Windows network. In most scenarios, DNS will be tried first, and if it can deliver a conclusive answer to a query, then that's what ends up being used to contact the target system. However, if DNS resolution fails, two other protocols kick in to help find the desired host: NetBIOS and LLMNR (Link Local Multicast Name Resolution). Both have been part of the Windows networking stack for ages, and both are equally vulnerable to poisoning and spoofing attacks. These attack techniques allow the malicious actor to act as "Attacker-In-The-Middle" or simply harvest credential material without bothering to give users an illusion that they communicate to a legitimate target.

While the techniques used to abuse LLMNR and NetBIOS may be similar, the conditions that lead to these protocols being used instead of DNS are different. LLMNR will try whatever host name or FQDN has been specified after the attempt to resolve that name using DNS fails. NetBIOS, on the other hand, is sometimes tried very early in the name resolution process (how early, depends on the application) and sometimes only attempted after both DNS and LLMNR have failed, but will specifically only try to resolve host names, as opposed to FQDNs (this behavior is alterable by group policy, usually leading to utter chaos). Since you

CHAPTER 4   ENGINEERING LOOKUP

absolutely want to avoid using host names in favor of FQDNs (we will talk about implications of that for authentication in the next chapter), disabling NetBIOS name resolution will help surfacing the applications that either depend on host names or have been misconfigured to use host names while perfectly capable of working with FQDNs.

Turning off LLMNR is straightforward – there is a group policy for it for domain members (see Figure 4-4) which can be reflected either in the local policy or directly in the registry for non-member machines. For NetBIOS, on the other hand, group policy can change behavior but not turn the protocol off completely. To achieve this, you'll have to either rely on DHCP or configure your TCP/IP stack statically to disable NetBIOS (GUI, registry, or WMI).

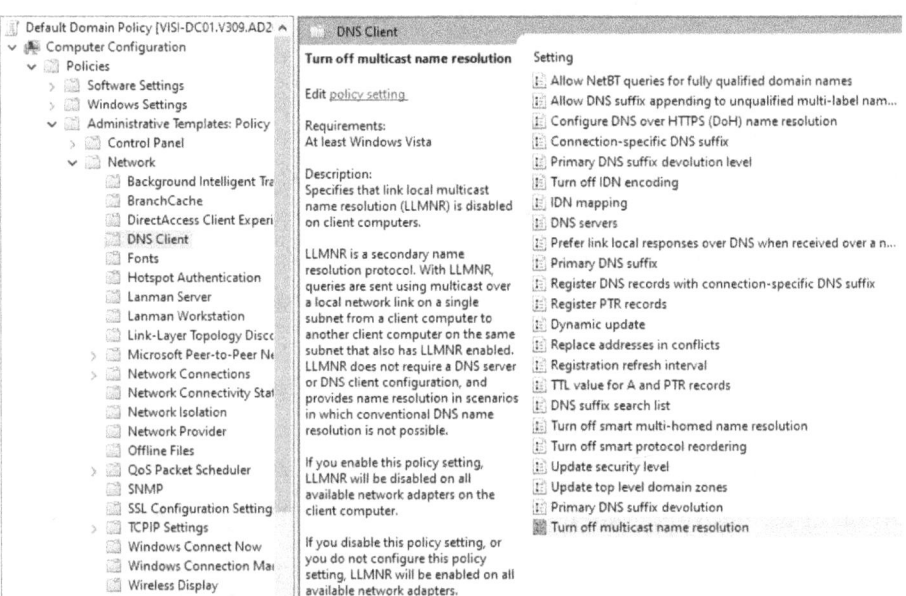

Figure 4-4. Many policies govern name resolution but none of them turns off NetBT

CHAPTER 4 ENGINEERING LOOKUP

Note If you identify applications that do rely on NetBIOS name resolution, the engineering approach dictates that you implement another legacy protocol you probably didn't want to hear about: WINS. It's part of every Windows Server distribution, including Server 2025 (at the time of writing in Insider Preview), and will allow you to prevent hostname sprawl, especially if your clients spend time in different networks other than on your enterprise LAN. Do not run WINS servers on Domain Controllers to avoid increasing their attack surface! Add all host records that are required for your legacy applications as static and set the migration flag to protect them from being overwritten by dynamic registrations.

Now that we got rid of legacy protocols, let us look at DNS and all the information that can be gleaned from it.

4.4.2 DNS and Reconnaissance

DNS holds a wide variety of records, grouped into zones or namespaces, which it will readily serve if queried. However, a DNS query has to be specific so that a nosy actor cannot retrieve all host (A) records the same way they could retrieve information about domain member computers by performing an LDAP search. The only way to bulk retrieve DNS information by using the DNS protocol is to request a zone transfer to a machine one controls. Windows DNS supports a zone configuration that allows transfers to any server that requests it; needless to say, this sort of configuration has no place in a well-engineered infrastructure. If you do need AD-hosted DNS zones transferred to non-AD servers, always specify them explicitly and make the admins of those systems aware that the data they will be receiving is sensitive information!

CHAPTER 4   ENGINEERING LOOKUP

DNS reveals IP addresses of hosts (A or AAAA records and their PTR counterparts), assignments of hosts to applications and services (CNAME for aliases, SRV for service records, MX for mail exchanger), and sometimes even port numbers specific services are listening on (SRV). A malicious actor is likely to want to obtain this information and store it for future use in order to not pop up on the defenders' radar by performing the same DNS queries over and over again. And although it is usually not very easy to access DNS records in bulk, most organizations follow naming conventions that can be abused to determine what hosts are actually there. Domain controllers can always be resolved from DNS – it is the basis for locating them in order to perform an LDAP lookup or Kerberos authentication. If the DCs retrieved from DNS bear generic names like SERVER73485, SERVER78556, and so on, one could assume that the server naming follows the pattern **SERVER\d{5}** and just try every host name from SERVER00000 to SERVER99999! Some well-known enterprise applications, like Exchange or Skype for Business, have hardcoded host names like autodiscover or lyncdiscover for service location; monitoring systems like Groundwork use this mechanism to provide automated onboarding to new machines. Although these records reveal valuable information about the environment to a potential malicious actor, they are necessary and must be present for the applications to work.

A special place in the world of name resolution belongs to DNS records of clients. In today's dynamic workplace where a laptop keeps moving between a docking station on an office LAN, a coffee shop WiFi across the street, conference room WiFi, and back on the LAN, not to mention working from home and dialing in through a VPN, organizations go to great lengths for keeping the records up to date (we will talk about it later in this section), but in reality, they are seldom of any real value. It may be necessary for things like Kerberos preauthentication that a client computer knows its own FQDN and the one it knows is identical with the FQDN stored in the **dnsHostName** attribute of its computer object. However, since no one should really be talking **to** client machines, having up-to-date name resolution for them is often not worth the effort. Your mileage may vary – some printer management systems have been known to resolve a client's name and compare it with the IP address the print job is being submitted from before accepting the job, but these are becoming more and more of an exception by the day. If you are in the business of providing up-to-date DNS records for client machines, reverse resolution (PTR) records may be of more value than A records; access logs often contain an IP address but not the host name, so, in order to correlate events from multiple sources, being able to resolve an IP back to its FQDN may indeed prove valuable.

In theory, you can restrict the blast radius slightly by using DNS Policies (available since Server 2016) and at least not disclosing service location information to DMZs, management networks, and other network segments where it wouldn't be of any use. However, policy-based DNS introduces a significant management overhead, which may not be justified by the benefit of hiding some records.

4.4.3 Other Ways to Bulk Access DNS Data

If your Windows DNS is AD-integrated (default configuration if you simply promote a Windows server to a Domain Controller), then each DNS zone and record is represented by an AD object. Depending on the replication scope, DNS zones are either stored in the **DC=ForestDNSZones,DC=root,DC=domain** partition or in one of the domain-specific **DC=DomainDNSZones,DC=some,DC=domain** ones. All this hierarchy is permissioned in a way that allows for a generic Read of both zones and individual records by "Everyone." So, if AD-integrated DNS is being used with default permissions, there's no way to hide DNS information from a malicious actor performing reconnaissance. However, there is a choke point in the permissions structure: traversing the **MicrosoftDNS** container placed underneath the NC head in order to get to DNS zone data requires either privileged access – or membership in the "Pre-Windows 2000 Compatible Access" group! By emptying that legacy group, you automatically hamper DNS reconnaissance using LDAP!

4.4.4 External DNS and Its Abuse

While hardening access to your legitimately stored DNS data, you shouldn't forget about the potential of DNS abuse for other attack techniques. To this day, many organizations put DNS forwarders to public DNS resolvers on their internal DNS servers and even allow internal DNS servers outbound access to those resolvers! This has been known to be abused for both data exfiltration and command-and-control traffic. In today's connected enterprise, client machines and possibly even servers may have to communicate with the outside world; however, more often than not, this communication is channeled through a proxy, which handles name resolution itself, without the requester having to bother about resolving DNS. If this is the case in your organization, you can just as well disable external DNS forwarding on your internal DNS servers.

If you do need external name resolution in your DNS, use a filtering DNS service or a filtering appliance within your network. Many firewall or content filter providers offer secured DNS resolvers that will consult lists of known malicious addresses and return an NXDOMAIN reply if a request contains a dangerous domain name or if the result of the next recursion returns an IP address known to be malicious from the provider's threat research. This also helps reduce the blast radius of phishing and drive-by downloads.

In any case, disable root hints on each internal DNS server as shown in Figure 4-5. If you are using AD-integrated DNS, forwarder and root hint configuration is not replicated between domain controllers. You can also replace the precanned root hints by secure DNS resolvers of your choosing. However, you cannot remove all of the root servers from the root hint configuration in Windows, regardless of them potentially being used or not.

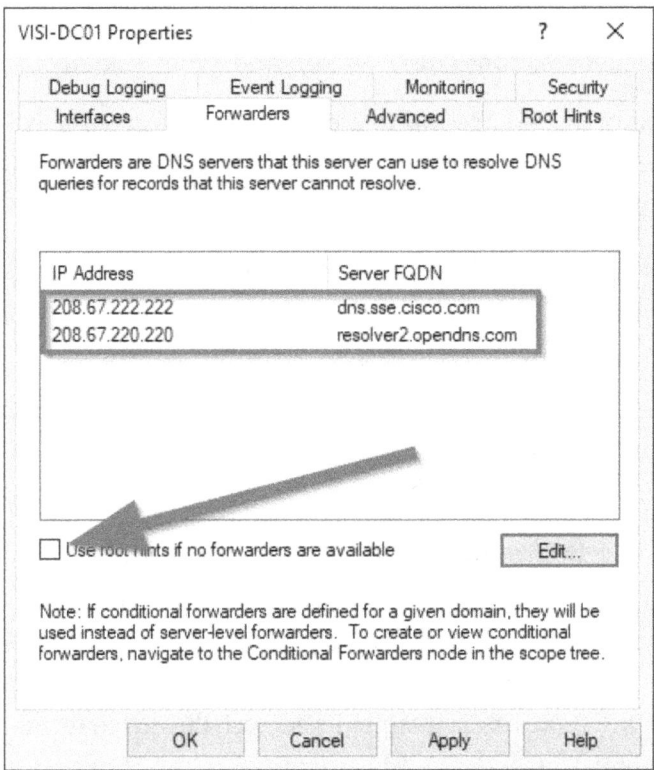

Figure 4-5. *Use secure external DNS and disable root hints*

4.4.5 DNS Record Creation

Although this chapter is dedicated to looking information up, this seems like the best place to talk about how DNS records get created in the first place. There are countless attack scenarios around Windows and AD that begin with the attacker abusing DNS to direct unsuspecting users to a server under the bad actor's control. There are four ways a DNS record can be introduced into an AD-integrated DNS zone:

- Using ADSI to create a record directly in AD which will then get read into the DNS server on zone reload

- Using DCOM or WMI to create a record through DNS server (that's what the DNS console and PowerShell are using)

- Using dynamic DNS registration from a remote computer

- Using DHCP to perform DNS record registration on behalf of a remote computer (if DHCP-DNS integration has been set up)

Using DCOM or WMI requires administrative permissions (local administrator or DNS administrator) on a DNS server. In the case of AD-integrated DNS, this means administrative permissions on a Domain Controller or a membership in the "DnsAdmins" Active Directory group. This is not a "well-known group" in the sense that it doesn't come with a fixed RID below 1000, nor is it considered "privileged" in terms of SDPROP and **adminCount**. However, for this exact reason, the abuse potential of this group is especially high and you should always keep an eye on its memberships.

Dynamic DNS registration is great for AD-related records provisioned by Domain Controllers. It is especially useful if the site coverage topology changes due to the introduction of new DCs or to changes in site links and bridges. Once the KCC regenerates the topology, DCs start registering their service records for the sites that they cover (and deregistering the records for the sites they are not responsible for anymore). However, opening dynamic registration to any server or client potentially means asking for trouble. The way it has been set up by default, "Authenticated Users" are granted the right to "Create all child objects." If you want to restrict dynamic registration to just domain controllers, you can remove the ACE for "Authenticated Users" from each DNS zone's ACL. If some computers are to be allowed dynamic updates and others are not, create a group for those computers and grant child object creation rights to that group. If only dynamic updates, e.g., on IP address changes, are to be allowed but not dynamic registration of new records, create the records using whatever provisioning process you have in place and then grant the corresponding computer object "full control" over the record.

Having DHCP create, update, and retire DNS records is the only way to reliably keep track of the rapid IP address changes typical for modern day's clients. DHCP will only create and manage A and, if so configured, PTR records, as opposed to dynamic registration that allows a remote computer to create any type of records. We will not go into details of the "DnsUpdateProxy" group and DNS service accounts in DHCP; suffice it to say that you should never run DHCP servers on Domain Controllers if AD-integrated DNS is in use, lest an attacker can manipulate your DNS by crafting DHCP requests to their liking and then abusing the godlike permissions a DC has in AD-integrated DNS. Before enabling DNS record management through DHCP, ask yourself if this kind of up-to-dateness really is necessary for your clients' records – or if those records are indeed required in the first place! There are cases where the answer to both questions will be positive, for example, if you are using clients that are not joined to AD and managed by a central instance reaching out to them on a proprietary protocol. Thin and zero clients often require this kind of management, and their management servers expect the clients' FQDNs to be resolvable to their current IP addresses.

If using DHCP with domain-joined Windows clients, you should choose one technology for DNS record management. Records created by DHCP will lack ACEs that allow them to be updated by "their" machines via dynamic update. Dynamically registered records, on the other hand, will not be associated with a particular DHCP lease.

4.4.6 DNS Security Enhancements

Microsoft DNS has had cache poisoning protection built in since at least Server 2008 ("Cache Locking"). However, in the early versions of Windows Server, it was not activated by default. If you're in the habit of in-place upgrading your Windows Server OSes, this could have carried over to your present Domain Controllers. If your servers have been installed fresh using at least Server 2016, then Cache Locking is activated by default, but it's always a good idea to check periodically.

In the context of this book, we will not spend much time on the new DNS protocol introduced, unsurprisingly, by the browser makers – DNS over HTTPS or DoH. At the time of writing, it bears no relevance for Active Directory operations. However, with the proliferation of DoH in client and, starting with Server 2025, even Server OS, you will want to find ways to engineer DoH management in a way that allows smooth resolution of any AD-related records. For now, though, DoH can offer a way to bypass DNS restrictions like the ones described above and allow for unchecked external name resolution and data exfiltration.

The DNS zone and record signing (DNSSEC) has been supported by Windows Server since version 2008R2. The benefits of having verifiable records, however, come at a price. First, DNSSEC is dependent on Public Key Infrastructure (PKI) that an organization may or may not have in place. Second, DNSSEC replies are much larger than DNS replies without signing because a signature is attached to every record returned by the server. This creates a potential for amplification attacks where a stream of DNS queries directed at a server results in huge amounts of data getting output and ultimately overloads the DNS server, causing it to become unresponsive or even crash. If the server in question happens to be a Domain Controller, this affects more than just name resolution. And, while DNSSEC offers reliable protection against DNS server spoofing (to clients that are DNSSEC-capable), it will not protect you against a record introduced into a zone by a malicious actor – that record will be signed and validated like any other in that zone! This is why DNSSEC is suitable for public Internet traffic and offers way less benefits for internal name resolution in the context of Active Directory.

4.5 Lookup in Perimeter Networks

Perimeter networks, or edge networks, or DMZs have a special place in the lookup design. Whether it's DNS lookup for internal systems or services or LDAP lookup for information from internally operated directories, allowing it to be performed from a potentially hostile network segment poses significant challenges. The pure doctrine of network security dictates that network connections between segments of different safety levels must be initiated from the safer zone and directed towards the less safe one, but not the other way around. Allowing LDAP or DNS from DMZ clearly goes against that principle.

4.5.1 DNS Lookup from the Edge

Before allowing internal name resolution in edge networks, you should always ask yourself (or the person in charge of that decision) what the purpose of it would be. Computer systems do not usually perform name resolution for its own sake, but rather as a precursor to initiating an actual connection which, again, would violate the principle of not connecting to safer regions from less safe ones. Under no circumstances should you just allow DNS from edge networks to your Domain Controllers hosting AD-integrated DNS if any of the zones are configured to accept dynamic updates.

The scope of name resolution is also an important factor. If a certain application in the DMZ only needs to connect to a handful of servers on the internal network and those servers' addresses are static, you might even get away with HOSTS files on the application's server or servers. If many applications from the DMZ seek to connect to a limited set of LAN targets, put a DNS server in the DMZ and have it serve just the required records. It goes without saying that there is a process component to this: If the IP addresses behind the names do change, this must be reflected in the HOSTS files or in the DMZ DNS. If your forest design is such that servers' DNS records live in a different zone than the clients', you could allow zone transfers in the server zone's configuration to a DNS server in the DMZ (which, even in this scenario, doesn't have to be a Windows server – zone transfer is part of the DNS protocol and perfectly possible between different OS families and DNS server products).

If you are ever in a situation where an edge network must resolve **clients'** names and/or addresses, there is something fundamentally wrong with your application design. Revisiting it to stick to more secure data pathways can go a long way towards securing the entire infrastructure.

4.5.2 LDAP Querying and Binding

The best way to protect your AD from LDAP-based attacks originating at the edge is by not allowing these connections in the first place. If it's just about looking up information from a domain partition, put an LDS instance in the DMZ (could even be "a" DMZ if you have multiple unsafe zones that are allowed to communicate with each other) and replicate the required attributes of the required objects to that instance, initiating the communication from the LAN side. It is very unlikely that a DMZ application would require information from the configuration partition or any of the application partitions.

If access to LDAP is required to authenticate a user rather than to just look up information using a static bind credential, consider implementing an LDS Proxy. We will talk about it in the next chapter. Although a proxy does not protect users from being locked out by a brute force attack against ADLDS, it reduces the blast radius by only providing proxy objects for users actually requiring this external authentication. At the very least,

CHAPTER 4   ENGINEERING LOOKUP

privileged users can't be probed from outside the LAN if you do not provision **userProxyFull** objects for them in the ADLDS directory. If a DMZ application requires lookup for a lot of users but authentication just for a subset of them, you can provision **organizationPerson** objects for all required users but **userProxyFull** objects for the ones that would have to authenticate.

In any case, secure the LDAP connection by using LDAPS (LDAP over TLS) to further protect the bind credentials used to access the directory. This is especially true if you do require access to the actual Active Directory. At the time of writing, Microsoft announced that simple binds using explicit credentials (which is exactly what DMZ applications are most likely to be using) will not be supported over unencrypted connections as of early 2025. Keep in mind that for certificate validation, the DMZ systems have to contact the validation authority, i.e., CDP or OCSP. Non-AD-joined machines will not be able to validate certificates if the only CRL that your PKI provides is stored in AD and can only be accessed via (authenticated) LDAP!

4.6 Modern Defaults

To provide "modern" defaults for your information lookup, start by gathering requirements. Do any applications that unprivileged users run require information from Active Directory? What particular attributes do they need? Does an application require information of users different from the one running it or groups the user is not a member of? Is this access conducted by the user starting the client application or by a service account running the middleware?

4.6.1 Restrict Read Permissions

Remove all memberships from the "Pre-Windows 2000 Compatible Access" group. If you are planning on using AD Certificate Services with the Certificate Managers feature, add computers running your CAs to the "Windows Authorization Access Group" instead. Mark a date in your calendar, maybe a year or two in the future, for the removal of the ACEs granting access to that group. If you have not encountered any legacy access-related problems until then, you are very unlikely to see any in the future. When you start removing legacy permission entries, don't forget that they exist in all partitions, not just in the domain partitions! The **AdminSDHolder** container in each domain also needs explicit attention since it does not inherit permissions from its parent object but will propagate its explicit ACL to all the administrative accounts.

Set the third character of **dsHeuristics** to "1" to enable Object List mode. If no value has previously been set, set the attribute to "001."

Remove all entries for "Authenticated Users" (AU) and "Print Operators" (PO) from the default security descriptor for the following object classes in the schema:

- User
- inetOrgPerson
- Group
- Computer
- OrganizationalUnit

If you are creating a fresh domain, reboot your domain controllers for the schema changes to take effect, or just restart the "NTDS" service.

Remove all entries for "Authenticated Users" and "Print Operators" from **AdminSDHolder** and all OUs and containers on the top level that are already present. Leave the entry for "LostAndFound" in place – it is required by AD! The "System" container and its substructure must be traversable by both computers and users, at least the parts that are needed for the GPO application. Feel free to leave "Read" permissions for "Authenticated Users" in place – everything disclosed by them is part of the base inventory of your domain and will hardly be of interest to the attackers. Other parts like "Password Settings Container" are hidden from "Authenticated Users" by default.

Remove the ACE for "Authenticated Users" from the "Infrastructure" object under the domain root.

Move all privileged objects with the exception of Domain Controllers into the "Privileged" OU.

Redirect new computer and user creation to a "New Objects" OU and severely restrict access to that OU. Link a GPO to it denying interactive and remote-interactive logon to everyone.

Remove all "Authenticated Users" ACEs from the domain head. After this change takes effect, a non-privileged user is still able to log on to a member machine; however, they will not see any objects in the directory, not even their own, and will also not be able to apply Group Policies because none of the OUs between the domain head and the user object are readable at this time. Computers that are not domain controllers will also not be able to process Group Policy. If you are creating a fresh domain, it should not be a problem. In a production forest, you should perform the procedures in the next two sections before removing "Authenticated Users" from the equation.

4.6.2 Provide Visibility to Non-privileged Users

Non-privileged users require three distinct sets of permissions:

- "List object" on every OU between the domain head and the user's parent OU in order to see own object.

- "Read all properties" on every OU between the domain head and the user's parent OU in order to apply GPOs.

- Whatever other objects your applications require to be readable by the user. This could be authorization groups, the computer object of the computer the user is logged on to or other parts of the infrastructure reflected in AD.

A good method of providing these permissions are "shadow groups," i.e., groups corresponding to OUs. By assigning the "List Object" and "Read all properties" rights to these groups and nesting the group into each other following the OU structure, you can achieve manageable permissions that restrict visibility while allowing functionality at the same time. A good globally unique naming convention and a simple monitoring script will help prevent permissions sprawl and ensure that group policies can be applied where needed.

Assign "List Object" permissions to individual objects as required.

4.6.3 Provide Visibility to Computers

Computers must be able to locate and read both their own OUs and those where the users logging on to them are located in order to successfully apply Group Policies (as of June 2016, the computer must be able to read the user part of the group policy in order to apply it to the user session). Create appropriate groups for servers and workstations according to their planned placement in the OU structure. Each of these groups has to be assigned the following permissions:

- "List object" on domain head

- "List object" and "Read all properties" on every OU between the domain head and the computer object

- "List object" and "Read all properties" on every OU between the domain head and any of the users that may be logging on to the machines in question

When deciding on the granularity of this structure, keep in mind that an attacker being able to execute LDAP searches in the SYSTEM context of a workstation is a perfectly viable scenario. After all the work you have done restricting your users, you should apply the same level of granularity to the computer objects. And even then, a computer will be able to potentially see more OUs in AD than any non-privileged user.

4.6.4 What Other Objects Have to Be Visible?

If you use groups, users, Ous, or other objects in Group Policy and especially in Group Policy Preferences, these objects must be visible by at least the computer applying the policy and, if the user part of a policy is involved, by the user as well. An example of this is a GPO to replace "Domain Admins" added to a member's local Administrator group as a part of domain join by a custom group. Both groups must be visible to the computer object in order to perform the operation. However, the groups' **membership** does not have to be readable by the computer object, so the potential for reconnaissance can still be limited.

4.6.5 Restrict Users' Own Visibility

Depending on the paranoia level of your planned hardening, you might consider removing some of the SELF permissions from user objects. Almost none of them are required to provide a successful logon and user profile creation. However, these restrictions are among the hardest to troubleshoot and to provide an exception to. For now, we can leave the default read permissions to SELF in place and turn our attention to other aspects of information retrieval.

4.6.6 Restrict DNS Access

By removing all memberships from "Pre-Windows 2000 Compatible Access," you have already ensured that DNS zones and records cannot be viewed using LDAP by a non-privileged identity. There is little you can do to limit the amount of information revealed by your internal DNS using the DNS protocol itself. To prevent abuse through DNS manipulation, check that the Cache Locking feature is active and consider severely restricting dynamic registration. If your servers do not change their IP addresses on a regular basis, the following can provide a good and secure name registration experience:

- Remove the permission for "Authenticated Users" to create child objects.

- Provision A and PTR records for servers, printers, and other network devices capable of dynamic registration statically as part of the server provisioning process. Do not forget to also include deleting those records in the server decommissioning procedure since static records will not age and therefore will not be scavenged!

- Use DHCP to provision A and PTR records for clients and disable dynamic updates on the clients altogether. This will help both ensure timely updates upon IP address changes and prevent the creation of unwanted records by means of DNS.

To further harden DHCP/DNS integration, you might consider creating (and permissioning) clients' DNS records in a way that DHCP can update and delete existing records but cannot create new ones.

Last but not least, you are not required to use Windows DHCP and DNS, let alone AD-integrated DNS, to run a well-functioning Active Directory organization. Modern DDI systems are hardened against rogue records creation better than Windows DHCP and DNS are and still provide good AD integration so that Domain Controllers can create all requisite records themselves to reflect the site topology and coverage.

Do not set up external DNS resolution in your internal DNS unless your internal clients and users can and must contact external targets directly. If your Internet access is channeled through a proxy, then the proxy will be responsible for name resolution, and internal machines do not need it. If you have to provide external DNS internally, use a secured DNS resolver (at the time of writing, Cisco Umbrella is a good example, albeit only one of many) or an appliance sanitizing your DNS requests (at the time of writing, PiHole has become a de facto standard, even in larger organizations). Do not forget to disable root hints and replace pre-canned root servers by your chosen secure DNS provider!

4.6.7 Provide DMZ Access If Needed

Do not provide inbound DNS or LDAP access from unsafe network zones to Active Directory and AD-integrated DNS until absolutely necessary. For name resolution purposes, you can work with DNS servers placed in the DMZ and holding a copy of the required zones; however, in most cases, manually created DNS records of a few select internal targets or even HOSTS files on the DMZ systems themselves will prove quite a manageable replacement.

For LDAP directory lookup, use an ADLDS instance placed within the DMZ and only holding the required objects with the required attributes populated from AD (in which case the synchronization connection will be from the safe zone towards the unsafe one). Even with this additional layer of isolation, use LDAPS to protect the bind credentials.

If an actual LDAP bind is required, you can work with an ADLDS instance on the LAN segment holding **userProxyFull** objects for select users and proxying authentication requests to AD in the background. This also allows for a single point of LDAP authentication across multiple domains and even forests. The initial setup of an ADLDS proxy is complex;

however, this is the sort of complexity that is taken care of by automation. Once setup, proxy authentication works reliably and provides a good, consistent access experience.

4.7 Summary

In this chapter, we looked at different scenarios involving information retrieval from an Active Directory environment. While AD needs to provide some information to its members and users, the default permissions are relaxed (for the sake of backward compatibility) to the point where "everybody can see everything" almost becomes a valid statement.

We provided a "modern defaults" framework that only grants access to the absolutely necessary information while ensuring that all core functionality remains unaffected. This is only the beginning of your permissions engineering journey because in this book we cannot incorporate all of your applications' requirements into general recommendations.

We introduced stealth techniques of privileged access, most notably the "shadow principals," allowing you to conduct "golden" forest administration from the Red Forest without any group membership being tracked back to the identities used.

We then looked at DNS as a means of information retrieval, a target of abuse, and a strictly required component for flawless Active Directory operations. There is not much in DNS that can be hardened in terms of information retrieval; creating, updating, and retiring DNS records provide multiple controls that you can put in place to restrict DNS abuse.

A special case of information lookup is making AD and DNS data available to systems in unsafe network segments (e.g., DMZ). We discussed various techniques of securing DNS lookup, LDAP lookup and – although not quite in the scope of this chapter – even LDAP bind as a means of authenticating AD users in external-facing applications.

CHAPTER 5

Engineering Authentication

While information lookup may not actually be needed for every identity using your directory services, authentication is a different matter. It is Active Directory's primary function and must be provided in a reliable and secure manner. For decades, reliability and, more generally, usability were IT organizations' primary focus, relegating security to the back seat. A series of devastating cyberattacks followed, leaving Windows and Active Directory with a bad reputation for authentication security. In this chapter, we shall mitigate authentication-related risk by careful engineering and generous use of security controls that modern Windows versions place at our disposal.

The risk associated with authentication is that of a usable credential being disclosed to an unauthorized third party and then used with malicious intent. This can happen in many ways:

- Cleartext usernames and passwords leaked by physical means (a Post-It note under the keyboard being a classic example, albeit not the only one – we have seen passwords written on a whiteboard visible on a public webinar)

CHAPTER 5   ENGINEERING AUTHENTICATION

- Cleartext usernames and passwords revealed by digital reconnaissance (even at the time of writing, there are admins who routinely put passwords into the **description** attribute of user accounts and even have that "process" automated; text files or scripts containing cleartext passwords were found in most of the organizations the author has audited for security)

- Cleartext passwords revealed from cryptographically secured sources (credential managers, encrypted configuration files, etc.) using previously obtained information unrelated to authentication, e.g., DPAPI backdoor keys

- Cleartext usernames and passwords revealed by successful guessing attempts – brute force or password spray

- Password hashes subjected to cracking, ultimately revealing the cleartext passwords ("a" password would actually be more precise, because there are more different passwords than possible hash values)

- Password hashes used directly to authenticate to services (Pass-the-Hash) or to obtain legitimate authentication tickets from the KDC (Overpass-the-Hash)

- Other authentication-related information subjected to brute-force cracking with the goal of obtaining a cleartext password (Kerberoasting being the most prominent example)

- Forged credentials, either following the disclosure of a different credential (e.g., "Golden Ticket" type attacks) or abusing flaws in enterprise cryptography (PKI misconfigurations)

Disclosing cleartext passwords bears an additional risk of a malicious actor inferring future passwords for the same user from the current one. If a password believed to be set in May 2024 was **R@ngers2405!** and the attacker discovers from reconnaissance that the user has changed their password in January 2025, **R@ngers2501!** is actually a very good guess, because humans *are* creatures of habit. In some cases, even brute-forcing a long, complex password or passphrase could be justified due to this additional attack vector. Even if it takes a GPU farm two months to crack **Rough winds do shake the darling buds of May,**, knowing that the password has only been changed once since this one makes **And summer's lease hath all too short a date.** an excellent proposition (*these lines are from Sonnet 18 by Shakespeare, in case you're wondering*)!

Our risk management strategy in regard to authentication will primarily focus on reducing the likelihood, i.e., making all attack vectors listed above as expensive and unattractive to a potential threat actor as possible. We will deal with the impact-limiting component of mitigating credential-stealing attacks in the next chapter. Some of the techniques for reducing the potential of credential theft from active or past logon sessions are directly related to AD; we will look at them in this chapter and also in Chapters 6 and 7. Other hardening methods belong in the domain of systems administration; we will mention those in passing in this and the following chapters.

5.1 Authentication Protocols in AD

Active Directory Domain Services supports two authentication protocols: the industry-standard Kerberos being at the heart of the Active Directory security model from its inception, and Microsoft-owned NTLM, hailing from the Windows NT era and kept for backwards compatibility purposes but also to support Windows in non-domain-joined scenarios. It is no

CHAPTER 5 ENGINEERING AUTHENTICATION

secret that Kerberos provides better authentication security (and, being a standard protocol, better interoperability with other systems), but it is also a well-known fact that NTLM is still widely used and not easy to get rid of. To better understand the implications, possible vulnerabilities, and mitigations of the two protocols, let us take a quick look at how they work.

5.1.1 NTLM: "Prove Who You Are"

NTLM is a challenge-response authentication protocol derived from "LAN Manager" (LM), which was the standard authentication protocol in OS/2. The cryptography used by LAN Manager was weak both in terms of design and the hashing algorithm used for hash generation. The reason we are mentioning LAN Manager in this book at all is that to this day it is possible to configure Windows to both store LM hashes and reply to LM authentication requests. If a system in your organization requires you to support LM, it has no place in a modern AD infrastructure and must go into an isolated bubble together with its own authentication provider.

Note Most security measures described in this chapter are worthless if your AD supports LM authentication.

NTLM improves upon LM in terms of cryptography, making the authentication flow more secure, albeit slightly. Looking at Figure 5-1, design weaknesses of NTLM become apparent:

- The "answer" component requires a password to derive the answer from. Any system using NTLM for authentication is stuck with passwords as the only possible authenticator.

- The MD4 function used to derive an NTLM hash from the password has been relegated to "historic" status in 2011 by RFC6150. While the hmac_md5 encryption of the nonce can still be considered solid, the MD4 hashing function is too weak even at the time of writing.

- No other cryptography than the MD4 hashing function is ever applied to the password. This makes the NTLM hash the "password equivalent" for any protocols and applications that do not require the user to type their password into a logon form.

- At no stage in the authentication flow must the client verify the user's identity to the Domain Controller. The client only talks to the resource (as it would in a workgroup scenario), and only the resource talks to the Domain Controller if it's a domain account that tries to authenticate (thus enabling a scenario where a workgroup machine is used to access domain-joined resources using a domain user's identity). In the first version of the NTLM protocol, this allowed for simple replay scenarios where NTLM handshakes sniffed from the network would be directly reusable to access a different resource.

- At no stage in this simplified authentication flow is the particular resource the client intends to access specified as a part of the authentication traffic.

CHAPTER 5   ENGINEERING AUTHENTICATION

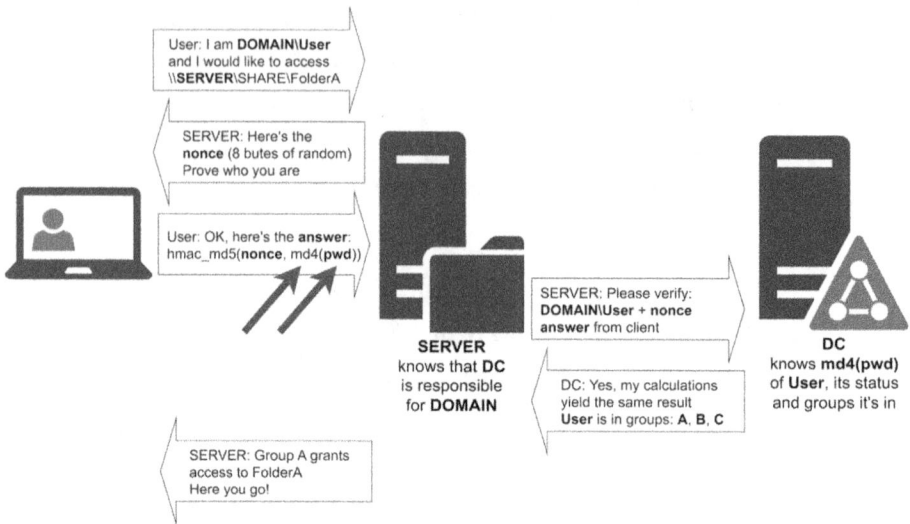

Figure 5-1. *NTLM authentication flow*

NTLMv2, which is the last and final version of the old protocol, improves upon NTLMv1 by adding session security and message integrity mechanisms to prevent direct reuse of captured NTLM packets. These extensions include both standardized techniques like signing or channel binding and proprietary mechanisms like service binding that make NTLM aware of the targeted resource. Even if abandoning NTLM altogether is not yet an option in your organization, the least you can do is restrict the protocol to only use NTLMv2. There is a group policy for it that you can also reflect in the local policy for non-domain-joined machines.

Note   Direct replay attacks that should not be possible anymore, even with NTLM (as long as v2 is used), are sometimes confused with NTLM relay attack techniques where a privileged computer, most notably a Domain Controller, is coerced into authenticating using NTLM to a machine controlled by the attacker. That authentication

CHAPTER 5　ENGINEERING AUTHENTICATION

request is then relayed to the intended attack target, which authenticates the (perfectly valid) request and performs actions requested by the attacker on behalf of the privileged identity.

Whatever hardening measures we put in place for NTLM, three fundamental flaws remain:

- Everything is tied to the password.
- NTLM hash is based on MD4 and potentially weak, allowing for brute-force cracking if the password is not long enough.
- NTLM hash of the user's password is all that is needed to perform successful NTLM authentication, unless manual password entry into a logon form is required and cannot be bypassed.

The best way of dealing with NTLM in a modern AD infrastructure is by disabling it altogether. We will discuss it in Section 5.3.

5.1.2 Kerberos: "Here's Who I Am"

Kerberos takes a different approach to authentication. Before providing any identification to the desired resource, the user verifies their identity against the central identity infrastructure, i.e., Active Directory. Using the verification (ticket) obtained from a DC, the client then provides verifiable proof of their identity to the resource, which then performs authorization and grants access in pretty much the same way it did with NTLM authentication.

Kerberos uses cryptography to check the veracity of the user's claim to their identity. However, the key material used to encrypt the challenge is not necessarily derived from a cleartext password. Kerberos provides a second option: using a certificate where the user performing authentication holds the private key (usually on a smart card or a crypto token), whereas the Domain Controller holds the corresponding public key.

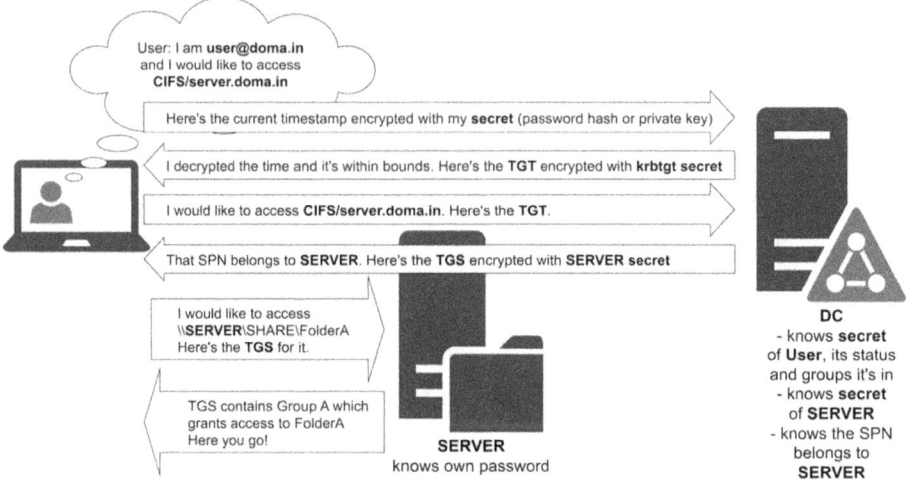

Figure 5-2. *Kerberos authentication flow (simplified)*

To really appreciate the benefits of Kerberos, consider the two kinds of tickets Figure 5-2 shows served by the Domain Controller to the user: Ticket Granting Ticket (TGT) and Service Ticket (TGS). None of the tickets is decryptable by the user but only by the entity they intended for – TGT by a DC from the user's domain, TGS by the service being accessed. What's even more important, these tickets have a lifetime (ten hours by default) during which they can be reused as needed, reducing the amount of traffic directed to Domain Controllers. Add to that potentially stronger cryptography, and you get a robust and secure authentication protocol.

Note In this and all the following chapters, "TGS" will be used in place of "Service Ticket" for the sake of brevity, following the slightly imprecise "terminology" many AD folks are accustomed to. The true meaning of "TGS" is, of course, "Ticket Granting Service".

CHAPTER 5   ENGINEERING AUTHENTICATION

One of the weaknesses of Microsoft's Kerberos implementation lies in the fact that there usually is more than one Domain Controller for every domain, or, in the Kerberos terminology, there is more than one "Key Distribution Center" (KDC) instance for every "Realm." This poses the challenge that a TGT obtained from DC1 must allow getting a TGS from DC2. Microsoft solved this challenge by adding a special user account named "krbtgt" to the directory itself so that every DC in the domain has knowledge of its password hash, which is the domain-wide secret used to encrypt TGTs. Knowledge of this account's password allows an attacker to create TGTs that are technically indistinguishable from those granted by a Domain Controller, a technique known as "Golden Ticket."

Another chink in Kerberos' armor in Active Directory is the cryptography used to create user secrets from cleartext passwords. With the release of AD in 1999 and all the way up to Server 2008, Kerberos only supported two protocols: DES (which was already considered too weak back in 1999) and RC4. RFC6649 from July 2012 deprecates RC4 along with DES and 3DES, and for good reasons: DES is what LAN Manager has been using, and RC4 is identical with the MD4 hash used by NTLM. So an NTLM hash harvested by network sniffing or by the coercion part of a relay attack has the potential of allowing the attacker to request Kerberos tickets using the NTLM hash in lieu of the RC4 hash ("Pass the Ticket"/"Overpass the Hash"). To mitigate this, Kerberos RFCs introduce the notion of "newer" encryption types. In Microsoft's case, this means AES128 and AES256 were first implemented by Server 2008R2 Forest Functional Level. This is going to be complemented by AES256 with SHA256 and SHA384 instead of SHA1 once Server 2025 is released, meaning that the FFL upgrade to 2025 will force the krbtgt password to be changed like the upgrade from any FFL below 2008R2 to 2008R2 or above did.

149

The decision to make the RC4 hash identical with NTLM one can be explained by the requirement of migrating from a Windows NT domain to Active Directory. With NT, DES and MD4 hashes were all that was stored in the domain database. Users and computers being migrated to AD had to be able to authenticate using Kerberos. Instead of forcing everyone to set a new password upon migration, Microsoft chose the path of just keeping the hash and making it valid in the target. This is just one of many examples of perceived usability and backward compatibility winning over better security.

Finally, you can introduce an additional vulnerability into your Kerberos authentication by setting the flag "Do not require Kerberos preauthentication" on a user object. The term "preauthentication" sounds like something optional, maybe offering additional security; in reality, however, the "preauthentication" is the part of the flow where the user sends the current timestamp encrypted with their secret to the DC in order to verify their identity and the freshness of the request! In a modern Active Directory environment, no user object, let alone a privileged one, should **ever** have that flag set. You can quickly find all accounts in your directory by using the following LDAP filter:

(&(objectClass=user)
(userAccountControl:1.2.840.113556.1.4.804=4194304))

It will find both user and computer objects with preauthentication disabled.

5.2 Engineering Kerberos for Security and Usability

Attacking Kerberos in order to obtain either reusable or crackable credential information usually boils down to the malicious actor either gaining control over a legitimate computer within the AD forest or tricking the users into communicating with a system the attacker introduced themselves and had control over from the beginning:

- Harvesting password hashes from current and past interactive logon sessions on workstations and servers. This is not specific to Kerberos, an NTLM hash can be used for a "Pass the Hash" attack if the environment supports NTLM authentication. We will look into getting rid of NTLM in the next section.

- Harvesting password hashes from AD backups. If the backup is recent enough, this allows for an immediate "Golden Ticket" attack.

- Harvesting service tickets submitted to a legitimate service the attacker brought under their control.

- Harvesting service tickets by just requesting them abusing a legitimate identity. By default, any identity in the forest can request and obtain a TGS to any service known to AD. The target identity can either be a subclass of **computer** using an explicit or implicit Service Principal Name (SPN) or a subclass of **user** in which case it needs an explicit SPN to be identified as a service account. We will talk about these in Sections 5.4 and 5.5.

CHAPTER 5   ENGINEERING AUTHENTICATION

- Harvesting TGT and forging TGS by abusing Kerberos delegation. There are multiple attack scenarios for each delegation technique, with different mitigations for them.

An additional source of password hashes and other secrets is replication from the live directory (DCSync). This allows for an immediate "Golden Ticket" attack since the krbtgt password hash obtained this way is guaranteed to be valid until the password is changed.

In this section, we will look at configurations and techniques that harden Active Directory against these authentication-based attack vectors. In the context of this chapter, we will always assume that an attacker is able to execute processes in the SYSTEM context of a machine they control (but this machine is NOT a Domain Controller). While it is by no means a trivial achievement, there are plenty of scenarios leading to this situation – over the years, we saw vulnerabilities in various Windows subsystems leading to remote code execution (RCE), vulnerabilities in Exchange (Hafnium), startup scripts and scheduled tasks deployed by GPP, and local administrator accounts gleaned from scripts, password lists, or even from misconfigured LAPS attributes. Limiting these possibilities is the administrators' first priority, and there are means to achieve this – endpoint protection, application whitelisting, limiting execution rights in the file system, just to name a few. However, mitigating this initial infection vector is not in the scope of this book.

5.2.1 AD Authentication the Engineer's Way

In the last chapter, we dispensed with the myth that "everybody can see everything in AD" – with a well-defined permissions framework we could hide privileged objects from unprivileged users' and computers' views, and by utilizing PIM Trusts, Shadow Principals, and Just-In-Time administration, even the traces of the true administrative identities could be hidden from a nosy actor's reconnaissance efforts. Now is the time to look at authentication in the same manner and see if we can prevent undesired authentication flows.

The first mechanism for restricting authentication capability was introduced in Windows NT in the form of the **userWorkstations** attribute that was carried over to Active Directory and retained its function. It's a string attribute that holds a comma-separated list of hostnames from which the user is allowed to log on. This attribute is checked before verifying the password so that by trying to log on from a disallowed workstation, the attacker will not lock out the user, nor will they be able to determine whether the password they used is correct. While it's possible to automate adding and removing hostnames of computers eligible for logon to users' **userWorkstations** attribute, this becomes unmanageable very quickly, even if using automation, and generates lots of Active Directory changes if the environment is dynamic. VDI farms are a great example of an infrastructure that does not lend itself well to managing logon restrictions this way because it's the highly dynamic virtual desktop names that need to be added to the allowed list. One could imagine automation that will add a virtual desktop's hostname on the fly as the designated user's **only** allowed endpoint. While certainly a fascinating proposition, any seasoned administrator will probably offer half a dozen scenarios off the top of their head where this can and will go wrong. Individual restrictions, albeit effective, just aren't the engineer's way to manage things. We always prefer using policies to using individual settings.

The first policy for restricting logon that was introduced in Active Directory is the "Allow logon"/"Deny logon" security policy managed by GPO in the "User Rights Assignments" section of the Computer part. This mechanism has been the administrators' preferred method of restricting logon for decades. There are, however, two major problems with this approach:

CHAPTER 5 ENGINEERING AUTHENTICATION

- Logon restrictions are processed on the endpoint, i.e., *after* successful authentication. A TGT will be issued and returned to the workstation for determining whether the desired logon type is allowed by policy. A user trying to log on from a disallowed workstation will know if the password was correct. They will also be able to lock a legitimate user out by trying wrong passwords once too often (in case account lockout policies are in place).

- For the logon restriction policy to be processed, it has to be applied in the first place. Devices outside of the admins' purview know nothing of this policy. If an attacker manages to unlink the logon restriction policy from an OU or move a computer account into a different OU, they may be able to circumvent this restriction.

With Server 2012R2, a major new feature was added to Kerberos in Active Directory: Kerberos Armoring. Armoring is not proprietary to Microsoft's Kerberos implementation; however, Microsoft contributed heavily to the RFC6113 that defines it. The generalized Kerberos technology behind armoring is "Flexible Authentication over Secure Tunneling" (FAST). In Windows, Armoring is activated by group policy and configured using Authentication Policies and Authentication Policy Silos. To identify authentication flows conformant with a specific policy, an additional qualifier can be used that was introduced into Kerberos authentication: Claims. Technically, claims belong to an authorization mechanism known as "Dynamic Access Control" (DAC), which was introduced with Server 2012. By default, armoring uses one special claim type, which is "Authentication Silo." However, the policy data model is flexible so that any user or device claim you create for use with DAC can be part of an authentication policy definition.

CHAPTER 5   ENGINEERING AUTHENTICATION

Authentication policies are extremely powerful. In addition to allowing or rejecting a TGT request, they

- Specify the lifetime of the TGT which can be shorter or longer than the default for the domain

- Allow granular control over source machines allowed for NTLM authentication

- Allow replacing the password hash by a random rolling secret in NTLM authentication flows

- Specify under what conditions a service ticket can be issued if the service is running under a user, gMSA, or computer account governed by the policy

In the 11 years that passed since Kerberos Armoring was released to the world, very little has been written about it. Most AD administrators the author has talked to either never heard of the feature or didn't realize the potential. This book will not provide a deep dive into how Authentication Policies work under the covers; however, we will use them extensively to achieve our engineering goals. Authentication policies are equipped with a graphical UI that you will find, exclusively, in the "Active Directory Administrative Center" (ADAC) in the "Authentication" menu folder on the left-hand side.

5.2.2 Protecting from Credential Harvesting

Every interactive logon session causes the Local Security Authority (LSA) to store at least the password hashes, calculated by supported encryption methods, in memory. They are needed to perform NTLM authentication or request Ticket Granting Tickets for Kerberos authentication. Some of this information is kept in RAM even after the user session has been logged off. Server 2008R2 and older would routinely store even cleartext passwords for the active sessions; this has been amended in the modern Windows

CHAPTER 5   ENGINEERING AUTHENTICATION

versions. If you enable WDigest or CredSSP credentials delegation on a machine, even the latest versions of Windows will have the LSA store cleartext passwords in memory because these protocols pass, supposedly in a protected manner, cleartext credentials to the target system.

To prevent WDigest from storing cleartext passwords in memory, set the REG_DWORD registry value **UseLogonCredential** under the key **HKEY_LOCAL_MACHINE\SYSTEM\CurrentControlSet\Control\SecurityProviders\WDigest** to zero. The value is respected starting with Windows Vista/Server 2008, but on older operating systems, you may have to add it because it's not present by default.

CredSSP is usually not insecure per se since the secrets used for TLS encryption of CredSSP messages are negotiated using the underlying authentication protocol, which is typically Kerberos. However, CredSSP requires Windows to store cleartext password in memory, which you want to avoid, even if it means not being able to log on seamlessly to some services. What credentials may be delegated for CredSSP is governed by group policy settings found under "Computer/Administrative Templates/System/Credentials Delegation." Some of these policies are required to provide a Single Sign-On (SSO) experience towards Remote Desktop Services servers or VDI farms and are primarily targeted at non-privileged users for whom this infrastructure is intended. However, a privileged user logging on to a workstation configured to delegate CredSSP credentials would be treated the same way, so additional protection is required for privileged identities.

The best way to protect a user's credentials from being harvested on a particular workstation or server is by not allowing them to log on to that machine in the first place. By default, Windows places the "Domain Admins" group in the local "Administrators" group on each member upon its joining the domain. This prompted generations of admins to just use their domain admin account as "the account that can manage every system," putting their admin credentials in extreme jeopardy. Remember, Server 2008R2 and prior versions would routinely keep cleartext passwords in memory! Since admins are humans and humans make mistakes, techniques widely known as "tiering" have emerged to prevent privileged accounts from logging on to unprivileged machines. Administrative tiering has been part of Microsoft's "Enhanced Security Admin Environment" (ESAE) model since its introduction around 2010, but the logon restrictions in most practical implementations were based on the "Deny Logon" group policies described above. It wasn't until early 2024, following the partial deprecation of the ESAE architecture, that Dagmar Heidecker, a Microsoft Security Consultant from Austria, published a blog post describing how to use Authentication Policies to achieve the required restrictions on the server instead on the endpoint side! The Authentication Policy presented in the post is the simplest imaginable and includes the minimally required setup for Kerberos Armoring. Since most of this work is applicable to other armoring scenarios we will encounter in this chapter, and because so little guidance exists on how to set it up, we will go through the implementation step by step. In this exercise, we will use the terms "FAST" and "Kerberos Armoring" interchangeably.

5.2.3 Implementing a Basic Authentication Policy for Tier 0

To recap: We want to allow Tier 0 admins to log on to Tier 0 systems (Domain Controllers, PAW workstations, and other Windows systems classified as Tier 0). Tier 0 admins must not be able to log on to any other machines in the forest.

The first round of preparations you only have to do once. Assuming the FFL of your forest is at 2012R2 or above, configure group policies for DCs and members to support or even enforce Kerberos Armoring. The policy for DCs is called "KDC support for claims, compound authentication and Kerberos armoring" and located in **Computer Configuration\Policies\ Administrative Templates\System\KDC**. Set it to "Supported" as shown in Figure 5-3.

CHAPTER 5 ENGINEERING AUTHENTICATION

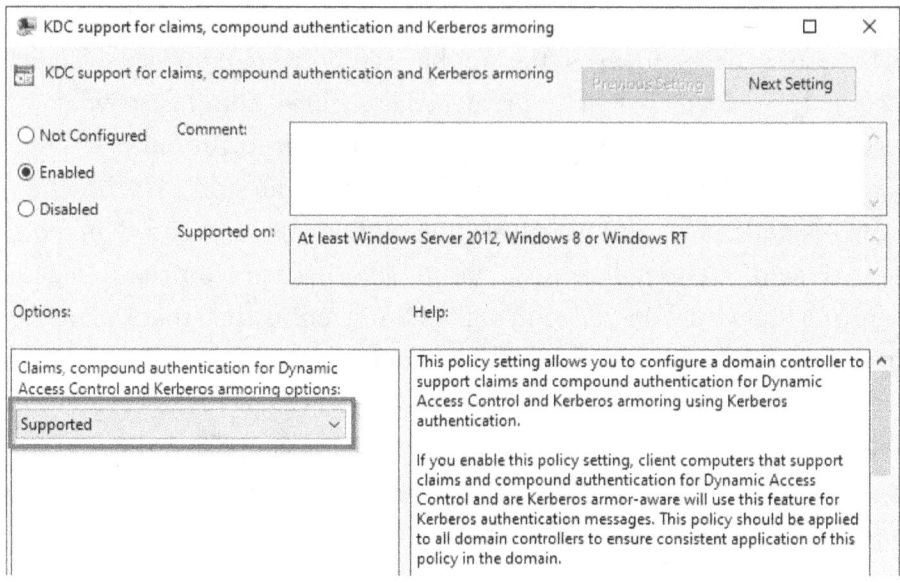

Figure 5-3. *"Supported" is a good setting to start with*

The corresponding policy for member machines is "Kerberos client support for claims, compound authentication and Kerberos armoring," located in **Computer Configuration\Policies\Administrative Templates\System\Kerberos**. You can also instruct the members to fail authentication if the domain is not offering Kerberos Armoring, but this is seldom done even in environments that have embraced Authentication Policies. In the context of hardening, this setting could help protect privileged credentials in case malicious actors manage to unlink the KDC policy described above from your Domain Controllers. The beauty of Authentication Policies is that you only need to activate Kerberos Armoring support on machines that will be *allowed for authentication*. If you are only protecting the Tier 0, you don't have to enable FAST on your entire member fleet just yet; the policy for Tier 0 accounts will automatically fail on those other machines, which is exactly what we need!

CHAPTER 5   ENGINEERING AUTHENTICATION

As you go along and extend the reach of your Kerberos Armoring to further use cases, remember to activate the Kerberos client policy on additional computers as described.

Once the GPO activating FAST has been applied to both DCs and privileged clients and servers, we can create an Authentication policy. We have to specify which member computers to treat as "privileged," and the easiest way to do that is to put them into a group named "T0Computers." Once that is in place and the computers' TGT has been renewed, either by rebooting or by waiting long enough for it to expire, we can create and apply the Authentication Policy that will protect the privileged users' credentials.

Create a new Authentication Policy named "Tier0 Access" and assign it to the privileged accounts you want to protect. To indicate that user settings are being configured, specify a value for the TGT lifetime. You can set it to the domain default of 600 minutes, or to the "Protected Users" default of 240 minutes, or to any other value of your choosing. To specify from which computers TGT requests should be accepted, create a condition for User Sign On as shown in Figure 5-4.

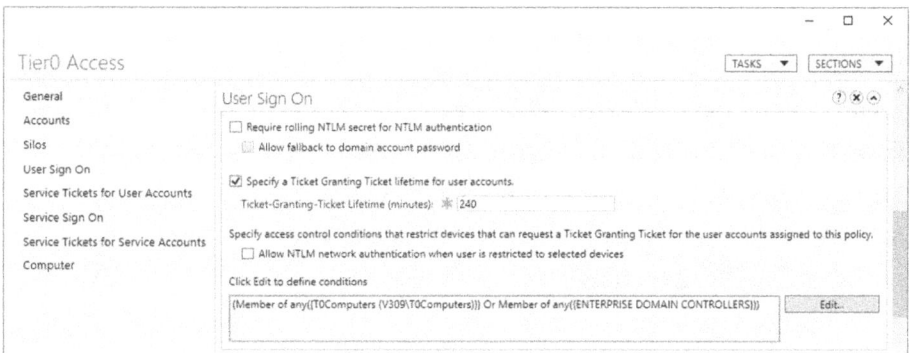

Figure 5-4. *Specifying computers to accept authentication from*

159

CHAPTER 5   ENGINEERING AUTHENTICATION

Warning   Do not assign Authentication Policies to Break-Glass accounts unless you are using the default administrator account with the RID of 500 as Break-Glass.

From now on, users assigned to the "Tier0 Access" policy will only be issued a TGT if they are logging on to a Domain Controller or a member computer that is a member of the "T0Computers" group. An attempt to log on from any other machine will not result in a TGT being issued. There is a small quirk in the graphical editor for Authentication Policies: in the condition for User Sign On, it will only allow you to add conditions for "User," whereas in reality you are describing *computers* eligible for authentication under this policy. This ambiguity is resolved in the parameter names of the PowerShell cmdlets. To create the policy described above on the command line, you would run the following code (existence checks and error handling omitted for brevity):

```
Import-Module ActiveDirectory
$policyName = 'Tier 0 Access'
$computerGroup = 'T0Computers'
$tgtLifetime = 240
$groupSID = (Get-ADGroup -Identity $computerGroup).SID.Value
$fromSDDL = "O:SYG:SYD:(XA;OICI;CR;;;WD;((Member_of_any
{SID($groupSID)}) || (Member_of_any {SID(ED)})))"
$authNPolicyParms = @{
    'Name' = $policyName
    'Enforce' = $true
    'UserTGTLifetimeMins' = $tgtLifetime
    'UserAllowedToAuthenticateFrom' = $fromSDDL
}
New-ADAuthenticationPolicy @authNPolicyParms
```

CHAPTER 5 ENGINEERING AUTHENTICATION

You can find the same code with additional checks and error handling in the code example **5.1-Simple-AuthNPolicy.ps1**.

You have probably already discovered the problem with this approach (which is taken verbatim from the blog post mentioned above so comes as close to "official Microsoft guidance" as it gets these days): A highly privileged account that does NOT have this policy assigned will not be protected simply by virtue of being privileged! Nor do Authentication Policies have anything to do with *granting or revoking* privileges, i.e., we cannot make an account privileged by assigning it a certain policy. So, tiering (and zoning, we will talk about it in Chapter 8) remains a two-pronged approach: Authentication Policy to prevent even the TGT issuance to well-managed admin accounts and logon restrictions GPO rolled out to unprivileged member machines to catch those that ended up not being assigned an Authentication Policy. Of course, you should use whatever automation you have available to ensure that all privileged accounts have the correct Authentication Policy assigned!

5.2.4 Next-Level Harvesting Protection: Credential Guard

An additional technology in Windows that does not prevent the LSA from storing password hashes or cleartext passwords in memory but restricts access even for applications running elevated or as SYSTEM to that memory is Credential Guard. This very effective protection has been introduced in Server 2016 and Windows 10. It isolates the parts of LSA storing credentials from the parts performing authentication by using Virtualization-Based Security (VBS), which means SecureBoot must be enabled and the hardware must meet the requirements for Hyper-V (although the Hyper-V role will not be activated as such if you enable VBS) and contain a TPM 2.0 conformant security chip. These system requirements can absolutely be met by virtual machines (VM), although the TPM requirement may introduce additional complexity into the hypervisor platform. Server 2025 will activate Credential Guard by default if the machine is a domain member, all prerequisites for Credential Guard have been met, and the technology has not been explicitly deactivated using Group Policy. On earlier OS versions Credential Guard must be *explicitly activated* even if all prerequisites have been met.

Not all credential flows are equally well protected by Credential Guard. Local accounts and Microsoft Accounts are exempt from Credential Guard protection since their password hashes are stored in the SAM database (part of the registry). Same goes for logon verifiers ("cached credentials") used for logging on offline with a domain account if Domain Controllers aren't reachable. CredSSP and WDigest cannot access the logged-on credentials, so applications relying on these protocols will prompt for explicit credentials, and **those secrets will not be protected by Credential Guard** anymore.

Warning Do not enable Credential Guard on Domain Controllers! It does not offer protection of your AD database but will disrupt the Domain Controllers' operations!

5.2.5 Protecting Against Service Ticket Abuse

Service tickets in Kerberos can be abused in two ways:

- Cracking a ticket to obtain the cleartext password of the service account or
- Requesting (and obtaining) a *valid and sufficiently authorized* ticket for a service of attacker's interest and submitting it in order to access the service

CHAPTER 5 ENGINEERING AUTHENTICATION

The first family of techniques is widely known as "Kerberoasting." The "roasting" part describes the brute-force machinery used to decode the cleartext password from the service ticket. The ability to break Kerberos encryption is based on the prior partial knowledge of the cleartext. Figure 5-5 shows the TGS structure where, knowing who *requested* the service ticket, the attacker knows a part of the cleartext starting at a fixed offset.

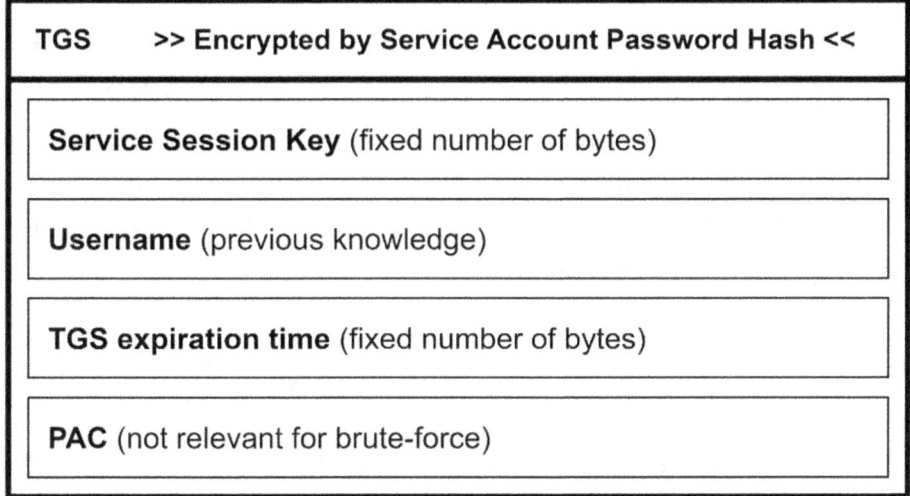

Figure 5-5. *TGS data structure*

Of course, brute-force decryption can only succeed within an acceptable (from the malicious actor's perspective) time frame if

- The encryption algorithm used to issue the TGS is weak, so RC4 is preferable to AES128, let alone AES256.

- The underlying password is not very long and not too complex.

- The time frame is long enough, i.e., the time needed to break the encryption is shorter than the password lifetime so that the cleartext password, once obtained, will actually be usable.

163

The last condition, even if the absolute requirement of the password still being usable upon decryption has been met, is still relative. For a service account that offers immediate domain dominance, burning GPU for a month can still be worth the effort. A password for a non-privileged user can usually be obtained by other means, although sometimes a service account, while not being highly privileged per se, possesses that crucial bit of data access that the attacker actually needs.

Note Be aware that the actual decryption work always happens outside of your environment and cannot be easily detected. GPU power is available from the public cloud on a Pay-As-You-Go basis. Service tickets are small and can be stealthily exfiltrated even using DNS, OCSP, or other techniques.

A service accessible from other systems (only such services require service tickets to begin with!) can be set to run under

- A "legacy service account," i.e., normal user account that has the "Log On as a Service" privilege (**seServiceLogonRight**) on the server
- A gMSA with the server allowed to retrieve the password from AD, or
- The server's SYSTEM context (LocalService and NetworkService as well as other virtual accounts fall into this category as far as Kerberos is concerned)

In the default Active Directory configuration, any authenticated user can request – and obtain – a service ticket for any service known to Kerberos. All that is needed is a Service Principal Name (SPN) of that service. This is where legacy service accounts differ from computer accounts and gMSA (also derived from computer class): while the former requires an SPN to be specified in its **servicePrincipalName** attribute, the latter two accept implicit SPNs combined from one of the allowed service classes and the value of the **dnsHostName** attribute. HOST is always allowed as an SPN service class; further classes are defined in the **sPNMappings** attribute of the **Directory Service** configuration object. By default, 53 additional service classes are mapped to HOST and can be used at will. This freedom of choice, however, is more than offset by both computers and gMSA rotating their passwords automatically (every 30 days in the default configuration for both) and choosing very long and very random passwords on each rotation. This leaves "legacy" service accounts as the lower hanging fruit for obtaining crackable tickets. With these accounts, there is no automated mechanism for rotating passwords, and the difficulty of a coordinated manual password change very often leads to the flag "password never expires" being set for these accounts. The following techniques help protect legacy service accounts from Kerberoasting:

- Restrict encryption types in Kerberos to not allow RC4 (or DES, but this should be self-evident by now).

- Implement a password rotation regime, preferably automated, using long and complex passwords. We will revisit this in more detail in Section 5.4.

- Remove SPNs from user accounts that do not need them and reduce the blast radius by restricting the privileges of the accounts that do. Believe it or not, attackers will try to analyze the potential benefit of spending GPU time on cracking a particular account's TGS!

- Last but not least, implement Authentication Policy to reduce the selection of users (and source machines) who are able to obtain a TGS for your services.

CHAPTER 5   ENGINEERING AUTHENTICATION

5.2.6 Strengthening Kerberos Encryption

Restricting encryption algorithms supported by Kerberos can be done on several levels, but everything boils down to the **msDS-SupportedEncryptionTypes** attribute every user and computer object has. This attribute contains a bit mask, each bit denoting a particular protocol:

Bit	Value (decimal)	Value (hex)	Protocol
0	1	0x01	DES_CBC_CRC
1	2	0x02	DES_CBC_MD5
2	4	0x04	RC4
3	8	0x08	AES128
4	16	0x10	AES256
5	32	0x20	AES256_SK

The last encryption type was introduced in November 2022. It is not surfaced anywhere yet but the bit is reserved and should be taken into account if performing searches or updates.

For modern encryption, you will want to see values of either 16 (0x10) or 24 (0x18) in that attribute, while the default since Server 2008 has been 28 (0x1C), which covers both RC4 and AES. For computer accounts that have an actual computer attached to them, this attribute is always populated because computers are allowed to write that attribute by default. This can be a double-edged sword – some third-party services have been known to set that attribute to DES, even though the service in question (a) does not accept or initiate any connections that would be "kerberized" and (b) is running on a modern operating system that supports any encryption available to Windows. For user accounts, this attribute is not populated by default, although they are also allowed to

CHAPTER 5 ENGINEERING AUTHENTICATION

set its value for their own object. If no value is set, Domain Controller will consult the registry value **DefaultDomainSupportedEncTypes** located in **HKEY_LOCAL_MACHINE\SYSTEM\CurrentControlSet\Services\Kdc**. The value stored there follows the same convention as the values above.

In the Microsoft GUI tools, AES protocols are surfaced as check boxes on the "Account" tab. However, there is no checkbox for RC4 so that the only way to see if RC4 is allowed or not is by examining the value of **msDS-SupportedEncryptionTypes**. If you set and then clear the checkboxes for AES, the result depends on the value set in **DefaultDomainSupportedEncTypes**. If that value allowed for RC4, the removal of AES will leave RC4 in place. If the registry value had RC4 disabled, then the GUI tools will leave the user with a value of 0 as shown on Figure 5-6.

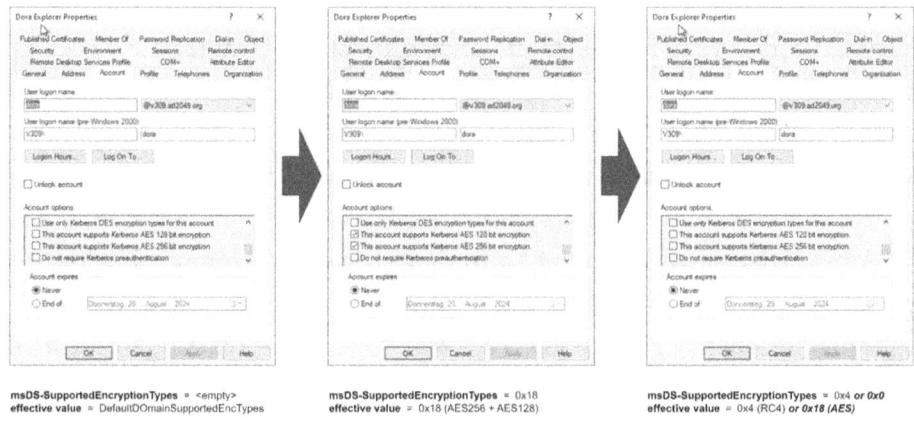

Figure 5-6. *Setting encryption types graphically may not be the best idea*

For Windows computers, the value for the **msDS-Supported EncryptionTypes** attribute is derived from the registry value **SupportedEncryptionTypes** located in **HKEY_LOCAL_MACHINE\SOFTWARE\Microsoft\Windows\CurrentVersion\Policies\System\Kerberos\Parameters** and usually set by the group policy "Network security:

CHAPTER 5   ENGINEERING AUTHENTICATION

Configure encryption types allowed for Kerberos." If you select "Future encryption types" in the policy editor, you will end up with a large number in the registry since all bits beyond 5 will be set to 1. Windows will translate it to what it knows, so "RC4 + AES128 + AES256 + Future types" will show as 0x7FFFFFFC in the registry, but the computer will set it to 0x1C in AD.

The encryption types set (or inferred from the defaults) for a principal have two effects:

- They determine what keys will be generated from the cleartext password on the next password change.

- They determine what encryption algorithms will be offered to issue Kerberos tickets.

Consider the following scenario: You set **msDS-SupportedEncryptionTypes** for a user to 0x4, only allowing RC4. You then change the user's password, upon which only RC4 key material will be generated and stored in AD. If you then change the **msDS-SupportedEncryptionTypes** value to 0x18, allowing AES but disallowing RC4, this user cannot obtain a TGT anymore until you either relax the allowed encryption types or reset the user's password.

Forest trusts are limited to RC4 by default so that accounts that are in the "Protected Users" group in their domain or are limited to AES by other means will not be able to access resources in the trusting forest. The "Active Directory Domains and Trusts" console allows setting a checkbox for AES encryption, meaning that *only* AES128 and AES256 encryption types will be supported on the trust. If you have the requirement to support both RC4 and AES on a trust, set the checkbox for AES and then use the KSETUP command as follows:

ksetup /addenctypeattr trusting.doma.in RC4-HMAC-MD5

You could, of course, just edit the **msDS-SupportedEncryptionTypes** attribute of the **trustedDomain** object (although in this case, it is a "trusting domain" that we modify), but the above procedure is the recommended and supported way.

5.2.7 Protecting Against Stealing Valid Service Tickets

Even if any authenticated user is able to request a TGS for any service, not every service ticket will provide an equal level of access. Malicious actors will therefore attempt to obtain a service ticket that is already privileged in the target service instead of trying to elevate their permissions by different means. To acquire valid service tickets from different users, attackers can

- Spoof DNS and lure service connection requests to a computer that they control, thus having valid TGSs delivered to them by the users themselves, or

- Abuse Kerberos delegation and use a service that they control to subsequently request TGS to the service that they want to target

We have already looked at DNS record registration and possible spoofing in the previous chapter. The ability to obtain valid TGS tickets by redirecting traffic to a host controlled by an attacker should be an additional reminder to harden DNS record management as much as possible in order to prevent this avenue of attack.

Kerberos delegation has been part of Active Directory since its inception and went through three iterations over the years. The purpose of all three is the same: to enable a service to access resources (i.e., other services) on behalf of the connecting user rather than by using the service

CHAPTER 5   ENGINEERING AUTHENTICATION

identity. The Kerberos feature used here is called "Service for User," or S4U. All three delegation methods are still configurable and usable even today:

- **Unconstrained delegation** was introduced in Windows 2000 and allows a service to cache any connecting user's TGT (decrypted from the TGS supplied to access the service) and request TGS using it. The trick in abusing unconstrained delegation is to coerce a highly privileged identity (e.g., a Domain Controller) into accessing the compromised service, thus leaving their TGT open to reuse for as long as it's valid.

- **Constrained delegation** followed in Server 2003 after it became clear that unconstrained delegation is not a very good idea. This configuration allows you to specify which SPNs a service is allowed to delegate user access to. However, the way S4U works allows attackers to swap the service class quite easily so that the effective constraint of Constrained Delegation is the host part of the SPN.

- **Resource-based constrained delegation** (RBCD) works in a similar fashion to Constrained Delegation but the configuration is not done on the front-end service ("This Front-End is allowed to delegate to those Back-Ends") but rather on the back-end service ("Those Front-Ends are allowed to delegate to this Back-End"), thus putting the burden of managing delegation relationships on the back-end (i.e., resource) administrators. Additionally, RBCD is configured using a binary blob rather than string attributes and userAccountControl flags, making the reconnaissance more expensive and noisy.

Both Constrained Delegation variants at the time of writing suffer under a design flaw that allows the front-end service (or the attacker controlling it) to "impersonate users out of thin air," as Elad Shamir put it in a blog post from 2019. Instead of waiting for a privileged user to submit a TGS to the front-end service, Constrained Delegation allows the service to request a TGS for an arbitrary user for this service. This TGS can then be used to request a TGS for that user but for a different service!

None of the delegation variants actually specifies which user or computer identities the delegation is valid for. From the delegating service's point of view, it's "all of them." However, accounts can be protected from being delegated by setting the userAccountControl flag "Account is sensitive and cannot be delegated." Out-of-box GUI tools only surface this flag for user objects, but you can use PowerShell or edit **userAccountControl** directly to enable it for computers and gMSA as well.

> **Note** Unless there are known services in your environment that require Kerberos delegation, no harm is done by setting the "Account is sensitive and cannot be delegated" flag as your new default. Even if delegation has to be introduced at a later time, removing that flag using PowerShell is a matter of minutes, even in larger environments.

5.2.8 Strong Protection for Interactive Administrator Sessions

No initiative for hardening and securing authentication is complete without the functionality offered by the "Protected Users" group introduced with the 2012R2 Domain Functional Level. For any user that is a member of this well-known group, the following restrictions apply:

CHAPTER 5   ENGINEERING AUTHENTICATION

- CredSSP and WDigest do not cache plaintext credentials regardless of what is configured on the machine.

- NTLM authentication is not possible. NTLM subsystem on the endpoint will not cache plaintext credentials or NTLM hash.

- Kerberos authentication using RC4 or DES is not possible. Kerberos on the endpoint will only create AES keys.

- No logon verifier is cached for offline logon.

- Kerberos delegation is not possible using any of the delegation methods listed above.

This looks like a membership in "Protected Users" takes care of many attack vectors we have talked about until now. Alas, this protection comes at a price. There is one last restriction that comes with it:

- TGT is valid for four hours and is not renewable.

This last restriction precludes computer and service accounts of either type from being a member of the "Protected Users" group. And even interactive users' working experience will suffer since all tickets will simply expire after four hours, leaving connections to resources and services suddenly unauthenticated. The user must then log off and log back on, or, if the applications tolerate it, lock the screen and unlock it again. For administrators, this is an acceptable price to pay for the level of protection that membership in the "Protected Users" group offers. If one intends on executing long-running scripts with administrative privileges, other methods have to be found to do that. Executing the script as a scheduled task in a privileged system's SYSTEM context is but one possible solution.

5.3 Getting Rid of NTLM

NTLM is responsible for crackable hashes (weak hash function), Pass-The-Hash (using a harvested NTLM hash for authentication), and Pass-The-Ticket (using a harvested NTLM hash for requesting a RC4 TGT). It is therefore not surprising that getting rid of the old protocol is high on the administrators' priority lists... until they try. And we will not pretend that it is not a daunting task in an environment that started out long ago and developed over time. But the engineering approach helps, and since we are more interested in the end result than in "quick wins" at this time, we will start by determining what the desired end result is and how to get there from the defaults. Once that is established, we will provide guidance on how to deal with existing services.

5.3.1 An NTLM-less AD Environment

Until Microsoft makes good on their promise to implement a local Kerberos KDC in every Windows installation, Domain Controllers will remain the only systems that can be "truly free of NTLM." Every domain member and every workgroup machine still needs to support NTLM for logging on with local accounts. Figure 5-7 illustrates possible situations where NTLM *could* be negotiated, i.e., between machines in trusted realms, and where NTLM *would have to* be used, i.e., wherever local accounts are involved.

CHAPTER 5   ENGINEERING AUTHENTICATION

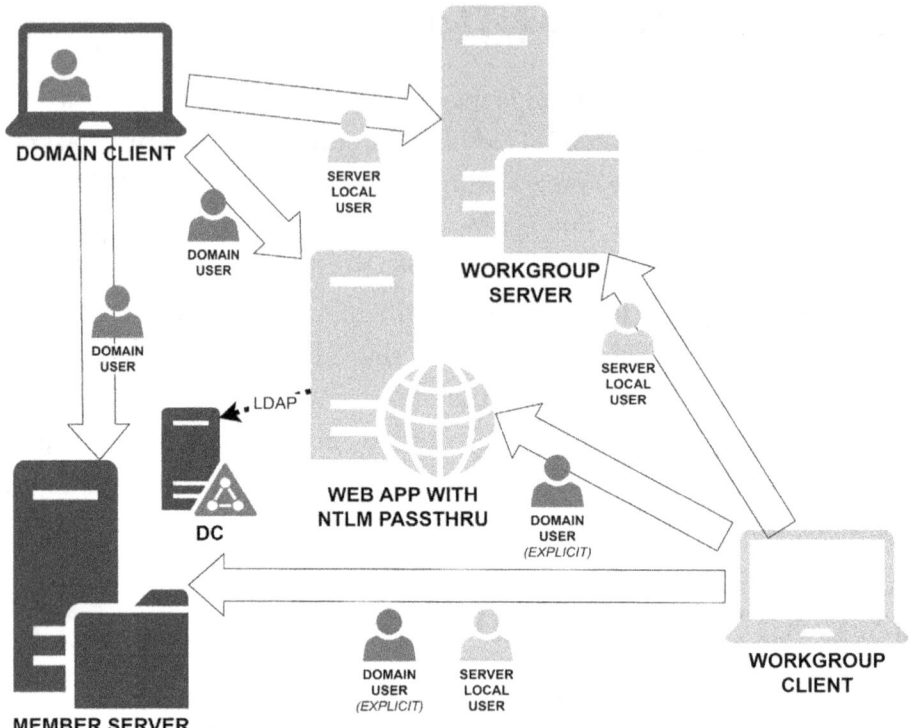

Figure 5-7. *Connections that can bear NTLM traffic*

From Active Directory's point of view, "getting rid of NTLM" means that the following is enforced:

1. All connections between machines in trusted realms are authenticated by Kerberos; NTLM is not used (which also means local accounts are not used between the member machines).

2. All connections from untrusted machines (workgroup or untrusted AD forest) to domain members or Domain Controllers using domain accounts are authenticated by Kerberos or rejected. Contrary to popular belief, it is not true

that Kerberos cannot be used to connect from an untrusted machine to a domain member or even DC. It certainly cannot if you enforce Kerberos Armoring or apply Authentication Policies preventing authentication from unknown workstations. Otherwise, as long as you use FQDNs and the connecting client has a line of sight to a Domain Controller, there's nothing to prevent the user from obtaining a TGT and a TGS.

3. All connections from untrusted machines (workgroup or untrusted AD forest) to domain members using local accounts from that machines' SAM are rejected. There may be use cases where an exception from this rule is possible or even desirable without compromising the security of your infrastructure.

4. Connections from domain members (or DCs) to untrusted machines, that would have to be authenticated by NTLM, are not possible. There is a special case of a web application that accepts an NTLM ticket from the browser and then uses it to perform authentication against AD without the web server being a domain member. You should always try to have the application modified in a way that would support Kerberos authentication using AES encryption.

There are group policy settings that allow you to enforce these restrictions. They have been introduced with Server 2008R2. If you have older Windows systems in your environment, you will not be able to restrict everything, but in that case, you are not running a "modern AD" anyway.

CHAPTER 5   ENGINEERING AUTHENTICATION

To prevent NTLM authentication within your AD forest, apply the group policy "Network security: Restrict NTLM: NTLM authentication in this domain" to your Domain Controllers and set it to "Deny all." There is a second policy that allows you to create exceptions for certain servers from which NTLM authentication requests will be accepted. This setting already takes care of the requirements 1. and 2. This does *not* prevent clients from generating an NTLM hash on interactive logons, the only way to achieve this is the "Protected Users" group or Kerberos Armoring.

To achieve 3., apply the policy "Network security: Restrict NTLM: Incoming NTLM traffic" to all domain members. If you have set the previous policy to "Deny all," you do not need to apply the incoming traffic restriction to Domain Controllers. Here you can make a distinction between domain accounts and local user accounts; however, you cannot allow domain accounts and deny local accounts – the options are "Deny all domain accounts" and "Deny all accounts" so domain accounts are always denied if you configure this policy.

Lastly, to cover 4., set the policy "Network security: Restrict NTLM: Outgoing NTLM traffic to remote servers" on all machines in your environments, Domain Controllers and members alike. This only gives you the choice between "Allow," "Audit," or "Deny." No distinction can be made between AD accounts and local ones.

This is easy – with just three group policy settings we have solved a 25-year-old problem of NTLM putting Active Directory environments in danger! Of course, as is often the case if Microsoft and backwards compatibility are involved, the reality is slightly more complicated.

If you're building a new IT environment from scratch, you could assume the "You Shall Not Pass!" stance, disable NTLM globally as described above, and tweak every new application until it's able to work under these conditions. You will probably be surprised more than once at what applications you'll have to throw overboard and what crude workarounds will be necessary to get other systems to work in a Kerberos-only AD. You will discover that some systems rely on NTLM at setup time

CHAPTER 5   ENGINEERING AUTHENTICATION

but will happily use Kerberos afterwards, while others only require NTLM for certain runtime features you won't discover until later, e.g., when the finance department tries to print the annual report that is already overdue. There is no experience like troubleshooting authentication of a black box in a calm, supporting environment.

More often than not, however, getting rid of NTLM happens in environments that have years or even decades of experience in not caring about what authentication protocol ends up being negotiated as long as everybody gets their work done and can go home at five. In these cases, you have to tread lightly and err on the side of caution.

5.3.2 First Things First: Fix What You Know

For each NTLM-restricting policy listed above, Microsoft created a policy for making exceptions from the restriction and another one for auditing the NTLM authentication or traffic without actually restricting anything. There is some guidance published both by Microsoft and independent bloggers on how to activate these policies and where to find the corresponding logs. Unless you have mad big data skills and lots of log storage, **do not do that just yet**! Otherwise, you end up drowning in logs and still not being able to come up with a plan of action.

Instead, start by fixing what you know. Disable NTLM for your administrator accounts by adding them to the "Protected Users" group. Depending on how friendly everybody is on your IT team, you might not want to protect them all at once. Educate the admins – this is a worthwhile task because they will have to educate the power users, who, in turn, will carry the knowledge to the masses. If someone complains that they are unable to connect to **\\10.0.101.241\ITFILES$**, verify that the share is indeed reachable under `**\\fileserver4711.domain.com\ITFILES$** and explain it to them. If it's not reachable by FQDN, you have a DNS problem. Fix it now.

177

CHAPTER 5 ENGINEERING AUTHENTICATION

Once the admins are sorted, look at your applications and user configurations. Make sure FQDNs are used wherever possible. In theory, many "kerberized" services either have explicit SPNs containing the hostname or will implicitly negotiate Kerberos if just the hostname is used in the TGS. In practice, however, you want to avoid ambiguity and guesswork, so just switch to FQDNs wherever possible. If you see IP addresses configured for accessing remote systems, you can be quite sure you have a winner. Creating an exhaustive list of places where to look for hostnames would be an impossible task, but here are the highlights:

- GPP for Drive Maps
- GPP for Files
- GPP for Shortcuts
- GPP for Shared Printers
- Scripts (logon, startup, scheduled tasks)
- DFS-N folder targets (if you use the wizard, it will register the targets as **\\SERVER\SHARE** – you have to copy and paste the UNC containing the FQDN into the wizard instead of browsing for the server and the share)
- SQL server connections in ODBC data sources, connection strings or applications
- Servers registered by IP address in Server Manager
- Servers registered by IP address or hostname in MMC consoles
- Failover Cluster nodes registered by hostname

Some applications will offer the possibility of replacing "NTLM" with "SPNEGO" or "NEGOTIATE" or even "KERBEROS" in some obscure configuration file, automatically switching the authentication protocol to

CHAPTER 5　ENGINEERING AUTHENTICATION

the desired one. Why didn't the person doing the implementation think of making that edit? Usually a rhetorical question. Be content that you found and eliminated another source of NTLM traffic in your network. Check for correct SPNs being assigned to the service principal *and* for correct FQDNs being used before you celebrate.

Then there are third-party systems like printers or network appliances that require AD authentication and offer an option of using Kerberos or NTLM for it. Often these devices lack proper DNS configuration, making them unable to participate in Kerberos or bad timekeeping that, again, prevents successful TGT issuance. Sometimes, these devices will require a Keytab file instead of a UPN and password. Remember to severely restrict the permissions of such identities and to include them in your password rotation regime lest the Keytab files get into the wrong hands and cause real harm! If you have lots of hardware that offers Kerberos authentication, brace yourself for the day when, after troubleshooting for an hour, you will discover that the vendor did not, in fact, implement Kerberos but already prepared the WebGUI for a future firmware release in which Kerberos support will be provided (true story).

Another area where you are likely to find NTLM fallback behavior without resorting to logs are clustered or load-balanced applications where the additional work required for providing Kerberos authentication has not been done. If multiple nodes are running the same application under a common FQDN, the respective SPN cannot be assigned to any one of the nodes because, in that case, it would be the only node capable of Kerberos! If the application is running under a service account (legacy or gMSA), this account will be the bearer of the SPN. If the application is running in the SYSTEM context of each node, as is the case, for example, with Microsoft Exchange, then you'll have to consult the documentation on how to enable Kerberos for it. In Exchange, you create a so-called ASA (Alternate Service Account), usually in the form of a computer object rather than a user, and have the servers roll the account's password and store it within Exchange configuration so that every node can decrypt TGSs issued to the shared name. Other applications will require you to generate and upload a Keytab file. In any case, plan for rolling this account's password on a regular basis. We will look into it in the next section.

Surprisingly enough, user name format has much less effect on the protocol being selected than the target server name. It is long-standing wisdom that you risk falling back to NTLM by using the **DOMAIN\user** syntax and that Kerberos will be magically achieved if you authenticate as **user@domain.com**. In reality, however, it all depends on the application. Windows and native Microsoft services are intelligent enough to perform a proper lookup and name translation in order to produce a UPN if Kerberos is an option. There are other applications that will translate UPN back to NetBIOS and authenticate using NTLM, no matter what name syntax you supply. You can do nothing about those except yell at the vendor and get them to fix the authentication package. In 2022, Microsoft performed an analysis over those customers where they were tasked with reducing NTLM usage. They found out that 52% of all NTLM authentication events were due to applications having NTLM authentication *hardcoded*. However, there is absolutely no harm in using UPNs for interactive authentication, service accounts, RDP connections, SQL server access, and other situations where you have to provide the username.

5.3.3 Start Logging Where It's Easiest

Once you have eliminated all NTLM traffic sources known (or suspected) in advance, it's time to embrace the unknown and start collecting logs. There are five parameters to any NTLM authentication flow:

- User performing the authentication
- Client they authenticate from
- Application (executable process) requesting the authentication

CHAPTER 5 ENGINEERING AUTHENTICATION

- Server they are trying to reach
- Resource (service) on that server that listens to the NTLM traffic

You can enable NTLM auditing on Domain Controllers (authentication), servers including DCs (incoming NTLM traffic) and clients (outgoing NTLM traffic). In all cases, events will be written to the "Microsoft-Windows-NTLM" EventLog stream and have "NTLM" as the event source. Figure 5-8 shows which authentication flow parameters listed above are logged where:

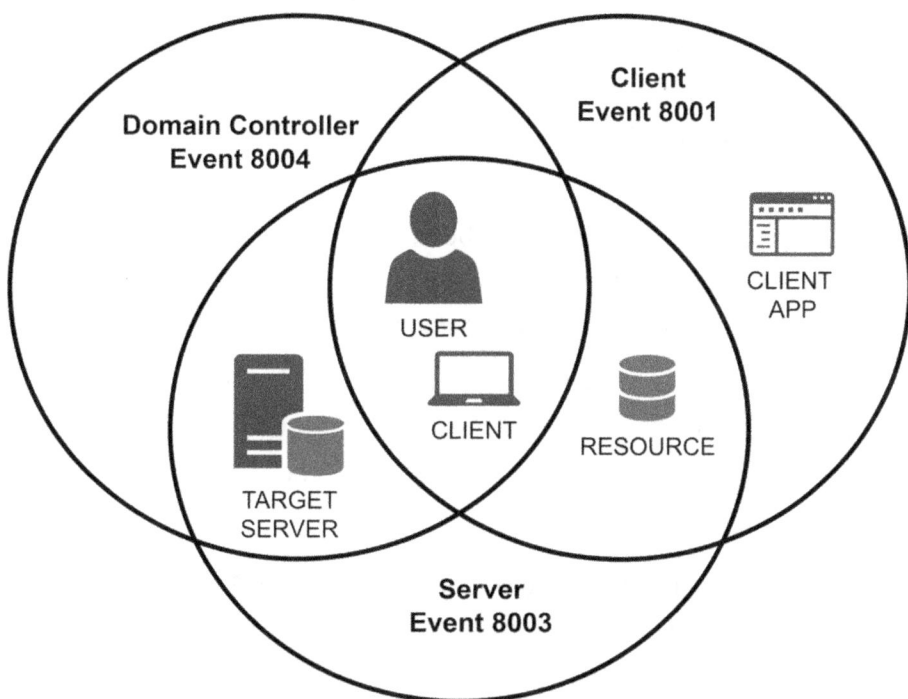

Figure 5-8. *NTLM log sources*

By activating the logging on Domain Controllers, you already get the data about which user is authenticating by NTLM towards which server(s) from which client(s)! The biggest benefit here is that you usually do not have as many Domain Controllers as you have member servers or clients. Aggregating logs will be much easier for just DCs than it will become once you start including member systems in the audit. These logs, of course, only cover domain accounts, but those are the ones we are most concerned about. Sometimes, the client is listed as an IP address – this could be a non-Windows device not providing or even maintaining a hostname.

Use this first wave of data to generate the following knowledge:

- What servers are being targeted by NTLM? Those are the only ones to audit for incoming traffic later.

- Can the service be inferred from the server? An SQL server is likely to be accessed by SQL, especially if the firewall is well managed and does not allow other inbound connections.

- Can the client application be inferred from the service? Database servers and even file servers often are purpose-built for a single business application.

- Are privileged accounts among the users being authenticated?

- Are service accounts among the users being authenticated?

- For a particular server, is NTLM the norm (lots of users and clients) or rather an exception? If everybody is using NTLM towards a file server, there may be a misconfigured drive map pointing to it – or a misconfigured DFS-N folder!

Once you have cleaned up the privileged users, the service accounts and the obvious suspects, you are ready for the next level of weeding out NTLM connections.

5.3.4 Down the Rabbit Hole

The next step would be enabling auditing on servers that are still being reported as passing through NTLM authentication to Domain Controllers. In these events, you will also see connections authenticated by local accounts (UserDomain is a hostname rather than a domain name). If you're lucky, most events will report a server process that has accepted the connection – a web server, a database server, or some other service known to be running on that machine. That gives you something to work with, and usually in these cases, you'll be able to troubleshoot and remediate the offending application without resorting to the client-side logs.

More often than not, however, the process name will be empty and the process ID reported to be 4. This is the SYSTEM process, and the protocol used for the respective connection is most likely SMB (CIFS in the Kerberos SPN parlance). If you enable NTLM auditing on the client reported in the event, you will probably see a CIFS-based SPN in the TargetName field. However, in that case, you will probably also see the process ID of 4 on the client side because SMB is generally being processed by the operating system in Windows. Finding the actual application can be a long and tedious process, but since the user responsible for the traffic is known, talking to them and looking at their user profile can help speed it up. Sometimes it's just an old desktop shortcut with the IP address in the UNC path that Windows tries to reach from time to time to refresh the shortcut icon. These things tend to take less time to fix than to find, but they also constitute the last portion of uncertainty that may just be worth the risk.

> The PowerShell script **5.2-Collect-NTLM-Events.ps1** illustrates collecting relevant NTLM events and condensing them into a common format. You can write these events into a central database or export to CSV and concatenate those files.

With Server 2025, Microsoft introduces the ability to reject NTLM-authenticated traffic just for SMB, which can help in dealing with servers where NTLM is used on multiple protocols. Microsoft also announced to expand this into a generalized ability to turn off NTLM on a per-protocol basis but did not commit to a specific date as per time of writing.

5.3.5 When You're Done with NTLM...

Once you have eliminated or drastically reduced NTLM usage, it's time to take care of RC4. As long as NTLM is not disabled for a particular user by Authentication Policy or by membership in the "Protected Users" group, an interactive logon will still create an NTLM hash. While it can't be used for Pass-the-Hash anymore, it is still usable for Overpass-the-Hash if the user in question supports RC4 encryption.

Once you disable RC4 for a user account, get them to change their password to invalidate the RC4 key material present in the Active Directory database.

5.4 Service and Task Accounts

Service and task accounts play a very important role in providing a well-engineered framework for authentication, because

- They have to have a password that is saved in other systems' credential stores.
- That password is often set to not expire because changing it is painful, but also set to a "human-typable" value, i.e., not very long or complex, for the same reason.

- In many cases, service and especially task accounts have permissions in other systems than those holding their credentials and often end up being highly privileged there, all the way up to Domain Admin or Exchange's Organization Management.

5.4.1 Service Account Typology

"Service Account" is not a standardized term, and different IT teams (or, worse still, different members of the same team) often have different understandings of what constitutes a service account. We have skirted the topic in the previous section when we talked about kerberoasting and delegation, but for the rest of the book, we will use the following convention.

First off, a "service account" or a "task account" is **never** a personal account. The use of personal user, let alone administrator, accounts for services must be banned, audited, and cleaned up as soon as possible.

A "service account" or a "task account" does not routinely perform an interactive logon. There are plenty of applications that either "work better if installed using the designated service account" or even state in their installation guides that it has to be done this way. Possible technical reasons for this are legion, and every one of them is an indication that the application in question is badly engineered. If you are dealing with this sort of software in your environment, you should verify whether the interactive logon permissions and/or local admin rights are needed permanently, and if they're not, design a permission regime that allows the application owner to assign these permissions temporarily for applying updates or rolling out the software to new machines. You could use temporary group memberships that come as a part of the "Privileged Access Management" feature we talked about in the last chapter to achieve this.

There are several types of accounts that fall under the general "service account" definition:

- A **"task account"** is an account that is used for running scheduled tasks on a Windows system. It needs the "batch logon" privilege on that system. Its password is stored in cleartext in the Windows Vault for the SYSTEM context. A gMSA can also be used as a "task account." Scheduled tasks using "task accounts" cannot be deployed using GPP and must be created locally using the Task Scheduler MMC, PowerShell, or SCHTASKS.EXE. While it is possible to start a process listening to incoming connections using a scheduled task, this is not done very often, so we can safely state that a "task account" should not need a Service Principal Name. If the tasks being run by the "task account" are not expected to take longer than four hours, it can be a member of the "Protected Users" group.

- A **"Windows service account"** is used to run a Windows service and therefore needs the "service logon" privilege on the system or systems where the service is installed. If the service in question just performs some local computations or reaches out to other systems but does not accept (authenticated) incoming connections, such an account does not need and should not have an SPN assigned. A "Windows service account" cannot be a "Protected Users" member, but it can be either a "legacy service account" (i.e., a user) or a gMSA.

- A **"service principal"** is an account that may or may not actually run a service but has a SPN assigned and is used to validate service tickets directed at the service designated by the SPN. It can be a user, a gMSA, or even a computer object. If it does not run a service but is simply used for ticket verification, this account never actually authenticates; its password has to be known (as cleartext or as Kerberos hash) to the systems running the service where it is stored either in the Windows Vault or by other means. Keytabs have also been known to be used with this sort of account, e.g., in VMware IDM's connector for Active Directory. "Service principal" accounts are the most likely candidates for having delegation configured on them (unconstrained or constrained) or for them (RBCD).

- A **"function account"** is a user account whose password (or Keytab) is stored on a system in order to authenticate to other systems. Typical examples include, but are not limited to: a script using credentials from a credential vault (or text file) to connect to a network device; a multifunction printer using a LDAP bind account to retrieve email-enabled users or groups. These accounts hardly ever have actual processes running in their security context; however, they do authenticate. A "function account" should not require an SPN but often cannot be placed in "Protected Users" because the application using it either requires NTLM or is not able to handle a non-renewable TGT.

From here on, we will be using the term **"service account"** to cover all sorts of security principals listed above.

5.4.2 Making Sense of "Service Account Sprawl"

All service accounts' credentials are in danger of being stolen, be it from the Windows Vault or from the multifunction printer's firmware. It makes rotating their password a necessity, both on a regular basis to prevent abuse and in an emergency situation where the abuse is already happening. The challenge here is not so much to reset a user's password in the directory but to make the new password known to every system where the account is being used. Not all of these systems support remote automation, and even those who do might not support replacing *secrets* by remote automation. This makes "controlled service account sprawl" a good thing.

Consider an LDAP bind account (that would be a "function account") for address book lookup used in 1000 unmanaged multifunction printers worldwide. If the password for this account has to be rotated, printer maintenance technicians have to be given that password to log on to each printer and replace the password in its configuration. Assuming that there are not 1000 technicians to rotate the password simultaneously on all devices, some printers will experience problems with address book functionality until the password has been updated. By creating separate bind accounts for different locations or different printer maintenance companies, we can shorten the downtime and reduce the blast radius of a password being compromised.

The problem around service accounts that many organizations are facing is twofold. An architect planning a new environment and an administrator managing an existing one will probably find different words for each part, but it's all about finding an optimal middle ground between few overprivileged, overexposed, and ultimately unmanageable service accounts and thousands or even tens of thousands of accounts that no human is able to wrap their head around anymore:

CHAPTER 5   ENGINEERING AUTHENTICATION

Greenfield environment	Existing environment
How do I plan my service accounts to balance between manageability and protection against credentials compromise?	How do I determine what service account is used where and in what capacity?
How do I plan for least privilege for my service accounts and still keep their number manageable?	How do I reduce the blast radius from potential compromise of a service account?

There are some battle-proven guiding principles that can help here:

1. **Automate password changes for service accounts as much as possible:** For Windows services and scheduled tasks, this can be done using PowerShell, command line, or by other means. There is one caveat in automating password changes on Tier 1 and Tier 2 members: You cannot use the same account to administer the target machines and to create the new password and set it in AD! For this, your automation needs access to some sort of a secret vault where Tier 0 can write to and all tiers can read from. Additional benefit: Figuring out how to automate password changes will help you automate password changes for krbtgt and DSRM passwords.

2. **Document all service account procedures:** This task belongs as much to application owners as it does to Active Directory administrators. Whoever is responsible for applications, servers, and service accounts in your organization, the team must be able to not only roll every password on a very short notice but replace *the entire service account* should the need arise. This leads us to the next rule.

189

3. **Looking at the typology above, no identity should fall into more than one category:** The only exception that can make sense is to have a Windows service account also act as a task account if it's limited to one machine or a very small set of machines running a common application and the service(s) in question do not require an SPN. Even if you're using "legacy" accounts, rotating the password for services and scheduled tasks on one and the same machine can be easily automated. And if the service account whose password is being rotated is limited to only one machine, administrators do not even need to know the new password, meaning it can be a randomly generated long and complex string known only to the automation in question.

4. **Removing SPN update rights granted to SELF can be a good idea:** In large and geographically spread Active Directory environments where replication convergence is an issue, it can be a good idea to take away the right to self-manage the `servicePrincipalName` attribute for service principals, including computer accounts, and manage it in a centralized manner using Tier 0 permissions. Services like MS SQL will register their SPNs on startup and remove them on shutdown, potentially leading to the SPN not being up to date in remote sites. Before removing permissions, always check if the SPN getting registered is indeed static. Specifically, if using named instances and

CHAPTER 5   ENGINEERING AUTHENTICATION

dynamic ports with SQL, the SPNs will change on each startup, in which case you should either let SQL manage them or talk to your database team and try to persuade them to stop using dynamic ports.

5. **For systems where automated password changes are not possible, consider rotating accounts, not passwords:** Let's get back to the 1000 printers example. Even if one tech is responsible for "only" 50 printers, there is still downtime between password change in AD and the update on the last printer, maybe even followed by a required reboot of the firmware. What if we created *two* accounts for every tech and would roll the password of the currently used Account #1 *after all the printers have been switched to Account #2*? They could have identical permission by being members of the same groups. The account that is not currently in use could be deactivated, and modern password managers' browser plugins allow to paste username and password into the printers' management UI in one go.

6. **Adopt gMSA as your new default for service and task accounts:** Not every application can work with gMSA even today. But instead of creating a legacy service account for a new application and hoping to revisit it soon, start creating gMSA as a matter of routine after checking with the application vendor whether they will support it. When chatting with the vendor, ask them if they have a minimum required password lifetime and set the lifetime as short as

possible, but slightly above the vendor's minimum. Remember: you cannot change the password lifetime for a gMSA after it has been created, so make it a habit to start asking these questions when a new application appears on the horizon!

7. **Define a naming convention and stick to it:** Since you will be restricting the visibility of your service accounts for unprivileged users and workstations anyway, no harm is done in beginning all account names with **svc** so that a privileged administrator is able to enumerate them all with a simple search filter. The part after that, the one that distinguishes each service account from the rest, should either be completely anonymous, i.e., just a number incremented with each new account, or very telling, i.e., contain a well-known (within your organization) moniker of the application the account belongs to. If an application requires multiple service accounts, the purpose of each account can also be part of the name, e.g., **svc-crm-sql**, **svc-crm-web**, **svc-crm-rpt,** and so on. Some administrators resort to AD itself for documenting service accounts usage (putting computer names in a multivalue attribute of a service account, creating a group and putting computers in that group, and so on). gMSA are, of course, self-documented because computers need to be added to the list of accounts permitted to retrieve the password from AD.

Server 2025 introduces a new variant of managed service accounts – "delegated MSA," or dMSA. This account type offers even more protection for the account credentials than gMSA does and comes with a migration wizard that supports migrating from legacy Windows service accounts to dMSA. An automated migration from gMSA to dMSA is not supported at the time of writing, even in preview.

5.4.3 Identifying Service Accounts

If a service account has been compromised (or the security team suspects that it could be the case), its password has to be reset. After that is done, the account is not usable until the password change has been reflected to the systems where the account is being used. For services, there is some inertia to this because a service account has a valid TGT even though the password has changed. For tasks or TGS decryption with service principals, the password change in AD is effective immediately. To minimize disruption, it is therefore important to know what service account is used where and in which function. This is where solid management processes, documentation, and naming conventions help survive the day. If you are in the situation where you do not have much to go by (e.g., as a consultant called in to help with an application that you are seeing for the first time), you have to extract this information from the live environment.

If you have to force-rotate a gMSA password (the PowerShell cmdlet to do that is **Reset-ADServiceAccountPassword**), you don't have to do anything else. Eligible computers will pick up the change and retrieve the new password from Active Directory at their earliest convenience.

For Windows service accounts and task accounts, you can use whatever inventory mechanisms you have in place to determine services that are set to run in the context of the account in question. If your configuration management does not cover servers, use WMI, here, for example, in PowerShell:

```
Get-CimInstance Win32_Service -Filter '(StartName="svc0815@v309.ad2049.org") OR (StartName="V309\\svc0815")'
```

To change the password in the Service Control Manager, WMI also offers a method:

```
Get-CimInstance Win32_Service -Filter '(StartName="svc0815@
v309.ad2049.org") OR (StartName="V309\\svc0815")' |
Invoke-CimMethod -MethodName Change -Arguments
@{'StartPassword'='P@ssw0rd'}
```

For scheduled tasks, PowerShell even offers ready-made cmdlets:

```
Get-ScheduledTask | Where-Object {$_.Principal.UserId
-eq 'svc0815'}
```

and

```
Get-ScheduledTask | Where-Object {$_.Principal.UserId
-eq 'svc0815'} |
Set-ScheduledTask -User 'svc0815@v309.ad2049.org'
-Password 'P@ssw0rd'
```

A service principal without a process running in its context you can only identify using its SPN. It may not be a server name, but you can still get the actual server from DNS. In some cases, the SPN or SPNs will contain a load-balancer name so that you must ask the load-balancer team to provide information about the "real servers" behind the load-balanced application. For Exchange specifically, you can enumerate the external and internal URLs of its virtual directories. The FQDN listed there must match the one in the ASA's SPN!

The most difficult case is that of a function account. If the naming convention does not allow you to pinpoint all devices where the account is used (one more reason to create many function accounts and assign them in a granular manner!), you have no other choice than to resort to logon events (4624) on Domain Controllers, provided your audit policy instructs them to generate these events. The problem with this approach is that you must wait long enough for the account to actually authenticate *and* query all Domain Controllers for those events! If you forward the 4624 and 4768 events to SIEM, it will be a tremendous help. Document your findings, compare them with the official documentation, and rectify whichever one is wrong – if you determine that a different service account should have been used on a particular system to begin with, it's an excellent idea to correct it right now!

5.4.4 Minimizing the Risk of Kerberoasting

With service principals, you should always try to leverage Authentication Policies to restrict who, and from what computers, is allowed to request a service ticket for this account in the first place. Trying to do that for an Exchange ASA is probably a waste of time since it's specifically the mail-enabled accounts, i.e., those most susceptible to phishing, that are *supposed to* request TGS for that service! If, on the other hand, you are setting up service accounts for a three-tier application (web frontend, middleware, and backend database) used only by a specific department, you can tighten security around it by creating three Authentication Policies:

- Only users who are members of "FinDept-Users" can request a TGS for svcFinAppFront, and only if they are logged on to computers that are members of "FinDept-Wks."

- Only svcFinAppFront can request a TGS for svcFinAppMid if that account is logged on to one of the frontend servers.

- Only svcFinAppMid and SQL administrators from the FinDept department can request a TGS for svcFinAppSQL.

Such policies can and should be created early in the process of onboarding the application. This gives you ample time to troubleshoot and iron out the kinks if need arises.

5.5 Computer Accounts

There are several AD-based vulnerabilities that involve computer accounts. Make no mistake – a computer is a special case of a user, i.e., a security principal capable of authentication. Microsoft treated computers very differently from users in the Windows NT security model, and a number of questionable defaults hail from that era. The anti-patterns that stem from those include, but are not limited to:

- Authenticated Users can create up to ten computer objects in a domain by default. We will revisit this in the next section, but the juicy bit is that if a non-privileged user creates a computer object, then that user gets and retains very far-reaching permissions over it.

- A computer account without an actual computer attached to it may be worth more to a threat actor than an actively used one. If you create a computer account by any (built-in) means other than ADUC, its initial password will be the computer name (SAMAccountName without the trailing $) truncated to 14 characters and converted to lowercase. This practice hails from the Windows NT times, and you can even emulate it in ADUC by checking the box for "Pre-Windows 2000 compatibility."

- A computer is always a "service" in the Kerberos sense. Left to its own devices, it will update its own **dnsHostName** and **servicePrincipalName** attributes, and SPN mappings in AD do the rest.

CHAPTER 5 ENGINEERING AUTHENTICATION

Computer accounts are often overlooked when administrators do maintenance and cleanup of their directory objects. While user accounts that belong to persons no longer working for the organization are disabled, put in separate OUs, stripped of permissions and attributes, and ideally deleted at some point, I have seen computer accounts initially migrated from a Windows NT domain coexist happily side by side with newly joined Windows 11 workstation accounts in the 2020s! Server accounts are even more dangerous since they have possibly been assigned permissions both in AD and in other systems so that services running as SYSTEM can access resources and perform tasks.

There is a long-standing anti-pattern from Active Directory's very early days to disable computer accounts' password changes in order to avoid them losing secure channel due to network disruption. Starting with Windows 7 SP1, this fear is unfounded because a member will not change its own password locally until the change in the directory has been confirmed by the Domain Controller. Nor do computer account passwords ever expire by themselves, following a password policy, or get locked out if a wrong password has been supplied. This makes abandoned highly privileged server accounts so dangerous – the attacker can spend as much time cracking the password as they need, and it will still be valid. To be fair, this will usually take a very long time.

A well-engineered authentication framework must always include a well-defined computer account lifecycle ending in the deletion of the account within an acceptable time frame following the last logon of the actual computer. When looking for computer accounts to clean up, remember that some of those that appear unused may be "service principals" as described in the last section.

5.6 From Domain Join to Domain Takeover

Building trust is hard. Even in human relationships, when someone or something goes from "untrusted" to "trusted," there are consequences. Making a computer trusted by joining it to a domain is no different. But even creating a computer object without attaching an actual computer to it can lead to elevation, credentials compromise, and domain dominance.

5.6.1 The Default Behavior

As mentioned in the previous section, every authenticated user can join up to ten computers to Active Directory by default. This reflects a scenario that the author has never experienced in three decades of doing both small business and enterprise IT:

- A user is issued a new, pristine workstation including an account with local admin privileges.
- They set the computer name themselves (maybe it comes preset from IT, but there's nothing to prevent the user from changing it).
- They join the computer to AD using their regular AD credentials (and still have an account with local admin rights unless that is managed by different methods like LAPS).
- After several years, they are issued a new workstation, and the process is repeated.
- The old workstation is decommissioned, but its account remains in the database.

CHAPTER 5   ENGINEERING AUTHENTICATION

This is probably where the number 10 comes from: If a user stays with the company for 40 years and is issued a new machine every four years, they will burn through ten workstations between apprenticeship and retirement. If you would like to know if this process has been practiced in your AD environment, search for computer objects with the attribute **mS-DS-CreatorSID** populated!

This "feature" is governed by two settings that are easily changeable:

1. The attribute **ms-DS-MachineAccountQuota** of the domain head that is set to 10 by default
2. The right "Add workstations to domain" set under "User Rights Assignment" in the Default Domain Controllers Policy (DDCP)

Don't let "workstations" fool you – there is nothing to prevent Joe User from adding a *server* to the domain! And in doing so, the account joining a computer retains very high explicitly assigned permissions on that computer's AD object – set dnsHostName and userPrincipalName, reset password, and lots more! It gets much worse if that server gets promoted to a Domain Controller – its privilege level rises quite dramatically, but the permissions the user who initially joined the computer to domain remain, as shown in Figure 5-9.

CHAPTER 5   ENGINEERING AUTHENTICATION

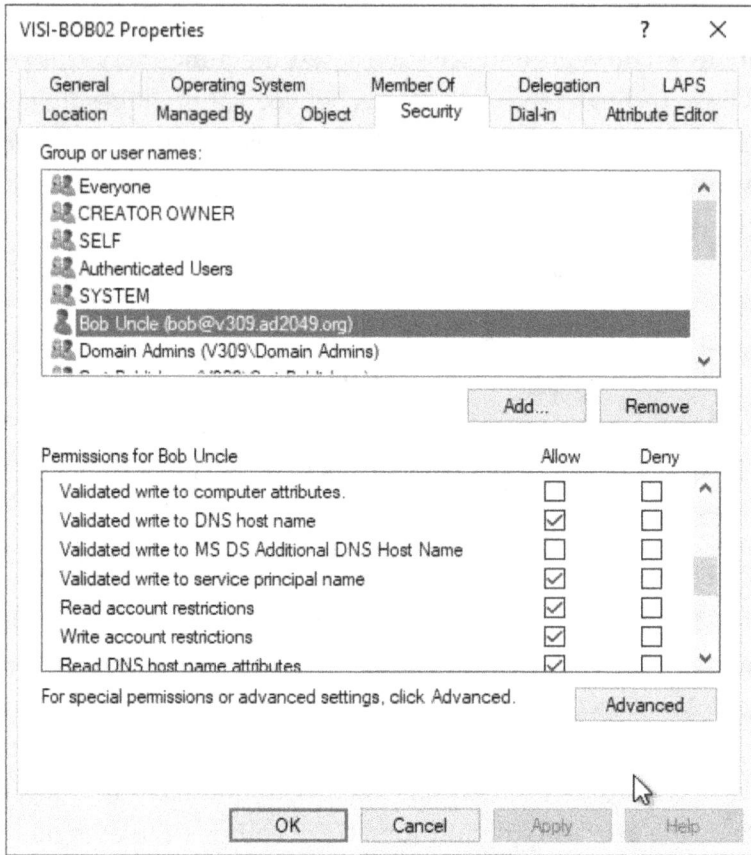

Figure 5-9.   You don't want to see these rights on a Domain Controller

Removing the default behavior is easy, and we suggest that you both remove the right from the group policy and set **ms-DS-MachineAccountQuota** to zero. As long as you don't *actually* let your employees add computers to the domain, nothing is going to break.

5.6.2 Let an Admin Do the Work – but Be on Your Toes

The obvious remediation to this is not allowing unprivileged users to add computers to domain, be it by process or by restricting this ability as shown above. However, in most organizations, computers are not added to AD manually but by automated deployment systems – which means whatever credentials are used for domain join must be stored in the deployment system, and more often than not they are either stored in cleartext (e.g., CustomSettings.ini file in MDT) or in a database with a known way to compromise them (for SCCM, Mimikatz has a dedicated scenario for retrieving domain join and agent push credentials).

So the next logical step in designing domain join for security-conscious organizations was to reduce the blast radius by "only" equipping the join account with the necessary permissions to join a computer to a certain container (because with the automated deployment systems it is almost always possible and sometimes even required to specify the location in the directory where the new computer object will be placed). However, there is a caveat to that.

5.6.3 The Joy of Ownership

To allow a user to join a computer to an OU in an Active Directory domain, it only needs five permissions:

- Create an object of "computer" class.
- Change password on "computer" objects (it's part of the official documentation, but the join process actually works without it).
- Reset password on "computer" objects.

- Validated write on **dnsHostName** attribute.
- Validated write on **servicePrincipalName** attribute.

The way the AD join process works, if a user performing the join is a domain admin *or if the default 10-machines-per-user facility is being used,* the ownership of the new computer object is assigned to "Domain Admins." If, however, the join user only has the rights listed above, the join account ends up being the owner of the new object! And this, too, doesn't get overwritten when the added computer gets promoted to a DC or given privileges to perform other Tier 0 tasks!

5.6.4 The Modern Domain Join Process

Since we cannot change the default domain join logic, in order to modernize the domain join process, we must split it into multiple tasks using the automation facilities at our disposal. For this, we need a "provisioning account" and a "join account." The "provisioning account" needs the permissions to create "computer" objects in one or more OUs as well as to modify their security descriptor and the owner. Additionally, the "provisioning account" is assigned the security option "Domain controller: Allow computer account re-use during domain join." The "join account," i.e., the one whose credentials are at immediate risk of being compromised, doesn't hold any permissions permanently.

- First, a "provisioning account" creates a computer object in the desired OU and grants the "join account" the permissions required for the new computer to take over the prepared computer object., i.e., "Validated write to dnsHostName," "Validated write to servicePrincipalName," and "Reset password."
- Then the computer is provisioned, renamed, and joined to the domain using the "join account."

- After the computer has been associated with the account in AD, the "provisioning account" removes the permissions previously granted to the "join account." Ideally, in a subsequent cleanup task, a highly privileged identity (a Tier 0 user or a Domain Controller) reassigns ownership to "Domain Admins" or another highly protected group and removes the explicit rights that were granted to the "provisioning account" by virtue of it being the creator of the object.

At the first glance, this may appear overcomplicated. However, since the goal is to minimize the blast radius of the join account being compromised, this is an approach that works really well. To harden this even more, you should create a procedure for regular password rotation of the domain join account.

> The group policy quoted above that declares certain computer object owners as trustworthy for account takeover was introduced in March 2023. Prior to that, an attempt to harden the domain join and account reuse process was made in October 2022, but that hardening change could be easily circumvented since the requisite setting (a registry key) had to be done on the machine being joined rather than in the directory.

A radically different approach for establishing trust and joining computers to a domain is the offline join using the DJOIN command. On the domain side, the computer object is provisioned using

DJOIN /provision /domain "V309" /machine "PC04711" /machineou "<OU path>" /savefile pc04711.join

The generated file must then be transferred to the correct computer (i.e., the one being provisioned), upon which it can perform the domain join by issuing

```
DJOIN /requestodj /loadfile pc04711.join /windowspath
"C:\Windows" localos
```

in the SYSTEM or local administrator security context.

The offline join file contains the computer password set for the new account in cleartext. The file is base64 encoded but not encrypted or otherwise protected. This way you can avoid having a join account whose credentials can be easily stolen. Instead, only the password of the new computer is at risk, and only until the computer actually joins the domain and rotates its password for the first time.

5.6.5 More Local Magic

Compared to the permission and ownership vulnerability, the other default behavior involved in the domain join process may appear harmless. When a machine joins, the "Domain Admins" group is added to the local "Administrators" group of the new computer. While not per se dangerous in an AD modernized and hardened by Authentication Policies and other tiering techniques discussed earlier in this chapter, this creates an incentive to use a domain admin account for local administration, thus putting domain admin credentials at risk.

You should always remove this nesting and add a custom group to the local Administrators. There usually will be several such groups, depending on the machine's role and tier placement. The most reliable way to achieve it is by GPP, but the machine account must have visibility over both the "Domain Admins" group being removed and the custom group being added!

5.7 Tickets from the Cloud

We have seen the domain join open numerous avenues for abuse and inherently expose at least one set of credentials to stealing. Workstations being joined to a domain also create reconnaissance and escalation attack vectors in addition to those based on user credentials. At the same time, users in many organizations spend a larger part of their business day using cloud applications authenticated against Entra ID than working with legacy applications that require on-premises authentication. Remote workforce is becoming the norm in numerous enterprises, making global laptop delivery logistics tricky to say the least – the machine must be delivered to an office location first to be joined to AD and then sent on to the designated user who also requires an initial password and a BitLocker PIN.

In the early days of Entra ID (which was called Azure Active Directory back then), Microsoft already offered SSO from a domain-joined client to cloud-authenticated applications. Since the COVID-19 pandemic, a domain-joined client steadily became a less and less attractive proposition. At the same time, mobile device management using Intune came a long way towards providing a client management experience on par with the previous, on-premises-based technology stack. Still, some business processes exist on premises and require Active Directory authentication.

To accommodate this requirement, Entra ID offers "Entra ID Kerberos." The goal of this technology is to allow a synchronized hybrid user access to on-premises resources **when logged on to a cloud-registered client using the cloud account**. For this, Microsoft leveraged a feature added to AD in Server 2008R2: Read-Only Domain Controller. Each RODC possesses its own krbtgt object in its domain, whose password is used to encrypt TGTs. When Entra ID Kerberos is set up, the **Set-AzureADKerberosServer** cmdlet creates a RODC object named "AzureADKerberos" in the default Domain Controllers OU along with a "krbtgt_AzureAD" account tied to that RODC

CHAPTER 5   ENGINEERING AUTHENTICATION

by virtue of the **msDS-KrbTgtLinkBL** attribute. The sAMAccountName of the krbtgt account follows the standard naming conventions for RODCs by adding five digits after the underscore. As shown in Figure 5-10, the cmdlet generates a password for the krbtgt_AzureAD user and stores its AES256 hash in the Entra ID cloud, where it is associated with the AD domain it came from:

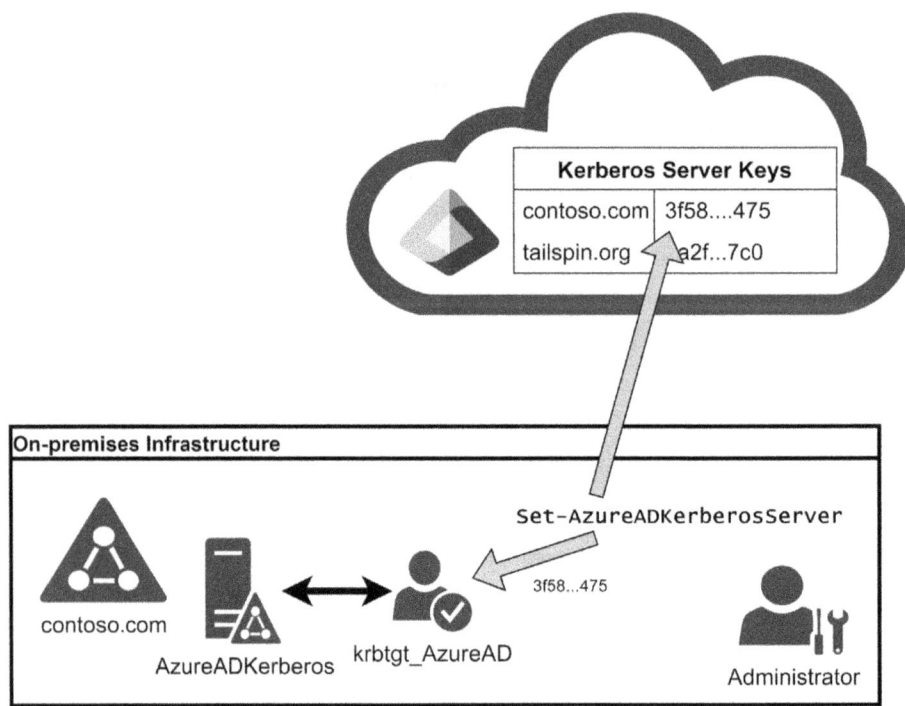

Figure 5-10. *Azure AD Kerberos is based on RODC*

Using the information synchronized from on-premises AD, which includes the UPN and the SID, Entra ID now can create a valid partial TGT, which, as far as AD is concerned, is issued by the "AzureADKerberos" RODC! When the client tries to access on-premises resources, this partial TGT is sent to a Read-Write-Domain Controller and exchanged for a full TGT, which can subsequently be used to request and obtain TGS tickets. A user logged on with a synchronized Entra ID account is able to access on-premises resources… as long as they accept Kerberos – NTLM authentication cannot be served in this way. By the way, the ability to craft a partial TGT is **not** dependent on the Password Hash Sync being enabled!

> At the time of writing, the PowerShell module for managing this functionality is still called "AzureADHybridAuthenticationManagement" and has dependencies on legacy modules also bearing "Azure AD" in their names. Be prepared to find this module deprecated and replaced by a different one. Not only has "Azure AD" been renamed to "Entra ID" but also the APIs published for managing the cloud identity are subject to regular change, everything being migrated to Microsoft Graph.

When you design your regime for rotating krbtgt passwords, you will normally want to include RODC-related accounts. However, to rotate the password of krbtgt_AzureAD, you **must** use the **Set-AzureADKerberosServer** cmdlet to have the password change replicated to the cloud! It is not done by Entra ID Connect or Cloud Sync.

5.8 Certificate-Based Authentication

Unlike NTLM, Kerberos supports a private/public key pair as an alternate authenticator beside the password. Usually this kind of authentication is facilitated by a smart card. The private key is stored in the card's cryptographic processor, whereas the public key is stored with the user object in AD and thus known to the Domain Controllers. The time stamp encrypted by the private key during preauthentication can be decrypted by the DC using the public key, allowing for the verification just like the DC used the password hash as a shared secret in the password-based authentication flow. Needless to say, certificate-based authentication is more secure since nothing that can be gleaned from AD or from a user's logon session that could be reused for an attack scenario. Well, almost nothing.

Generally speaking, you can issue every user a smart card, and if all endpoints are equipped with a smart card reader, everything will continue working as usual. Locking and unlocking the session can be facilitated by removing and reinserting the smartcard, making this element of physical IT security even more comfortable. If all your applications accept passthrough authentication from Windows, you can even enforce the smart card use by setting the corresponding bit in **userAccountControl** (surfaced as the "Smart card is required for interactive logon" checkbox in the account properties). There is, however, one caveat to this.

If an application requires NTLM authentication (and the user is not prevented from providing it by being a member of "Protected Users" or having an Authentication Policy assigned), Windows and AD will oblige. To facilitate this, the PAC structure of the TGT contains "NTLM_SUPPLEMENTAL_CREDENTIAL" which is, as the name suggests, an NTLM hash. If the smart card usage has not been enforced, it is simply the hash of the current password of that account, which is subject to the password policy that is in effect for the user. If the smart card authentication *is* enforced, however, the user is exempt from the normal password rotation regime and may, in theory, never have received their initial password in the first place! In this case, AD generates a long and complex password for the user, similar to that of a gMSA, and uses its hash for NTLM authentication. How often this password is rotated depends on the value of the **msDS-ExpirePasswordsOnSmartCardOnlyAccounts** attribute of the domain head. If your domain was created using Server 2016 or later, the value is TRUE, and the password expires and is rotated as per effective password policy. If your domain was upgraded from Server 2012R2 or earlier, the value is FALSE and the password will never expire, making the

NTLM hash slightly more attractive for cracking but vastly more attractive for reuse in Pass-the-Hash attacks! The attribute is surfaced in ADAC by the checkbox "Enable rolling of expiring NTLM secrets during sign on, for users who are required to use Microsoft Passport or smart card for interactive sign on." The "Microsoft Passport" technology mentioned here has evolved to "Windows Hello."

If you run a hybrid environment, consider switching interactive logons for regular users to Entra ID accounts and "Windows Hello for Business," leveraging Azure AD Kerberos as described in the previous section, before you start issuing smart cards to everyone in the organization and upgrading endpoints with smart card readers. Windows Hello for Business allows you to use biometric protection and FIDO keys, which do not require special hardware but can simply be connected to an existing USB port. More expensive USB keys may even contain a smart card-compatible cryptographic processor in addition to FIDO functionality, accommodating even more use cases.

5.8.1 Next-Level Privileged Access

For privileged access, smart card authentication in Windows holds an additional functionality that helps make administration both more secure and more comfortable. It is known as "Authentication Mechanism Assurance," or AMA, or, because it's based on smart cards, SCAMA. Setting it up is rather involved, but once everything is figured out, it becomes a very powerful instrument of privileged administration. The way it works, in a nutshell, is this:

- You create universal security groups and delegate permissions for administrative tasks to those groups. **Do not add any members to these groups!**

CHAPTER 5   ENGINEERING AUTHENTICATION

- For each group, you create a new issuance policy in your enterprise PKI and assign it an OID from an internal numbering scheme you have to come up with. If you're looking to make your OIDs unique, you can request a "Private Enterprise Number" (PEN) from the "Internet Assigned Numbers Authority" (IANA) and start your OID namespace with 1.3.6.1.4.1.<PEN>.

- In the OID branch of your "Public Key Services" configuration, you locate the OIDs you just created and set the attribute **msDS-OIDToGroupLink** of each OID to the **distinguishedName** of the corresponding group.

- You create a smart card certificate template (to use modern cryptography, it must be a v3 template, so at least Server 2008R2 compatibility level!) and assign it the issuance policies for the required privileged groups.

- An administrator enrolls their smart card for a certificate from the template you just created.

You do not have to enforce smart card authentication for this to work. If the administrator logs on using their name and password, it is not assigned any of the privileged groups you created for AMA. If, however, they log on using an appropriate certificate on their smart card, their logon token contains the privileged groups' SIDs along with those they are members of! Given that more expensive smart cards are capable of holding multiple certificates, you can provide a very user-friendly privileged administration experience where switching between roles or even tiers is done by selecting a different authentication certificate from the smart card.

If you are not using Microsoft ADCS but a third-party PKI, you can still use both certificate-based Kerberos authentication and AMA. For authentication, you just have to import the CA's certificate into the NTAuth store. However, if the PKI product of your choice does not offer creating the issuance policies in AD, you will have to create the requisite **msPKI-Enterprise-Oid** objects for AMA mappings yourself.

We have already mentioned several times that a computer account is in essence a user as far as authentication and authorization are concerned. This is true in regard to certificate-based authentication as well. The computer certificates must have the OID of 1.3.6.1.5.2.3.4 (PKINIT client authentication) in their EKU, and you have to make absolutely sure that these certificates are only issued to legitimate devices! Microsoft states that manual enrollment is the only way to achieve this level of trust.

5.9 Engineering Trusts

Trusts between Kerberos realms have been around for a long time. Active Directory introduces specific types of trusts that are only relevant for AD domains and forests but provide additional functionality. We already learned about the PIM trust earlier in this chapter. PIM constitutes a very specific use case for privileged administration utilizing a Red Forest. In this section, we will look at the more general trust usage.

If you follow the recommendations from Chapter 3, you may end up running multiple forests serving either identities or resources, or both. Assuming that all those forests are part of an overarching application and identity infrastructure, cross-forest access will be required, and trusts will have to be established between the forests.

A complete typology of forest and domain trusts is not in the scope of this book. There are, however, general considerations for each new trust that you plan for your AD organization.

5.9.1 Dimensions of a Trust

When planning a trust between forests, you have to decide on the following attributes of the new trust:

- **Direction:** Which forest needs to trust which? In a classic "user forest + resource forest" scenario, the resource forest must trust the user forest, but not the other way around.

- **Scope of authentication:** Many trusts are created using global authentication so that any user from the trusted forest can authenticate to any service in the trusting forest, and it's up to that service's authorization to deny or grant access. However, this may put credentials from the trusted forest at risk if the Authentication Policies have not been configured in the trusted forest to protect them. To manage cross-forest authentication more tightly, you should set up selective authentication where appropriate. Selective authentication requires a user from the trusted forest to be granted the "Allowed to Authenticate" permission at least on one service principal in the trusting forest in order for the trusting forest's KDC to issue that user a TGS.

- **SID History:** Between "production" forests (i.e., user or resource but not Red forests), SID History should only be used to facilitate a migration and only for as long as this migration is ongoing. Even if the trust as such is still needed (why?) after the migration has been completed, SID filtering on the trust should be reenabled.

CHAPTER 5   ENGINEERING AUTHENTICATION

- **Transitivity:** A transitive trust allows identity from a trusted forest to authenticate not only in the immediately trusting forest but also in the "next" forest that trusts that trusting forest but does not share a direct trust with the user forest. Security researchers have shown that due to the way cross-trust authentication works in Windows, declaring a trust as "non-transitive" does not prevent a sufficiently versed attacker from authenticating to the "next-hop forest." However, authentication using trust transitivity causes the DCs to generate multiple referrals for the same authentication flow, so it might be a better idea to just create a direct trust instead of relying on transitivity. A PIM trust must always be created as transitive, even if there are only two forests in the whole organization.

- **Encryption types:** We discussed the encryption support over a Kerberos trust earlier in this chapter. At the time of writing, the question should not be "do I enable AES?" but rather "is there a reason to allow RC4?" But if the answer ends up being "yes" to both questions, there is a supported process of setting the trust up this way.

If both the trusted and the trusting forest consist of multiple domains, you might want to consider creating a shortcut trust if users from a particular child domain (of the user forest) authenticate frequently to services located in a particular child domain (of the resource forest).

213

5.9.2 Trust Anti-patterns

The worst anti-pattern encountered in multi-forest environments is creating bidirectional trusts to make administration less painful. This usually stems from placing resource administration in the resource forest rather than in the user (or, better still, Red) forest. If that is the case, adding a principal from the user forest to an application joined to the resource forest can be challenging because principals in the resource forest have no visibility into the user forest! The answer to this is not in enabling the trust in the "wrong" direction but in moving the administration into a different forest, thus creating the requisite visibility. Of course, there will always be applications that are not designed to work that way. You should talk to business about retiring such applications, at least long-term. If there is only one or two of these, breaking out of the forest topology design and placing them in the user forest may be a viable workaround for the interim.

5.9.3 Fortifying a One-Way Trust

Just like we learned in 2021 that non-transitive trust can, in fact, be traversed, a one-way trust has never been truly impenetrable (in the wrong direction). A trust between two domains or forests is facilitated by a pair of **trustedDomain** objects, one placed in the trusting domain and the other in the trusted domain. There is, however, an additional object of class **user** that is found in the trusted domain but bears the NetBIOS name of the trusting domain followed by a dollar sign. This account has a password that is rotated on a regular basis and is reflected in the **trustedDomain** object for that domain. Once the trusting domain is completely compromised, the attacker can dump Kerberos keys for the outgoing trust *which are identical with the password hashes of the user account.* This allows the attacker to get a foothold in the trusted domain. It's just a "Domain Users" member at first, but, depending on how the trusted domain has been hardened, it may be enough for both reconnaissance and kerberoasting!

Server 2025 will provide built-in protection against this type of attack. If your environment is not yet on that OS and functional level, you can leverage the fact that the trust user account does not normally authenticate but simply serves as a container for the password hashes. Enable Kerberos Armoring in the trusted forest and assign an Authentication Policy to the trust account that will always fail (e.g., computer belongs to group that is empty), effectively preventing the account from authenticating.

5.10 Authentication in Perimeter Networks

Many applications and systems hosted on premises have to be accessible from the Internet and thus are placed in perimeter networks (edge networks, DMZ, etc.). We discussed the challenges that arise if such applications have to look up objects from internal directory services in the previous chapter. But what if an external system needs to actually authenticate internal users in order to grant them access to information?

Assuming that the application on the perimeter is web-based, the most secure proposition is to have it use SAML authentication – either by means of an on-premises ADFS instance or, if you already utilize hybrid identity, by authenticating to the edge application using Entra ID. This last method offers additional security by enabling application proxy, conditional access, and strong authentication as needed. If, however, the application in question does not yet support modern authentication but insists on performing an LDAP bind based on username and password, you need to secure this access in order to prevent credentials compromise.

Even if you do not have this requirement on the immediate horizon, be prepared for it to surface one day. The worst anti-pattern you can follow when it does is to improvise instead of carefully engineering this critical access path.

5.10.1 Logon from the Perimeter

The most secure way to provide LDAP bind on the edge is by allowing LDAPS access to an ADLDS instance hosted on the internal network. This directory can hold, as far as users are concerned, two kinds of objects:

- A generalized **user** object. It is able to authenticate, but its password is stored in the LDS directory. It does not need a corresponding object in AD so can be used for creating additional user identities for the edge applications, e.g., for partners, customers, or contractors. It can also be created mimicking attributes of an actual AD user, thus providing the basis for information lookup.

- An **organizationalPerson** object with the additional subclass of **userProxyFull**. This adds the **objectSID** attribute to the object schema. However, the SID is not governed by the LDS directory (it does not have that functionality) but serves as a pointer to an Active Directory user object. An LDAP bind using this object as the bind DN will create a Kerberos authentication request towards the directory, and the result of that request is returned to ADLDS, which will grant or reject the bind.

A word of caution is in order. While this will take care of authentication and even offer additional benefits like consolidating multiple AD domains into one LDAP endpoint or allowing schema extensions that are undesired in AD, some applications may not like it when it comes to authorization. Nested group memberships, for example, are not very likely to work well with proxy authentication if the application was developed with the full-blown Active Directory in mind rather than with a more generic LDAP directory.

Provision an ADLDS instance ahead of time so that, once an edge application requiring AD authentication via LDAP bind comes along, you have the basic infrastructure and the user provisioning processes figured out.

5.10.2 User Access from the Wild Wide World

A different kind of access from the perimeter is a user trying to access an on-premises resource from an untrusted network in the same manner they would access it from a trusted one. It can be a domain user logged on to a domain-joined endpoint (either using cached credentials or just disconnecting from the LAN while logged on and walking across the street to a café to have a meeting there) or a synchronized Entra ID user trying to use Azure AD Kerberos from a cloud-joined client but without "line of sight" to a writable DC to convert the partial TGT from the cloud to a full TGT and request a TGS using it.

There is a relatively little-known feature in Windows Server that has, at the time of writing, just started to get significant traction due to new work styles taking hold worldwide: KDC Proxy. It can be hosted on the resource itself (provided it is run on a Windows Server), or you can provide a central KDC proxy for all your external authentication needs. KDC proxy has been around since Server 2012 and was initially introduced to provide Kerberos SSO to RDS server farms in conjunction with RDS Web Access and RDS Gateway. However, this generic functionality can be leveraged for any Kerberos authentication without line of sight to a DC.

Nothing in Active Directory itself has to be changed to enable the KDC proxy. On the server or servers providing the functionality, you have to create or import a TLS certificate (KDC proxy uses HTTPS) and bind it to the selected port (this example assumes that you are running the commands from an elevated PowerShell window):

```
$appid="{$([Guid]::NewGuid().Guid)}"
$certhash = Get-ChildItem "Cert:\LocalMachine\My" |
Where-Object Subject -eq "CN=proxy.contoso.com" | Select-Object
-ExpandProperty Thumbprint

# reserve the URL and bind the certificate
netsh http add urlacl url=https://+:443/KdcProxy user="NT
AUTHORITY\Network Service"
netsh http add sslcert ipport=0.0.0.0:443 certhash=$certhash
appid=$appId

# if smart card is not used, run this:
Set-ItemProperty -Path "HKLM:\SYSTEM\CurrentControlSet\
Services\KPSSVC\Settings"`
-Name HttpsClientAuth -Value 0
Set-ItemProperty -Path "HKLM:\SYSTEM\CurrentControlSet\
Services\KPSSVC\Settings"`
-Name DisallowUnprotectedPasswordAuth -Value 0

# set to autostart and start service:
Set-Service kpssvc -StartupType Automatic
Start-Service kpssvc
```

On the client side, you must configure the group policy setting "Specify KDC proxy servers for Kerberos clients" found in Computer/Policies/Administrative Template/System/Kerberos. The value of this GPO is a list of domain-to-proxy URL mappings. Wildcards are allowed, including mapping every domain (*) to the same proxy. For clients not joined to AD but living natively in the cloud, you must deploy this setting using the Mobile Device Management (MDM) of your choosing.

5.11 Modern Defaults

The "modern defaults" for AD authentication start with using Kerberos rather than NTLM. In a greenfield environment or during a prolonged migration, you can enforce it from the outset and treat any NTLM-bound application as "hostile"; you will usually not have this luxury when modernizing an existing environment. In that case, start the NTLM removal process, clean up the obvious suspects, and define the exceptions. We will revisit this in Chapter 11.

If the vast majority of your users do not need the NTLM-bound applications and your organization has embraced the cloud, start the discussion about removing the clients from AD and moving to Azure AD Kerberos with business and client management as early as possible. Highlight the possibilities that become available, such as MFA, Windows Hello for Business, password quality checking, and conditional access even for applications hosted on premises.

5.11.1 Password Policy Defaults

As long as NTLM and RC4 are possible in your environment, the "Post-Burr password policy" with its very long password lifetimes is not for you, no matter how long the passwords end up being. With Pass-the-Hash, you cannot prevent a stolen hash from being used, so the only way to reduce the damage is by restricting the time it can be used, beside restricting the permissions, of course.

Unless every user is issued a smart card and its usage is enforced, you also have to provide a good framework for account lockout policies. A static lockout policy (X failed logon attempts during Y minutes) as offered by Windows does not lend itself very well to engineering a brute-force protection mechanism. But, if the password quality is good enough, a policy observing up to 100 failed logons within 150 minutes is a better proposition than observing 10 failed logons within 15 minutes, although the average logon rate is the same. The latter can absolutely stem from normal user activity after a prolonged vacation, whereas the former definitely indicates that something is awry.

Both for password and lockout policies, the fact that an attacker who already has acquired standard user permissions knows what's set on the domain level doesn't make the environment more secure. That is why you should set the actual policies in the FGPP, even for normal users, and set the Default Domain Policy to values that could dissuade an attacker from trying to brute-force passwords, e.g., 14 characters minimum and lockout after two unsuccessful attempts. As long as the malicious actor cannot read FGPP, they have no way of knowing that the effective policy has different settings.

5.11.2 Kerberos Defaults

Enable Kerberos armoring as early as possible. You might not be able to ever enforce it, but it is still needed for Authentication Policies to work.

Unconstrained delegation should be banned as early as possible. When setting up constrained delegation, keep in mind that the service class part in the allowed SPNs is much less binding than the hostname part, so that artificially restricting the number of SPNs for the same host may be a waste of time.

Set the encryption to only support AES as early as possible. Keep in mind that any changes to encryption types require a password change to really become effective.

If planning to use smart cards in a specific domain, check the **msDS-ExpirePasswordsOnSmartCardOnlyAccounts** attribute value, especially if unsure whether the domain was created using Server 2016 or an earlier version.

5.11.3 Privileged Access Defaults

Every privileged user should have the flag "Account is sensitive and cannot be delegated" activated. Admin accounts belonging to persons belong in the "Protected Users" group.

Ideally all privileged access is carried out from the Red Forest; the only Tier 0 identities in the "golden" forests are break-glass accounts. Use SCAMA for privileged administration; use PIM Trust and Shadow Principals if SCAMA is not possible.

5.11.4 Session Protection Defaults

Enable Credential Guard wherever possible. For virtualization, evaluate providing vTPM to your VMs and enabling Credential Guard even there.

For RDP access, use Remote Credential Guard or at least the older and slightly less powerful Restricted Admin mode.

Avoid communications that require CredSSP or WDigest as these may lead to passwords being stored in cleartext in memory.

5.11.5 Service Account Defaults

Use gMSA (and, once your environment has been updated to Server 2025 or newer, dMSA) wherever possible. Use gMSA for scheduled tasks as well. This has the downside that you cannot deploy the tasks using GPP, but if you accept making unsupported edits, you might be able to get it to work by editing the XML files of your GPOs directly. When creating gMSA, select the password lifetime as short as possible and as long as required by the application – you cannot change it after the fact.

For service principals, evaluate how many users will require a TGS and if those are end users, whether there already is a group they must be a member of to be able to use the service. If specifying the allowed users by group or claim is possible, apply an Authentication Policy to the service account to restrict who can request a TGS.

If using legacy service accounts, design an automated password rotation regime. Remember, a documented "service account sprawl" is a good thing.

5.11.6 Trust Defaults

All trusts from a "golden" forest to the Red Forest must be unidirectional, possibly configured as PIM trusts but with global authentication.

For all other trusts, evaluate selective authentication. If the user forest has 10,000 users but only 20 of them use an application provisioned out of a resource forest, there is no need for 9,980 users to be able to authenticate to that forest at all!

Harden the trust in the trusted forest by preventing the trust user object from authenticating by Authentication Policies until Server 2025 relieves you of this task.

5.11.7 PKI Defaults

Any PKI not designed to issue smart card certificates is removed from the NTAuth container.

Smart card certificate templates should be v3 to use the modern key storage provider.

5.12 Summary

In this chapter, we looked at various aspects of authentication in an Active Directory-based environment (except for federated authentication provided by ADFS). Since authentication is the most important functionality in AD, there is a lot to consider. Besides providing a robust authentication experience, the most important task of a "modern AD" is securing highly privileged credentials from being stolen and abused. This involves getting rid of NTLM and RC4, putting privileged accounts in a Red Forest, using Shadow Principals and SCAMA, protecting Tier 0 accounts from logging on to unprivileged computers and many other techniques. Kerberos armoring an Authentication Policies should have a fixed place in your toolbox.

Domain join involves creating a trust relationship and therefore is a very sensitive operation which has been hardened by Microsoft in recent years but still requires careful engineering. Providing LDAP proxy authentication in perimeter networks and Azure AD Kerberos for today's hybrid work environments helps authenticate securely from potentially untrustworthy sources.

CHAPTER 6

Engineering Authorization

After a user has found the service that they want to access in the directory and authenticated to it, the service will have to validate their access and decide what features the user is allowed to use and what data they may access within the service. This is called authorization. In Active Directory-based applications, authorization is mostly performed using group memberships: when a ticket is issued to a principal, the SIDs of the groups it is a member in, including nested (transitive) memberships, are added to the ticket along with the user's own SID. The application performing authorization will evaluate permissions assigned to each SID and produce an authorization verdict.

In this book, we will not be covering in any detail a Server 2012 and newer authorization feature that, while very promising in principle, remains largely unused in the real world: Dynamic Access Control (DAC). It uses generalized claims to provide authorization information about the user trying to access resources. Group memberships are also valid claims, but in DAC, claims can be based on a multitude of attributes and also on the computer the resource is being accessed from. With Authentication Policies, we are able to deny TGS or even TGT issuance if the wrong workstation is being used; with DAC, this principle can be applied to individual files, based on various attributes. Some of the file attributes can be generated automatically by analyzing the content; this is known as "automatic classification."

CHAPTER 6   ENGINEERING AUTHORIZATION

For customers who decided to move their documents from file servers and on-premises SharePoint farms to M365, Microsoft Purview shows how content-based classification and access control can work across applications, providing a unified policy-based access and lifecycle management for information of various types. DAC was intended to offer the same experience on premises even before it was available in the cloud but never managed to cover more than just file servers. All DAC features for file classification and dynamic access control are still under active support at the time of writing. This includes even the integration with ADRMS so that documents can be automatically classified and encrypted based on attributes derived from their content. If you cannot put your sensitive documents into Microsoft's cloud just yet, you can at least provide modern classification and access control using your on-premises file servers. Covering the required planning, engineering, provisioning, and ongoing operation of an enterprise-grade DAC and ADRMS implementation is more than enough to fill another book.

6.1 Working with Groups and Object Hierarchies

Assigning permissions to groups is usually straightforward enough, and old admin wisdom dictates that permissions be **always** assigned to groups rather than to individual users. While this sentiment is not per se wrong, the reason it has carved itself in the Windows admins' collective stone lies not so much in the engineering way of thinking but in the fact that Windows, and specifically NTFS, is really bad at propagating permissions through deep and wide hierarchies! Assigning a permission to a single empty folder is easily done. Fill that folder with 20 levels of subfolder hierarchy and millions of files, and it will take hours, if not days, to effectively add a second user to the top of the folder tree. Everyone who ever made a mistake to perform this act using Windows Explorer also knows that this is a blocking operation, making your admin session unusable for the duration. The same applies to permissions in Active Directory if set on top OU levels when there are lots of Sub-OUs and objects in them.

To avoid this situation, we assign permissions to groups, hopefully very early in the creation of the application in question, and let them propagate down through the hierarchy while it's still small. When we add data, e.g., folders and files, on the lower levels of the hierarchy later, they will just inherit the permissions from the parent object as a part of the creation operation.

Another old admin wisdom, specifically that of file server admins, dictates that the depth of the hierarchy where permissions are explicitly applied be very limited. Three levels of hierarchy are the widely accepted maximum, although the author has seen organizations go for as deep as seven. Whatever the number, all permissions below that level are dictated by what is set above. This may not apply to any application – for example, even if a wide cohort of users are given some limited permissions on virtual machines in a vSphere cluster, there are unlikely to be three levels of folder hierarchy to take care of the granular permissioning.

While the technical aspects of assigning and propagating permissions in all the different applications are not in the scope of this book, there are general principles that apply everywhere. Methods your teams decide to follow for applying permissions in the applications will have direct consequences for group management in Active Directory.

6.1.1 Nested Groups vs. Propagated Permissions

Thinking of a shared folder hierarchy within the first levels where the permissions are explicitly applied, there are multiple management models that your organization can utilize. Look at the simple three-level hierarchy in Figure 6-1. There are multiple ways to delegate the management of this folder tree.

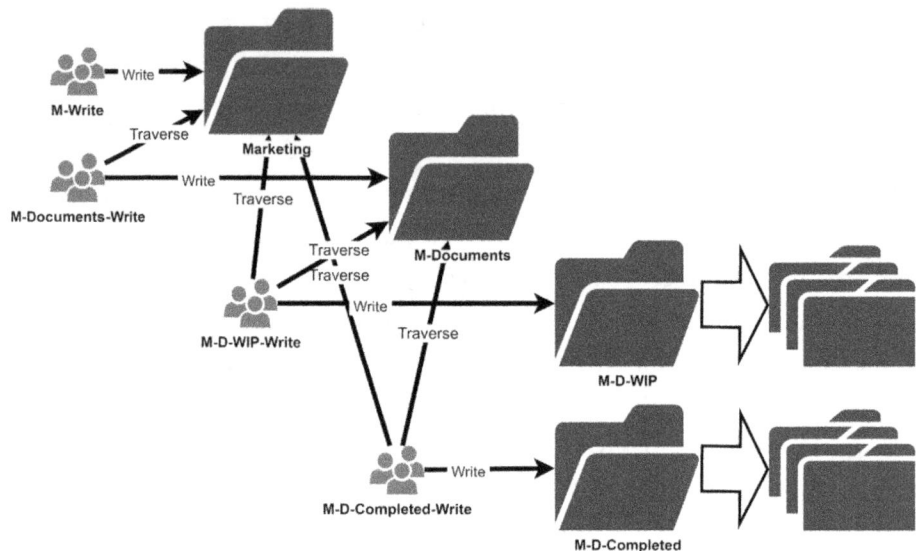

Figure 6-1. The management model dictates how permissions are assigned

1. **Explicit assignment.** Every group is only assigned permissions on the level it is intended to (plus traverse permissions above it); they are not propagated. On the deepest level, permissions are propagated down so that the folder subtree below "M-D-WIP" has the same permissions as that folder itself: The group "M-D-WIP-Write" has write access and can create subfolders; the group "M-D-WIP-Read" has read access; and so on. If a user has to be given write access to the "M-Documents" folder, they have to be added to the "M-Documents-Write" group explicitly. Each folder is assigned one read ACE and one write ACE, and the folders higher up in the hierarchy are also assigned multiple Traverse ACEs, one for each subfolder. However,

the management model in many organizations dictates that permissions given on a higher level be retained on the levels below it. This requirement can be satisfied in three ways (we do not consider just giving the user memberships in all the required groups because it is not "automatic," although this method would satisfy the effective access requirement).

2. **Explicit assignment on multiple levels.** In this construct, the "M-Documents-Write" group is given explicit write permissions on "M-D-WIP" and "M-D-Completed," and the "M-Write" group is given write permissions on the "M-Documents" and its subfolders. This way, every folder on the third level has three read ACEs and three write ACEs deployed to it; every folder on the second level has two read ACEs and two write ACEs, and so on. Traverse ACEs are not needed if the Traverse right is granted along with Read/Write.

3. **Explicit assignment with nested memberships.** The propagation of effective permissions can also be achieved by nesting the "M-Documents-Write" group into the "M-D-WIP-Write" and "M-D-Completed-Write" as well as nesting "M-Write" into "M-Documents-Write." This way, a member of "M-Write" will effectively have write permissions on the entire "Marketing" subtree without creating more ACEs.

4. **Permissions inheritance.** By leaving permissions inheritance active, you can also solve the requirement of having permissions trickle down from the top. This is the "go-to" method of assigning permissions in many organizations. Traverse ACEs are still needed on the upper levels.

The last approach is different from the other three in that for high-privileged users it yields the least group memberships stored in the token – a "top-level reader" or "top-level writer" only has one group for the whole hierarchy! The least desirable approach for these users is the third one (or the equivalent method of assigning all required memberships directly to the user which, to be fair, can be taken care of by automation and IAM). In this case, the token contains all the subfolder-specific groups!

For users with granular access to the lowest-level folders (which will probably constitute the majority), there is not much difference in effective behavior, no matter what delegation methodology your organization chooses. However, if you choose to propagate permissions from the top down, you have to make 100% sure that they will not change in the future – repermissioning a top-level folder with inheritance enabled all the way down can cause major disruption of the file server's performance.

Warning   A mistake in day-to-day administration may also lead to resource exhaustion due to unintended repermissioning – always lock down the right to change permissions and use automation wherever possible!

CHAPTER 6   ENGINEERING AUTHORIZATION

6.1.2 The Much-Dreaded Token Bloat

Why is it important how many groups end up being stored in the security token anyway? The answer lies in the token size and restrictions different systems put on it. Each group the user is a member of, directly or via nesting, contributes to the size of the token. If a migration is ongoing and both users and groups have **sidHistory** populated, SIDs contained in that attribute (of the user itself and of any nested group) are also included, unless the access occurs over a trust and the SIDs contained in sidHistory are filtered out.

There are actually two kinds of data structures that impose restrictions on the number of groups:

- The **Kerberos token** ("Authorization Context") is part of the PAC structure of the TGT. If DAC is used, it also contains the user's and computer's claims information. The number of groups that the token may contain is not limited as such, but the token size is. The registry value **MaxTokenSize** allows values of up to 65,535 bytes; the default value for modern Windows version is 48,000 bytes and that for Windows 7 and older was 12,000 bytes. It is not recommended to set this limit higher than 48,000 because many applications have a hard data transfer limit of 64k and use base64 encoding that adds 33% to the data size. Different kinds of SIDs contribute differently to the ticket size.

- The **LSA access token** generated on the endpoints the user logs on to has a hard limit of 1,024 SIDs, which includes well-known SIDs, leaving space for 1,010 custom SIDs. This limitation is not specific to Kerberos but applies equally if using NTLM for authentication.

CHAPTER 6   ENGINEERING AUTHORIZATION

The Kerberos token size calculation used to be an exact science, but since Server 2012 introduced resource SID compression and DAC claims that are also part of the PAC, the ticket size became slightly less predictable. If you **know** that DAC claims have not been defined, you may choose to ignore the SID compression, in which case the ticket size can be calculated as follows:

- The base value is 1,200 bytes.

- Every SID from sidHistory (user or any group) contributes 40 bytes.

- Every universal group from a different domain contributes 40 bytes.

- Every global group, universal group from the same domain, or a domain local group contributes 8 bytes.

- If unconstrained Kerberos delegation will be used, double the lot.

So, in a single-domain forest with sidHistory cleaned out for all objects, the default maximum value allows for 5,850 group memberships (or half that if the token is to be used with delegation), which is well beyond the limit for the LSA token. To reduce the number of SIDs being added to the LSA token, resource forests can be a great help, and the plural is important. Looking back at Figure 6-1, all groups displayed there could be – and usually they would be! – Domain local groups from the file server's domain. *Remember, Domain Local groups can only be assigned permissions in their own domain but accept members from everywhere, including trusted forests.* When the TGT is generated, domain local groups from other domains and forests are not included. It is when the user tries to access a resource in a different domain that the LSA on the resource builds their access token (adding server's local groups if any of AD groups is nested into them!) and recognizes Domain Local group memberships. By placing resources in different resource domains or forests, we can reduce both the TGT PAC size and the LSA token size quite significantly!

> **Be prepared!** If you end up having too many groups in the token no matter how you split the resources, and the business is not prepared to review their delegation model and granularity, it may indeed be time to start evaluating Dynamic Access Control for file server access. You would be putting a certain additional load on the file servers, but the token size should be able to shrink quite drastically. If you are not using Windows file servers, they may still support a subset of DAC features (NetApp, for instance, supports most of them on CIFS shares with NTFS emulation).

It is worth noting, if only for the sake of completeness, that those who go against the decades-old wisdom and assign permissions to individual users instead of groups do not have to deal with token bloat. The phenomena they *do* have to deal with, though, are usually much worse and harder to get under control.

6.1.3 Enumerating Group Memberships

Since the groups that make up the token are so important, how can we quickly evaluate how many groups will be included in it? Active Directory user objects have multiple constructed attributes that offer insights into the group memberships:

- **msds-memberOfTransitive** includes DNs of all nested groups from the same forest, including distribution groups and their parents, but excluding domain local groups from other domains and also excluding the primary group

233

- **msds-tokenGroupNames** includes DNs of all groups that become part of the token: global, universal, and domain local from the user's own domain

- **tokenGroups** includes SIDs of all groups listed in **msds-tokenGroupNames**

- **msds-tokenGroupNamesGlobalAndUniversal** includes DNs of all global and universal groups that become part of the token

- **tokenGroupsGlobalAndUniversal** includes SIDs of all groups listed in **msds-tokenGroupNamesGlobalAndUniversal**

- **msds-tokenGroupNamesNoGCAcceptable** includes DNs of all groups from the same domain as the user, including domain local groups from the user's own domain

- **tokenGroupsNoGCAcceptable** includes SIDs of all groups listed in **msds-tokenGroupNamesNoGCAcceptable**

Attributes listing the SIDs were part of the Active Directory schema from the beginning; **msds-memberOfTransitive** was introduced with Server 2012R2, and the "Names" attributes became available with Server 2016. Bear in mind that the "Names" attributes take a while to include groups from different domains. **tokenGroups** is usually updated fairly quickly.

As is mostly the case with constructed attributes, they cannot be returned in a search result unless the search was focussed on one object only – the user in question. The following PowerShell code returns the tokenGroupNames of a user:

```
Get-ADUser -SearchBase "<User DN>" -SearchScope Base -Filter *
-Properties "msDS-tokenGroupNames" |
Select-Object -ExpandProperty "msDS-tokenGroupNames"
```

the distinguishing factor here being **-SearchScope Base**, which specifies that only the base object will be searched. The script code **6.1-Estimate-TokenSize.ps1** briefly demonstrates token size calculations. To precisely calculate the token size, the **sidHistory** of both the user and any of the groups has to be taken into account, and also if the universal groups are from the user's own domain (8 bytes) or from a different one (40 bytes).

6.2 Role-Based Access Control (RBAC) Models

For applications like file servers that use the Windows security model for authorization exclusively, the entire RBAC must be built using group memberships and nestings. Many application vendors do not use the Windows security model directly but follow the same process: build an access token from all groups, including nested memberships, add the user's own identity on top, then evaluate each principal in the token against the permissions on the desired resource.

> **Note** Authorization in Windows file servers can be more complex but we agreed to leave DAC out of the equation, and File Server Resource Manager (FSRM) is not in scope of this book.

All role-based access control models are based on the assumption that for each person's current role in the organization it is known what resources in what applications they will need to access to perform their duties. This is not necessarily restricted to one application (although most examples found in books and on the Internet only deal with file servers). For example, a Marketing Manager could need

CHAPTER 6   ENGINEERING AUTHORIZATION

- Write access to file shares where spreadsheets about marketing campaigns are stored
- Read access to file shares where marketing materials like PDFs, videos, or graphics files are stored
- Startup and Shutdown access to a number of VMs performing media scraping
- Write access to a SQL database that holds keywords for media scraping
- Read access to a PostGreSQL database that holds the results of media scraping
- Read access to a telephone directory of press partners
- Read access to ERP for pulling performance indicators for correlating them with marketing activities
- Normal employee access to the time-sheet and time-off application for themselves
- Manager access to the time-sheet and time-off application for their team

The list goes on and on. The idea behind RBAC is that, if tomorrow a second Marketing Manager would be hired to split the workload with the existing one, assigning the manager to the same role or selection of roles would be enough to immediately provide them the same application and data access the current manager has. If identities to be assigned roles are Active Directory accounts, it makes sense to base the roles themselves on Active Directory groups!

When designing RBAC, keep in mind that "Deny" permissions should not be used with RBAC groups. Otherwise, adding a user to multiple roles may prove to be not entirely additive in terms of permissions granted.

6.2.1 AGDLP – Lots and Lots of Groups

When researching RBAC in conjunction with Active Directory, the AGDLP model as pictured in Figure 6-2 is the most frequently quoted design. Accounts (**A**) are added to global groups (**G**), which, in turn, are nested into domain local groups (**DL**). Those groups are assigned permissions on actual resources. In the more generalized RBAC jargon, the global groups are "Role Groups" and the domain local groups are "Authorization Groups."

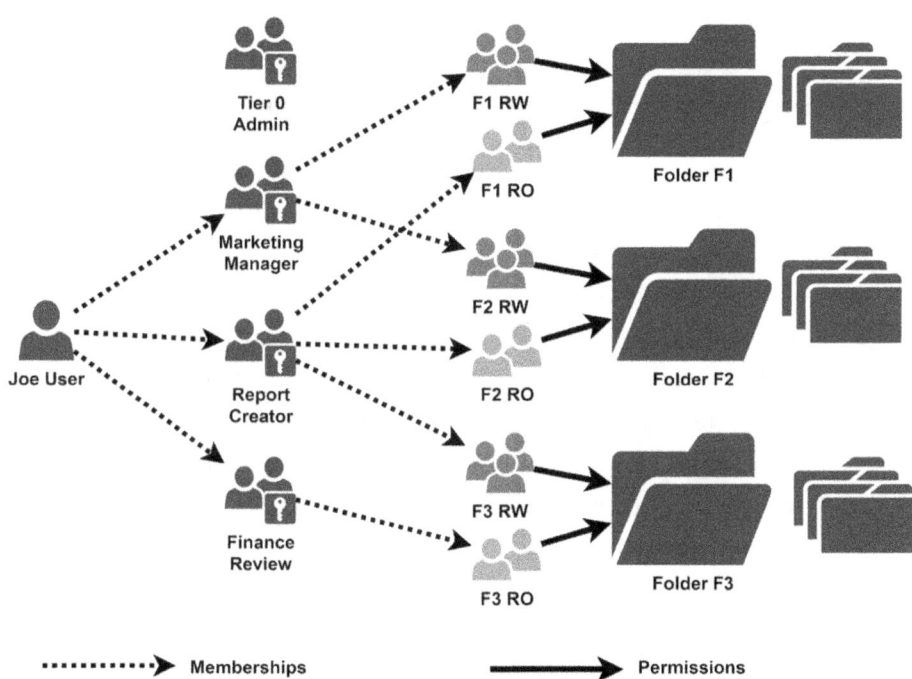

Figure 6-2. Joe User has write permissions on all folders, albeit through different roles

If you visualize not one but three folder hierarchies and many more folders on each level than depicted here, it becomes clear very quickly that an organization embracing this sort of granular control will end up

CHAPTER 6   ENGINEERING AUTHORIZATION

having lots of groups, which, by the way, is not a problem per se if naming conventions are adhered to and the process of creating and permissioning groups is automated as part of the process of creating the actual resource. There are third-party tools for that, or you can roll your own using whatever automation you have in place. However, it is also clear that persons who have many roles (or roles requiring access to many resources) are in acute danger of token bloat.

In Figure 6-2, we intentionally did not give any of the folders (resources) names that would hint at their purpose. It was just to illustrate how permissions are granted using AGDLP. The sad truth is, though, that RBAC does not always make sense, even if it weren't for token bloat. There are several scenarios that do not lend themselves well to role-based access control:

- Project-based resources (**AGP** or **AP**). In many organizations, there are thousands of such initiatives floating around at any given time, with cross-departmental and cross-role access requirements to resources. However, structures to be accessed within the project are usually flat (one shared folder, one SharePoint site, one VMware vApp, etc.). After the project is done, resources are partially destroyed, and the rest is archived. Providing authorization groups for these resources for a limited period of time is a waste of effort. If a project can be mapped to existing roles, grant access to the role groups. If only a handful of people are working on a project, granting permissions to users without creating any groups can be easier on the token size, especially if supported by automation.

CHAPTER 6　ENGINEERING AUTHORIZATION

- Swap folders (**AGP** or **AP**). This is a special case of a project resource with an extremely short life span. Since it is known in advance that the folder and all permissions granted on it will be gone in a few days or weeks, creating dedicated groups for this doesn't make much sense. Grant permissions to existing roles or even individual users – this is not a problem, performance-wise, while the folder is empty.

- Process-based resources (**ADLP**). This is an extreme case of a project resource in that persons from all over the organization are involved but none of the predefined roles would apply; however, a process is usually a permanent fixture, so managing permissions on a per-user basis is not a good fit; create a domain local group for the process and add the participants to the group directly.

- Applications that do not support nested groups, cross-domain nested groups, or cross-forest nested groups. This can always happen if a particular application does not rely on Windows to build an authorization token but evaluates the memberships themselves using LDAP. You can usually work with **AGP** in these cases.

Since all of the use cases listed above are fairly common in today's organizations, AGDLP in particular and RBAC in general usually fail to deliver on what is often considered the most important part of their value proposition: **You cannot reliably determine what permissions a particular user has in the overall environment simply by looking at their direct group memberships.**

6.2.2 AGDLP, AGUDLP, or AUDLP?

When designing roles based on groups, always consider what realms the users will be coming from. Global groups can, despite the name, only contain members from their own domain. In a multidomain forest, AGDLP dictates a separate role group per domain which is not very intuitive. To allow adding users from multiple domains to RBAC, Microsoft and others formulated the AGUDLP model where the global role group is nested in a universal group, which in turn is nested into the many domain local groups granting the role its permission. There is still a separate global role group per domain, but the domain local groups only have one membership – that of the universal group.

Since every slot in the authorization token is extremely valuable, there is a lot to be said for forgoing the global groups altogether and just adding the users to the universal group (AUDLP). This approach has the additional benefit of being able to use the role group directly in modern and cloud-based applications (Exchange prefers universal groups since 2007, and Microsoft also recommends this group scope as the best candidate for synchronizing to Entra ID; at the time of writing, the "Group Writeback" feature will always create universal groups).

If users who are to be granted permissions by RBAC come from different forests, you are stuck with multiple per-forest global or universal role groups, which can then be added to per-domain domain local authorization groups. Do everybody a favor and name them identically across all forests!

6.2.3 Leveraging Distribution Groups

If you suspect a particular application of analyzing group memberships instead of the authorization token, you can try assigning permissions within that application to distribution groups instead of security groups. Despite several publications in the last 25 years stating otherwise, distribution groups do actually have a SID. However, it is not added to the Kerberos token, nor to the LSA token. And if you add a distribution group to a security group, the SID of that group is also not added to the token. The membership as such, however, is like any other: LDAP search for transitive memberships using `(memberOf:1.2.840.113556.1.4.1941= <Group DN>)` works, and, if you add a distribution group to a well-known privileged group, the distribution group and all its members get `adminCount` set to 1 after the next SDPROP cycle.

6.3 Delegating Administrative Tasks

While creating and maintaining RBAC for application and file access may not be up to the Active Directory team (until the day the users start suffering from token bloat, that is), delegating administrative tasks – both in AD and on member machines – is the Tier 0 administrator's prerogative. Since admin accounts will not usually participate in the general RBAC, token bloat is less of a concern. Still, a good delegation framework for administrative tasks is in order.

Even if hitting the 1,010 groups limit for administrative accounts is highly improbable (it would suggest a "God mode" account that should be avoided anyway), other size-related considerations may apply. If, for instance, you decide to adopt SCAMA for authentication, every group membership granted by a smart card certificate means an additional issuance policy included in the certificate template, blowing up the certificate size and putting its compatibility with cryptographic hardware in jeopardy. Keep this in mind when creating your delegation model.

> If the user overburdened by groups is a local administrator on the endpoint, violating the 1,010 groups limit will not prevent them from logging on. It is, however, very hard to predict which groups will be included in the LSA token and which ones will not.

CHAPTER 6   ENGINEERING AUTHORIZATION

In this section, we will list the typical tasks that are part of everyday administration and can be delegated explicitly using either permissions or memberships in specific well-known groups. As discussed in Chapter 4, an account (or a group) with read permissions on all objects in the forest, including those not normally visible to non-privileged identities, is a good idea. It goes without saying that this group should be empty when not actively used, and its memberships must be guarded by Tier 0 admins in the same closely managed manner all other memberships in Tier 0 groups are maintained.

If your organization qualifies as "enterprise" in terms of the definition in the Introduction, and hopefully even if it does not, you are probably using third-party technology that simplifies, automates, and delegates administrative tasks all the way up to Tier 0, so you may ask yourself, why bother? The answer is twofold:

- A malicious actor may not be willing and/or able to go after your enterprise management technology (which is good), but they can and will go after your AD. If the default overpermissioned methods of administration are still open but just not being used every day, they are still open for the attacker, too.

- We have seen every technology fail at least once. Your management product may fail, or your AD may fail, get recovered, but put the management and automation out of commission in the process. You will fix that too, eventually, but do you really need the pressure?

Remember what we said about a Red Forest earlier: A well-designed and well-managed Red Forest replaces big parts of almost any third-party management add-on at no cost and using technology that you already know inside and out.

6.3.1 Delegating AD Administration: Tier 0

Tier 0 administration of AD objects happens on several levels:

- Basic AD infrastructure: Forests, Domains, Trusts, Schema, Topology, and Configuration (Authentication Policies, Fine Grained Password Policies, permissions, global directory service configuration, etc.)

- Management of Tier 0 OUs, users, and groups

- Management of OUs and tiering groups for the lower tiers

- Creation of unprivileged users and groups for the lower tiers

- Management of computer accounts and service accounts for Tier 0 facilities

- Management of Kerberos encryption and delegation for all objects (application administrators setting up constrained delegation or RBCD was a nice idea, but this ability should not be given to Tier 1 admins – it is clearly a Tier 0 task that even has a potential to increase the token size for a high number of users)

Permissions needed for some of these tasks can be subdivided into individual rights or consolidated into a more generic "Tier 0 Admin" role without breaking it up in too small chunks. The most important distinguishing factor should always be the frequency of the task being delegated. Users, groups, and computers for Tier 1 and Tier 2 are provisioned every day. Management of Tier 0 accounts can be a biweekly occurrence, whereas schema updates, new trusts, and changes in Tier 0-related OU structures are much less frequent. They do not have to be delegated to everyone, even within the Tier 0 team.

6.3.2 Delegating AD Administration: Lower Tiers

In the lower tiers, administrators should be allowed basic management tasks for "their" AD objects:

- Managing group memberships

- Setting groups' description and "Managed By" (but without the ability to allow the manager to edit membership if this permission wasn't delegated by Tier 0)

- Managing the users' job, address, and communication attributes

If the administrator isolation framework adopted by your organization includes "zoning" rather than "tiering" (different applications isolated from each other in the same way Tier 0 is isolated from Tier 1), some of the tasks may have to be "zoned" as well, increasing the overall number of groups for application administration.

6.3.3 Delegating Group Policy Administration

Managing Group Policies involves the following tasks:

- Creating Group Policy objects and managing their delegations and WMI filter, including the creation of new WMI filters

- Editing Group Policy content

- Linking Group Policies to (and unlinking them from) Tier 0 objects like Tier 0 OUs, domains, and sites

- Linking Group Policies to (and unlinking them from) OUs in lower tiers

There are quirks in the behavior of the Group Policy Management Console (GPMC) and the Group Policy Editor that make granular delegation of Group Policy management not as straightforward as it could be. We will unwrap them in Chapter 7.

6.3.4 Delegating DNS Administration

If your organization decided to forgo AD-integrated DNS and use a third-party technology, you can skip this section and read up on proper management delegation in that product instead. But whatever the technology underneath, consider the following tasks:

- Creating or editing a DNS zone (including adding NS records and managing permissions for zone transfers)
- Managing conditional forwarders (they are really just a special case of zones)
- Deleting a DNS zone
- Managing records related to Domain Controllers and AD services, both in the _msdcs zone and in the domain zones
- Adding a new DNS record
- Updating an existing DNS record
- Deleting a DNS record

If you *are* using AD integrated DNS, the goal of administrative delegation must be to be able to keep the "DnsAdmins" group empty since it's grossly overpermissioned. Ideally, you would want to reduce the permissions of this group, too, but then you have to repeat parts of this operation for every new Domain Controller. Scripting this, therefore, is an excellent idea.

6.3.5 Delegating Server Administration

We have already established that the default nesting of "Domain Admins" in the local Administrators group of every machine joining a domain needs to be removed. An easy replacement is putting a custom group, ideally an application-specific one, into the local Administrators group of each server belonging to that application. However, in addition to that group, you might want to delegate application-specific administration more explicitly. Hyper-V, DHCP, WSUS, and several other Windows Server roles automatically create local security groups for themselves that are usually a good fit for the typical administrative tasks.

In other cases, all the privileges an "Application Administrator" would need are write access to certain folders and the right to restart a certain service, maybe to reboot the entire application server machine. These types of permissions can be delegated by Group Policy. Do bear in mind that, in order to edit startup and shutdown permissions for a service, you must edit the policy on a computer where the service is actually installed (but as a user with permissions to edit a GPO!). A scheduled task running as SYSTEM and deployed via GPO may be a better option. We will discuss that in more detail in the next chapter.

6.3.6 Delegating Client Administration

For client administration, temporarily obtaining local administrator permission is usually granular enough. Normally, client administration **interactively on the device** shouldn't ever happen. If you are doing it on a regular basis, you are doing it wrong (as an organization). Automate recurring tasks like deleting a file from a user's profile through your existing configuration management – its agent runs as SYSTEM and does not need any additional permissions to do the work. If you do need to access a client device interactively, retrieving a password for a local account from LAPS could be enough in many cases, and you don't need an account permanently assigned local admin rights on a large portion of your client fleet!

We will revisit several aspects of administration delegation in more detail in Chapter 8.

6.4 Modern Defaults

Authorization is influenced by the IT environment and the organization's accepted working practices more than any other Active Directory function. But since AD is not offering a premade (and not very well-engineered) authorization framework to begin with, there is no need to formulate "modern defaults to replace the legacy defaults." Instead, "modern defaults for authorization" are guidelines to solve your authorization requirements in the most efficient and secure way.

6.4.1 RBAC Is Not Always the Answer

Remember that Role-Based Access Control is not always the answer, even from the process perspective. Sometimes delegating permissions to people directly reflects the desired business process better. Sometimes one of the RBAC layers is not needed – either the roles layer or the authorization layer! Some systems simply will not be able to use the same role groups that you provision for business applications and file server access.

If in multi-domain forests, AUDLP is your AGDLP. Given that more and more applications give preference to universal groups, AUDLP might just be your new AGDLP even in single-domain forests! Stick to naming conventions: in a multi-forest organization, a group for the same role must have the same name in every forest.

CHAPTER 6   ENGINEERING AUTHORIZATION

Monitor the number of SIDs in your user`s **tokenGroups** on a regular basis. You don't need to do it in real time, but doing it once a month helps establish a trend and start corrective action long before it becomes a problem! Keep in mind that as soon as users access resources cross-forest or even cross-domain **tokenGroups** does not represent a complete answer. If you are actively using AGDLP or AUDLP at scale, keeping track of domain local group memberships definitely helps to follow the token size more closely.

6.4.2 Ask Where They Get Authorization Info From

Differentiate between applications that evaluate the Windows security token for authorization and those who enumerate group memberships on their own. If an application uses an LDAP bind for authorization, there may be two caveats to this:

- More often than not, nested group memberships, especially those spanning multiple domains or even forests, will not work.

- The bind account (either "the" bind account or the user for whom authorization is being performed) possibly must have visibility over the group objects!

6.4.3 File Servers Are Still at the Core of Most Authorization Frameworks

Plan authorization for file server access carefully and keep an eye on the overall number of groups a user may end up being a member of. There is no other application likely to introduce as many groups in as short a time frame! Avoid nesting permission groups as much as possible – a couple more ACEs, even if they have to be propagated far and deep before they take effect, are a small price to pay for not having a hundred additional groups in the token. If you don't see any reasonable way to reduce the number of groups for everybody, consider splitting file services over multiple domains or even forests. If all else fails, start drafting a Dynamic Access Control framework for your file services. But remember: DAC will only help if the number of permission groups is reduced by an order of magnitude without introducing as many claims into the token as groups removed from it.

The best way to reduce the management overhead, including that for authorization, of file servers is by restructuring the processes to move documents your users work with to different platforms like SharePoint. Funnily enough, file servers you will *never* be able to get rid of (Document Management, shopfloor automation, etc.) usually require the least amount of granular permissions since there are only a handful of function or service accounts accessing them on behalf of the users.

6.4.4 Administration Is Different

Authorization of administrative tasks (outside of AD) usually requires authorizing functions access as well as (or even more than) file and data access. For applications, you will have to find a balance between exposure to lateral movement and micromanagement.

For client management, authorization may involve reading the local admin password from LAPS rather than granting actual admin permissions to AD accounts or groups on a permanent basis.

6.5 Summary

In this chapter, we looked at authorization from the identity provider perspective. While AD does not offer an authorization framework in the same form it presents us with a lookup and authentication framework, there are still hardcoded behaviors and limiting factors. In a multi-domain, multi-forest environment, the question of "Have I got too many groups?" becomes even more difficult to answer reliably than in a single-domain environment.

The RBAC model of administration, while looking extremely good on paper, will always require exceptions. The earlier you catch the trend of exceptions becoming more frequent than the rule, the smoother your transition to a more dynamic, business-case-oriented model will be.

We would have loved to provide a detailed insight into Dynamic Access Control introduced with Server 2012. However, it is as complex as any other AD feature, or maybe even more so since it involves ADRMS integration if done properly, but only covers file servers as an actual use case.

Last but not least, remember the two "backlinks" from authorization to authentication:

- Kerberos delegation reduces the number of groups a user can be a member of by doubling the memory required for each SID.

- Claims created for DAC can be used in Authentication Policies.

CHAPTER 7

Engineering Configuration

When a Windows device joins Active Directory, it not only becomes a security principal with permissions on AD objects and structures but also subjects itself to configurations handed down from the domain it is now a member in. There have been attempts by third parties to extend this relationship to Linux endpoints as well, but they did not get much traction, even in organizations that do routinely join Linux devices to their AD-based Kerberos realms.

In this chapter, we will concentrate on delivering configurations to Windows servers and clients by means of Active Directory technologies.

7.1 AD and Configuration Management

One of the most popular misunderstandings about Active Directory is that it provides "management" functionality of various kinds, configuration management being named quite often, along with identity and access management. While "management" is not a very well-defined term, some features of a configuration management system clearly are missing in AD:

- Impact estimation: If I change X, on how many systems (and which ones) will it lead to an actual change in configuration?

- Lifecycle tracking: Who introduced this configuration and when? Who changed the setting X in the area Y, and when did the change occur? And, sometimes even more important: When was the change delivered to device Z, and when did it take effect there?

- Versioning, which closely ties into lifecycle tracking: If I know the configuration was good last Friday, is there a quick and reliable way to get back to that state?

None of these questions can be answered by AD alone, and the author never encountered a third-party tool that would provide these insights across all areas of configuration delivery that AD supports.

7.1.1 Configuration Delivery – What's in the Box?

Active Directory offers three ways to deliver configurations to its members and domain controllers:

- Hardcoded behavior that is triggered by AD join (e.g., adding "Domain Admins" to the local "Administrators") or by promotion to DC (disabling the local SAM database and switching interactive authentication to AD).

- Information stored in AD objects that causes the machine or the user session to behave in a certain way (e.g., setting the logon script and home drive attributes of a user causes the logon process to run the script, map the network drive to the specified letter, and redirect various file operations to that drive).

CHAPTER 7   ENGINEERING CONFIGURATION

- Information stored in Group Policy. This is without a doubt the area of Active Directory most administrators associate with "configuration management." Numerous books have been written on the topic; in fact, at the time of writing, at least one new book is in the process of being published! As client systems slowly transition out of Active Directory and into the public cloud, administrators in those organizations are struggling with the task of providing an identical management experience both to AD-joined clients and to "modernized" ones.

Operating system behaviors based on AD attributes can be problematic in modern dynamic working environments:

- A different behavior may be desired, e.g., mapping a home drive on terminal servers and hardwired workstations but not on laptop clients

- A consistent behavior may be desired but not possible in all situations, e.g., a logon script cannot run after an offline logon

Sometimes it is not the operating system itself but an application that takes advantage of data stored in AD (user object or computer object). Outlook, for instance, will use the value from the logged-on user's **mail** attribute to create a new MAPI profile. If AD is not available at that moment, Outlook autoconfiguration will not be as smooth as in an online situation.

Examples of attributes with hardcoded behavior of the user session are:

homeDirectory (local path or UNC path)

homeDrive (if set, the UNC path from **homeDirectory** is mapped to this letter)

CHAPTER 7   ENGINEERING CONFIGURATION

profilePath (if set, the user profile will be considered roaming)

scriptPath (logon script relative to NETLOGON)

If your clients are mobile and you are not enforcing pre-logon VPN so that your users may end up logging on offline, you'll have to consider the behaviors governed by these attributes – a network home drive will not be mapped unless you enable the "Offline Files" feature and allow the users to take their home drive on the road with them. Logon scripts will not run – if they perform actions that are important for the overall user experience, you have to find another way to initiate these actions. Roaming profiles and the problems that arise from using them in dynamic work scenarios could easily fill an entire chapter – luckily for us, they are not in the scope of this book! However, you really should think twice before you start populating any of these attributes – there may be a better way to provide the same functionality without sacrificing flexibility.

Dial-in attributes (**msNP*** and **msRADIUS*** attributes) are present both for user and computer objects but rarely used in the modern days since network access controllers and dial-in (VPN) concentrators prefer their built-in management to the AD settings. The latest remote access features of Windows itself – Direct Access and AlwaysOn VPN – both ignore these settings. Some third-party vendors like Fortinet use **msNPAllowDialin** to control the ability of users and devices to establish a VPN connection, mainly because it's surfaced in ADUC as a checkbox.

A special case of a behavior-defining attribute is **userParameters** where the remote desktop connection configuration (RDS profile path, RDS home folder and so on) is stored. Although defined in the Active Directory schema as a "unicode string," it contains a specially encoded data structure. The data itself is illegible without proper decoding, but a quick peek at the string reveals field names like CtxCfgPresent and CtxCfgFlags, hinting at the origins of this structure – Remote Desktop Protocol was originally developed for Microsoft by Citrix!

CHAPTER 7   ENGINEERING CONFIGURATION

7.2 Engineering Group Policy

Group Policies have been around longer than Active Directory has. Windows NT borrowed System Policies from Windows 95 and added the ability to apply user policies not only to individual users but to groups of users, and so the concept of a "Group Policy" was born.

Group policies are a very powerful way to transfer – and, if everything works as expected, apply – a variety of configuration settings to Windows systems and users logged on to them. However, since there is no built-in technology to *manage* these configuration settings, we must engineer our policy framework in a way that supports systems management rather than add unnecessary complexity and reduce the processing performance.

Performance of group policy application has been a topic of many a heated discussion over the decades, because policies, at least user policies, are applied immediately after logon and their processing time counts into the "time to desktop," a performance metric often used to gauge the quality of the end-user desktop experience. If you research this topic, you are likely to find statements like the following:

- Many individual policy objects each governing individual features or applications are processed slower than a monolithic GPO that has tons of unrelated settings in one object.

- WMI filters are detrimental to processing performance.

- Disabling the unused part of the policy (User or Computer) improves processing performance.

- Administrative templates must be deployed on every computer in the environment.

- Loopback processing only works for terminal servers.

Not all of these statements are true, and none of them is true in every situation.

7.2.1 Factors Influencing Group Policy Engineering

To provide a long-lasting framework for group policy management in your organization, consider the following:

Having lots of GPOs in your environment is not bad per se if you get the naming convention and the visibility right. Only the accounts who will either apply or manage/edit/view a certain policy need to know it exists in the first place. The process of building the Resultant Set of Policy (RSoP) begins with enumerating the **groupPolicyContainer** objects to which the "Apply Policy" right has been granted. This is done by the most performant facility in the whole process – the Domain Controller.

Since June 2016, the computer performing the actual policy processing needs to have "Read" (but not necessarily "Apply") rights to every policy that should be applied, even if it only contains user settings. Still, objects that cannot be seen will not be part of the enumeration, so no policy except the DDP should ever be filtered on "Authenticated Users" or "Domain Computers." Use dedicated targeting groups for this.

WMI Filter processing happens on the client very early in the process of building the RSoP. Avoid queries that are known for their poor performance, especially file system queries. Registry, AD, and SQL are further examples of queries that promise great flexibility (for administrators) but mostly end in tears (for end users). The hardcoded limitation of 30 seconds per filter doesn't really help much.

There are literally millions of WMI query examples published both in books by well-known experts and by independent bloggers, not counting discussion forums and newsgroups. Every single one of them begins with **SELECT ***, instructing the WMI provider to return objects full of properties to the Group Policy Client, while the latter only needs to know whether a result has been found at all! You should break out of this cycle and just

CHAPTER 7 ENGINEERING CONFIGURATION

return one property, the ones you filter on being good candidates. It will not give your users whole minutes of their lives back, but in a high-density VDI farm, these things can actually be measured.

Potentially long-running filter queries are not only found in WMI filters but also in the definitions of Item-Level Targeting (ILT) of GPPs.

Each Client-Side Extension (CSE) introduces its own load time. It is not easy to keep track of all the different CSEs that get activated once the RSoP has been built, but if you have a thousand individual settings in the RSoP and one particular CSE is only loaded for one of them but on many machines, it may be worth the while to look into providing this functionality by different means. While the performance profile of Microsoft native CSEs is relatively well known, third-party CSEs may introduce performance effects that are hard to troubleshoot. PowerShell code **7.1-Get-CSE.ps1** illustrates how CSE information can be gathered and visualized. Of course, only the CSEs actually installed and registered on the machine applying the policy will be processed.

Cross-domain or cross-forest GPO application, while technically possible and sometimes even desirable, doubles the time for Domain Controller discovery and RSoP computation. See if the existing profile management solutions can take care of user settings that really require access to the user forest so that for the majority of settings, Loopback processing can be used.

Do not use the software installation part of the group policy. Just don't. There are many ways to install software on a bunch of computers, and only two of them are really bad: manual installation on each device and group policy. You blow up your policy's size, you need MSI files of the highest quality, and you still do not get to know where the software has been successfully installed and, even more importantly, where it has not.

Local GPO can be used to provide a robust configuration baseline. To maintain security, it must be reinforced by domain GPOs serving identical settings and, of course, the exceptions to the baseline. But having the enterprise hardening and configuration baked into the local GPO can help maintain a certain level of configuration consistency in case a machine drops out of scope of its intended policies.

CHAPTER 7   ENGINEERING CONFIGURATION

An old admin wisdom dictates that DDP and DDCP should not be modified, or at least that only settings should be edited that have been set by default. The true reason for it is that certain settings can **only** be configured in these GPOs in order to take effect (password, lockout, and Kerberos policy in the DDP, security settings for Domain Controllers in the DDCP) so that if these GPOs become corrupted, they cannot just be replaced by a different custom GPO but have to be recreated using the DCGPOFIX command. Settings outside the predefined areas would be lost.

Note   Some of the settings are not only applied exclusively from the two default policies but also reflected back *into* them if introduced by other means. For example, password policy settings are transferred from the DDP to the domain head upon GPO application. But if we change the attributes directly on the domain head, the PDC Emulator will write them back into the DDP as shown in Figure 7-1! Changes to the local security policy on a DC are written back to the DDCP and propagated to all the other DCs in the domain.

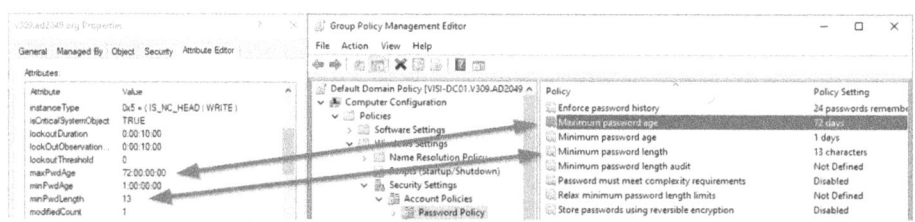

Figure 7-1. *Password settings are synchronized both ways between the domain head and DDP*

Keep these factors and peculiarities in mind when creating guidelines for your GPO administration.

7.2.2 Group Policy Security Considerations

From the security standpoint, Group Policy is a "gift that keeps on giving." Listing all the attack vectors that involve group policy is a gargantuan task, but just the highlights are scary enough:

- Cleartext passwords found in the Preferences of older GPOs. Well, almost cleartext – they are encrypted, of course, but the key is static and hardcoded in Windows. Inevitably, that key was leaked in 2014. Microsoft reacted by removing the ability to create new problematic GPPs from the group policy editor, but existing policies still work, meaning that if they are linked to something, then the passwords stored there are probably still valid! The problematic areas are: Data Sources, Local Users and Groups (specifically users), Scheduled Tasks and Services.

- Elevation and persistence through User Rights Assignment.

- Elevation and persistence through Restricted Groups (GPO) or Local Users and Groups (GPP).

- Defense Evasion through Audit Policies and Event Log configuration.

- Elevation and Persistence through Scheduled Tasks and Logon/Startup Scripts.

- Lateral movement and elevation through Desktop Shortcuts.

- Evasion and persistence through AppLocker policies and System Services.

- Persistence and elevation through Registry and File System rights.

CHAPTER 7   ENGINEERING CONFIGURATION

To make matters even worse, most of the GPO areas listed above are stored in the form of plaintext files (.inf and .csv for GPO, .xml for GPP) that are readable, searchable, and even editable, access rights permitting. This is yet another reason to manage access rights to GPOs very closely, both in AD and in SYSVOL. Remember: In SYSVOL, "Authenticated Users" have "Full Control" permissions at share level by default so that NTFS rights are all that is standing between an authenticated malicious actor and all the different attack vectors listed above.

7.2.3 The Right Tools for the Job

This section assumes that your team will be managing Group Policy using the built-in tools, i.e., the Group Policy Management Console. It is not a secret that these tools are lacking any "management" functions we discussed earlier in this chapter. At the time of writing, Microsoft is still offering Advanced Group Policy Management (AGPM) to Software Assurance holders; however, the future of this offering is uncertain – while the extended support end date was moved from July 2024 to April 2026, there is no published roadmap for the time beyond that.

Managing group policy in a highly specialized forest like the Red Forest or a resource forest specifically created to isolate domain local groups is easy and usually does not require any additional tooling. The policies are usually few and fairly static, managed by a small number of highly trusted personnel. Sticking to the overall guidance we are about to provide and to the naming convention agreed upon within your organization is enough to keep the group policy infrastructure in these smaller and simpler forests operational. It is in general-use forests where user accounts and/or client devices are located that you may benefit from a third-party solution to create and maintain a lifecycle and a delegation regime for your policies.

Before you start evaluating third-party offerings for group policy management, it is a good idea to consult your overall digital workplace strategy. If the clients are going to be cloud-joined with the next hardware

CHAPTER 7   ENGINEERING CONFIGURATION

refresh, most of the policies in effect now will become obsolete anyway. Instead of bringing in a new solution to manage the policies in AD, you should start developing a strategy for bringing them over to Intune or whatever MDM solution your organization is envisioning. Until then, a toolbox that allows you to (a) compare two states of the same policy and (b) restore its contents to a previous state may be just enough. For the first part, there is a Microsoft tool named "Policy Analyzer" shipped with the Microsoft Security Compliance Toolkit (SCT). For the second part, a bit of automation around **Backup-GPO** might just fit the bill. Since Policy Analyzer uses GPO backups to perform the comparison, it is a combination that can help achieve good results with very little effort. The code in **7.2-Backup-ChangedGPO.ps1** illustrates how this can be automated by keeping track of the state so that only changed GPOs get backed up on each execution.

7.2.4 Creating the Framework

In every good GPO framework, there are two layers: the baseline and the individual configurations. The baseline is usually derived from a hardening benchmark like CIS or SCT but can also contain configuration settings that are not security-related. Optimize the baseline for performance – no scripts, software installations, drive maps, and other long-running CSEs. Follow the CIS guidance and activate even those settings in the baseline that just reinforce the default behavior of the operating system. The defaults may change in the future; your desired behavior will not.

There will be multiple baseline GPOs – probably at least five (Domain Controllers, hardened servers, general servers, general clients, and relaxed clients like kiosks or shopfloor equipment). If you have regulated areas in your organization, you may end up with even more baselines, depending on the hardening you need to impose in the particular area. Even if it's not clear from the outset what differences there will be between the baselines, try to identify areas in advance that would *potentially* require a different baseline and put the policies and the permissions in place early, even if the contents of the policies are identical at first.

There is also a user part to the baseline. To decide on its placement, ask yourself (and the business) this: How often will a typical user switch not just between different computers that belong into the same baseline but also between areas with different baselines applied to them? Usually, it's not a very common occurrence, and you can put the user baseline into one GPO together with the computer baseline for the same area.

Much has been written in the last two decades about linking of GPOs within an OU structure. One recurring pattern here is the warning against both breaking inheritance and using GPO enforcement. The main reason for steering clear of these techniques is that it becomes increasingly difficult to visualize the RSoP if you use them extensively, especially if you enforce multiple GPOs that contain overlapping settings. If you manage your policies closely, you will not be needing these techniques:

- Do not delegate policy linking to application owners, leave it to Tier 1 or Tier 2 admins (Tier 0 admins for the domain head, Tier 0-related OUs, default containers, and sites).

- Only delegate editing the settings, not the security filtering, to application owners. Be aware that the default "Edit settings" permission includes changing the WMI filter applied to the GPO.

- You cannot limit editing of a GPO to only certain settings, areas, or CSEs. Therefore, if you delegate editing of policies to application owners, these policies must have a **lower** priority than the baseline! Exceptions to the baseline must only be made by trusted admins from the respective tier.

CHAPTER 7 ENGINEERING CONFIGURATION

- Link both the baseline and the individual settings as close to the targeted object(s) as possible, even if it results in many linked OUs for the same policy. Consider inheritance – no custom settings policy should be linked closer than the baseline!

Individual settings come in two flavors: Exceptions to the baseline (i.e., settings that are also present in the baseline, overriding it) and "application settings." The former must have **higher** priority than the baseline, but their editing must only be delegated to very trustworthy admins who know what they're doing and are intimately familiar with the baseline they will be defining an exception to. The latter must have **lower** priority than the baseline to prevent settings made by application admins from overriding the baseline. For targeting individual settings, you should apply the same wisdom that dictates that permissions on file structures be only applied at 1 to 3 levels. Compare Figure 7-2 through Figure 7-4. In the former, the admins followed the decades-old pattern and relied on OU placement which led to the application GPOs effectively overriding the baseline!

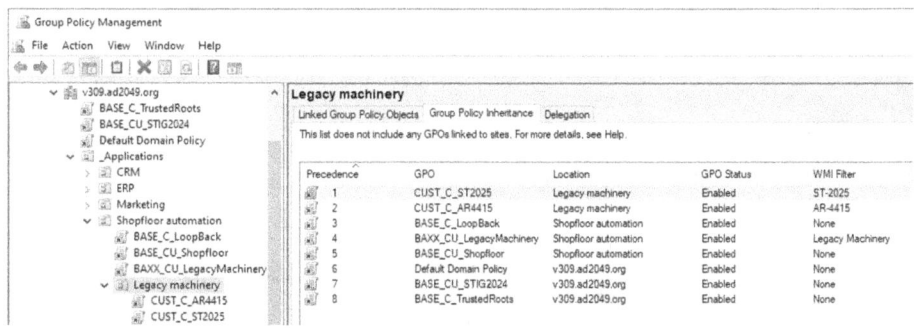

Figure 7-2. *Unintended effect of close linking*

263

CHAPTER 7 ENGINEERING CONFIGURATION

By enabling enforcement on the "Shopfloor automation" level, we could remediate this as shown in Figure 7-3.

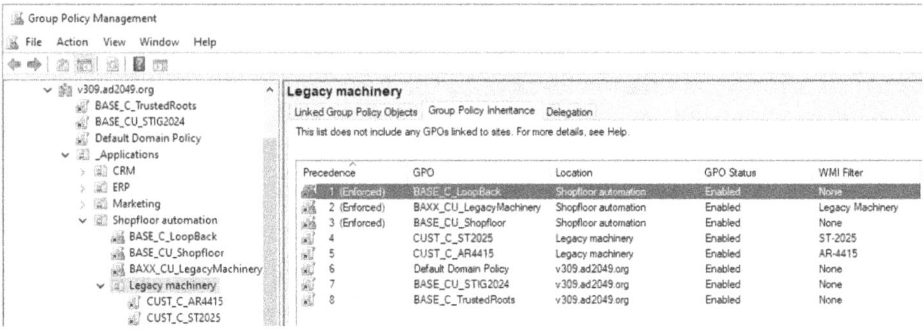

Figure 7-3. Enforcement restores the right order but makes it less obvious

If there were lots of Sub-OUs below "Shopfloor automation," it might even be a somewhat elegant solution. However, since the custom policies are already closely targeted using an equipment-specific WMI filter, linking everything on the "Shopfloor automation" level could provide the same result without resorting to enforcement, as shown in Figure 7-4.

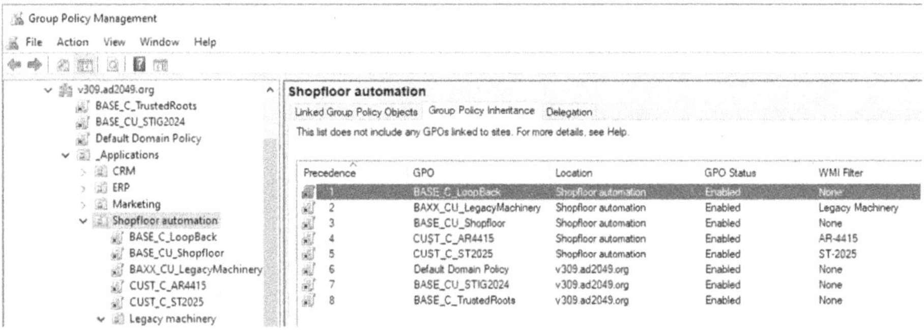

Figure 7-4. Stop linking at baseline level

While the custom policies are not in danger of overriding the baseline anymore, they still override the DDP and the Trusted Roots. The DDP should not be a problem since it only contains settings relevant to the behavior of the domain. If you want to protect Trusted Roots, link it to the baseline-level OUs. Do not delegate the "Link GPO" permissions on OUs below the baseline level.

Targeting individual settings can be achieved in several ways. Depending on the delegation model you choose, having hundreds of individual GPOs can be a great solution approach because each group a particular GPO's management has been delegated to will only see that GPO and not the others in the console. If a small group of highly privileged administrators are tasked with implementing individual settings on behalf of application owners, avoid the anti-pattern of creating "monster GPPs" with hundreds or thousands of item-level targeted settings. Each of the ILT filters will be evaluated on every computer and/or user session the policy is targeted to! It is also easy to make a mistake and edit the wrong item.

A naming convention will be an important part of your GPO framework. Avoid the anti-pattern of beginning the names by "GPO" – it's not like the names will be used (or visible) anywhere else, and you have to avoid confusion. Including a "C" or "U" in the policy name to indicate that it contains computer or user settings is a good idea on paper. There is, however, hardly an area of group policy management where the author observed more configuration drift over the years than here. You could make it a habit of disabling computer settings in "U" policies and vice versa – something that can be quickly analyzed and monitored. Do keep in mind, though, that the "Edit Settings" permission also allows changing this part of the configuration! Contrary to popular belief, disabling truly unused (i.e., empty) parts of the configuration does not have any measurable effect on processing performance, because a. each GPO is always downloaded in full, and b. if one part of the policy *is* empty, then so is the **gPCUserExtensionNames** or **gPCMachineExtensionNames** attribute, respectively.

Warning Access rights permitting, an administrator can create OUs from the Group Policy Management Console. These OUs are created without the "Protection from Accidental Deletion" applied by default if creating OUs in ADUC!

7.3 Advanced Group Policy Techniques

There are several GPO-related techniques that are not part of the GPO management framework but are still worth discussing since they have the potential of making your life hell – or saving you valuable time!

7.3.1 Do Not Use the Central Store

The "central store," i.e., the PolicyDefinitions folder in your policy store in SYSVOL holding ADMX templates for use when editing the GPOs, is one of those ideas that looked good on paper. It was introduced with Windows Vista/Server 2008, and its use has been warmly recommended countless times over the years. Voices against this technological gimmick have been few and not very loud, yet the author, albeit guilty of using the central store in the past, would like to add his voice to this small but constantly growing choir. Microsoft showed first signs of not standing firmly behind the central store idea as well by introducing Windows 11 policy settings that were incompatible with identically named settings for Windows 10! But even if it weren't for technical incompatibilities: Do not use the central store. If you want to keep your policy definitions up to date and add ADMX files for new applications in a centralized manner, use your software distribution facility, scripting automation, or good judgment to just copy the correct template files to the local PolicyDefinitions folder of your PAW.

7.3.2 Leverage Starter GPOs

If you delegate policy creation for certain recurring use cases, consider leveraging Starter GPOs for it. You cannot use them for creating baseline-type policies since they only contain settings presented by administrative templates (so no "Starter GPP" objects either), but for those, you can quickly create, say, a Microsoft Office GPO with all the different settings relevant for your organization already prepopulated. Starter GPOs aren't for everyone, but if your organization happens to require the exact use case described above, they can be a great time-saver.

There is a small potential for confusion here – once enabled, by default, "Authenticated Users" are permitted to see the "Starter GPOs" folder and even click "New..." to create a starter object. The seemingly relaxed permissions end here though – only explicitly allowed administrators will be able to actually create an object; everybody else gets an "Access Denied" message.

7.3.3 Only Link GPOs to Sites If Absolutely Necessary

Linking GPOs to sites provides location-based settings and can be used, for instance, to direct the Windows Update client to a WSUS server that is within the site or closest to it. Same goes for drive maps if you are not using domain-based DFS-N, which is site-aware by default (or if your drive mapping conventions do not follow site coverage).

The problem with site-linked GPOs is that they can insert settings not applied by GPOs linked to domains or OUs, regardless of enforcement, which creates a conflict of interest: On one hand, you might want to delegate the site-specific content to the local administrators of those sites; on the other hand, you absolutely do not want those teams to touch any settings that would augment the baseline. Site policies also do not appear in the Group Policy Inheritance view – you have to perform a full-scale modeling run to have those taken into account.

There is only one solution to this: Both linking policies to sites and editing the content of policies that are intended to be linked to sites are Tier 0 tasks and cannot be delegated below that tier. Having every single possible setting set (to some default value) in the baseline would, in theory, relax this requirement, but in practice, it would make the baseline clunky and unmanageable.

7.3.4 Use Loopback Correctly

Loopback policy processing is a great technology, and some of the best-managed AD organizations the author has experienced use it throughout the environment. If you are not intimately familiar with loopback, here's a 101:

- Normally, with Loopback disabled, a separate RSoP of Machine and User policies is computed and applied.

- With Loopback in Merge mode, after the policies linked and filtered to the user have been included in the RSoP, the **user part** of the policies linked and filtered **to the machine** is applied on top of it, causing "computer scoped user settings" to override "user scoped user settings."

- With Loopback in Replace mode, user scoping is skipped completely, and only user settings found in the GPOs belonging to the computer's RSoP are applied to the user session.

Replace mode can have rather dramatic positive effect on policy application performance, especially in cross-forest or cross-domain scenarios where only the machine domain is examined for GPOs. VDI logon times can also benefit tremendously from having Loopback in Replace mode activated on VDI pools, especially if the resulting user part is ultimately empty and the user profile is managed by the VDI's own user environment management facility.

Merge mode has a much more pronounced negative effect on the ease of administration and configuration drift than it has on logon performance, in spite of many sources stating otherwise. However, configuration drift is one of the things your GPO framework must help prevent, and the recommendation of this book is to avoid Merge mode. If you do need user-targeted settings, they are usually fairly few, and you can provide them in a computer-scoped policy using GPPs with item-level targeting.

Create a separate loopback baseline GPO and have everyone tasked with editing GPO content commit to *never ever* setting Loopback-related policies in any other GPO. Specifically disable loopback in the baselines – until the day you find the loopback GPO linked everywhere, then you can reverse the logic.

7.3.5 Policy Caching and Wait for Network

In all Windows versions supported at the time of writing, GPO caching is enabled by default. It is believed by many that "GPO caching" somehow means "RSoP caching." There is no need for that – settings from the last computed RSoP have been applied to the machine already. What is *actually* being cached is the content of the GPOs downloaded from SYSVOL. Confusion tends to arise around the questions "When does this cache get updated by re-downloading the files from SYSVOL?" and "When is this cache actually being used?". The answer to the first question is easy: on every policy update, whether scheduled or manual. The second question is trickier: the cache is used *only on synchronous policy application*. The "synchronous" part applies to the entirety of CSEs. If you have folder redirection or software installation configured, the complete RSoP will be processed synchronously, and the cache is not used.

This leads to a situation many administrators have inherited from times long past: The policy "Always wait for the network at computer startup and logon," introduced with Windows XP, is enabled. This treats every computer restart and every user logon as *synchronous*, i.e., the cache will always be used, although we have waited on the network before beginning the application of policies! The problem here is that if someone makes a change to a policy and reboots a computer in scope of that policy immediately afterwards, the cache has not yet been updated, so the cached previous version will be used – the opposite of what the administrator intended by rebooting!

To remediate this, disable either the cache (there's a policy for that) or the "Wait for network" policy. If you are not using these synchronous CSEs, cache disablement will have zero effect on the policy processing performance.

7.4 Engineering Domain Controllers

After discussing configurations your Domain Controllers are delivering to members, let's take a look at configuring Domain Controllers themselves. This, of course, should also be done by policy as far as possible to ensure conformity. An old Active Directory admins' wisdom says, inspired by Gertrude Stein, "DC is a DC is a DC." If something happens to the hardware, the operating system, or the NTDS database on one particular DC, replacing it should be a standard task, easier and faster than restoring from a backup and reconciling the state of AD. This can only be achieved if no additional functionality beyond AD, DNS (in case AD-integrated DNS is used), and DFS-N (DCs only acting as namespace servers, not holding the actual data) is deployed to DCs. Here is a list – by no means exhaustive – of "foreign" functions routinely found on DCs:

CHAPTER 7   ENGINEERING CONFIGURATION

- Certification Authority
- DHCP Server
- File Server
- Print Server (this function effectively precludes you from disabling the spooler service on this DC, opening up multiple avenues of attack)
- Licensing Server for RDS
- Key Management Server
- Licensing Server for third-party applications
- WSUS
- RDS Gateway (exposing the DC to potentially hostile network zones)

The list could go on, and every single function poses the same three problems: They all have some sort of data in them, introducing a different backup, restoration, and migration regime; they all have the potential of introducing undesired load on OS and hardware; and they all increase the attack surface of your DCs! Are you prepared to declare management of all the features listed above Tier 0 tasks? The alternative is allowing lower-tier personnel to manage configurations of your DCs.

7.4.1 Domain Controller Sizing

Physical resource sizing of a DC has never been an exact science. Not adding unrelated roles and features helps focus the sizing calculations on the actual AD workload. Microsoft provides some guidance here, mostly admitting that the best way to gauge the performance needed is to overprovision and then monitor the performance counters provided with Windows and NTDS for this purpose to deduce a more precise sizing.

One of the "Active Directory internals" books available on the market can provide more detailed guidance, but those values too will be heavily influenced by the attributes actually populated in your directory (a user object is estimated to require 3,7-5KB database space; if you add two certificates and a JPEG photo to it, you can increase this consumption tenfold) and by additional features such as Recycle Bin (storing enriched objects until they age out, are stripped of content and converted to tombstones). In a multi-domain forest, other domains contribute to the database size by adding their objects to the Global Catalog. The CPU requirement of 1 core per 1,000 concurrent users depends heavily on the applications but also on the Kerberos encryption protocols used in the environment. The recommendation to equip your DCs with so much RAM as to hold the entire NTDS database may not always be feasible in large organizations, especially if Domain Controllers are virtualized.

7.4.2 Domain Controller Networking

Avoid having multiple active TCP/IP configurations on your domain controllers. If you absolutely cannot avoid this, at least ensure that all the subnets the domain controller in question ends up belonging to are part of the same Active Directory site.

Do not *ever* disable IPv6 by unchecking the protocol in adapter properties. IPv6 support has been known to cause confusion among Windows systems in certain scenarios; however, the only correct way to remediate these problems is by either telling the network stack to prefer IPv4 over IPv6:

```
reg add "HKEY_LOCAL_MACHINE\SYSTEM\CurrentControlSet\Services\Tcpip6\Parameters" /v DisabledComponents /t REG_DWORD /d 32 /f
```

or, if that doesn't help, by turning of all IPv6 components in the stack:

```
reg add "HKEY_LOCAL_MACHINE\SYSTEM\CurrentControlSet\Services\
Tcpip6\Parameters" /v DisabledComponents /t REG_DWORD /d 255 /f
```

Literally every single "IPv6 for Windows" book begins with the description of the numerous Windows functions relying on the IPv6 stack being active and why it's a bad idea to uncheck it in the LAN adapter properties.

For the same reason, you should never disable the Windows Firewall. You should use Windows Firewall as extensively as you can; it's a great technology. But even if you decide, for whatever reasons, to not filter traffic on your Windows systems, leave the firewall enabled and set it to "Always allow inbound + Always allow outbound."

7.4.3 PDC Emulator

The Domain Controller currently holding the PDC Emulator FSMO role must be reachable and able to answer requests directed specifically to the PDCe in a timely manner. It also runs a number of PDCe-specific tasks like SDPROP and others. This leaves less headroom for normal DC and DNS operations so that you might want to shield your PDCe from participating in those operations, at least to an extent.

The first design consideration here is to not offer the PDCe as a candidate for DNS lookups to domain members and other systems. This is not something you can influence as an AD administrator (setting DNS servers per GPO has been briefly introduced with Windows XP and then very quickly deprecated), but you can offer guidance to that effect to your network teams. This agreement, of course, must include all regular candidates for holding the PDCe role.

Deprioritize the PDC emulator for LDAP lookups by reducing the relative weight of its SRV records. This is done by modifying the registry as follows:

Windows Registry Editor Version 5.00

```
[HKEY_LOCAL_MACHINE\SYSTEM\CurrentControlSet\Services\Netlogon\Parameters]
"LdapSrvWeight"=dword:00000100
"LdapSrvPriority"=dword:00000002
```

The values shown here are the defaults. By setting **LdapSrvWeight** to a lower value than 100, you decrease the priority of the SRV records registered by this DC. Of course, if you move the PDCe role, you have to change these registry values both on the old and the new PDCe. These settings take effect immediately, without restarting NETLOGON, which is why you can (and absolutely should!) distribute these registry values to your DCs using group policy. To target the DC currently holding the PDCe role, apply a WMI filter using the following query:

SELECT DomainRole FROM Win32_ComputerSystem WHERE DomainRole=5

You should assign this policy a higher precedence than the policy holding all the other domain controller settings (e.g., the domain controller baseline).

To exclude the PDCe from serving authentication requests and policy files, consider placing the PDCe into a separate site and making the link to that site very expensive (but without restricting the actual connectivity). This will effectively remove the PDCe from all traffic except the PDCe-specific requests.

The (root domain) PDCe is also the only server *in the entire forest* that must be configured to synchronize its clock with an external time source. Every other machine in the forest should use the NT5DS time provider for NTP. You can use the group policy targeting the PDC Emulator we discussed above to configure an external time source. Talk to your firewall team to enable *all* PDCe candidates to connect to the external time source(s)!

7.4.4 All Other Writeable DCs

In this book, we cannot offer an exhaustive list of controls that might influence the behavior of your DCs and that you could use to engineer that behavior to your organization's requirements. The purpose of this section is to provide some of the most prominent examples of DC-specific configurations and to encourage you to read up on this topic in one of the excellent AD how-to books available on the market.

In larger, globally distributed AD organizations, the default DC behavior of pushing every password change explicitly to the PDCe via NETLOGON, before replicating it to replication partners even within the DC's own site, can cause problems if the PDCe is located far away from the DC performing the password change or even not reachable at that specific moment. The same is true for the password conflict resolution feature: if a user tries to authenticate using a wrong password, the DC that received the authentication request will forward it to the PDCe to take care of the situation that the password was changed very recently and the change didn't reach the DC yet. This is very possible in a hub/spoke topology with replication schedules if the password was changed in one spoke and authentication is attempted in a different spoke. Both behaviors can be turned off simultaneously by setting the registry value **AvoidPdcOnWan** to 1. The value is found in **HKEY_LOCAL_MACHINE\System\CurrentControlSet\Services\Netlogon\Parameters** and absent by default, which equals to the value of 0. You can deliver this value on a per-site basis using GPP and item-level targeting.

Another feature that can play a significant role in speeding up authentication in multi-domain forests is Universal Group Membership Caching. It is disabled by default so that a Global Catalog instance is required to perform user logon (the SIDs of universal groups have to be included in the TGT). To enable the caching, edit the properties of the NTDS Site Settings object as shown in Figure 7-5:

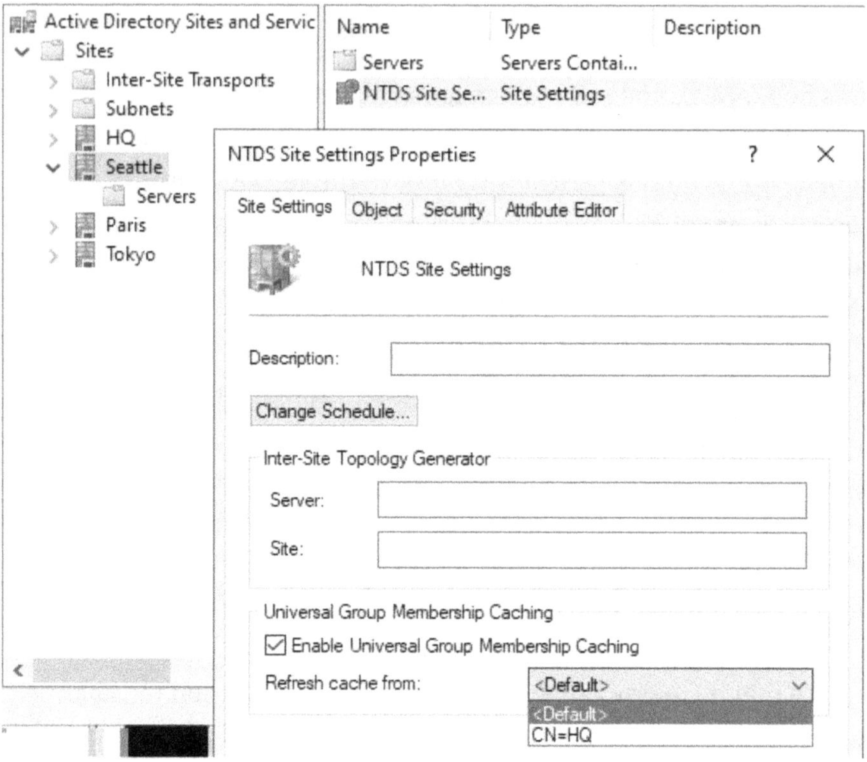

CHAPTER 7   ENGINEERING CONFIGURATION

Figure 7-5. You can specify the site to replicate universal group memberships from

You can then tune the behavior of the cache using the following registry values:

```
Windows Registry Editor Version 5.00

[HKEY_LOCAL_MACHINE\SYSTEM\CurrentControlSetServices\
Services\NTDS]

"Cached Membership Refresh Interval"=dword:000001e0
"Cached Membership Staleness"=dword:00002760
"Cached Membership Refresh Limit"=dword:000001f4
"Cached Membership Site Stickiness"=dword:0001fa40
```

CHAPTER 7   ENGINEERING CONFIGURATION

The values above are the defaults (480 minutes = 6 hours, 10,080 minutes = one week, 500 groups at once, 129,600 minutes = 90 days). If you need to adjust these values for a certain site, you can also deliver them by GPP with ILT to ensure a new DC provisioned in that site will inherit them without manual intervention.

If you find yourself in a situation where the DC holding the RID Master FSMO role is not reachable from a certain site due to network topology but you have to provision large batches of SID-enabled objects, i.e., users, computers, or groups, from within that site, you might want to increase the size of the RID pool issued to that site's domain controllers from its default size of 500 RIDs per block. To achieve this, deploy the following registry setting to the domain controllers in the site:

Windows Registry Editor Version 5.00

[HKEY_LOCAL_MACHINE\SYSTEM\CurrentControlSetServices\Services\ NTDS\RID Values]

"RID Block Size"=dword:000001f4

the value above being the default of 500. You can increase the block size as far as 15,000. After you change the registry value, invalidate the current RID pool and request a new RID pool while there is a line of sight to the RID master. To invalidate the RID pool, Active Directory offers a special LDAP operation that you can leverage using PowerShell as follows:

```
$Domain = New-Object System.DirectoryServices.DirectoryEntry
$DomainSid = $Domain.objectSid
$RootDSE = New-Object System.DirectoryServices.
          DirectoryEntry("LDAP://RootDSE")
$RootDSE.UsePropertyCache = $false
$RootDSE.Put("invalidateRidPool", $DomainSid.Value)
$RootDSE.SetInfo()
```

277

After this is done, request a new RID pool while still maintaining line of sight to the RID Master by trying to create a SID-enabled object. The attempt will fail, but the DC will receive a new RID block of the configured size.

7.4.5 RODCs

Read-only Domain Controllers do not usually require any local configurations beyond those of the writeable DCs. Their core functionality, password caching, is configured using their Active Directory object, and the local administration delegation (remember: DCs do not have local administrator groups, and RODCs are no exception) is achieved by setting the **managedBy** attribute to the desired user or group. This is a rare example of an AD-delivered (rather than GPO-delivered) configuration having an immediate impact on Tier 0 security.

7.5 Securing Domain Controllers

Domain Controllers, being arguably the most critical systems in your entire infrastructure, deserve the best you can provide in terms of securing and hardening. Most of the general Windows server security guidelines apply to Domain Controllers verbatim (with the notable exception of activating Credential Guard).

If you have followed the guidance of keeping Domain Controllers free from other software, both first and third party, you don't have to worry about ports and protocols not required for Active Directory. Enable Windows Firewall and manage inbound traffic rules closely. Unfortunately, Active Directory needs a lot of communication channels in order to function properly. Using a firewall that understands RPC, such as the Windows Firewall, you can restrict the RPC subprotocols allowed inbound to LSA, SAM, NETLOGON, and DFS-R only. Remember to allow ICMP

Ping from members to DCs to allow keeping long-running LDAP queries alive. And don't forget to allow Port 389/udp that domain members use to perform the initial RootDSE request.

7.5.1 SYSVOL Share Hardening

Restrict permissions that unprivileged users have on the share level to remove any sort of write access. By default, "Everyone" has "Read" permissions on both NETLOGON and SYSVOL, but "Authenticated Users" have "Full Control" on SYSVOL. This allows delegating the entire group policy management lifecycle to an otherwise unprivileged user. It also allows an attacker who discovers a GPO folder where a user they control has write access to modify the content of the GPO directly by editing the files – the most critical ones being .inf, .csv and .xml! You will be engineering this process more closely so every time you delegate editing a particular GPO to a group, you will allow that particular group write access – but not full access! – on the share. Unfortunately, you'll have to do it separately on every Domain Controller so that repermissioning the shares is a good candidate for automation.

If all your domain members are at least Windows Vista/Server 2008, you should enable UNC path hardening by applying the policy setting "Hardened UNC Paths" found in "Administrative Templates/Network/Network Provider" for both NETLOGON and SYSVOL, requiring at least "mutual authentication" and "integrity." The value names will have the format of ***\NETLGON** and ***\SYSVOL**, the values themselves should be set to **RequireMutualAuthentication=1,RequireIntegrity=1**. There is a third parameter, **RequirePrivacy=1** which means SMB encryption and requires at least Windows 8/Server 2012. You have to roll out this setting to all your member systems that support it, which means it should ideally be included in the baseline. The current CIS benchmark requires it to be set as described above.

CHAPTER 7   ENGINEERING CONFIGURATION

7.5.2 LSA Protection

A credential protection technique that is still not very widely used at the time of writing but has been around since Windows 8.1/Server 2012R2 is "additional LSA protection." You already know that you can't enable Credential Guard on Domain Controllers to isolate and protect both the LSA process and its memory. And even on member machines, Credential Guard can introduce incompatibilities and cause applications to present the user with logon dialogs that will leave credentials unprotected.

To offer at least partial protection for all the privileged information that LSA processes, it's possible to have it start as "Protected Process Light" (RunAsPPL). This feature is based on "HyperVisor-assisted Code Integrity" (HVCI), and although it does not protect the process memory as effectively as VBS does, it protects the LSA process itself by disallowing any unsanctioned code injection. LSA plug-ins and drivers that have to inject code into the LSA process in order to perform their functions must be signed by Microsoft. This mode of execution of plug-ins was intended primarily for antimalware products but has found other uses since its inception.

On modern systems featuring UEFI and SecureBoot, PPL can be enforced by setting an UEFI variable so that it cannot be disabled from within the operating system. On other systems, a simple registry setting and a subsequent reboot activate PPL for LSA:

Windows Registry Editor Version 5.00

[HKEY_LOCAL_MACHINE\SYSTEM\CurrentControlSet\Control\Lsa]
"RunAsPPL"=dword:00000001

The setting of 1 will store the PPL setting in the firmware if UEFI and SecureBoot are enabled. The setting of 2 will not store this information in UEFI, but it is not enforced on any server version older than 2025.

7.5.3 BitLocker on DCs

There have been many discussions over the years around enabling BitLocker on servers in general and on Domain Controllers in particular. To answer this question for your specific infrastructure, it is important to understand what BitLocker is about:

- It will protect disk volumes at rest if they have been separated from the computer on which they were BitLocker-protected (stolen disk/stolen SAN/stolen backup performed at storage level).

- It will protect disk volumes connected to "their" computer on the system startup, provided an additional protector has been enabled on top of the TPM chip. This could be a PIN or a recovery key.

- It will **not** protect disk volumes connected to "their" computer once Windows has been successfully booted, unlocking the "Full Volume Encryption" (FVE, the internal name for BitLocker) either by a user supplying the PIN on boot or by the TPM being the sole protector configured for the boot volume.

- Protectors for secondary data volumes are stored on boot volumes if those are BitLocker-protected.

If your threat model requires that you protect DCs from the drives being stolen but not from the actual machines being stolen, enabling BitLocker with TPM is sufficient and, apart from a very small uptick in CPU consumption, it will not introduce any problems. Test your backups though – if they are created at storage level, the recovered disks will be encrypted, but the TPM chip holding the key is probably lost. In this case, you will need the full recovery key... which, more often than not, is only stored in Active Directory. For Disaster Recovery, assuming all DCs have been lost, you should either store the keys differently or perform AD backups using an agent *within* the Domain Controller.

In case your threat model has to accommodate an entire DC being stolen and able to power up in the malicious actor's lab, TPM protection is not enough. In this case, by enabling PIN or Password protector on top of TPM, you create a situation where every reboot requires a. console access (may not always be possible) and b. administrator interaction *and* knowledge of the PIN (precludes you from automatically booting DCs at night). You can evaluate BitLocker Network Unlock which will allow BitLocker-protected machines to boot into Windows without user interaction as long as they're connected to the organization's LAN while requiring PIN and/or password otherwise. "Otherwise," of course, includes all Disaster Recovery (DR) situations where the Network Unlock server is not available.

7.6 Domain Join as Priority One Design Area

We already looked into threat vectors emerging from the seemingly innocuous act of joining a computer to domain, especially if said computer is running a Server operating system. It goes without saying that in a well-engineered network non-privileged users will be stripped of their ability to add up to 10 machines to domain both by setting **msDS-MachineAccountQuota** to 0 and by removing the "Add workstations to domain" entitlement for "Authenticated Users" from the DDCP.

7.6.1 Know Your Provisioning Scenarios

To create a domain join process that satisfies the organization's requirements without exposing the identity store to an additional risk, it is important to acknowledge that there is no "one size fits all" domain join

CHAPTER 7   ENGINEERING CONFIGURATION

scenario. In a typical modern enterprise that has not yet managed to ban domain-joined client endpoints, you will have to analyze the following scenarios at least:

1. A new client device or a device refresh after hard disk replacement (provisioned in a secured area and then handed out to the designated user).

2. An existing client device refresh (reprovisioning after a security incident, possibly in situ, at least for LAN-bound devices).

3. An "out-of-policy" client (a conference room device, a piece of manufacturing machinery, or – these things happen even today – a super fancy laptop the company owner just bought) that has to be joined manually.

4. A virtual client provisioned by a VDI broker component.

5. A physical server provisioned within the datacenter by an automated process.

6. An "out-of-policy" physical or virtual server that has to be joined manually.

7. A virtual server joined to the domain by the virtualization platform's template provisioning process (VMware calls this facility a "customization specification").

8. A virtual server provisioned by an automated software installation process that includes domain join.

Not all of these eight types of domain joins exist in every organization, and there may be variations of these types coexisting side by side within your particular environment, but the principal distinction is between

- Scenarios involving an administrator joining a machine manually and
- Scenarios where the domain join is facilitated by a set of credentials stored in a provisioning system (VDI, hypervisor, configuration management, on-boot deployment system, etc.)

7.6.2 Administrator Entering Credentials

To join a machine to a domain, the person performing the act not only has to have certain rights in Active Directory, but they also need local admin privileges on the computer itself. This is what prevents any security-conscious organization from even contemplating the "user gets a new PC and joins it themselves" workflow envisioned by Microsoft in the 1990s. The domain part could be taken care of by preprovisioning the object in AD, giving the designated user the "Reset password," "Validated write to dnsHostName," and "Validated write to servicePrincipalName" permissions on that object and removing them after the join. It's the uncertainty about what the person could do between being handed the computer, including the admin password, and joining it to AD, rebooting, and losing that access that is untenable.

In all manual join scenarios, therefore, the person performing the join will be one that can be trusted with local admin rights on that system. Most organizations these days are inclined to assume that such a person can also be trusted with protecting their own join credentials – sometimes this assumption is justified, sometimes it's not, and sometimes humans

CHAPTER 7   ENGINEERING CONFIGURATION

just make costly mistakes. In any case, the join account should not be the person's primary work account, nor their regular admin account, no matter which tier it belongs to! Anyone trusted with manually joining systems to AD receives a join account. To streamline the automated part of the join process, all these join accounts are added to a "join group" for the scenario in question. There will certainly be different groups for clients (Tier 2) and servers (Tier 1, potentially escalated to Tier 0). All of the "join groups" are added to the GPO, making them trustworthy owners of reusable computer accounts (see Section 5.6 for details).

The join workflow then looks as follows:

- The person performing the join sets the machine name and the IP configuration and confirms line of sight to DC, maybe also sets the time if it's off in the hardware.

- An admin (it could be the same person but using their admin account) triggers the automation (it could be a simple PowerShell script triggered from a PAW or from an admin server) and supplies computer name and the OU the computer has to be joined into.

- The automation creates a computer object in the target OU, sets the "join group" as its owner, and grants it the permissions required for object takeover.

- The person uses their join account to join computer to the domain and reboots it.

- A dedicated automation task, either running on demand or periodically, reassigns the ownership of the new computer object to "Domain Admins" and removes the rights assigned to the "join group."

CHAPTER 7   ENGINEERING CONFIGURATION

Join accounts should be allowed interactive logon at least to some workstations in order to change their password. Alternatively, delegate the right to *reset* the join account's password to its owner's admin account. Put the join accounts under a Fine-Grained Password Policy (FGPP), restricting their password lifetime.

7.6.3 Automated Domain Join of a VM by a Third-Party System

In the list above, this would be scenarios 4 and 7. Since these systems are usually of the "black box" variety, the best you can do here is

- Restrict to what OUs the join account is allowed to join machines by only granting the right to create a new computer object on those OUs.

- Evaluate automated password rotation for the join account (for vSphere customization specification this is easily done using PowerCLI, for Horizon View there is an API for this, your mileage with other systems may vary quite significantly). Once you have figured that out and tested it to ensure the robustness of this process, you can establish an automated rotation regime, thus minimizing the blast radius of possible credential compromise.

7.6.4 Automated Domain Join You Can Influence Directly

If you provision machines, physical or virtual, using an automated system that involves a domain join, you can use the same procedure as described for the manual join. Restrict access to the system or systems holding the

CHAPTER 7   ENGINEERING CONFIGURATION

join accounts credentials as severely as possible. If the in situ ("under the desk") reimaging of workstations is not part of your organization's endpoint lifecycle, the installation server for clients only has to be accessible from the secured area where new machines are prepared. The installation server for server machines doesn't have to be reachable from client or printer network segments, from perimeter networks, or from the VPN concentrators' networks.

A different approach to protecting domain join credentials would be to not use such credentials at all. The workflow would look like this:

- The automation performs a **DJOIN /provision** operation, creating a computer object in the desired OU. It can reset the ownership to "Domain Admins" already.

- The offline join file generated by DJOIN is saved on a web server that is only accessible from the designated provisioning networks.

- The provisioning task sequence contacts the web server and requests the file named after the computer being joined, e.g., **https://joinserver.domain.org/SRV4711.join**.

- The provisioning task sequence then performs an offline join with **DJOIN /requestodj** using the downloaded file.

- The cleanup task running after the fact deletes the file from the web server after making sure the computer has actually taken over the object.

This way, the (randomized) computer password is revealed for a certain amount of time, but it can only be used once and only for this specific computer!

7.6.5 Monitoring and Cleanup

Whatever provisioning and join processes your organization decides to put in place, use your automation to ensure that no stale or unused computer objects are left in the directory. Typical search patterns include

- Computer objects created a week or longer ago but never logged on

- Computer objects created an hour or longer ago with dnsHostName and userPrincipalName populated but not containing the name (**CN**) of the object

- Computer objects not owned by either Domain Admins, the automation account responsible for provisioning, or one of the "joining groups"

- Computer objects with relevant properties initialized but not logged on for 90 days or longer

- Computer objects with relevant properties initialized but password not changed for 90 days or longer

Alert administrators of the tier (determined by OU) about the object found using these and other relevant searches. Maintain a white list of computer objects to be excluded from monitoring (e.g., an Exchange ASA will usually pop up in the first two searches and, depending on how it was provisioned, maybe even in the third!). In some OUs, such as VDI desktop pools OUs or the default "new computers" container, you can delete stale accounts "on sight"; for server OUs, the admins should be given the chance to review the object before deletion.

7.6.6 Removal of Default Local Group Nestings

Regardless of the join procedure being used, the default nesting of "Domain Admins" in the local "Administrators" has to be removed and replaced by a more suitable group or user. We covered that in previous chapters. The default memberships in the "Users" group are also interesting – both "Domain Users" and "Authenticated Users" are nested into this group by default! "Domain Users" often make little sense, especially if the machine and the user logging on to it come from different domains. "Authenticated Users" includes users from any trusted domain or forest, which is definitely more than you would like to see. If you have appropriate groups already ("Laptop Users" or "Finance Department Users"), you could just add those. Leave the "NT AUTHORITY\SYSTEM" in place to ensure the proper function of user desktop sessions.

> **Reminder:** Both the removal of default group nestings and the addition of your custom groups can be very easily and reliably performed by GPP. The trade-off is that the computer account must have visibility over any group involved in the process – both the less-privileged specific ones and the privileged "Domain Admins." Replacing the "Domain Admins" as a one-time scripted step in your provisioning process and dealing with the less-privileged members of local "Users" by group policy could constitute an acceptable workaround in many cases!

7.7 Default Containers

In a well-engineered and well-maintained Active Directory environment, "accidental" creation of user or computer objects should not be possible because these are normally only created by automation, and automation always specifies the target container.

> When writing automation scripts for AD object creation, always include verification that the target container actually exists (i.e., is visible to the automation account) prior to attempting object creation!

However, a wisdom older than IT itself dictates that it's better to be safe than sorry. All automation notwithstanding, it is good to provide a safe place for the "accidental" objects to be placed in. Assuming that you have delegated object creation rights correctly, the only principals capable of creating an object by accident are "Domain Admins," "Administrators," and "Account Operators" (the last one should be empty, and you should be monitoring for that on a constant basis). These groups have the requisite rights by default, and once you redirect the default containers for users and computers using the **REDIRUSR** and **REDIRCMP** commands, respectively, ensure that

- No other principals can create objects in the new locations.

- No one can create objects in the old locations by adding a Deny entry for "Create child Computer object," "Create child User object," and "Create child inetOrgPerson object" to "".

7.7.1 "Intended Accidental" Object Creation

Every now and then, you will encounter an application installer that insists on creating the required accounts and groups itself but does not allow you to specify the target container for them to go to. On the other hand, installing software, even in Tier 0, by a member of "Administrators" is not an acceptable workaround. If you encounter this, you will have to temporarily add an ACE for the user performing the installation, allowing that account to create users in the default OU. This topic should be included in the next business review with the application vendor, preferably with your CISO present.

There is a special place in hell for those applications that not only insist on creating their service accounts and authorization groups themselves but also

- Store them internally as DNs so that they can't be moved or renamed after creation.

- Create them in the "CN=Users,DC=domain,DC=com" instead of looking up the well-known object path for the new objects target container.

In this case, the discussion about suitability of such a product for a modern enterprise should be conducted *prior* to installation, resulting either in a hotfix by the vendor to change this behavior or in the cancellation of the contract by your organization. The second outcome is much preferable, by the way, because software designed in such a manner is bound to have even more "landmines" buried within it. More often than not, it will ask for the service account being a domain admin quicker than you can say "domain domination"! Avoid such products at all costs, because they have the potential of reducing all your engineering and hardening work to almost nothing. If a department insists on having such a low-quality product in place, a security admin's first thought is to provision a separate forest for the application and bill the department for operating it. Don't get your hopes too high though – cross-forest access will probably not be the application's strong suit either.

7.8 Summary

In this chapter, we examined different ways Active Directory helps deliver configurations to its members and even to Domain Controllers themselves. We have looked at Group Policy as the most frequently used Active Directory feature for configuration delivery and indeed one that many IT people, administrators, and decision-makers alike confuse with "Configuration Management." To manage your group policy framework successfully even without third-party tools, you need good planning, very explicit delegation, and a naming convention everyone is familiar with. Even then, closely managed delegation, e.g., of the right to link GPOs to privileged Ous, is all that is standing between you and dozens of attack vectors involving group policy.

Some configurations specific to Domain Controller operations must be done on DCs directly; they can be applied by GPP if all DCs have uniform configurations. Uniformity is key to an efficient Domain Controller lifecycle, including unplanned replacement due to a hardware or operating system malfunction.

Domain join is a first-rate attack vector so that no AD engineering initiative will be complete without establishing close management processes for all its flavors.

CHAPTER 8

Engineering Administration

A common anti-pattern in Active Directory administration is the idea of building out the production environment first and hardening the administration later. Almost every AD organization created before Server 2016 has been built this way. The complexity of abandoning legacy administrative identities and management processes and moving towards tiered permissions, restricted authentication, and Red Forests is one of the reasons the ESAE model (introduced well before that) did not get enough traction on the market and ended up being officially deprecated by Microsoft. On the other hand, Microsoft continues using ESAE in their internal infrastructure even at the time of writing, once again reconfirming the viability of the concept.

ESAE takes care of two major shortcomings in the Windows and AD identity lifecycle: Tiered administration and Privileged Access Workstations protect privileged credentials from being stolen off a compromised workstation or member server, while the Red Forest takes privileged administration out of the production identity infrastructure, thus minimizing both the discoverability and exposure of highly privileged objects. Organizations will benefit the most from implementing ESAE guidelines if they have the two parts working together. However, each of the two major ESAE concepts can be put in place independently of the other and offer a substantial increase in security:

CHAPTER 8　ENGINEERING ADMINISTRATION

- By moving 100% of actively used privileged identities to the Red Forest and implementing a hardened one-way trust (possible since 2012R2) and Shadow Principals (possible since 2016), organizations can make highly privileged accounts nearly undiscoverable by a malicious actor until/unless they authenticate to a computer controlled by the attacker.

- By putting tiered administration in place in the "golden" forest(s), organizations can protect privileged credentials from being captured on a lower-tier device controlled by the attacker, even if these credentials come from the same forest and are discoverable by unprivileged reconnaissance.

Add the concept of a "Privileged Access Workstation," which was introduced together with ESAE but assumed a lifecycle of its own down the road, and the visibility restrictions we discussed in Chapter 4, and you are looking at an Active Directory environment that is already pretty heavily fortified! There is still no guarantee that it will withstand the attacker long enough for the Blue team to detect the malicious activity, but it's definitely a better starting point for defending the identity infrastructure than the default installation.

The secret to a successful implementation of secure administration is to view it as an integral part of the overall AD management. Just as we did with configuration defaults, do not assume that what comes out of the box is the "normal" way and everything else is a "hardened" way. Try viewing the secure way as the "normal" and the default way as the "bare bones," and you will quickly develop the right attitude!

8.1 Privileged Access

The concept of "privileged access" has many aspects to it, and by confusing them, security architects often create administration frameworks that end up not being secure enough, usable enough, or both. Security and usability cannot be viewed separately from each other, and "10 Immutable Laws of Security Administration" acknowledge this in Law #2:

> Security only works if the secure way also happens to be the easy way.

Privileged access exists in various flavors, but in the context of engineering a secure administration framework, we have to make the distinction between network access and interactive access. Network access is inherently more secure because raw authenticators like cleartext passwords and smart cards never even come near the target system. Service tickets could potentially be abused if the target has been compromised and the service tickets were captured, but it is not trivial and usually way more "noisy" than other attack techniques. Apart from event log entries, network access does not usually leave traces on the target after the work is done. Interactive privileged access, even if protected by Shadow Principals, SCAMA, "Protected Users," and Credential Guard, still creates a logon session, a user profile, and potentially even (also privileged) service tickets directed to other services within the target environment ("golden" forest).

One of the goals of a well-engineered administration framework will, therefore, be reducing interactive privileged access to an absolute minimum, ideally to zero.

8.1.1 Interactive Administration

For decades, security-minded individuals have been telling administrators not to log on interactively to Domain Controllers in order to perform some management tasks on AD or SYSVOL. This guidance often fell on deaf ears, and in some cases, it is not actually applicable. In a tiny environment where there is only a DC, a server for an accounting application, and the users' workstations, logging on with a domain admin account directly to the DC is actually more secure than logging on with the same credentials to a workstation being used for the daily work. But for any decent-size network, managed by a dedicated IT team rather than by the owner's nephew, interactive administration of a Windows system should be an exception.

Microsoft tried to reinforce the benefits of remote administration twice, starting with Vista/Server 2008: by implementing UAC (making remote administration less painful than local one) and by offering Server Core as a more lightweight option for teams accustomed to remote administration. Both received significant pushback from the user base, and the guidance on disabling UAC was quickly more abundant on the Internet than the explanation why UAC is actually a good thing. Server Core was ahead of its time: many server installations around 2008 were still on physical hardware, and hardware vendors failed to provide Core-compatible drivers and installers quickly enough. This was most pronounced with network card teaming which, for Server 2008, had to be implemented in the vendor's driver stack. Many teams tried Core back in the day and discarded this deployment option as unmanageable. In retrospect, the release of Server 2012R2 would have been a great moment to introduce the Core option: deployments moved further towards virtual, Microsoft's own hypervisor matured significantly, network teaming was relegated to Windows' own network stack, and the driver installers evolved. But the reservations against Core were already there, and it will take a generation of admins to overcome them again.

CHAPTER 8　ENGINEERING ADMINISTRATION

Let us analyze the situations prompting for interactive administration. The most important question we should be asking ourselves doing this is, what overall level of access is really required for this operation.

Scenario	Required local privileges	Required network access
Something broke, and the system is not accessible from the network anymore.	Since cached credentials for privileged AD accounts are not possible anyway, a local admin with a LAPS-provided password is the only practical way to access Windows.	Since the network is broken, network access is impossible anyway.
A software package must be installed, and an unattended installation is not supported by the vendor.	Local administrator with a LAPS-provided password should be enough to perform the installation. If an AD user is required, try starting the installation as an unprivileged AD user with the right to log on locally and elevate to local admin if UAC asks for it.	It is very unusual for an installer to require access to network resources. As a last resort, if the UAC approach fails, create an AD user account, elevate it to local admin, provide access to the desired network resources, perform the installation, then remove the user from the local admins, remove the access granted to it and roll its password in AD.

(*continued*)

297

CHAPTER 8   ENGINEERING ADMINISTRATION

Scenario	Required local privileges	Required network access
Troubleshooting requires a tool that can only be run locally (e.g., ProcMon by Sysinternals).	Local administrator with a LAPS-provided password should be enough to perform the troubleshooting. If the reason for troubleshooting requires access to AD or to resources secured by AD, then a parallel session of an unprivileged AD user might be sufficient. Alternatively, log on as the unprivileged user in question and elevate the troubleshooting tool using RunAs and a local administrator.	Network access for the unprivileged part of the session is possible, the privileged part shouldn't normally require it.

Scenarios that **do not** require an interactive, let alone interactive *and* privileged, logon session include but are not limited to

- Rebooting a machine
- Restarting a service
- Reading Event Logs
- Creating a file share
- Managing disks, partitions, and volumes
- Viewing, creating, deleting, or modifying a registry key
- Setting permissions in a file system or in the registry
- Installing a software package from a well-composed MSI

CHAPTER 8   ENGINEERING ADMINISTRATION

- Installing certificates
- Managing failover clusters
- Performing a forced group policy update
- Managing local users and groups
- Viewing and installing Windows updates
- Connecting to AD, DNS, DHCP, Certification Authority, WSUS, SQL, or IIS to administer these services

The vast majority of day-to-day tasks are perfectly suitable for remote administration. In fact, it can even benefit from the "remoteness" since UAC does not get in the way of operations triggered by network access – your remote access token already has all authorized privileges assigned to it!

It goes without saying that having to combine multiple user contexts to perform an installation or troubleshooting task is not as comfortable as working with a "God-mode" account that has admin privileges in all systems at once. But trying to find a middle way usually leads to compromise. If you absolutely cannot avoid having to perform a certain operation in "God mode" right now, create a completely new account, give it the required privileges, do the work, and destroy the account afterwards.

In all scenarios listed above, if the system in question is a Domain Controller, many system engineers immediately think of a "BUILTIN\Administrators" member in lieu of a "local administrator." Do not do this. If you do not have time to create a custom group and grant it the required local permissions on Domain Controller by adding them to the DDCP, that's what the built-in "Server Operators" group is for! However, if your "domain controller interactive administration" account is in the same domain (at this point, you should ask yourself *"Why? It should have come from the Red Forest..."*), making it a member of "Server

CHAPTER 8   ENGINEERING ADMINISTRATION

Operators" will put it under SDHolder/SDPROP control, making it discoverable as a potentially privileged account (which, of course, it is).

> **Remember:** Being able to log on locally or execute a process, even without elevated privileges, on a highly privileged system enables a number of "Potato" attack scenarios and should be delegated sparingly!

AD accounts designated for interactive administration must be "Protected Users" members, even if it means that every single session is limited to four hours. Ninety percent of the actions requiring interactive logon are finished well within that time range. But the best protection is still to use LAPS governed local accounts rather than AD identities for local administration.

8.1.2 Remoting Protocols

Remote administration requires different protocols to connect to different applications. Early versions of Windows used DCOM and WMI for remote administration, and it's still the basis of many of the built-in administration APIs. Both protocols are based on RPC and therefore require authenticated network access to the RPC endpoint mapper and the ability to communicate on the RPC high ports the client receives from the mapper. RPC relies on Windows for authentication, so unless you are using IP addresses to connect to the target systems, Kerberos will be used. All MMC-based management consoles use DCOM and WMI to connect to both local and remote servers.

With the advent of PowerShell (it became part of Windows Server with the release of Server 2008R2), remoting over WinRM became ubiquitous in Windows networks. WinRM is the Microsoft-specific implementation of the industry standard "WS-Management" protocol, which describes a SOAP (webservice) approach to remote systems management. WinRM is based on HTTP and listens on Port 5985 (unencrypted) or 5986 (HTTPS). These ports can easily be changed as long as the client applications connecting to the WinRM listener support custom ports as well. In conjunction with PowerShell, WinRM offers a set of authorization and delegation capabilities known as "Just Enough Administration" (JEA). If PowerShell is part of your remote administration framework, you absolutely must become familiar with JEA. It offers elegant solutions to many delegation requirements you will not be able to satisfy as easily using the legacy protocols.

Windows Admin Center, a relatively new browser-based server management offering introduced 2017 as "Project Honolulu" and generally available since April 2018, is based on PowerShell remoting and, to a smaller extent, remote WMI.

If you use the built-in PowerShell module for Active Directory that has been part of the ADDS RSAT since Server 2008R2, it does not use LDAP as you might have expected. The connection to ADDS – or even to an ADLDS instance – is facilitated by the "Active Directory Web Services" (ADWS) – a SOAP wrapper for ADSI, listening on port 9389. Keep this in mind when planning firewall rules for administering your AD.

SMB can be considered a "remote administration protocol" as well, because it allows accessing files and folders on the target machine using the administrative shares (`<drive>$` for each disk drive plus `ADMIN$` for the Windows installation folder). If you prefer to not have these shares on your privileged systems, add a REG_DWORD value `AutoShareServer` to `HKEY_LOCAL_MACHINE\SYSTEM\CurrentControlSet\Services\LanmanServer\Parameters`, set it to 0, and restart the LanManServer service (or reboot the computer). On desktop versions of Windows, in case you decide to also restrict this access on your client machines, the value is named `AutoShareWks`.

WMI and PowerShell remoting can also be used for working with file systems. Of course, you will not be presented with the familiar Explorer experience, but the directory listings including file metadata will be there.

CHAPTER 8   ENGINEERING ADMINISTRATION

The latest addition to the Windows remoting protocols family is SSH. The PowerShell team at Microsoft maintains an OpenSSH port since September 2015. The client component has been a part of Windows since Windows 10/Server 2016. The OpenSSH daemon started out as a separate download and became a Feature-on-Demand (FoD) in Server 2019 and 2022. Server 2025 comes with an SSH server preinstalled but not activated. The activation is possible from Server Manager with a single click of a mouse (but not from SCONFIG if you are on Server Core).

In early preview versions of Server 2025, SSH presented a grave security problem. It comes with password authentication enabled by default. Since the daemon uses impersonation to create a session in a user's context, it uses the logon type 8 (network logon with explicit credentials). This allowed any user to connect to a privileged system that SSH enabled with default settings. They would not have any additional privileges in that session, but being able to communicate from a Tier 0 system is an attack vector in and by itself. This has already been hardened at the time of writing, i.e., pre-release, by adding an **AllowGroups administrators "openssh users"** clause to the SSH daemon configuration. There is, however, another SSH-related phenomenon that may require your attention.

If you create a dedicated management group for managing certain member servers, you may want to deny that group permissions that would put its member's credentials at immediate risk: "Log on locally," "Log on using Remote Desktop," "Log on as a service," and "Log on as batch job." Since the members of that group are meant to be able to administer the servers remotely, you cannot deny them network access to the servers. If you now nest the management group into local "Administrators" and enable SSH with default settings on the member servers, the members of the management group will be able to log on via SSH, and since it is a logon type 8 (Network with explicit credentials), an actual user profile will be created for that session, and the user's credentials will be stored to the same extent as if they were logged on interactively!

8.1.3 Remote but Interactive

There is a special logon type which is probably used more often than the dreaded Interactive logon: Remote-Interactive, which means connecting to a Windows system using Remote Desktop Protocol (RDP). This creates a desktop session and has the potential of exposing credentials in the same manner as a "true" interactive logon session does. VBS and Credential Guard protect these sessions as well, but this technology cannot always be enabled – on virtual machines, prerequisites for VBS are not always met, and on Domain Controllers, Credential Guard cannot be enabled regardless of the hardware platform.

Since RDP is routinely used for Windows Server administration, Microsoft provides two methods of protecting remote logon credentials from unauthorized access in case the targeted machine has been compromised by a malicious actor: "Restricted Admin" and "Remote Credential Guard." Both require the Credentials Delegation policy setting "Remote host allows delegation of non-exportable credentials" to be set to "Enabled" on the target servers.

Restricted Admin mode has been around since Server 2008R2 – more specifically, it was introduced with Server 2012R2 and then backported to those older systems. The way Restricted Admin works is to allow Windows to create an interactive desktop session using only an NTLM hash or a Kerberos TGS as proof of authentication. The user attempting the connection must be a member of the local "Administrators" group on the target system. The supplied authentication material is not stored on the target system, so it cannot be extracted by the attacker controlling that system. However, this information is stored on the client from which the connection is being initiated. **This means that "Restricted Admin" mode cannot be used to administer a privileged system from an untrustworthy client.** But in a well-managed infrastructure, this should be the rule anyway, and ideally, RDP (port 3389/tcp or /udp) should not be allowed from client subnets by the datacenter firewall or by the

CHAPTER 8   ENGINEERING ADMINISTRATION

Windows Firewall on the target systems. If the clients are configured to "Require Restricted Admin" as shown in Figure 8-1, the Remote Desktop Client will initiate a protected connection automatically. If the last option, "Restrict Credentials Delegation," has been set, administrators can select "Restricted Admin" mode by adding the **/RestrictedAdmin** switch to the MSTSC command.

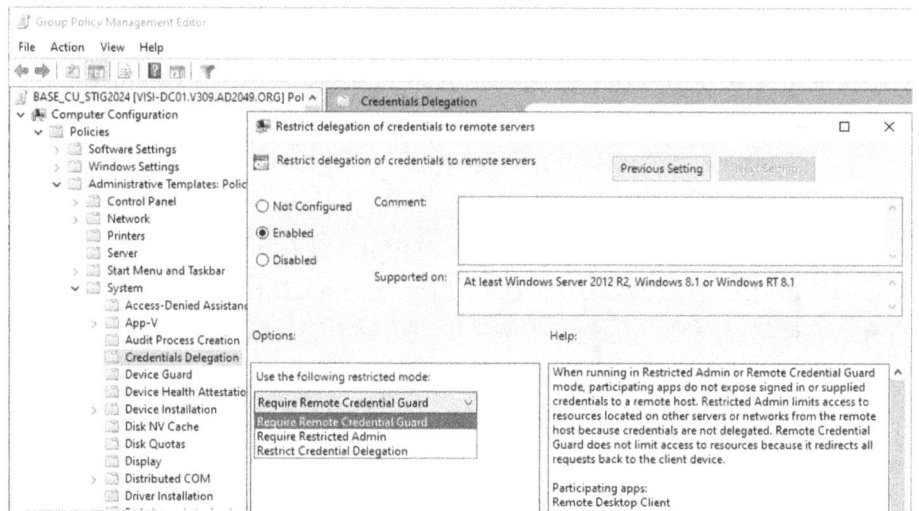

Figure 8-1. *The desired administration mode must be configured on the client side*

Since a Restricted Admin session does not store any cryptographic material about the user, an outgoing connection from that session will not be authenticated as the user but rather as the machine identity of the target host. If the target host is a Tier 0 system, it means immediate escalation of privileges (the user must be a local administrator to use Restricted Admin so would be able to escalate anyway, but this is a zero-step escalation).

Remote Credential Guard (RCG) does not require local administrator permissions, just the permission to log on using RDP. However, the

CHAPTER 8   ENGINEERING ADMINISTRATION

connection will be established using Kerberos on behalf of the account logged on to the client. Although no Kerberos tickets are passed as such from the client session to the target server, the server session is still able to request TGS for resource access. This makes an RCG-secured session capable of a "second hop" in the connecting user's security context. If the target has been compromised, the attacker can abuse the session to access resources as the connected user. If RCG has not been specifically enforced by the policy shown in Figure 8-1, option "Require Remote Credential Guard," the user can initiate RCG by using **mstsc.exe /remoteGuard**.

RCG is not intended for privileged administration but rather to help protect regular users' credentials if connecting to terminal servers, VDI, or remote workstations. It is by far more secure than using credential delegation techniques required for RDP SSO without RCG enabled. Since RCG creates a secure channel between the client and the server to pass TGS requests and service tickets back and forth, only direct connections without a Remote Desktop Gateway are supported. The TGS submitted from an RCG session does not contain claims, so if compound authentication must be used for authorizing access to certain resources, that access will be rejected.

Popular RDP connection managers like RDCMan from Sysinternals or Remote Desktop Manager from Devolutions support both Restricted Admin mode and RCG.

Note   Despite all protective measures for RDP, you must have a documented way of accessing privileged systems via console – physical KVM, server hardware management, the virtualization platform's console like VMware's VMRC, and so on. The reason for this is threefold: First, if something wrong happens with the network, RDP is not available. Second, console access allows you to close the host firewall completely for inbound access, e.g., for privileged automation hosts we'll be discussing in Section 8.3. Third, only at the

CHAPTER 8   ENGINEERING ADMINISTRATION

console can you perform a direct smart card logon if your accepted privileged management paradigm requires it! Ironically, the very advanced technologies in virtualization that are designed to prevent hypervisor admins from escalating to Tier 0 identity admins, like shielded VMs in Hyper-V, also prevent console access!

8.1.4 Break-Glass Accounts

Sometimes things break, even in a well-maintained environment. Sometimes malicious actors manage to break through our defenses and start wreaking havoc in our identity infrastructure. If that happens, some of the facilities we put in place to make AD management both secure and efficient are not at our disposal anymore, stripping us of capabilities we became accustomed to. These are situations where the concept of a "break-glass account" comes in.

A break-glass account for Active Directory must be able to login interactively, at least locally to a Domain Controller, if all else fails, and have enough permissions to either *be* a domain administrator, *be able to elevate itself* to a domain administrator, or *be able to create* a domain administrator, which is ultimately amounts to the same thing. This account should not be restricted by any measures preventing it from authenticating in an emergency – again, at least locally to a domain controller.

It is clear that a break-glass account for a certain domain must belong to that domain – in a scenario where one domain controller is left standing (or could be recovered), accounts from a different domain or forest cannot be used. An ideal break-glass account for every domain is the built-in Administrator (the one with the RID=500). You probably heard many times that you should not use it for day-to-day Tier 0 administration tasks, and this is absolutely true – give it a very long and complex password, print it out, and put it in a safe. Most security auditing tools for AD specifically check for when the RID-500 account has last been used and issue an alert if it has logged on recently. The built-in Administrator is ideal for break-glass scenarios because it cannot be locked out by brute force and cannot be prevented from authenticating by assigning an Authentication Policy to it. It also cannot be removed from the "BUILTIN\Administrators" group, at least not using the regular management APIs.

If you have established a good regime for rotating DSRM passwords and storing them securely but independently from AD, you can disable the built-in Administrator account to prevent it from being used accidentally and also to deter possible malicious actors from conducting brute-force attacks against it. The downside of keeping this account disabled (don't do this by policy!) is that in a disaster scenario you have to boot the DC into DSRM first, mount the NTDS database, and reenable the built-in Administrator.

If you create custom break-glass accounts (to be able to put different passwords in different safes, for example), you have to establish regular checks to make sure they are not locked out, assigned an Authentication Policy, or polluted with **userWorkstations** values that would prevent them from logging on in a disaster recovery situation.

8.1.5 Workstations and Jumphosts

When talking about privileged access and well-engineered administration, there are few concepts as ubiquitous – and as often misinterpreted – as that of a "Privileged Access Workstation" (PAW). To understand what a PAW is, what it can and cannot do to secure your privileged administration, and what deployment options you must consider before finalizing your privileged administration framework, here's the definition that consolidates both patterns and anti-patterns of PAW design:

CHAPTER 8   ENGINEERING ADMINISTRATION

A PAW is the first device in the privileged administration flow, the one persons performing administration physically log on to, either by entering their password or by inserting a smart card and entering the PIN to activate the desired certificate. A PAW is not (necessarily) the device from which the target system is contacted in a highly privileged security context in order to perform administrative tasks on that system.

This is not to say you can't administer AD from the PAW directly. Figure 8-2 illustrates this use case, and there is a lot to say in its favor, because it is the simplest way to benefit from SCAMA and Shadow Principals, especially the former.

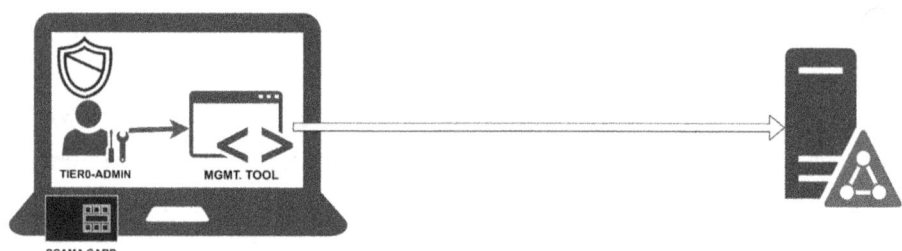

Figure 8-2. *Direct administration from the PAW offers the optimal support for SCAMA but works best in LAN*

However, this approach only works if there is a line of sight from the PAW to the system being managed. For workstations located in the office, i.e., with direct access to the enterprise LAN, this is a great opportunity to create a streamlined and very secure privileged access experience. If using SCAMA, this even allows a person who has Tier 0 and Tier 1 admin responsibilities to have a single PAW for both, just not at the same time – the permissions follow the OIDs in the smart card certificate currently being authenticated with!

CHAPTER 8 ENGINEERING ADMINISTRATION

Organizations that harden their PAWs "to the gills" but then still don't trust them with protecting interactively logged-on credentials, or those experimenting with "Cloud PAWs," sometimes resort to a different approach, illustrated by Figure 8-3.

Figure 8-3. *RunAs administration does not solve the source networks problem*

Here, an unprivileged (but still heavily protected) user logs on interactively to the PAW and starts the desired management tools in a security context of their choice using RunAs or other impersonation techniques. This does not actually solve any real technical problems (if you don't trust your PAW for interactive logon, you shouldn't trust it for RunAs either) and still requires a line of sight from the physical endpoint to the privileged infrastructure.

To alleviate the line of sight problem, many organizations implement "jumphosts," i.e., Windows machines placed close enough to the privileged infrastructure to always have a line of sight to it and secured to the standards of their respective tier. The privileged administrator either connects via RDP using admin credentials, as shown in Figure 8-4, or connects using an unprivileged account and uses RunAs. The RDP connection to the jumphost can go through a VPN, thus allowing the administrators to work from home or generally to be on the road.

309

CHAPTER 8   ENGINEERING ADMINISTRATION

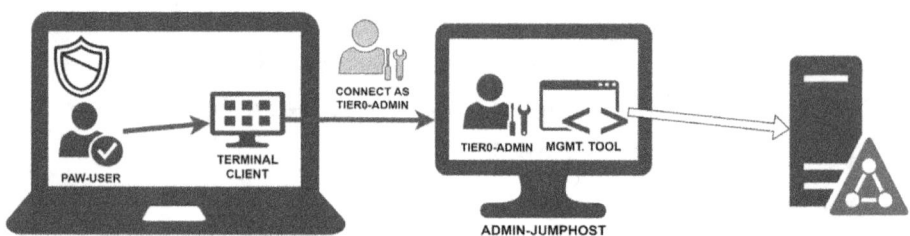

Figure 8-4. *Using jumphosts solves the remote networks issue but creates an attractive target*

A privileged RDP connection is actually preferable to RunAs from the credential protection perspective – if you implement Credential Guard on your jumphosts, RDP session credentials are fairly well protected. This cannot generally be said about the credentials entered in cleartext *within the session.*

Many administrators instinctively think about terminal servers when they hear "jumphosts." This does not need to be the case in all organizations – if your Tier 0 team only counts 5-10 members, personalized virtual or even physical machines as jumphosts are totally feasible! Remember, it's generally easier to enable Credential Guard on a modern physical PC than on a virtual machine. Of course, these machines have to be treated like Tier 0 systems that they are and locked in a datacenter, possibly in a separate cabinet. Dedicated VDI implementations have been known to serve as "ephemeral" jumphosts, destroyed after each logoff and leaving no traces of privileged credentials passing through them. This looks great on paper, especially if the person looking at the paper is from the security rather than from the infrastructure department. However, there may be severe problems with this approach, even security-wise. Most VDI systems have the user authenticate not directly to the target virtual machine but to the connection broker. The broker then passes the credentials on to the virtual desktop once it has been provisioned and assigned to the user. The way the credentials are transferred introduces new attack vectors placed very close to the core of your privileged infrastructure!

8.1.6 A PAW Needs Its Claws

The assumption about the PAW is that it is hardened to the extent that it can be considered "secure enough to enter highly privileged credentials on." This means:

- No physical keylogger. If the workstation is deskbound and wired, all cables must be visible in full length at all times, and it's the administrator's responsibility to perform a visual examination before logging on. The case must be locked and ideally glued shut to prevent a malicious actor with physical access from slipping a keylogger dongle into the case, between the USB port and the mainboard, rather than attaching it on the outside. And of course, wireless keyboards and mice of any kind must not be used with a PAW. Laptops must be kept visible or locked away when not in use.

- No unsanctioned data connections. Bluetooth must be disabled in BIOS. Excess USB ports of deskbound PAWs must be disabled, closed, or glued shut. Installation of USB devices must be restricted to known device IDs to avoid "rubberducky" type attacks.

- No network access beside the route that is needed for the privileged administration. Specifically no Internet access. If wired access is provided, WLAN must be disabled in BIOS. There are design options for an Internet PAW that enforce AlwaysOn VPN as the only network connection. Since the underlying Internet connection still has to be established somehow before AlwaysOn VPN is in effect, this design is not universally accepted.

CHAPTER 8   ENGINEERING ADMINISTRATION

- No camera or fingerprint.
- Full Disk encryption with PIN, password, or smart card protector on top of TPM.

Both Microsoft themselves and independent sources emphasize that the hardening of the PAW hardware must begin at the procurement stage, working with trustworthy manufacturers, resellers, and shippers and maintaining the chain of custody from the factory to the setup workbench to the admin's desk. If your organization can negotiate such contracts at all, then this should probably be true of *every* piece of computer equipment they buy, not just the privileged ones. If this sort of trusted supply chain is not feasible, you can make use of the fact that PAWs are usually very few and do not necessarily need high-end hardware and just engage in "security by dodging," i.e., order these devices outside of your usual supply chain or, better still, buy them physically in a store.

Hardening of a PAW's OS and BIOS must be done to the highest standard. Always separate hardware configuration from the software as much as possible. If your hardware vendor offers a driver and a PowerShell module to "comfortably" manage the BIOS from the OS, do not install them. If this sort of manageability can be turned off on the hardware level, then that's what you should do.

The single most important measure to implement with your PAWs is application whitelisting. Applied consistently, it will mitigate most of the actionable threat vectors that could be used against a PAW. In the Windows ecosystem, there's nothing more effective than Windows Defender Application Control (WDAC). Although WDAC is missing a granular human-friendly control and configuration interface (Intune and "AppControl for Business" are trying to mitigate this shortcoming at the time of writing), specifically for the PAWs, the implementation is usually very straightforward: create a PAW image and apply a WDAC policy only allowing what's in there. You will want to restrict drivers, too, so using uniform hardware for your PAWs will save you a lot of work. Don't put any third-party EDR/XDR on your PAWs, even if your organization has a policy of using one on all devices, *especially if it's using a cloud service for its detection and prevention logic.* Microsoft Defender, if combined with WDAC, is good enough, and you have less publisher certificates and executable names to consider in your whitelisting policy.

Generally, don't spend too much time designing a "management regime" for your PAWs. This time is better spent designing a *rotation* regime. If a PAW has a problem, or if a vendor has published a firmware update, prepare a replacement and just replace the computer, period. There should be nothing on the PAW in terms of files, settings, or – God forbid! – stored credentials. And if there were, then it's a good thing the machine got pulled. Once you have the previous machine in the workshop, reimage it and flash the BIOS. It's absolutely OK and even desirable to have a separate physical deployment server for the PAWs.

8.1.7 A Word on "Cloud PAW"

In terms of becoming an established part of the enterprise privileged access ecosystem, Cloud PAWs are now, at the time of writing, where the physical PAWs were eight years ago. I am sure that if there is a follow-up to this book in ten years' time, Cloud PAWs will be a fixture there.

In short, a Cloud PAW is a virtual PC running in a public cloud that can be accessed from a variety of physical devices, not all of them necessarily hardened to the accepted PAW level. The physical devices are assumed to be hostile in terms of leaking keystrokes or password hashes. This is why cleartext passwords cannot appear anywhere in the chain of communications between the administrator's desk and the target system to be managed. It's fairly easy with cloud services, where passwordless authentication is rapidly becoming the norm. However, to manage a kerberized on-premises system using the Cloud PAW approach from a potentially hostile device, several levels of isolation will be needed. Figure 8-5 demonstrates one approach used today:

CHAPTER 8   ENGINEERING ADMINISTRATION

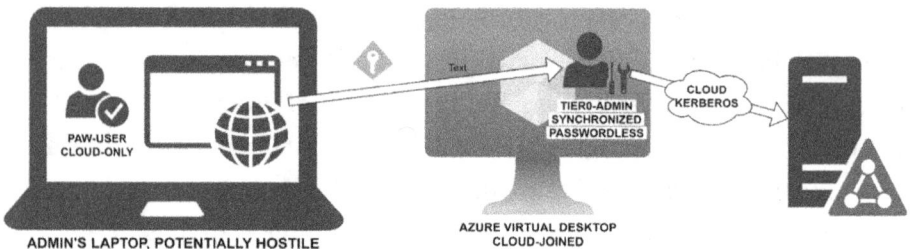

Figure 8-5. *A simplified Cloud PAW management flow*

The Tier 0 admin user in this approach must be synchronized into the cloud in order to simultaneously support passwordless logon on a cloud PC and cloud Kerberos towards on-premises resources. This calls for a "Red Entra ID Tenant," synchronized to a Red AD Forest, to isolate privileged identities from the production applications.

> **Remember:** However many layers of abstraction and virtualization you put between the admin's chair and the crown jewels, if you don't trust the metal, cleartext passwords are forbidden!

8.2 Delegation of Privileges While Reducing the Attack Surface

Most IT teams whose responsibilities include managing Active Directory have already adopted some level of delegation of administrative privileges. Even if logging on as a member of "Enterprise Administrators" still is a daily occurrence in many IT departments, "Schema Admins" is usually empty even in those infrastructures. Every administrator has the right to self-elevate to Schema Admin, but the group is empty 99% of the time and only populated when needed. It is a small step, arguably in the **wrong** direction – if you look at the "privilege ray" in Figure 8-6, you will recognize that the engineer's way of creating a privileged identity is not by creating an overprivileged one and then removing the *excess* permissions, but by starting at zero, or at least at the default user level, and then assigning the *required* permissions granularly.

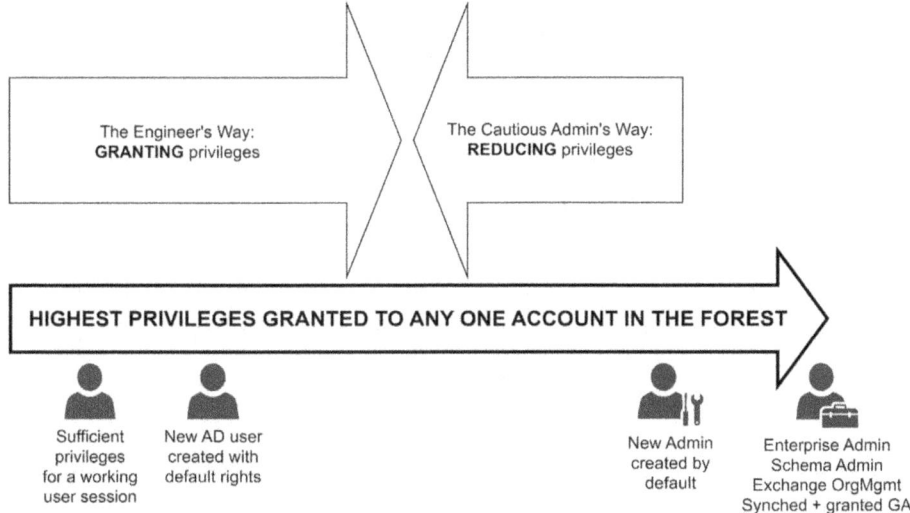

Figure 8-6. *Privileges should be granted, not taken away*

Removing default admin rights can be a daunting task, because the way Windows assigns management permissions by default is not very granular.

8.2.1 Granular Permissions, Red Forest, and Task Recurrence

Organizations embracing the Red Forest concept are often unsure whether the removal of highest-privileged identities from the production forest makes granular permissions obsolete. If a "God mode" identity is hidden from view and presumably cannot be taken over, maybe it's OK to use one? The question is to be taken very seriously, because it is indicative of a "shortcut-taking" mindset.

CHAPTER 8   ENGINEERING ADMINISTRATION

Even if your Tier 0 team only consists of two people with identical job descriptions, knowledge, and backgrounds who fill in for each other, there is still value in not delegating every permission on a permanent basis. Schema Administration is a great example everybody can relate to: A lot of damage can be done by abusing that privilege, and the changes it is needed for are few and far between. If an administrative identity does get compromised, the more privileges it holds at that time, the more potential avenues of abuse you have to investigate before declaring your AD to be in a clean state! In a small Tier 0 team, two levels of privileges may be enough, with the ability to self-elevate (like the "Schema Admins" group a domain admin can add their own account to). Self-elevation should be done on a time-restricted basis by using "Just-In-Time Administration" (JIT) introduced with the Server 2016 "Privileged Access Management" feature. A good criterion to distinguish between tasks requiring elevation and those allowed by default is their recurrence – any permission that is not needed for at least a month during normal operations should be delegated explicitly once the need arises.

The more people perform privileged tasks on a daily basis, the more levels of privilege could make sense, and at some point, the team should agree that not all privileges can be self-elevatable even in Tier 0! Since the authorization model in Windows does not allow for "anyone but myself" types of claims, a separate identity will have to be created for authorizing elevations to the highest level.

Note   On-demand elevation is not easily achieved for automated tasks, but it's not impossible. A more sophisticated runbook automation engine could be used to first elevate a task account using a "God mode" account and then trigger the actual task using the freshly elevated account. Since all automation accounts should be restricted to only authenticate from the automation server(s) anyway, abuse of the "Elevator" account is not very likely.

A Red Forest helps not so much to facilitate these elevation and self-elevation operations but to hide them from the malicious actor's view. Every time a Tier 0 administrator accesses a "golden" forest, they come with certain privileges attached to them. The less the bad guys know about how these privileges got assigned, the better!

8.2.2 Delegating AD Administration

Following the methodology laid out in the previous section, management of AD objects can be subdivided into at least four levels:

- AD Infrastructure management: Schema manipulation, site and subnet manipulation, promotion of demotion of DCs, creation and configuration of trusts, integration of PKI, etc. Editing of DDP and DDCP should also be delegated at the highest level. These are tasks that are usually performed in a maintenance window after a change review and approval process.

- Tier Zero management: Creation, configuration, and deletion of OUs, users, computers, groups, group policies (including baseline policies), and authentication policies designated for Tier Zero operations. If viewed as a role, this is a self-elevating one since the permissions management for global infrastructure also falls under its remit.

- Tier Zero operations: Creation and assignment of FGPP, creation of users and groups, including those for Tier 1 and Tier 2 administration, OUs, and group policies outside of the privileged management container. Complete management of any and all AD objects outside of Tier 0. Provisioning of computer accounts also falls under Tier Zero operations.

CHAPTER 8   ENGINEERING ADMINISTRATION

- Tier One operations: Management of attributes that are not authentication-related for unprivileged users, computers, and groups. Management of group memberships for Tier 1 and lower-privileged groups.

In almost every organization there is also a "Helpdesk" layer, mostly granted permissions to reset user passwords and unlock locked accounts for non-privileged users, retrieve BitLocker recovery keys for workstations, and edit personal information like the telephone number or the job description. Try to avoid granting these permissions directly to service desk personnel but rather solve these requirements through automation. Personal information and especially job-related attributes should come from a different data source anyway – Identity Management or Human Resources being the most preferable candidates. Password resets and account lockouts should always generate a service request ("trouble ticket"), and the ticket system can serve as the data basis for automation. BitLocker keys may be an exception if you do not manage your clients at all, but if you do, your configuration management tool most certainly offers the function of retrieving a BitLocker key that is way more comfortable than looking it up in AD.

An interesting case of rather problematic delegation is the permission to retrieve a local administrator password for a workstation from LAPS. At the first glance, it appears to be a Tier 2 task; however, if the written policy in your organization (*or the common sense*) does not prohibit Tier 2 administrators from sharing this information with end users, it becomes an extremely sensitive task that should always involve the most trustworthy personnel.

To physically delegate permissions on AD objects and containers, you can use ADSIEdit, ADUC (for domain partitions), PowerShell, or the built-in "Delegation of Control Wizard" that has been part of the AD toolkit since Server 2003. There are a number of third-party tools available on the market that will assist here as well, mostly based on templates, which make application of permissions easily repeatable. The built-in wizard also uses templates that you can easily customize – the preinstalled file **C:\Windows\System32\delegwiz.inf** contains examples for typical parameter sets, and Microsoft published an even more comprehensive example in the knowledge base 20 years ago. Not all of the tools allow creating templates that already contain the actual principals the permissions are intended for (the built-in wizard doesn't).

There are lots of projects on the Internet that aim to deploy a delegated administration framework to an existing AD domain or forest. In the author's experience, none of them will fit your business requirements, team structure, and personal preferences completely, so you will probably end up borrowing code from multiple projects and creating your own delegation provisioning script – or scripts, depending on how you choose to structure them.

Don't forget the AdminSDHolder container – its ACL must reflect your "Tier Zero Management" delegations since all groups covered by SDHolder are most definitely Tier 0!

8.2.3 Delegating GPO Administration

When creating a GPO administration framework, there are seven operations you need to take care of:

- Creation of a GPO (from scratch, from a Starter GPO, or from an existing GPO by copying it)
- Viewing the GPO's properties and content (those are different permissions but the author never saw anyone differentiate between them)
- Editing the GPO's properties (including WMI filter and branch enablement/disablement)
- Editing the GPO's content

CHAPTER 8   ENGINEERING ADMINISTRATION

- Linking a GPO to (and unlinking it from) a domain, a site, or an OU (the first two always being a Tier 0 operation)

- Deleting a GPO

- Blocking GPO inheritance on an OU

If you use the GPMC to create these delegations, be aware that the right "Link GPO" grants write permissions to both **gpLink** and **gpOptions** attributes, as shown in Figure 8-7.

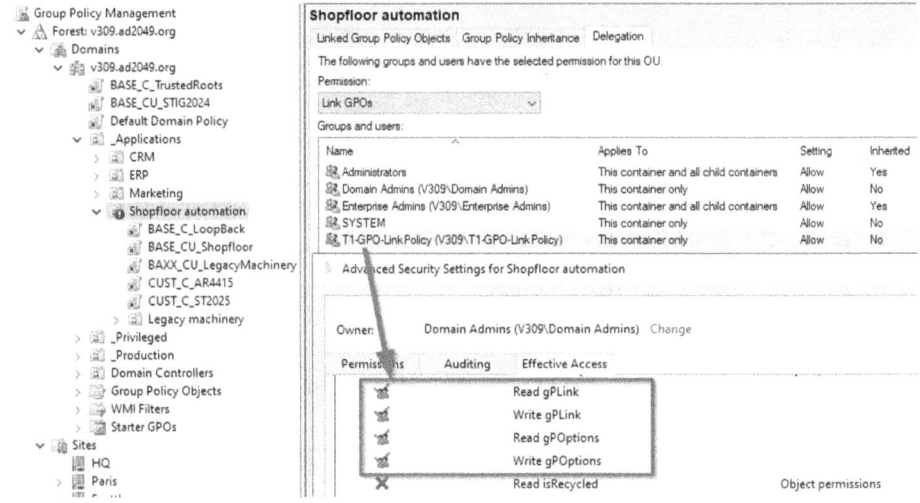

Figure 8-7. *The built-in "Link GPO" permission is not granular enough*

This gives any principal you allow to link GPOs to an OU the ability to also break the inheritance (setting **gpOptions** to 1) and cancel out all GPOs handed down from the domain and from the parent OUs! You can remove the write permission to **gpOptions** without breaking anything.

Creation of GPOs requires, beside the right to create a **groupPolicyContainer** object in the "Policies" container, the permission to create the corresponding folder and file structure in SYSVOL. You can delegate both rights simultaneously using GPMC, and Microsoft does a decent job of not overpermissioning the newly created object; however, the problem we already encountered while creating computers in AD in Chapters 5 and 7 presents itself here as well – the **user account** creating the object ends up being assigned both ownership and write permissions over it, both in AD and in the file system, unless the account chains up to "Domain Admins"! There are multiple solution approaches to this:

- Since creating new GPOs *is* a Tier 0 task anyway, chain the respective group up to Domain Admins.

- Automate the creation of GPOs, including the application of the correct permissions *and* removal of the creator's user object from the ACL.

- Preprovision a lot of GPOs using a domain admin and delegate the right to set permissions on them to a Tier 0 group. This way, the objects will already be created with correct permissions, and when the edit rights are delegated, it will not result in a user identity being added to the ACL. Remove visibility for lower-privileged identities from unused objects so the console view of other administrators is not too cluttered. In any case, start the names of preprovisioned GPOs with "ZZZ" so that they are displayed at the bottom of the list.

- Use **Copy-GPO** with the **-CopyACL** switch and a correctly permissioned template object for creating new GPOs.

The GPMC-supported delegation of "Edit settings" is also not granular enough, because it creates a "Write all properties" ACE on the AD object. This allows renaming the policy (**displayName** attribute) and changing the WMI filter (**gPCWQLFilter** attribute), which may not actually be desirable since it has the potential of changing the scope of the policy! The only

CHAPTER 8   ENGINEERING ADMINISTRATION

attributes a "settings editor" does need write access to are **versionNumber**, **gPCUserExtensionNames**, and **gPCMachineExtensionNames** plus the right to create some child objects for the more obscure areas of the policy. However, if you limit write access to these properties, GPMC will refuse to let you edit it. Another reason to delegate GPO tasks sparingly if you use the out-of-box tools to manage your environment!

8.2.4 Delegating DNS Administration

If your organization uses AD-integrated DNS, give some thought to who will be responsible for operating it and how to separate the management of records pertaining to privileged operations from the rest.

Note   Even if your organization opted for using a third-party DNS service for production forests, there is much to be said in favor of using AD-integrated DNS for the Red forest. This removes an external dependency on third-party DNS and encapsulates your "crown jewels" within themselves. The Red Forest will probably be fairly static as far as host records are concerned, so that even disabling Dynamic updates after the topology has been reflected in DNS can be a viable option. At the very least, remove the permission for "Authenticated Users" to create new objects – you will not have that situation in the Red Forest.

Delegate the ability to "Create all child objects" and "Delete all child objects" on DNS server level to a specially created Tier 0 group – this affects the creation and deletion of DNS zones and conditional forwarders – both can be extremely security-sensitive. The DNS server security descriptor is shared between all DCs in the domain and applied to the "MicrosoftDNS" container you will find in the "System" branch of your domain tree. You can nest your specially created universal group into the built-in domain local group "DnsAdmins" – it already has the requisite permissions. This group is also not monitored by SDHolder so that it will not mess with your permissions. However, this group is *de facto* privileged enough to have the same ACL you assign to the "AdminSDHolder" container.

8.2.5 Delegating PKI Administration and Certificate Issuance

If your organization will be using a Microsoft enterprise PKI (ADCS) for Kerberos authentication, it should reside completely in the Red Forest. For SCAMA or simply for admins logging on using a smart card, the authentication needs are already covered by this, since they will be authentication against the Red Forest.

If you want to offer smart card authentication in the "golden" forest, just import the Issuing CA certificate from the Red Forest PKI into the NTAuth container and make sure Domain Controllers can reach the CDP or OCSP.

> **Note** You should always prefer OCSP to CDP with smart card authentication because it allows you to enable deterministic revocation checking, i.e., certificates will be rejected not only if they have been revoked but also if they have not been issued by the correct CA in the first place!

PKI administration and even certificate template delegation within the Red Forest is easier than in a production forest, because there are no "accidental" ACLs opening up control paths to a phished user from Marketing. Still, for smart card certificates, you should use enrollment agents and have a very limited group of persons issue smart cards to everybody else.

CHAPTER 8   ENGINEERING ADMINISTRATION

Things become much more interesting if the business requires autoenrollment for users (S/MIME) or computers (802.1X). You cannot use your Red Forest PKI for this because these entities cannot authenticate towards it, nor would you want them to. If you create a new Issuing CA as a "subordinate enterprise CA" in the "golden" forest (it can be signed by the same offline root CA as the Red Forest one or by a different root), you might be forced to leave its certificate in the NTAuth container **if you run Windows NPS for 802.1X, Direct Access, or AlwaysOn VPN** because all of them require the Issuing CA's certificate to be added to NTAuth. In this case, you might end up running a more complex PKI structure than you had originally bargained for.

Whatever PKI infrastructure you decide (or are forced) to create in the "golden" forest,

- Have Domain Controller certificates issued strictly by the Red Forest PKI, even if it means that they will not autorenew and you have to automate the process or do the job manually

- Assign any and all permissions to the CA and certificate templates to Tier 0 groups, except for "enroll" and "autoenroll"

- Use "Tame My Certs" or a similar commercial product, if available, to prevent creating authentication certificate for privileged identities

Before you provision a PKI in the "golden" forest, take some time to evaluate whether the lifecycle processes for users and computers allow equipping them with certificates from the Red Forest-based PKI in a secure manner.

8.3 Using Automation

Automation is one of the most important parts of the "modern AD" administration framework. It helps overcome the seeming complexity of thousands of repetitive tasks and avoid typical human mistakes like reading from the wrong row in a spreadsheet or editing the wrong file. It makes scheduling of recurring privileged operations like **krbtgt** or DSRM password rotation. It also helps keep highly privileged credentials out of humans' hands – at the price of having to keep them in a place where machines can make use of them.

8.3.1 On Schedule and on Demand

When tasked with automating administrative activities, IT teams usually have little problem implementing scheduled operations. There is always the Task Scheduler in Windows, and if managed manually (vs. deployed by GPP), the tasks can even run under a gMSA. Of course, there are other methods of triggering a task or a script on schedule, but Task Scheduler is a very robust, battle-proven technology, and no one has ever been fired for using it (at least, not for using it in a proper way). If you're contemplating a third-party alternative, it should deliver at least the following two features Task Scheduler lacks:

- A mechanism to securely deliver a credential object to a task (with Task Scheduler, you have to roll your own and put it in every script you schedule that requires explicit credentials)

- A mechanism to react to the result of the task execution, especially if the result is not 100% positive (in Task Scheduler, the task itself must take care of it, which means that it absolutely cannot error out in the middle!)

CHAPTER 8   ENGINEERING ADMINISTRATION

If an "enterprise runbook automation" system cannot deliver these features, then in most cases it is not worth the effort of implementing it.

Running a complex task on demand is something many administrators never seem to figure out how to implement properly. Here's where those "enterprise runbook automation" products really shine – you feed a script or a runbook into a user interface, create a task to run this item against system X using credentials Y and do Z after it finishes (close the ticket on success, escalate the ticket on failure, send an email, or whatever), and delegate the task to admins A, B, and C. Some of these products will support scheduled execution as well, others will require you to license this feature separately. In general, it is a good idea to use a well-tested product from an established vendor for your automation needs rather than roll your own. Before you commit to using a certain technology for automating your highly privileged tasks, evaluate the two factors that matter most: effort of deployment (you will need at least two separate instances just for Tier 0 and Tier 1 and may end up needing more) and protection of "runas" credentials. From the security standpoint, the latter is paramount. While the built-in secret storage facilities in Windows are not ideal (we will discuss this in the next section), their vulnerabilities are known and so are techniques to protect against them being exploited. A "super secure secret storage" provided by your chosen product may not be as secure as the name suggests (the author has seen a user-readable SQLite database holding cleartext passwords in a product that cost five-digits per year). Be equally wary if the solution supports using a well-known external vault like Azure KeyVault or Thycotic SecretServer for credentials storage. In most cases, you need a secret to retrieve credentials from a vault, and the way your runbook automation product stores that secret is all that is standing between an attacker and your highest-privileged credentials!

If you decide to take a shot at providing on-demand automation yourself, do not let past experience limit your imagination to seeing "executing a task" as "running a script and getting the result back." Firstly, you'll have to run the script using highly privileged credentials; secondly,

CHAPTER 8   ENGINEERING ADMINISTRATION

you need both access to the script *and* the assurance that you're running the current version; and finally, this also requires direct network access to the target system. Here is but a small selection of techniques that allow you to accomplish this in a more secure and scalable manner:

- Have a scheduled task run as SYSTEM on your task server every five minutes. The script in the task contacts a file share or a SQL database admins have write access to and looks for signals (files or records in a database table) to start a certain job. If such a signal has been found, the task triggers another task (SYSTEM can do that!) that performs the required actions. This approach can also be used to automate privileged actions based on the ticket system, which is usually Tier 2 and thus cannot be used to trigger Tier 0 automation actively!

- Delegate permissions to run scheduled tasks to less-privileged accounts and let the administrators connect remotely using the Task Scheduler console and trigger the tasks. It is a non-trivial exercise that, too, can and should be automated if you decide to go down this path.

- Use PowerShell JEA to trigger scheduled tasks or even run scripts as a privileged virtual user. The administrators' user experience will be that of running a script, but this script will not be run privileged, nor shall it be doing the actual work.

327

8.3.2 Storing and retrieving credentials

To perform privileged actions against any system using Kerberos in Active Directory, including Active Directory itself, you have five choices:

1. Run the tasks on the target itself (e.g., on a Domain Controller) as SYSTEM (thus replacing the manual task of doing the actual work by the manual task of managing automated tasks on that computer).

2. Run the tasks on a domain-joined task server as SYSTEM and grant the required privileges to the computer account of the task server ("required privileges" being those required by any of tasks being run there – this has the potential of escalating to "God mode" very quickly).

3. Run the tasks on a domain-joined task server as a gMSA and grant the required privileges to the gMSA (this has the advantage of being able to use different gMSA for different tasks).

4. Run the tasks on a domain-joined task server as SYSTEM, local service account, or non-privileged gMSAs and provide privileged credentials to those tasks.

5. Run the tasks on a workgroup task server as SYSTEM or a local service account and provide privileged credentials to those tasks.

The first choice has only made the list for the sake of completeness. No one does that, and for good reason. One example where it actually *can* make sense is the rotation of the domain controller's own DSRM password. In this case, the secret management challenge is not providing a secret to the scheduled task but getting the new password *out* in a secure manner. This is solvable using "Cryptographic Message Syntax" (CMS) where the script encrypts the new password using a public certificate of which the trustworthy Tier 0 admin holds the private key, so that the admin is the only person able to decrypt the password.

A "God mode" computer account in approach 2 is THE target for malicious actors trying to take over your AD; we discussed possible risks of computer accounts in Chapter 5. However, if the server in question is joined to the Red Forest and the firewall on it rejects any inbound connection attempts, this solution may just be acceptable. Still, highly privileged service tickets coming from a computer account mean asking for trouble in the long run.

Method 3 can work well enough and be considered sufficiently secure if you choose a short gMSA password lifetime of 1–2 days for all the gMSAs involved. Since the scheduled tasks do not usually run that long, it shouldn't be a problem. If joined to the Red Forest, gMSA can work with (and hide behind) Shadow Principals when performing actions against a "golden" forest.

Sometimes Kerberos SSO from the task server to the target systems is not enough, and explicit privileged credentials must be used. If you use a runbook automation solution that offers truly secure credentials delivery, you should make use of that. Document the procedure of rolling a password both in AD and in the automation product's credential store and check if that, too, can be automated. This would allow you to automate rolling the passwords of function accounts used in automation! In case your chosen automation solution does not provide secure credentials delivery, you will have to handle credential retrieval within your task scripts.

The difference between 4 and 5 becomes apparent when you realize that whatever you do to retrieve credentials from whatever store – Windows Vault, certificate, Credential Manager – is protected by DPAPI in the end. On domain members, DPAPI-protected secrets of both computers

CHAPTER 8   ENGINEERING ADMINISTRATION

and users can be easily unprotected using a domain-wide "DPAPI BACKUP Key" (the author caught himself calling it a "backdoor key" many times in his career). This key is generated at domain creation, and no supported procedure exists, at least at the time of writing, to ever rotate that key! Imagine a malicious actor discovering a ten-year-old backup of your DC that your predecessor created quickly before performing a schema upgrade and never bothered to delete. All passwords have been changed since then, but with the backup/backdoor key found in the backup, the attacker is able to decrypt everything that's been protected by DPAPI ever since. Keeping that in mind, a task server not joined to a production forest becomes a very attractive proposition. However, managing privileged workgroup machines carries risks of its own. Joining the task server to your "Red" forests where you don't leave old backups lying around is an excellent compromise.

> Using CMS with "Document Encryption" certificates became the author's favorite solution to the problem of secret delivery over the years. If you have an enterprise PKI with autoenrollment enabled, you can have your task servers and gMSAs request certificates themselves, so that no one ever gets to see the private key. You can grab the public part of the certificate from the CA or from the task server. Once you have the public key, use **Protect-CMSMessage** to encrypt the password and make the encrypted text available to the script. In the script, use **Unprotect-CMSMessage** to retrieve the cleartext password.

When running tasks using explicit credentials, always verify where the actual authentication takes place and limit the ability of the function accounts to authenticate to as few computers as possible using Authentication Policies or other techniques we discussed in Chapter 5.

8.3.3 Do Not Compete with Your Own Automation

Keep track of the tasks you have automated in your AD management ecosystem (including closely related areas such as deployment, domain join, GPOs, DNS management, certificate lifecycle management, and so on). Once a particular task has been automated, do not do this work manually, even if your muscle memory allows you to do the required change in AD faster than you would create and trigger an automated job. If you need any justification at all for this recommendation, consider these two factors:

- Every time you do a modification directly to a Tier 0 system, you expose your Tier 0 credentials. Automation exposes its credentials on a regular basis anyway.

- Any automation worth that name will log every action that it has been instructed to do, the exact time and duration, as well as the success of that action. If you do the work manually, you have to log it yourself, and it will probably not be in the same logging facility.

8.3.4 Prevent Automation Sprawl

A common anti-pattern often encountered in organizations that love automating things but do not have a clear idea how to do it in an efficient manner is a multitude of automation engines and tools. Try to avoid this "automation sprawl" and automate all your privileged administration using one set of tools and machines. This helps prevent situations where you end up troubleshooting a task in one engine – only to find out that the same task is being executed by a different engine as well! If your automation methodology includes storing and using explicit credentials, automation sprawl increases these credentials' exposure to all sorts of risks.

8.3.5 Sign Your Scripts

If you use PowerShell, sign your script code. More specifically, sign every version you consider production-ready and leave development-grade versions unsigned. If you set the execution policy in your production environment to "AllSigned," you will at least get a warning if trying to run a dev version in production.

> **Note** PowerShell execution policy is not a security feature – a well-versed attacker knows at least 15 different ways to circumvent it. However, it is awesome for keeping admins from shooting themselves in the foot.

Code signing certificates you use for signing PowerShell scripts can be used for signing any other executable code that supports Authenticode or similar technologies like Java Code Signing. Protect private keys of these certificates, ideally by not allowing them outside the key store of your development workstation.

8.4 Using Desired State

A special kind of automation is "Desired State Configuration" (DSC). DSC is a general term, although it has been used as a feature name in PowerShell and in Microsoft SCCM. The idea behind DSC is as simple as its real-world implementations are complex:

- A configuration of a certain system (e.g., Active Directory) is described outside of the system itself. Usually markup languages like JSON, XML, or YAML are used to hold the desired state. The description can require the presence or absence of a certain object

CHAPTER 8   ENGINEERING ADMINISTRATION

and, if the object must be present in the desired state, certain properties of the object to have certain values.

- An automation facility (DSC engine) is empowered to configure the target system. It parses the desired state data and utilizes the target system's configuration interfaces to create the desired state.

DSC helps prevent configuration drift. It has been used with great success by IT teams to keep application servers, network devices, or even database clusters configured in a certain way without human intervention. Extending DSC to identity systems requires the ability to "undelete" and "uncreate" objects, which may or may not be easily achievable.

At the time of writing, the best attempt made so far to create a DSC facility for an Active Directory forest is the "Active Directory Management Framework" (ADMF) for PowerShell created and maintained by Friedrich Weinmann. It does not offer every little bit of configuration that we discussed in the previous chapters, but it does an excellent job of keeping permissions and GPO links at the predefined standard.

ADMF is designed to be domain-agnostic which allows the same configuration to be applied to multiple forests. It can be a great help if you have several resource forests designed to have identical configurations (e.g., file server forests for domain local groups isolation). Specifically, site and subnet configuration is part of the desired state, and you definitely want to keep those synchronized.

Time will tell whether ADMF or any other DSC project, open source or otherwise, that may surface in the future will become a universally accepted standard for modern AD management. If it does, a future AD engineering book may contain heaps of JSON or YAML files!

8.5 Summary

In this chapter, we examined administrative activities that require an interactive logon to the target system and those that can be accomplished remotely. We looked at protocols used for remote and remote-interactive scenarios, their authentication and authorization capabilities, and possible risks of their usage.

We discussed the correct delegation of typical administrative privileges for AD, DNS, and group policy administration. We glanced over PKI integration and the challenges it presents for secure administration. And since automation has been a big part of the "modern AD" engineering effort from the very beginning, we described possible solution approaches for providing this capability and security implications of these solutions.

CHAPTER 9

Building a Modern AD

Now that we have collected most of the pieces that make up a well-engineered Active Directory implementation, it is time to put the puzzle together. In this chapter, we will engage in the very rare exercise of building a sizable production-ready AD organization from scratch, i.e., on a "green field." While the greenfield approach is not immediately applicable to real-life transitioning situations (we will take care of those in Chapter 11), the prerequisites, decision-making processes, and implementation milestones are much more visible here, making this approach perfectly suitable for the "what could have been/what we should aim for" conversation.

In this greenfield implementation, we will deliberately not consider the reasons that led to building an Active Directory organization from first principles. We will leave this, too, for Chapter 11. Even today, at the time of writing, these things happen, and we will do our best to gather, evaluate, and ultimately fulfill the business requirements in a manageable, resilient, and secure manner.

There are distinct anti-patterns observed in many AD implementations that can derail even a greenfield deployment:

- Spending too much time and effort on formal requirements engineering and design questions like naming conventions. Both requirements engineering and conventions are important, but there is a world of difference between theorizing what could be and analyzing concrete applications that the new AD will support from day one.

CHAPTER 9   BUILDING A MODERN AD

- Building Tier 0 systems in an insecure environment, or in one that is only temporary and will have to be migrated in the near future.

- Trying to implement the complete security operations stack at once.

- Neglecting either the backup regime or backup security, or both, in the early stages of deployment.

We will try to avoid these mistakes in our build process.

9.1 Fast-Tracking Design

This book began with the clear distinction between "Design" (defining the requirements) and "Engineering" (fulfilling the requirements). And although the design part is usually not up to you, it is ultimately your job to extract the requirements from "the business" (upper management and business units), the application owners, the policy makers (security, compliance, data protection, and so on), and the physical world surrounding the enterprise. The sad truth is: you will never get people to tell you what they need, and the very few exceptions the author encountered in over 25 years of consulting simply reinforce the rule. This is why you should always choose a different approach and let them surprise you if you stumble upon one of those exceptional cases.

9.1.1 Gather Only the Most Significant Requirements

There are some constants you just can't do anything about. Email domains, and sometimes even email addresses, are determined by Marketing, domain availability, and HR policies (e.g., those of not abbreviating the employees' names unless the 255-character limit is violated, and even in that case, one HR team the author had the pleasure of working with did not go down without a fight). Email addresses define UPNs, because a. in a hybrid infrastructure, Microsoft applications work better if the two are identical, and b. you want to be able to tell the employees to "just logon with their email address." UPNs define the suffix namespace – or namespaces, if the organization runs several mail domains. Remember, even a single-domain forest can have as many supported – and routable – UPN suffixes as you like!

Another set of requirements you can do little about is geography and the topology of the organization's physical WAN. You can, however, reason with the network team if the topology provided by them would cause functional problems or force you to choose an overcomplicated and unsustainable forest design. We discussed this in Chapter 3. The question of office locations with poor physical security is also one to take care of at the very beginning. Do not *offer* to provide local authentication in those sites – no one will ever say no to this offer. Instead, try to establish in every single case that they *do not actually need* local infrastructure. Remember, an RODC only provides real value if you can define – and describe by technical means like a group membership – the users whose passwords need to be cached there. The only other benefit is that GPOs will load faster if there is an RODC present in the site, but "poor physical security" does not necessarily mean "poor network connectivity," so this benefit may end up not being worth the effort and the risk.

Collect the top 20% of the most important applications used in the organization. What an "application" is is not necessarily defined by the executable the users will start on their endpoints. Whether they create and share Word documents, Excel spreadsheets, or PowerPoint presentations is of no consequence. It is, however, important how those files are stored and how the access will be authorized, so "Office programs with documents stored on a file server" is a different "application" in terms of AD design than "Office programs with documents stored in SharePoint." Each application has a frontend (sometimes even multiple – Exchange can be used with Outlook, with Web Access, and with mobile devices, each fronted adding to the requirements in a different way), a backend, and interconnections with other applications. The "importance" of an application is determined by its criticality for the business and by the number of users working with it on a constant basis.

If the organization does not yet exist but is in the process of being created, you will not have the advantage of being able to talk to application owners actually running the application in question about its specific behavior. When dealing with non-standard software that you do not happen to intimately know from past experience, talk to the vendors. Sometimes you have to tread really carefully here, so as to not tip them off about an imminent purchase of their product. Keep an eye out for applications that are potential candidates for a resource forest – either due to legacy requirements, or to an overblown authorization structure, or both.

Application delivery is not in the scope of an AD implementation project, but it is inseparably tied to it. Make sure to talk to the application delivery team – maybe there is a "Digital Workplace" project already underway, and all those remote sites with bad physical security will consume business application via terminal services or VDI anyway! On the other hand, application delivery can have requirements of its own, for example, in terms of reusing computer accounts or creating new ones, or using keytab files for authentication.

Talk to the infrastructure team, unless you are yourself a part of it. It may have relevant requirements defined already, e.g., for a Guarded Fabric which, in turn, requires a host attestation forest. Both the datacenter infrastructure team and the network team probably have systems under their purview that require DNS, authentication, certificates, or maybe all of the above, while being placed in network segments that should not necessarily be allowed to communicate with Tier 0 identity systems.

Last but not least, at this stage, you need a clear understanding of what the typical enterprise client device will look like and whether it will be AD joined (why?), Entra ID joined, or even hybrid joined (usually the worst possible choice). Do not be afraid to ask critical questions if they are pertinent to the design.

9.1.2 Create a Design Proposal

We're still in the "design" phase, so the next logical step is creating a design proposal. You have now established what UPN suffixes will be used, which applications will have to be delivered and to what sites, and how well these sites are a. connected and b. physically secured. You also know at least the basics about what sort of endpoints this infrastructure will be accessed from. You probably don't know many things yet that will become important later on, e.g., whether authorization requirements will call for additional resource forests.

Your design proposal is directed, first and foremost, at management. Make it manager-ready, start with a "Management Summary" (this is where the reasoning we intentionally left out in this chapter comes in), and continue by briefly summarizing the requirements and then describing the Active Directory infrastructure you are proposing to build in order to fulfill these requirements. Do not bore your audience with fringe cases at this stage. Your proposal may not even reach large parts of the intended readership, but if it does, each person has to see why it is relevant to them. Use graphics rather than tables, especially when describing the physical topology. Tables are for techies, and there will be tables galore at the next stage.

You should point out at the design stage (if that's the case, of course) that the planned design will include several forests. Describe their purpose briefly so that a manager can understand the intention and a techie can visualize the implications. Include the Red Forest in the very first draft. You do not need any more justification than "for providing secure privileged administration" at this stage. The earlier you get the seed planted and the concept signed off on, the less friction you will encounter down the road.

CHAPTER 9 BUILDING A MODERN AD

Apart from involving the corporate leadership and getting them to approve the design, the design proposal you create plays a very important role even before being presented to the management. This is the first time your new modern AD manifests itself not as ideas but in the form of a concrete description. If you cannot get 100% behind the design proposal yourself, your engineering effort will either fail, or it will deviate so much from the proposal that even managers might notice the discrepancy. Discuss the proposal with members of your team or with an experienced AD person not involved in the project. The author has had the privilege of being that person in several high-profile engagements, and the expert conversation around a design put on paper always was much more valuable than theoretical musings about the intricacies of AD or some application relevant to the project.

9.2 Secure from the Beginning

The modern Active Directory organization must be built to the security standards you envisioned in the design, even if they are not detailed in the design proposal document itself. The secret to building a secure AD is to *build securely*. Even a greenfield organization comes with a number of requirements, most notably applications it has to support, that have the potential of reducing the overall security posture. Twenty years of the world's experience running AD show that starting at a reduced security level and hoping to harden afterwards is not going to get you to where you want the security posture to be.

Running a modern AD is to be prepared for change. We will deal with it in a more general way in Section 9.4, but in terms of security, "change" begins with accommodating requirements that do not fit the planned security framework, even before that framework has been implemented.

9.2.1 Deal with Insecure Applications You Know About

The most frequent security-reducing requirement introduced by applications, even to this day, is to support NTLM authentication. Microsoft determined in 2022 that 52% of NTLM authentication is due to it being hardcoded in applications. Your AD forest, of course, comes with the modern authentication defaults and has NTLM disabled. To find a way to accommodate this requirement, analyze the application. Does the NTLM requirement come from the server side of the application or from the client piece? Is NTLM only required for internal communications, e.g., between the middleware and the database server, or for client-server communications? Will the users only access the application from a predefined set of client devices (e.g., shopfloor or medical devices)? Qualified answers to these questions allow you to find solution approaches that may help reduce the application's impact:

- Use a different authentication provider, e.g., SQL authentication from the middleware to the database instead of Windows authentication if "Windows" has been hardcoded to NTLM by the vendor.

- Create an Authentication Policy for the service account in the backend only allowing NTLM if accessed from a list of designated source devices.

- Create exceptions to the NTLM restriction policy only for the servers that actually need to be authenticated against by NTLM.

- If there is a particular workflow requiring NTLM that is only executed every couple of months, an automated task adding the required server(s) to the exception and removing them afterwards helps reduce the attack surface.

Another typical application requirement that leads to diminished security is having service accounts of certain types or having excessive permissions assigned to them, be it on the machine where the service is running or in other systems like database servers or file servers. Analyzing and reducing these requirements must become standard procedure very early in the implementation process. Document it well, and have an after-action discussion with your team. Critically questioning requested permissions and legacy protocols must become a part of your operational DNA if you want your team to survive the next 25 years.

9.2.2 Start with Proper Delegation Early

You are building an AD organization that is supposed to operate under delegated, secured administration for decades to come. It is only natural that you should start implementing this operational paradigm as early in the process as possible.

Create the groups for your delegated administration and assign them the required permissions as early as possible. Start by adding an administrative user from the group's own forest; you can move all privileged administration to the Red Forest later if the groups are in place. This gives you the ability to preflight your identity provisioning and AD management processes, make adjustments, and ultimately document the complete procedure.

> **Note** Do not use the built-in Administrator account more than once. The first order of business after each new forest is instantiated is to create a new account – it can well be a copy of the "fresh" RID-500 Administrator! – for each Tier 0 administrator who will participate in the forest buildout. There should not be more than a handful of those – there is no point in provisioning accounts that will not be used since they will all be deleted at a later time.

CHAPTER 9 BUILDING A MODERN AD

If you are using a predefined procedure to configure your forest, you might need to skip one important step at this stage:

Note Do not enable the Recycle Bin feature until all temporary God-mode accounts have been deleted! Alternatively, enable the Recycle Bin early and delete the initial God-mode objects from it using ADSI - this will bypass tombstoning the object and delete them irrevocably.

Remember that group scopes matter, and you will not always be able to convert them after the memberships have been populated:

- Fine-Grained Password Policies are only processed if assigned to **global** groups. The graphical management interface in ADAC will protect you from assigning an FGPP to a universal group; however, a domain local group can be added without a warning. The PowerShell cmdlet **Add-ADFineGrainedPasswordPolicySubject** will add any group from the same domain without checking the scope.

- SCAMA requires the mapped groups to be of **universal** scope. This means that you cannot map Domain Admins via SCAMA.

- Shadow Principals can be mapped to **any security principal with a SID**, i.e., can be not only a group but also a user or even a computer object.

- **Domain local** groups in cross-domain and cross-forest scenarios are only included in the access tokens issued within their own domain.

Deploy all "golden" forests you know you will be needing from the beginning: User, File Server, Exchange, Host Attestation for Guarded Fabric, etc. Since you already knew from the Design Proposal that you will be needing several forests, you scripted or otherwise automated at least

- Creation of sites and subnets
- Removal of default permissions and group nestings
- Provisioning of Tier 0 groups for delegated administration
- Default Domain Policy and Default Domain Controller Policy
- Baseline policies, their filtering, and linking

You can have your script for privileged groups provisioning also prepare migration tables for GPO transfer from your first forest. Since migration tables are just XML files that work mostly with NetBIOS names, creating them becomes a trivial exercise if you use the same naming convention in all the forests:

> The process of copying GPOs between forests of your organization becomes even easier if you give groups of the same designation *identical* names across all forests. This, however, comes at a price – you will always have to look at the domain part in the distinguished name to determine which forest the group in question belongs to! In the author's experience, the additional (perfectly automatable) complexity of maintaining a migration table for each forest pair is a small price to pay for the ability to instantly visually determine where a certain group comes from.

9.2.3 When to Introduce the Red Forest

If your privileged administration framework is based on a Red Forest (as it should), do not deploy one just yet. Prepare everything Tier 0-related in the "golden" forests and test it with local accounts so that you can transfer your administration model to the Red Forest quickly when the moment comes.

You know that you're finished with Tier 0 once you start onboarding the first application (Tier 1) and/or the first client device (Tier 2) into their respective forests. We will return to the stage of Red Forest deployment in Section 9.6.

9.3 Creating Prerequisites

You are building an identity infrastructure that is supposed to cater to the organization's authentication and authorization needs for the next 25 years. If it were a house, you would probably insist on having a solid foundation in place before you start laying bricks. You should apply the same principles here.

If you are tasked with engineering and implementing a new Active Directory, chances are that other teams are busy building out the global WAN, the LAN segments in the office and datacenter locations, storage and virtualization platforms, and all the other parts of a global IT infrastructure that are even closer "to the metal" than authentication and authorization. Use this time to prepare your bricks and your mortar – naming conventions, scripts, and so on – but do not accept temporary platform solutions for the parts of the infrastructure that are bound to reduce the security of your AD!

> **Note** Even at the time of writing, some organizations insist on setting up centralized Active Directory authentication for server hardware management, storage arrays, network devices, virtualization hosts, and other infrastructure components. In a "modern AD," this should not be possible already due to the fact that the management interfaces of those systems must be encapsulated in the "Tier -1" management network that has no access to production AD. On the other hand, centralized account management to log on to thousands of network devices is definitely a very good thing to have. If the infrastructure team does not possess any workable knowledge to set up their authentication authority on a different basis than AD, build a separate, isolated forest just for the infrastructure authentication purposes. Hyper-V will obviously always require AD in any enterprise-grade deployment – here, too, a separate forest just for the purpose of supporting Hyper-V clusters is a better solution than opening virtualization management to be accessed from production networks and vice versa. Remember, a Hyper-V cluster can *start* without AD being available so that you can even virtualize the "management network forest" on the platform itself without creating a dependency loop. You have, however, to take very good care of network isolation if you do that.

9.3.1 Prepare and Maintain a Test Environment

You will always need a test environment, and an early stage of an Active Directory deployment is the ideal moment to create one. It must reflect the security controls you put in place in production and it's a good idea to put objects into the test Active Directory that are similar to production in terms of numbers, placement, and attribute values that are populated. The test environment does not have to reflect the entire physical topology of your production AD, although it is a very good idea to provision a network segment and an AD site without Domain Controllers in it and also a site only containing an RODC if such sites exist or are planned to exist in production.

Many specialized backup and recovery solutions for Active Directory tout the ability to "quickly create a downsized test environment from production backups." This is indeed a very attractive proposition if the actual content of your AD is what's needed for testing. If you decide to take advantage of this feature, always keep in mind that all the secrets in such a test environment, including the virtually immutable DPAPI backup key, are those of your production AD at the time of backup! A test environment created in this way must be physically secured to the same standards your organization defined for production. In most cases, a copy script that simply creates identically looking objects in a new forest, without copying the actual identities, is a much more secure method that does not reduce the usefulness of the test environment created that way!

9.3.2 Storage and Backup

You already know that taking physical control of a Domain Controller – even a RODC – leaves a malicious actor in possession of DPAPI backup keys that enable them to unprotect any and all DPAPI-protected secrets in that domain going forward. For this reason, do not put a Domain Controller on a storage device access to which is not restricted to personnel authorized for Tier 0 operations!

> **Remember:** Storage and virtualization admins for devices that host Tier 0 identity systems are Tier 0 admins. If someone leaves the administrator password for a storage array at its default value or sets it to "12345," anyone with network access to the storage management interface is a Tier 0 admin.

CHAPTER 9 BUILDING A MODERN AD

These considerations apply to backup as well, and you should be extremely wary of "platform backups" if the platform is intended to host Tier 0 data. If the backup team cannot provide written documentation on who, and at what point in the data lifecycle, has read access to backups and, in case backups are encrypted, access to encryption keys, then that facility should not back up Tier 0 components, period. We will talk about backup, restore, and DR processes specific to AD in the next chapter.

If you activate BitLocker on your Domain Controllers, the situation shifts a little, but you still have to do your due diligence and trace the whole data lifecycle of the backups that are intended to protect Tier 0. For BitLocker, you need TPM, and for virtual machines, TPM data must be stored somewhere. With VMware vSphere, for instance, an external Key Management Server will protect the virtual TPM chips, but if that KMS is implemented on a vCenter appliance and that appliance is part of the same backup set as the BitLockered Domain Controllers, then the key is stored on the backup media right alongside the lock!

In every AD infrastructure the author has ever had to deal with, Windows Server Backup was used to create Domain Controller backups at some point in time. It is widely believed that a "wbadmin backup" is the only backup procedure supported by Microsoft for a complete forest recovery. In reality, though, Microsoft will usually not help you restore your first Domain Controller from backup anyway but will only support the subsequent forest recovery workflow. And if the solution used for backup and hopefully restore is based on a VSS BACKUP job, then the result will probably be indistinguishable from a WSB-restored machine. The author cannot, of course, offer any guarantee whatsoever about what Microsoft support will or won't do for a high-profile paying customer; however, past experience suggests that they will try to help you get your feet back on the ground after a cyber disaster. The particular backup technology that has been used may still come up as a topic of conversation later, in the legal and commercial aftermath of the incident.

If you, for whatever reason, decide to create a WSB backup of a DC yourself, give it the lifecycle it deserves:

- Do not place the backup on network storage devices you do not control, especially if you cannot control snapshots being created or content being replicated to other devices.

- WSB cannot encrypt the backups, so you'll have to encrypt the media you're putting them on.

- Destroy the backup files as soon as they are not needed anymore.

Until you have implemented a specialized backup solution for your Active Directory that encrypts the backups early in their lifecycle, keep an eye out for changes in the platform backup regime that can put your hard work and the organization's most precious IT assets at risk.

9.3.3 Permanent and Temporary Networks

You are not ready to start engineering, let alone implementing the AD infrastructure, until you know the network topology you will have to work with, including concrete IP address ranges, their geographical placement, the routes between them, as well as the bandwidth and latency characteristics of these routes. The networks will not necessarily have been built out to that specification when you start deploying. In a greenfield implementation, you should keep your AD confined to the central datacenter location(s) as long as possible and only fan out to the remote sites when it's time to serve clients and users there. This allows you to provision schema, configuration, and permissions updates without having to wait for (and verify the success of) replication. This way you also do not have to coordinate global changes to your "seed AD" with the network teams working on WAN connections to remote sites.

In the early phases of almost every AD implementation, there is some volatility in terms of networks both Domain Controllers and systems consuming AD services are attached to. If moving a DC to a different IP segment, remember that it will not change its site affiliation automatically even after a reboot. If a DC is supposed to be moved to a different site, you have to do it manually. Avoid having DCs in a wrong site at all costs! If changing IP addresses of production systems is something that your organization is known to do on a regular basis, put in an automated task comparing DCs' IP addresses with their site affiliation in the replication topology!

Changes in network placement also require changes in firewall rules. Plan for that to have processes in place to both roll out changes in Windows Firewall policies quickly and to communicate them to the firewall team and verify that the necessary rules have been activated.

Under no circumstances should you allow temporary LDAP binds to your new AD from insecure network zones. Whatever you have planned in the final architecture – ADLDS instances, a third-party LDAP directory attached to AD or to Identity Management systems – if these facilities are needed early in the implementation process, then they have to be implemented early, period.

9.3.4 Time Source

Before you start deploying Tier 0 systems, agree with the infrastructure people on a common, authoritative time source for the entire environment. If it ends up being an internal system like a GPS receiver or a dedicated time signal receiver (at the time of writing, DCF77 is still very popular in Germany; NIST runs several stations in the USA), have it put in a dedicated DMZ so that production and platform management can access that address independently. If you agree to rely on Internet time provided with excellent quality and availability by a number of major universities and standardization bodies (NIST alone runs 25 time servers out of four US locations), it may be worth the effort to provide a next stratum NTP server on the internal network. It should be a hardware device with an onboard clock module (so a Raspberry Pi is out of the question). All major operating systems, including Windows, offer both NTP server and NTP client functionality and can serve as an "NTP substation."

If you decide to take advantage of external network time, remember "Segal's law":

> A man with a watch knows what time it is. A man with two watches is never sure.

If you can register three external time sources to your NTP device or directly to your PDCe, then you can protect against one of them malfunctioning. If you only get two time sources to choose from, choose one and stick with it. Major IT vendors like VMware incorporated this guidance in their official documentation years ago.

9.4 Preparing for Change

As Heraclitius put it 25 centuries ago, "there is nothing permanent except change." Little did the philosopher know about the sheer velocity of transformation we are confronted with today when trying to provide a foundational set of services designed to last 25 years. Other than in building construction, "foundational" in our case does not mean "set in stone." Active Directory is traditionally being viewed as flexible enough, technically, to accommodate any requirements (the author remembers having a conversation with a customer about providing anonymous access to the directory as late as 2022). Unfortunately, it has also been viewed as not important enough, strategically, to actually *reject* some of these change requests – until ransomware payments worldwide started to soar and security analysts determined that AD played a pivotal role in 9 of 10 successful cyberattacks. It did not, however, raise awareness about secure

CHAPTER 9   BUILDING A MODERN AD

AD engineering and operational practices everywhere, not even among organizations that have actually been hit by ransomware. In numerous affected organizations, "awareness" took the form of blaming Microsoft for providing an inherently insecure technology (not true) and formulating a strategy of getting rid of AD soonest (not realistic in most cases). Whatever the cyber situation in the world at large, change requests within your own organization will continue pouring in, and it's your job to prepare systems, people, and processes for dealing with them.

9.4.1 Changes in Requirements vs. Changes in Infrastructure

In this book, we will not be dealing with changes to underlying infrastructure. If the organization decides to move the network stack from Aruba to Cisco and the datacenter firewalls from Sophos to Fortinet, AD shouldn't even notice as long as IP ranges, routes, and firewall rules stay in place. If the hypervisor platform hosting virtualized Domain Controllers changes, it can have implications on both configuration (e.g., vTPM that cannot be migrated) and security (new administration delegation, storage, and backup regime have to be reevaluated), but this only requires the Active Directory team to be prepared to roll out new domain controllers, to migrate existing ones, or to be able to quickly map out possible access paths in order to determine what systems and persons constitute the new Tier 0 perimeter after the change.

Changes in network topology are more interesting from the AD point of view, especially if they impose new restrictions on replication or relax the previously existing ones. If the WAN topology changes from multi-hub/multi-spoke to a fully meshed design, a multi-domain forest you were forced to implement becomes obsolete. While it is not necessary to migrate the subdomains into the root domain at once, the complexity you would be removing by doing so makes that migration a very attractive proposition, even in the short term. And if your organization decided to provision Domain Controllers on physical servers, removing domains will save on hardware, power consumption, and cooling.

We do not even want to contemplate a change in WAN topology that would force the AD team to *create* a multi-domain forest that initially was not required. Today, identity should have representation on the Change Advisory Board (CAB) in any decent-sized organization. The person representing Active Directory is responsible for catching these transformations early in the process and making their implications on the manageability and security of AD known to the business.

But changes in infrastructure are expected to have a big impact on the entire IT environment, so they are usually not introduced hastily nor approved without giving the implications proper consideration. At the time of writing, legislators in many countries aim to make business leadership personally liable for damages resulting from neglecting cyber security. If (or rather when, at least in Europe and in the US) this sort of regulation becomes law, it will hopefully strengthen the representation of identity and security in all IT strategy and change advisory bodies. Until that happens, however, it's the smaller changes that we should fear more and examine more closely, because they often "fly under the radar" or come under the guise of "urgent business needs." Requirements that come along with these changes often have the potential to send you back to the drawing board – or to compromise the security posture of the entire organization.

9.4.2 New Technology

Application developers (and embedded applications in multifunction printers, industrial machinery, or digital signage are no exception) sometimes come up with the strangest ideas. For decades, it was Active Directory administrators' job to just silently accept the requirements and provide the requested facilities, protocols, and permissions. Today, it's your job to question the "needed" if it does not fit into the well-engineered

CHAPTER 9 BUILDING A MODERN AD

framework of a modern AD. Requirements you may be confronted with due to a new system or application being purchased (or considered for purchase) are

- NTLM authentication
- Legacy service accounts
- Legacy service accounts with local admin rights on the application server(s)
- Legacy service accounts with write permissions (or admin rights) in AD, on SQL servers, or other shared resources
- File shares with SMB1 enabled
- Using SMB1 against Domain Controllers for authentication (rather than for actual file transfer)
- Unsecured LDAP binds to the directory
- Keytabs for function accounts having privileges in AD above those of a regular user
- Client components requiring local admin rights at runtime
- Client components requiring local admin rights *and* AD management permissions at installation
- Lower DFL/FFL than currently possible, or in any case, lower than 2016
- Changes to default schema permissions
- Anonymous directory access
- DES encryption in Kerberos
- Reversible encryption for password storage

CHAPTER 9 BUILDING A MODERN AD

Some of these requirements may seem antiquated; however, the above is the "list of shame" the author *started* keeping around 2019, so, at the time of writing, these are actual requests submitted by application vendors in the last five years! Software development has a frightening level of inertia to it, so be prepared to have these conversations in the future. You may have ready-made answers to some of those already, e.g., unsecured LDAP binds can be provided using an ADLDS instance as a frontend "bastion" directory. To others, a separate resource forest may be a valid solution. If your organization has adopted the culture of explicitly billing central services to business units, making this a commercial rather than simply technical discussion can help keep it short and to the point (a cost of running two DCs as compared to the risk of taking down the entire business *should* be a no-brainer after all).

Note Under no circumstances should it be allowed to make concessions in regard to Active Directory's security or functionality for a "Proof of Concept" installation of a business application or of a piece of machinery. That's what a test environment is for, and the additional effort of moving the application from test into production after successful evaluation and purchase must be understood by the business as the price of your team keeping the business secure!

In view of the potential liability of the C-level and even board for damage inflicted by cyber criminals, it's only prudent to include IT security and identity in the organization's purchasing decision for everything that has an IP address. Do not forget "the cloud" when formulating the "contract" about the AD team's veto rights on purchasing. Even today, a LOB application that has all the trimmings of a "Software as a Service" (SaaS) product may suddenly require an LDAP bind for lookup and/ or authentication from the public cloud or from the provider's rented infrastructure. Having a process in place to clarify this sort of requirements helps avoid costly purchasing mistakes.

355

9.5 Preparing for Disaster

Disasters happen. Not all of them are cyber breaches – the worst IT catastrophe, in terms of financial loss it incurred, between 2018 and 2024, although caused by a cybersecurity software company (CrowdStrike), was not a security incident but a bad update pushed out to millions of Windows systems simultaneously. And even flood, fire (in March 2022, a fire at an OVH datacenter in France stripped thousands of customers of their IT applications), or hurricanes (climate change causing them to appear in areas that were considered safe earlier) have the potential of causing major disruption to organizations' IT services.

Disaster preparedness, historically viewed through the lens of natural disasters, includes disciplines such as Fault Tolerance, High Availability (Active Directory has both of them built in, but you have to plan and build for it), and Disaster Recovery. However, threat models related to natural disasters usually do not include logical data corruption. If you add cyber disasters to your threat landscape, priorities change dramatically. A major cyber incident does not necessarily make AD services unavailable in terms of Domain Controllers not listening to authentication or lookup requests – but they may refuse authentication to users, deliver wrong results to queries, and allow privilege elevation for users that absolutely should not have that ability. As the attack progresses, it may be part of the malicious actor's endgame to actually take down your AD by encrypting or wiping it – and then again, it may not, if their target is some LOB system they just want to be the sole user of for a while! Being prepared for this sort of disaster requires more than just careful datacenter and network planning and an isolated backup storage.

9.5.1 Disaster-Resilient Design Options

For any kind of disaster, be it physical, logical, or cyber, a single-domain forest is a more resilient design option than one that consists of multiple domains. MAERSK experienced the benefits of this design firsthand after becoming a victim of the "NotPetya" malware in 2017 – the single Domain Controller salvaged from a site in Ghana that happened to suffer from a power outage while the rest of the organization suffered from malware allowed for a workable, albeit not instant, recovery of AD functionality. Split your identities across many domains with cross-domain permissions, group memberships, and policy linkings thrown into the mix, and you have a recipe for disaster waiting to happen.

Have Break-Glass accounts in every domain. If parts of your infrastructure are destroyed, an isolated Domain Controller may be all that you have left at your disposal.

Keep FSMO roles on one machine. This way, you do not have to guess which ones to transfer and which ones to seize if not all of your DCs have survived.

Have a bag of emergency tricks ready and tested in your test environment: A script to roll the **krbtgt** password twice, a script to roll **all** passwords twice, a script to disable all privileged accounts, and so on. Do not rely on documentation – create a single script for each task, name them accordingly, but **do not store them on your infrastructure**. Store them on a USB drive, along with Break-Glass account passwords and other critical pieces of information. And, of course, you should always have **two** of these drives stored in separate physical locations and a documented procedure for refreshing and verifying their contents.

Have at least one Domain Controller per domain deployed either on physical hardware or on a virtualization infrastructure completely separated from the rest, including management interfaces. This way you have something to start troubleshooting and recovery with in the event of a complete takedown of your production infrastructure.

If your user forests are deployed in a hybrid fashion, always enable Password Hash Sync (PHS) to Entra ID, even if it's not the primary authentication mechanism currently adopted by your organization in the cloud. This way, if you have to sever the connection between on-premises and cloud directories, or if an attacker severs the connection for you, cloud users will still be able to authenticate and use cloud-bound applications!

9.5.2 A Special Kind of Disaster

Admins make mistakes, too. If you are logged on with a "God-mode" account, all it takes to delete thousands of production objects is one line of PowerShell. All it takes to prevent everybody from logging on is one setting in one Group Policy. It goes without saying that you will do all that is necessary to prevent this kind of mishap from happening:

- Use automation to minimize the amount of interactive work done by humans in identity systems.
- Use zoning on top of tiering to limit the blast radius of any single mistake.
- Test scripted changes in the test environment before rolling them out to production forests.

But even with these precautions in place, there is still a residual risk of human error and, alas, also the residual threat of a disgruntled admin on their last day of employment. To mitigate these risks, you will have to resort to specialized tools offering one or both of the following:

- Granular tracking and reversal of undesired changes of AD objects, ideally without relying on AD for authentication (otherwise, deletion of the tool's own service account cannot be reverted, and neither can any other change until the service account has been reprovisioned)
- Very fast recovery of the entire forest on top of the existing infrastructure

The latter may not always be practicable in a large, geographically distributed environment, so if your planned toolbox does not allow for the former, you must familiarize yourself and your team with the mechanics of the authoritative restore in AD and provide both precise documentation and scripts to support this highly sensitive operation should the need arise.

9.6 Deploying a Modern AD in a Secure Manner

Once all prerequisites are in place and the deployment details have been hashed out and pre-flighted in the test environment, you are ready to deploy your modern AD for production use. Start by deploying a "seeding cell," that is, two Domain Controllers for each planned domain in one AD site. If some domains or forests are not designed to be present in this seeding site, you can still deploy them there in the beginning and then move the Domain Controllers to the desired destination after all the necessary object structures and permissions have been created.

Confining the initial deployment to a seeding cell offers the advantage of not having to work with hardened PAWs and other secure administration facilities in the very early stage of deployment.

After the seeding cell deployment is completed, deploy the necessary systems and agents of your designated Active Directory backup solution, be it the platform backup or a custom product specifically purchased to back up and recover AD. If none of these are available, prepare an encrypted medium (at the time of writing, you can buy a hardware-encrypted 1TB SSD disk for $300 that should easily hold backups of 20 to 30 DCs, and you only need one per domain for this temporary workaround) and create WSB backups on it. Even if your DCs are virtual, you should create WSB backups rather than VM exports because a. exports of TPM-infused VMs depend on the platform and b. scripts and tools for authoritative restore, should the need arise, are usually designed to work with WSB backups.

CHAPTER 9 BUILDING A MODERN AD

9.6.1 Remote Seeding Cells

Initial deployment of "remote" domains (i.e., those that will not be present in your seeding location according to the topology you created) works differently for domains belonging to a multi-domain forest and for forests that are going to be "remote" in their entirety. For "remote" forests, you can choose to place the seeding cell in the designated primary location for that forest, as long as you can connect to all necessary interfaces from the location you work from – or have a trusted member of your Tier 0 team on site there. If deploying a remote seeding cell remotely, keep in mind that you need console access which should not normally be part of the general routing topology. If your network team already has a management jumphost at that site, you can use that. A "management jumphost" is a machine with multiple network interfaces that you can connect to from the production WAN and use the other connection to manage virtual machines or physical servers. It goes without saying that this access must be secured to the highest standard and only allowed from designated trusted network segments or individual addresses on the production side.

To provide a remote seeding cell for a subdomain, either deploy its Domain Controllers in the central seeding cell and have them shipped (by a trusted shipping partner – these already are Tier 0 systems at this point) to that location or use AD replication to extend your primary seeding cell to the desired one and then remove the excess DCs as shown in Figure 9-1 (it reflects the partially routed site topology from Figure 3-6).

CHAPTER 9 BUILDING A MODERN AD

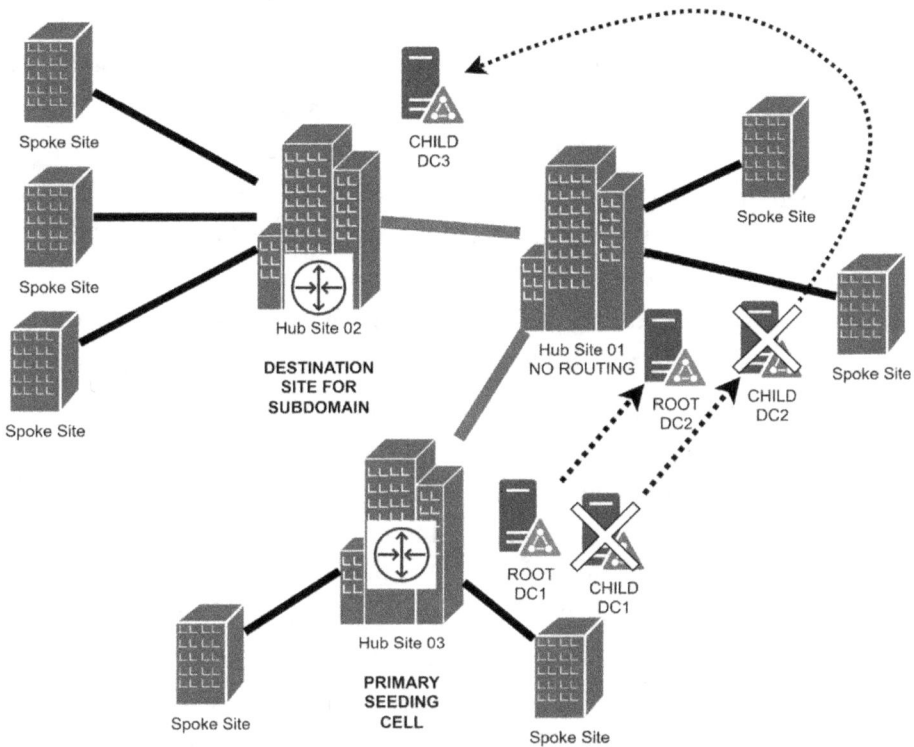

Figure 9-1. *After the CHILD domain is established at its site, temporary DCs are demoted and removed*

Depending on your topology, several temporary DCs per domain may be required to facilitate the seeding of a remote site. If you managed to avoid multi-domain forests in your AD, you can chalk up the saved effort of the remote seeding of subdomains as an additional benefit of your chosen design!

9.6.2 Red Forest and PKI

Once the seeding cells are in place, you should start deploying the Red Forest. It will usually have few (but very well connected) DCs, so you can deploy them all at once, infrastructure permitting. Establish the requisite

CHAPTER 9   BUILDING A MODERN AD

trusts and make sure they are replicated throughout the "golden" forests. Create the trusts towards the Red Forests as PIM trusts if you intend to use Shadow Principals (you absolutely should do that!); however, a PIM trust requires disabling sidHistory quarantine, which should be considered less secure *if not actively used*. Harden the trusts on the Red Forest side by disallowing authentication as soon as they are created. We covered this in Chapter 5.

The second subsystem to be deployed in the Red Forest, beside the Domain Controllers, is the PKI infrastructure, especially if you decide to use Microsoft technology, i.e., ADCS. You may have created an offline root CA already to provide an issuing CA to your infrastructure team – network devices and servers all have browser-based interfaces nowadays that benefit hugely by having internally trusted certificates bound to them. Create the requisite CAs, sign them by the offline root CA's certificate, and publish them all as needed. Do not forget to put the revocation checking infrastructure in place. Web servers for HTTP CDPs and/or OCSP servers should never be collocated with CAs, but they are still Tier 0 systems and must be treated accordingly.

Use the time before rolling out to production to set up deterministic revocation checking in your OCSP, provision certificate templates, set up delegated template management, and issue Domain Controller certificates for "golden" forests from an appropriate template. At the time of writing, ADCS comes with three templates created with Domain Controllers in mind: "Domain Controller," "Domain Controller Authentication," and "Kerberos Authentication." In all but really rare fringe cases, a clone of the most recent "Kerberos Authentication" template should be used. If you do not intend to use smart card authentication in that particular domain or forest, you can remove the "Smart Card Authentication" and "KDC Authentication" EKUs from the template clone. If you would like to obtain a PEN from IANA for your OID namespace, this, too, can take a week, so plan ahead. But if your organization has been running IT for a while already, a search of the PEN database may reveal that one has already been assigned years ago.

9.7 Putting AD into Production

After you have finished deploying the core infrastructure of your modern AD, one more task remains before you can start provisioning identities and onboarding applications: deploying of Domain Controllers to all the sites that require them according to your topology. When deploying the Windows Servers that will become Domain Controllers, remember that they become Tier 0 systems the moment you promote them, which is why they must be part of a very secure lifecycle from the very beginning.

If you're going to be deploying application servers using an automated system (rather than migrating existing ones), now is the time to put that system in place as described in Section 7.6, and the Domain Controller candidates can serve as your first "guinea pigs" for the new deployment procedure. You are still in the secure zone, so even if you discover something in the deployment process that bears correcting, you do not have to throw away or reimage your new machines before promoting them – just adjust permissions as needed and move on.

Your domain controllers do not hold a lot of data at this point: administrative groups, Tier 0 accounts, permissions, and baseline policies. If you have many Domain Controllers to deploy into remote sites and your organization's network spans long distances, it can still be a good idea to use an "Install From Media" (IFM) file set to promote DCs in remote locations. First, you can preseed the data locally before starting the promotion so there will not be much additional load and WAN-induced latency to the promotion operation. Second, it *can* make the promotion operation that little bit faster even if there are not millions of objects to be replicated.

9.7.1 Onboarding Applications

At this stage, you already know what applications the new Active Directory will have to support, what service and function accounts, and what authorization groups and servers they require. This gives you time to

CHAPTER 9   BUILDING A MODERN AD

create all requisite AD objects, permissions, Authentication Policies and group policies well before the actual deployment. If a certain application shows a level of complexity that requires the vendor to come in and assist with the installation (or if the vendor included this service with the license fee anyway), you have a formal reason to send that data to the vendor and to request their comments on the infrastructure created for them ahead of time. Most of the time, the vendor will love it and provide the feedback you asked for. If they don't, your conscience is clean in case there is some holdup with the installation due to AD prerequisites not being in place. If they're unsure, offer them a test drive in the test environment – not to re-evaluate the whole application but to validate just how well the application's authentication and authorization needs fit into your modern AD framework. The author had to deal with applications more than once that required an awful lot of authorization groups but would not allow them to be of domain local scope, making it impossible to deploy this application in a resource forest. Some vendors are unsure whether or not their application server will play well with group managed service accounts, in a hardened environment, or in a multi-forest scenario. Don't blame them – they, too, have limited resources, and if you can validate it in your test infrastructure, it's a win-win. The author might be a bit biased here, though, having worked in software presales for a while.

Track what the vendor, or the in-house application owner, is doing with the permissions they granted. If they take shortcuts, have them document the overpermissioned artifacts and roll them back to the requested permission level after the deployment is completed. Some installers have the ability to create databases, folder structures, or Exchange mailboxes but need higher privileges in order to do so than those required to run the application. Leaving "installation-level permissions" in place after the installation has been finished is one of the most common reasons for elevation paths found in AD infrastructures.

Once the authorization structures for your organization's applications and resources are known, you can start estimating the number of group SIDs that will become part of the users' logon tokens. If your environment is not very large and the overall authorization structure is not overly complex, you may be able to skip this step. When in doubt, simulate a user provisioned to a certain role or roles and count the token groups. This allows you to move applications into separate resource forests before the token bloat forces you to – and before there are millions of files or database records to be repermissioned within those applications!

If your Tier 1 framework includes zoning (i.e., "horizontal tiering," isolating Application A from Application B in the same way Tier 0 is isolated from Tier 1), provision all zone-related objects and policies together with the application prerequisites.

9.7.2 Onboarding Users

The process of onboarding users to the new Active Directory should begin long before the first user account is ready to be created and assigned memberships in roles and/or authorization groups. The information about both the users' metadata (surname, given name, email address if that has already been determined, etc.) and their application authorization settings (group memberships, Authentication Policies, etc.) must come from somewhere. Determine the authoritative sources of that information and ways to provision users and assign application-specific logic to them that can be used within your organization. There is no need to reinvent the wheel – sometimes organizations already have an identity management (IDM) system in place. If that is the case in your environment, then you are probably contractually bound to use it. However, IDM systems will not always be able to account for the placement and naming conventions, let alone FGPP and Authentication Policy assignments in your specific environment. In this case, you will need additional automation to adjust users created by IDM to fit your framework. Many IDMs support scripted actions: after having the IDM driver or connector create the AD object, a script is executed to modify it according to the policies of the AD organization.

Sometimes IDM will come integrated with access management, thus offering full IAM capability. In this case, newly created or existing users are automatically added to a number of groups according to their "entitlements" or "roles." This is where role-based access control models integrate really nicely into the overarching identity lifecycle.

Once accounts have been created, synchronized to the cloud, and granted permissions, you can test the final piece of your architecture under real-life conditions: handing out laptops, communicating the initial password to users, and taking them through the first-logon process. If your clients are cloud-bound and the primary logon account is the cloud one, the process will be different and require enrolling an MFA device, granting consent to cloud applications, and only then accessing the on-premises parts of the infrastructure authenticated and authorized by Active Directory.

9.8 Summary

In this chapter, we walked through a greenfield implementation of a "modern AD," from the initial design proposal through the first deployment steps and all the way to the onboarding of production applications, users, and endpoints. Since security is paramount in identity systems, we created the environment to the planned security standards, started delegated administration early, and introduced the Red Forest into the mix when all prerequisites for moving the privileged administration credentials to the secure enclave.

The modern AD tenets of being prepared for both a change in requirements and a catastrophic failure are an integral part of every engineering and implementation effort, which is why they deserve a separate section each in this chapter. You will notice throughout the chapter that you're going to spend a lot of time talking to people. Keep that in mind if you are working with persons for whom communicating with humans is a challenge.

We will discuss the operational aspects of the modern AD in the next chapter and the challenges and chances of transitioning to a modern AD from a preexisting infrastructure in Chapter 11.

CHAPTER 10

Operating a Modern AD

Active Directory, deployed in a modern, dynamic organization, is a living organism. Change is ubiquitous, threats are as advanced as they are persistent, regulatory requirements evolve, and people in charge of managing the identity infrastructure change as well. This makes operating a modern AD a way of life rather than a checklist to follow, although checklists do play a very important role in getting through the day safely and securely.

From day-to-day operations to disaster recovery, there are challenges every IT team has to deal with if they want their Active Directory infrastructure to continue serving the lookup, authentication, and authorization needs of their organization for decades to come.

10.1 Day-to-Day Operations

In Active Directory's early days, a typical administrator's daily task list consisted of creating users and groups, changing group memberships, editing GPOs, resetting passwords, and unlocking accounts. Everything else was an event out of the ordinary and, depending on the ability of the IT team to predict the impact of each particular occurrence, was either prioritized and taken care of, or just chalked up as "probably OK, who knows what's going on under the hood in AD." In large, geographically spread AD forests, checking replication status and change convergence time were part of the daily routine. Monitoring backup status and performing restore or disaster recovery tests seldom were a regular activity.

Times have changed, although there certainly still are "sneakernet" type admins struggling to keep businesses online out there somewhere. However, if your AD infrastructure qualifies as "enterprise" according to the definition at the beginning of this book, you have probably embraced automation, monitoring, and offloaded users and groups lifecycle to the Human Resources and/or IAM systems your organization has in place. Your disaster recovery tests are automated (at least as long as they are successful). At the same time, IT environments have become more dynamic, with new requirements and new integrations to be taken care of every day. Instead of spending your day dealing with standard changes like adding a user to a group, you have to engineer solutions on the fly for singular ones like onboarding a new site or a new application. The only recipe for survival is to have solutions for typical requirements in place so that you can pick a more complex change apart and have most of the partial answers ready.

10.1.1 Battling Configuration Drift

Unless you have implemented Desired State Configuration for everything (we visited the topic briefly in Section 8.4) and literally no one touches AD manually except in an emergency, configuration drift will inevitably occur. Automated processes are created by humans and not guaranteed to be 100% error-free so that configurations are sometimes enforced incorrectly even by automation. You cannot possibly hope to detect deviations from the desired state by manual inspection, so a part of your team's everyday chores will be refining and debugging the automated tasks that verify adherence of your actual configurations to the desired state. This sort of configuration deviation report is known in some organizations as the "morning coffee" report because it's usually delivered per email at the beginning of the administrators' working day to be consumed with the first cup of coffee or whatever office beverage you prefer. Typical checks in these reports are

- Default privileged groups contain identities outside of a predefined whitelist or container.
- Accounts placed in privileged management OUs do not have an authentication policy attached to them.
- Accounts placed in privileged management OUs do not have the "account is sensitive and cannot be delegated" flag set.
- Accounts placed in privileged management OUs are not members in "Protected Users."
- Objects in the "New Objects" container.
- Groups referenced by OIDs for SCAMA are not of universal scope.
- Groups referenced by FGPP are not of global scope.
- Groups in "authorization groups" OUs are not of domain local scope.
- Users with tokenGroups count above predefined threshold.
- Circular groups nesting (while not dangerous in itself, it can put a significant load on Domain Controllers).
- Users with "password never expires" flag set and "use smart card logon" flag not set and no authentication policy attached.

- If object-specific OUs are in use: objects of wrong class in an OU.
- OUs with group policy inheritance disabled (unless used intentionally).
- Group policies linked below specific OU level.
- Group policies with enforcement enabled (unless used intentionally).
- Unexpected CSEs in group policies (unknown GUIDs or CSEs the organization agreed on not using, e.g., printer mapping).
- Printer queues published to AD (unless used intentionally, in which case they should have a location value).
- Sites or subnets without a location value or with a misconfigured one.
- OUs outside of the agreed-upon structure.
- Permissions outside of the agreed-upon structure.
- Sites, subnets, and site links deviate from the topology description used for deployment.
- Legacy service accounts or function accounts not logged on for 30+ days.
- Member computers with Server OS not logged on for 30+ days.

The list can go on forever, but in a well-managed modern AD, the report should be empty most of the mornings. We did not include GPO content in the list because drift in GPO settings is much harder to detect than drift in AD or DNS configuration. Deciding whether to roll back to the previous state or to accept the changed configuration as the new standard is harder still. But if you like the challenge of parsing the XML files generated by **Get-GPOReport**, you can absolutely check for critical settings like "Loopback Processing" or "Always Wait for Network" in the policies where they do not belong.

When you detect systematic configuration drift, make sure the necessary adjustments are fed back into your automation facilities to prevent the particular deviation from reoccurring.

10.1.2 Implementing Changes in Topology

Every time a new physical site becomes part of the organization's network, the AD team needs to reflect it in the replication/site coverage topology. In a multi-forest deployment, you definitely want to automate site and subnet creation, but your topology description still has to be extended manually to include

- The new site's name and location (if the **location** attribute is being used in your organization)
- Additional settings like universal groups membership caching
- Subnet definitions belonging to the new site (including the location information if applicable)
- Site links containing the site

Before Domain Controllers, writeable or read-only, are deployed to the site, verify that all requisite firewall rules are in place, both in your Windows Firewall configuration and on the datacenter firewalls between the physical subnets. Countless hours are spent every day on troubleshooting applications just because an overworked firewall admin created the necessary rules on the firewall, closed the change, but forgot to *commit* the updated configuration to the actual firewall. For connectivity verification, **Test-NetConnection** may not always be good enough, because some firewalls have traffic inspection capabilities that will make them "accept" any connection, regardless of the ruleset and the target host's existence, causing the port connectivity test to succeed where in reality the connection will fail.

When deploying AD components to new sites, always make sure someone from the network and firewall team is on call.

10.2 Incorporating New Technology

New applications, systems, and infrastructure components are introduced into organizations' IT every day. Most of them have requirements that affect Active Directory operations and potentially the security posture of the entire environment. Not all of these requirements are exceptional, and some of the new applications are going to fall into the area of "day-to-day activities." Others need careful consideration and thorough engineering.

10.2.1 Changes in Platform Technology Foundational to AD

Changes to platform components like server hardware, virtualization, and storage are always exceptional because they require a reevaluation of all prerequisites, technical and organizational alike, that have been put in place prior to hosting Tier 0 components on that infrastructure:

- The new virtualization platform's guest components (VMware tools, XenTools, Hyper-V integration components, etc.). Are there known vulnerabilities? How is the lifecycle of these components managed?

Do the components allow instant elevation by running processes within the VM without providing VM-specific credentials? Do the components enforce host time synchronization, and how can it be disabled?

- The new virtualization platform's security features (vTPM, SecureBoot, VBS, and HVCI support).

- Same questions for new server hardware in case of physical deployment of Domain Controllers or other Tier 0 systems.

- Storage and virtualization access controls, privileged management regime, and data lifecycle.

- Possible reintroduction of platform backup if Tier 0 systems were exempt from it in the past.

Sometimes platform components come with "comfort features" that allow some sort of AD integration. Make sure that platform administrators' Active Directory credentials have not been used to enable such integrations by permanently storing them in the platform.

10.2.2 Exceptional Application Requirements

If you are confronted with "exceptional" requirements of the sort we listed in Section 9.4, it helps to have at least some answers ready, preferably in the form of an officially looking PDF that you can send back to the requesting party and ask them if they would like to have the suggested workaround implemented for this particular application. For the author's "list of shame," it could look like this:

Requested feature	Pre-approved solution	Exceptional workaround
NTLM authentication	Not supported in this environment.	Provisioning of server components in a separate forest and of client components on a secured VDI farm.
Legacy service accounts	gMSA, justification for legacy required. Password lifetime will be limited to 60 days; password rotation is the application owner's responsibility.	None.
Legacy service accounts with local admin rights on the application server(s)	Not supported in this environment.	Placement of server(s) in a resource forest.
Legacy service accounts with write permissions (or admin rights) in AD, on SQL servers, or other shared resources	Not supported in this environment.	Application will be declared as Tier 0; application owner has to be trained and provided a PAW and Tier 0 credentials.
File shares with SMB1 enabled	Restriction of SMB and RPC access by firewall to a small number of client systems.	None
Using SMB1 against Domain Controllers for authentication (rather than for actual file transfer)	Not supported in this environment.	Placement of components in a separate low-security resource forest without trusts to production.

(continued)

Requested feature	Pre-approved solution	Exceptional workaround
Unsecured LDAP binds to the directory	Application must support SASL with Kerberos for unsecured binds.	ADLDS instance with restricted object selection.
Keytabs for function accounts having privileges in AD above those of a regular user	Not supported in this environment.	Application will be declared as Tier 0.
Client components requiring local admin rights at runtime	Not supported in this environment.	Separation of this application and Browser/Mail/Document sessions by VDI, terminal services, or local VMs.
Client components requiring local admin rights *and* AD management permissions at installation	Installation will be performed by a Tier 0 admin.	None.
Lower DFL/FFL than currently possible, or in any case, lower than 2016	Not supported in this environment.	A separate resource forest with limited trust to production.
Changes to default schema permissions	Not supported in this environment.	Justification and careful evaluation by Tier 0 team with long-term impact analysis and approval through the change advisory board.

(continued)

Requested feature	Pre-approved solution	Exceptional workaround
Anonymous directory access	Not supported in this environment.	ADLDS instance with extremely limited selection of objects and attributes.
DES encryption in Kerberos	Not supported in this environment.	An untrusted resource forest with separate identity.
Reversible encryption for password storage	Not supported in this environment.	An untrusted resource forest with separate identity.

Some of the application owners the author had the pleasure of working with, once confronted with a similar table, took the initiative into their own hands and put pressure on the vendor to reevaluate the requirement and to make necessary changes in the product. But those were companies with enough clout to have that discussion with a software or equipment manufacturer. You cannot assume that application owners will always be that forthcoming – or, in fact, that they will communicate at all.

10.2.3 At the End of the Lifecycle

If your organization has been doing IT using Microsoft technology for the last 25 years, chances are your Active Directory environment is just as old. Not every business process, application, or piece of machinery can boast a lifecycle that long, so offboarding applications and systems is as important a part of the overall IT Service Management as onboarding them. Unfortunately, not every application owner is diligent enough to communicate "their" applications' end of life to all teams it concerns, including AD.

If the application owner fails to give notice of a particular application or system not being used anymore, they might choose to shut down the corresponding application servers or uninstall the actual application. In this case, you can determine the applications' end of life through service accounts and maybe even computer accounts popping up in your "morning coffee" report as not logging on anymore (this is yet another advantage of using tightly focussed service accounts instead of reusing them for many applications or systems). If, however, the application is not "out-managed" but simply abandoned, i.e., left running without actually being used, you're out of luck.

Keep track of systems that caused exceptional measures that you would like to roll back sooner rather than later. If a piece of machinery required SMB1 to be enabled on a particular file server (or maybe even on DCs in a certain site), it might be worth the while to start monitoring SMB1 usage a couple of years after the implementation. If the old protocol stops being used, maybe the vendor upgraded the firmware and it supports SMB3 now – or maybe the machine broke down and was sold for scrap. In each case, you can now disable SMB1, and in doing so, move your security posture up a notch. If a file server cluster came with an authorization structure so voluminous that it mandated a separate forest and those documents are now all migrated to SharePoint Online, you can scrap a whole forest (if the domain local group separation was done by adding a *domain* to an existing forest, it is arguably an even more significant event).

10.3 Security Operations

A big part of security operations in a Tier 0 infrastructure is reactive, i.e., monitoring, log analysis, and incident handling. We will look at these in more detail at the end of this chapter. But there are activities that are proactive in nature and belong in the "security operations" category.

10.3.1 Ongoing Systems Hardening

Active Directory teams are traditionally involved in hardening of Windows systems at large: hardening settings and procedures are often delivered by GPO, and much of Windows hardening targets the protection not so much of the systems being configured but of Active Directory supporting them. Hardening of Windows and applications running on top of it, however, is not a static discipline but is in constant flow. Every now and again, the operating system is enhanced by new security features that need evaluating, configuring, providing with exceptions, and rolling out (including the exceptions). But the security frameworks the systems are hardened against are also dynamic and change with the evolving threat landscape.

Having a test environment that reflects the level of hardening deployed to production helps evaluate new settings (or new guidelines for configurations that have already been deployed) in a way that makes rolling them out a relatively easy task: identical policy, container, and group names allow for transferring GPO backups from test to production with a minimum of translation effort.

10.3.2 Supporting Security Scans and Pentests

A different sort of activity that can end up consuming a lot of the AD team's resources is supporting offensive security efforts targeted at the organization's IT. Normally, a system not allowing any inbound connections would pass a penetration test. If, however, the evaluation run commissioned by the CISO or the CIO is of the "credentialed vulnerability scan" variety, it comes with multiple requirements a security-conscious AD admin should always be unwilling to agree to

CHAPTER 10 OPERATING A MODERN AD

- Opening firewall ports throughout the environment to a small number of source hosts but on a huge number of ports, basically, "all of them"

- Providing a God-mode account having local admin privileges on a multitude of systems

- Providing a demigod-mode account having at least local logon + network access rights on a multitude of systems

The fact that most environments the security consultants setting up the scan have experienced so far are not as well protected as your "modern AD" does not help when trying to put these requirements into context. "Just add it to the Default Domain Policy," dropped in the CISO's presence, is not good for the team's morale. From an AD security expert's viewpoint, the consultant making that statement should be escorted off the premises at once; unfortunately, managers are not AD experts but would like to get the evaluation done in a timely manner.

Like with unreasonable application requirements we talked about in the last section, your best strategy is to prepare a two-tier answer: one you can live with but the vendor does not want to hear, and another one the vendor possibly can live with but leaving whoever brought them in in charge of the red tape and justification of costs. Of course, this strategy does not play out every time, and in some organizations the author had the misfortune consulting for it simply wouldn't work "because the boss said so." If that's the environment you have to work in, prepare a standard document detailing a risk, possible consequences, and due diligence you have done until now, and send it to an appropriate distribution list. At least no one can say afterwards they weren't warned. But mark your calendar for the projected end of the vulnerability scan engagement – no one will inform you that permissive firewall rules and scan credentials are no longer needed!

10.4 Backup and Restore

A customer the author was consulting for in the mid-2000s, when asked about their organization's backup plan, gave a rather unexpected reply that, albeit not technically 100% precise, made a lot of follow-up questions moot before they were even asked:

We do not have a backup plan. We have a restore plan.

This simple statement reflects the true nature of the entire "backup/restore" discipline better than all backup vendors' marketing slogans combined, although some of them have already discovered the power of this truism at the time of writing. It should be your guiding principle when engineering the backup regime for your Active Directory – start with the restorability requirements and let them dictate what backup facilities and data retention policies are needed and ultimately what tools are able to provide them.

10.4.1 Anti-patterns Galore

No one likes backups. And humans, when tasked with things they don't like, tend to not go about them with the same level of dedication and thoroughness they show when allowed to do things that appeal to them. It's human nature, and several anti-patterns the author has observed hundreds of times over the decades, have developed as the result:

- "We've been making backups for years!" In a business, the main database server died after years of faithful service. The systems integrator that had installed the system was brought in, only to find that a couple dozen of backup tapes stored neatly in the safe were all empty. Nobody ever bothered to verify a backup or perform a test restore, and company lore handed down from one junior onsite IT person to the next equated "making backups" with "swapping tapes once the previous one is ejected." They lost eight years worth of digital data that day.

- "HA is enough as backup," originated in the last century as "RAID1 is enough as backup." There are countless variants of this principle implemented out there, and Microsoft explicitly maintained in the early days of Exchange Online that four database copies are enough redundancy so backups are not needed. The problem with this statement is that it is formally true for Exchange Online (or any online service delivered under the shared responsibility model), but many organizations followed it blindly even for on-premises implementations, replacing backup with HA. If there is a problem with the content (e.g., objects or documents deleted or altered), it doesn't help much that the problem is highly available.

- "Replication is enough as backup" is a modern variant of the previous fallacy, again not taking into account that problems with the data itself are no less common than problems accessing that data!

- "Yearly backups are kept for 15 years for regulatory reasons." There is nothing wrong with this statement per se, but what many organizations subject to such regulation have failed to recognize is that IT is an extremely fast-changing business, and a backup set created 15 years ago by a technology that was already mature at that time will probably not be readable by any hardware readily available on the market. Ultrium LTO, a very popular tape technology since 2000, prescribes that a drive must be able to read tapes 2 generations back. A new generation has so far been licensed and manufactured every 2 to 3 years so that organizations required to keep old backups must either keep (and verify functionality of) old drives as well or copy old backup tapes every time a new generation is implemented – which, by the way, might be prohibited by the same regulation that prescribes the long-term retention!

- "Archive is enough as backup." This is the reverse principle to "HA is enough as backup" – it will protect against data alterations but not against loss of functionality as such – unless, of course, archives are kept on media that are independent of the systems reading them (e.g., DVD, BlueRay, or similar technology) and have an offsite copy (in which case, there actually *is* a backup in place).

- "We put weekly tapes in a bank safe deposit box." Unless the organization making that statement *is* the bank, there are at least two questions that must be asked before ticking the box on it. First is the chain of custody. Who, as a person, is responsible for delivering the tapes to the bank? Are these persons aware that they are transporting the modern day's crown jewels? Could they be persuaded by a third party to let them have a peek inside the tape magazine? The second question is not about employees' integrity but rather about the lack of basic understanding of physics – a skill a courier or a low-level clerical employee is not formally required to have! If subjected to high temperatures, digital media tend to deteriorate and "forget" what was stored on them, and tapes are especially sensitive. Half an hour in the trunk of a car in the Texas summertime can be all it takes to render a bunch of backup tapes unusable – and this will remain undiscovered unless the tapes are actually needed one day!

In this book, we will not provide guidance on how to design a general-purpose backup and restore facility for an organization but rather concentrate specifically on requirements for restoring identity systems. You have to rely on the backup team to provide the restorability (RPO) they promise in the time frame they have specified in their SLA (RTO).

10.4.2 The Case of AD Restore

What are the cases that call for a "restore" operation in Active Directory? The often-quoted case of a "fat-fingered" admin deleting a couple of user objects can be mitigated by the AD Recycle Bin feature. It's been available since Server 2008 R2 and offers much quicker and richer recoverability of deleted AD objects within their "Deleted Objects Lifetime" (180 days by default) before the objects are tombstoned for the duration of "Tombstone Lifetime" (another 180 days by default). AD Recycle Bin is surfaced by ADAC and PowerShell, although the former only allows viewing the contents of the "Deleted Objects" container and restoring objects from there **in domain partitions** as shown in Figure 10-1.

CHAPTER 10   OPERATING A MODERN AD

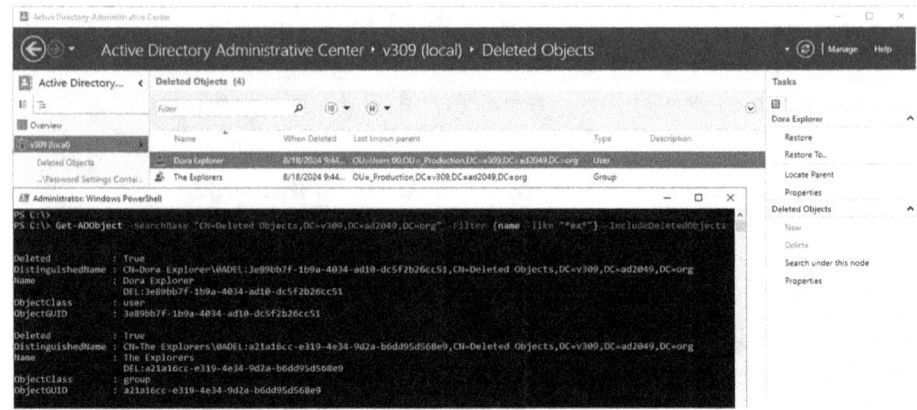

Figure 10-1. *In a domain partition, PowerShell and ADAC allow for viewing and restoring objects from the Recycle Bin*

Objects deleted from application (DNS) and configuration partitions can also be viewed and recovered from the Recycle Bin but only using PowerShell:

$configRecycleBin = 'CN=Deleted Objects,{0}' -f ([ADSI]"LDAP://RootDSE").configurationNamingContext[0]
Get-ADObject -SearchBase $configRecycleBin -Filter * -IncludeDeletedObjects -SearchScope OneLevel

There is a downside to the Recycle Bin that led several larger organizations to ultimately not enable the feature: It keeps the deleted objects in their entirety, so that they consume the same amount of NTDS database space they did before deletion. Organizations experiencing high seasonal churn, e.g., universities creating and deleting tens of thousands of student accounts every semester, are particularly affected. If your backup solution for AD allows for quick and comfortable restore of deleted objects by tombstone revival, it's perfectly OK to leave Recycle Bin disabled. If your backup tool of choice does not provide this capability but churn or data protection regulations prevent you from keeping fully populated deleted objects for a prolonged period of time, you can still consider enabling the Recycle Bin but setting the Deleted Objects lifetime considerably shorter than the suggested default. This is governed by the **msDS-DeletedObjectLifetime** attribute of the **Directory Service** object in the configuration partition, i.e., the lifetime of deleted objects in the Recycle Bin cannot be set to different values for different partitions.

> **Remember:** Once enabled, the Recycle Bin feature cannot be disabled in a supported manner.

However, accidental deletion of objects is but one use case out of many, and, in the author's experience, it's not even the most common one in day-to-day operations. As is often the case, data corruption is far more invasive and harder to take care of. Accidentally moving objects between containers in a complex OU structure and changing attributes in bulk on many objects without the previous value being recorded anywhere are situations most AD teams have experienced, and neither is easy to remediate. When planning for AD restore, you should pay special attention to these capabilities. If the Active Directory team is not going to own AD-specific backup facilities, validate the end-to-end process with the backup team – there may be additional steps necessary on their part, like mounting the correct backup set for restoration, that must become part of the documented item-level restore procedure.

10.4.3 Not Everything Is Stored in the Database

Many, if not most, backup-related discussions revolve around restoring objects and their attributes stored "in AD," that is, in the NTDS.DIT database. And, while that certainly is a very important part of the overall recoverability of your directory service, you should never forget about the other parts of what makes up a workable Active Directory organization.

Group policies are very often changed in an undesired manner, and the out-of-box tools do not offer any change tracking, versioning, or rollback functionality. If you detect a change in GPOs but are not able to easily pinpoint and correct it manually, you have two methods to get back to a known good state:

- If your team has made a habit of creating "native" GPO backups prior to changing the content of a policy or creating a GPO backup in a scheduled manner like we showed in Chapter 7, you can use the GPMC or the **Restore-GPO** cmdlet to restore your policy or policies to a previous state.

- If all you have available are Domain Controller backups (system-state, VM level, or similar), you can, in theory, extract the GPO folders and files from an appropriate backup set and replace that data in SYSVOL. However, the version information stored in the GPO payload and maybe even the CSE list will differ from the one in the AD object. If permissions have been changed since the known-good state, copied files from the previous SYSVOL version may not reflect them properly. Besides, without the version number being incremented, the background GPO processing will not pick up the change made to the files so that it can take a long time for the "restored" settings to take effect. A better way to perform a restore of a single GPO with out-of-box technology is by restoring a DC without network connectivity, backing up the desired GPO using GPMC or PowerShell, and then restoring that backup in production. This will take care of versioning, the CSE list, permissions, and all the other parameters.

CHAPTER 10   OPERATING A MODERN AD

When planning for operational restorability of group policies, always consider the possibility of undesired content changes and validate this capability in your chosen backup/restore tooling.

DNS, if not hosted by AD itself but provided by a third-party system, should also be "in sync" with what AD itself "knows" about geographical service placement and replication. If you rely on your network or infrastructure team to provide DNS for AD operations, you must evaluate and document their backup and restore processes along with your own.

If you use smart cards for logon or Domain Controller certificates for LDAPS, PKI is not just another application consuming AD for configuration and authorization but rather an integral part of AD. Include at least Certification Authorities in the same backup regime you have established for Domain Controllers and other identity-related systems. Validation Authorities like CDPs or OCSP servers can be rebuilt if all else fails, but for CAs, you may even have to go back to a previous state of the database one day. In any case, create an out-of-band backup of CA **certificates**, including private keys, as well as CA configuration settings from the registry and the **capolicy.inf** file, and store it in a very secure location. Last but not least, a Microsoft CA has a built-in backup tool. If you schedule that to back up the database on a regular basis, you can even get away with crash-consistent backups of a CA in a pinch.

10.4.4   A Restore Is the Only Proof That a Backup Exists

Consider the opening statement of this section. How does your team know what backups are in place? The only way to know for sure that a backup set is suitable for a restore if need arises is to actually perform a restore. Anything short of that is an assumption, and, as Jack Reacher used to say, "in the field, assumptions kill." Unfortunately, Active Directory does not allow to "just restore to some temporary location" – you need a network segment isolated from the production infrastructure, you need the ability to transfer the backup to that area, perform a restore, and validate that the restored artifact actually has AD data inside. This last ability is where general-purpose backup products usually fall short even if they offer the feature of a "sandbox restore" of a backup as soon as it has been created. But having a VM come up and not crash on boot is already way more than just assuming that a backup will be usable because the backup set was created and is of certain size.

AD restores work best if the backup you are restoring from has been created using the VSS BACKUP operation, whatever first- or third-party technology was applied after that. If you do not own the backup subsystem, agree with the backup team on the following:

- All DC backups are application consistent (as opposed to "crash consistent," which is what you get if you simply copy the storage blocks of the disks, ignoring possible open files and cached writes).
- If there are VSS errors in DC backups, the AD team is to be notified.

Still, a restore is the only way to **know** that you can recover your Active Directory objects to the state of that particular backup set.

10.4.5 How Many DCs Should You Back Up?

We have already discussed the value of the uniformity of DCs in Chapter 7. Assuming your engineering effort has heeded this guidance and your DCs are all "just DCs," then technically a verified backup of one DC per domain is what it takes to restore any object and SYSVOL file to the state of the backup set. There is, of course, some ambiguity introduced by replication (if a change was made in a remote site prior to backup time but arrived at

CHAPTER 10 OPERATING A MODERN AD

the location of backup *after* the backup was taken), but apart from that, you only need one DC backed up.

The "suspenders and belt" mentality has saved every seasoned admin's day more than once, so AD teams will usually request that at least two DCs per domain be backed up. This is old admin wisdom, and although we banned "we have always done it this way" from our vocabulary in the context of this book, you should not disregard it lightly. However, backups of multiple DCs make a lot more sense and offer a lot more value if

- Created by different technologies (do not put all your eggs in one basket)
- Created in different locations (there may be a site outage, planned or otherwise)
- Stored on different media (although this can be accomplished within one backup solution as well)

A decades-old practice of backing up over WAN so that each site holds backups from a different site (lower half of Figure 10-2) offers zero benefit compared to backing up each DC to its own site (upper half of Figure 10-2) if the DCs are "just DC."

CHAPTER 10 OPERATING A MODERN AD

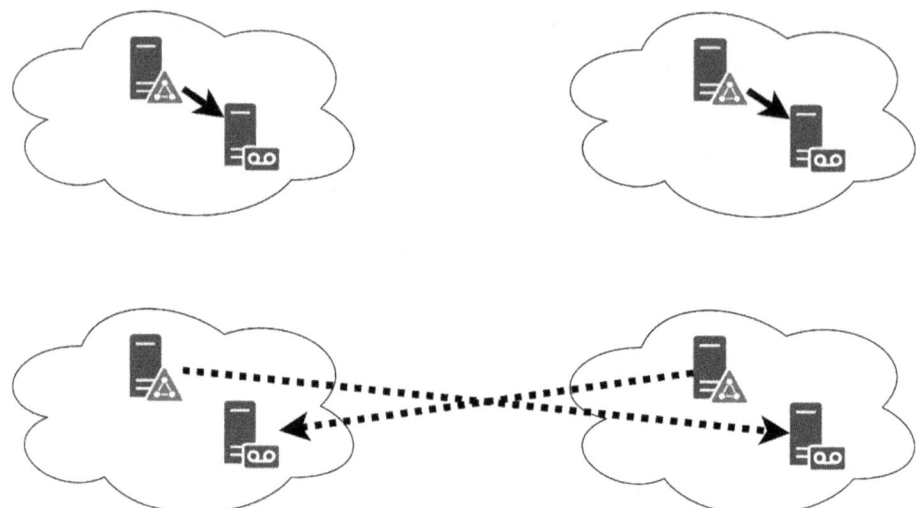

Figure 10-2. A "crosswise" backup offers zero benefit and puts additional load on the WAN

For operational backup/restore, it is usually of no consequence which particular DC is holding which FSMO roles. This may play a part in planning for disaster recovery, which we will discuss in the next section, but for object-level day-to-day recovery operations, FSMO role assignments are not important.

10.4.6 Is There Operational Value in WSB Backups?

If your regular backup regime is not based on WSB backups, there are still cases where an admin would want to create such a backup – for example, before performing a change, the success of which is not guaranteed. The author has not seen these "last-minute safety net" backups used very often for an actual rollback, but here, too, restore rules – if you know what problems this backup set will solve and exactly how you will go about using it, then and only then an out-of-band WSB backup is of any value.

Remember to treat this data with the reverence befitting the crown jewels. If possible, store it only on Tier 0 systems (any device you store it on *becomes* a Tier 0 system just by virtue of you doing so!), ideally on the Domain Controller itself. If you absolutely have to move a WSB backup set off its DC, use whatever technology is available, at the very least a password-protected archive, to encrypt the backup!

Many of what was said about backups and restores, in general, also applies, on a technical level, to Disaster Recovery. However, it is a discipline with its own rules of engagement and worthy of its own section.

10.5 Disaster Recovery

When talking to IT teams about disaster recovery (DR), the following questions always come up:

- We discussed backup and restore already – is it not the same thing?
- Is DR an operational or an organizational topic, i.e., is IT the right audience at all?

The answer to the first question is a very definitive "no." Restore is engineered, set up, and operated on the assumption that the infrastructure as such is intact and it's only one application, albeit in the case of AD, a foundational one, that has been impacted, and only on the content rather than on the infrastructure level. The assumption behind disaster recovery must be that the entire infrastructure and everything running on it has been destroyed. Only if this extreme case is accounted for in your disaster recovery plan are you prepared to face the next 25 years of AD operations with confidence.

10.5.1 AD Disaster Typology 101

Depending on whom you speak to, different levels of infrastructure loss will be qualified as "disaster" and thus fall under the topic of "disaster recovery" rather than a simple "restore from backup." The scenario most admins are unsure about, and the only one discussed here that the author would be prepared to put into the previous section is the physical loss of one Domain Controller while having at least one other DC from the same domain online and operational. The official Microsoft guidance suggests that you perform the following actions if you find yourself in this situation:

- Seize all FSMO roles the suddenly deceased DC has been holding using NTDSUTIL

- Clean up the missing DC's metadata from the replication topology, again using NTDSUTIL

- Verify replication of these changes to all remaining DCs in the entire forest (if connectivity permits, you can force the forest-wide replication by running **repadmin /syncall /AdeP** on the DC you connected NTDSUTIL to)

- Add a new server to the domain using the previous DC's IP address and machine name

- Promote the new server to a Domain Controller (using IFM if the domain is large and the network connecting the new DC to the next site slow or unreliable)

Unless you have implemented a specialized AD disaster recovery solution that automates all these operations for you, this is **exactly what you should be doing** if you lose a DC. The step in the middle, "verify that the changes in topology have replicated," is **not optional**. Neglecting to do this (and to wait some time) let many administrators become extremely averse to reusing DC names, which is completely unjustified. They probably would be as averse to reusing IP addresses too, but the pain of changing DNS settings on thousands of devices is even worse. There is nothing to fear and much to gain in reusing DC names, especially if third-party DNS is in play.

A simultaneous loss of all domain controllers hosting a particular naming context (domain or application partition) leads to the loss of this naming context and constitutes a disaster, at least for users and applications using objects from that naming context. As per official Microsoft guidance, one of the DCs has to be restored from backup and the rest metadata-cleaned out and then repromoted. If the NC in question was a domain partition, trusts with the other domains in the forest have to be validated and repaired if needed. Depending on the freshness of the backup, the Global Catalog in a multi-domain forest may have to be dropped and recreated.

If you lose the entire forest, for example, as a result of a ransomware attack, you have to perform a full forest recovery as per the Microsoft forest recovery whitepaper. Every administrator who has ever been in this situation probably learned to love single-domain forests because in this topology, the forest recovery procedure, albeit tedious, is nearly trivial regarding things to keep track of and possibilities to introduce a human mistake that would negate the whole progress made so far. In a multi-domain forest, the root domain has to be recovered first, although it often does not contain any objects relevant to recovering the business, and every other domain has to be reconciled with its parent or with the other trees of the forest. If you run a multi-domain forest, you definitely need a third-party tool to automate this process for you, including the rebuilding of the global catalog. In a single-domain forest, a third-party AD recovery solution helps maintain peace of mind and drastically reduce the RTO, but a single-domain forest recovery is something that every AD admin can accomplish by themselves in a pinch.

A corruption of data in an AD partition can constitute a disaster as well, depending on the partition that has been damaged. A large-scale damage in schema or configuration calls for a forest recovery. A custom application partition can sometimes simply be recreated and repopulated by the application using it. Domain partitions, on the other hand, are trickier since authentication and manageability of the domain may be impacted if partition data is corrupted. In this case, performing an authoritative restore of the complete partition is the only chance you have. In cases of partition corruption, you should always perform a backup – a crash-consistent one, if need be – to later determine the root cause of the data corruption, since you absolutely want to prevent this event from repeating itself!

10.5.2 AD Disaster Recovery Anti-patterns

The questions quoted at the beginning of this session show that many IT people have much less firm a grasp on the reality of disaster recovery than they do on the run-of-the-mill backup and restore. Microsoft included this observation as Law #1 into the "10 immutable laws of security administration":

Nobody believes anything bad can happen to them, until it does.

This leads to the first, most common, and most serious anti-pattern in disaster recovery planning: Assuming that too much of the pre-existing infrastructure is left standing. This is not a problem related to AD in particular or IT in general – even the overarching DR planning for your organization may be based on too generous assumptions. While you probably cannot do much about that except point it out to the person in charge of the DR plan, you should engineer AD disaster recovery based on realistic assumptions and not necessarily on those from the global DR plan. For example, even if the DR plan assumes that power is still being delivered to the central office locations, you should include a prolonged power outage in your planning and prepare for a scenario where someone

CHAPTER 10 OPERATING A MODERN AD

has to drive to a location that has power and connectivity and begin disaster recovery of the foundational network services in a public cloud. In that case, having recovery data already present in the cloud helps speed up the process quite significantly.

A second anti-pattern often observed in DR is over-reliance on the onsite team's skills. Even if the team does have the skills to complete a realistic disaster-recovery exercise within the expected time frame, in a real-life disaster recovery situation it will have to work under different conditions, under much more pressure, with much less infrastructure, access, and tooling, and probably with less people, too. Murphy's Law dictates that a global AD outage will happen when the most knowledgeable AD person is on vacation and unavailable, and the second-most knowledgeable one is down sick. The author was once called in to assist with a disaster recovery procedure because the person who was believed to have it all perfectly in hand literally got run over by a bus on the way to the office!

The third anti-pattern that bears pointing out, and one that is way too common in these difficult times, is that of never even performing a DR exercise or restricting it to a "tabletop gameplay." By neglecting DR drills, IT teams prevent the most important abilities from being developed: muscle memory and communication under pressure. Without these, the best AD know-how will only get you so far if a real disaster strikes.

Note There is a decades-old myth stating that a system-state backup older than the tombstone lifetime cannot be used for recovery. In reality, it only cannot be used *to recover a DC into a forest where other DCs are still running and replicating with each other*. But you normally wouldn't want that anyway if all that your DCs are doing is hosting AD and DNS. If you have lost your entire forest and all you have is a two-year-old backup, you can absolutely recover from that to the state of two years ago – without any recovery-induced inconsistencies in the resulting forest.

There are specialized tools available on the market that will automate the entire disaster recovery process and ensure that the recovered forest is technically healthy. Of course, if the loss of your AD infrastructure is due to a cyber incident, you will have to perform a forensic investigation and the necessary cleanup of the recovered artifact, no matter what technology you use for the Active Directory-specific part of the process. This is only possible with the intimate knowledge of the IT infrastructure surrounding your AD, of the applications consuming its services, and of the management processes you and your team have put in place. And this answers the second question we quoted at the beginning of this section: Yes, DR is an operational discipline, and a DR drill for Active Directory is as much part of the yearly routine as rolling **krbtgt** passwords or deleting stale objects.

10.5.3 AD Disaster Recovery as Part of a Global DR Effort

Almost every subsystem and application in your entire IT infrastructure depends on identity. This is why it is not only very important to know what is required to perform a disaster recovery in case of a complete loss of the environment, but also to be able to reliably predict how long it is going to take until lookup, authentication, and authorization are available again and to what extent these services will be degraded after the initial recovery steps have been completed.

Document every recovery drill and make the timeline and the end result available to other infrastructure teams and application owners. Even if the overarching DR plan does not include concrete timelines, knowing when identity becomes available helps other teams to plan their disaster recovery steps and request external assistance at the right time.

If your organization has developed enough operational awareness to not treat an IT disaster, especially one of the cyber variety, as an "IT problem," there is probably some kind of "crisis communications framework" in place to keep in touch with internal and external crisis responders, law enforcement, shareholders, customers, and the press. You will probably want to tap into this facility as well – at the point in your post-breach cleanup where you decide to roll every user's password to contain possible user-based persistence vectors. Having a channel of communication in place that the users are trained to receive this sort of information on helps speed up resuming normal operations. It also helps prevent post-breach phishing, where the users are contacted by a malicious actor (not necessarily the one responsible for the current breach) and lured to official-looking password reset websites.

10.5.4 Disaster Recovery in a Hybrid AD

A modern AD is hybrid, which is why you must be aware of the peculiarities of a synchronized AD/Entra ID directory and prepared to recover both in the right way and order. A part of the challenge of being prepared is the limited ability to visualize the possible disaster on the cloud side of the directory. With an on-premises AD, a seasoned administrator can easily imagine a Domain Controller refusing to boot, a whole OU tree getting deleted, or a schema extension wreaking havoc in the partition. With Entra ID, a loss of functionality or data is much less intuitive, especially because there *are* outages there on a regular basis and no one but Microsoft can do anything about it.

A common anti-pattern in preparing yourself for a hybrid disaster is captured in the following response from a customer:

> "All relevant identities are synchronized from the on-premises AD anyway so that we can just reprovision users if they have been damaged."

CHAPTER 10   OPERATING A MODERN AD

There are at least two things wrong with this statement:

- If "all relevant identities" includes administrators, all the way up to Global Administrator role holders, your hybrid AD is a sitting duck waiting to be shot. Whoever gains control over the on-premises AD has everything at their disposal to take down the cloud tenant completely, including all the applications that use Entra ID for authentication and authorization. And if some of the synchronized accounts are privileged on premises and you have set up Cloud Kerberos, then a takeover of your cloud tenant leads to a very quick takedown of Active Directory. On the other hand, if you do not synchronize your administrators to the cloud, then you *do* need a plan to protect and recover the cloud-only parts of your Entra ID tenant.

- But even if all synchronized identities are just regular users both on premises and in the cloud, there are still tons of things to consider before you can reenable Entra ID Connect (or Cloud Sync). Some of the applications you have attached to your tenants anchor by Object ID which is not retained if the object was hard-deleted (security groups, at the time of writing, are always hard-deleted; there is no Recycle Bin for them in Entra ID; of course, this may change very quickly like everything cloud-related).

And then, of course, there are all the other object types that are not users, groups, or computers and cannot be synchronized from on-premises. There are links between all the different objects both within Entra ID and outside of it, and many of them make use of the Object ID. Last but not least, if you are using Entra ID Connect, then you are responsible for keeping track of the synchronization configuration, including custom attribute transformations, filter rules, etc.

For Entra ID Connect, once your configuration has stabilized, export it using **Get-ADSyncServerConfiguration** and save the resulting JSON file in a secure location.

To prepare for a hybrid disaster, you must consider all possibilities and have a documented workflow for each of them:

- On-premises AD is compromised, but the cloud tenant is not showing any signs of compromise yet.

- On-premises AD is compromised and the cloud tenant is showing unusual behavior but is still operational.

- On-premises AD is not showing any signs of compromise yet, but the cloud tenant is showing unusual behavior or has been taken over so that you have no administrative control over it.

Include the procedure for breaking up synchronization between on-premises AD and Entra ID and converting synchronized cloud users into cloud-only users in your DR drill. You should really go through this exercise every time because with Entra ID, not only the graphical user interfaces are updated on a regular basis but also the PowerShell-based tools and the APIs these tools communicate with. You should also include gap analysis and resynchronization procedures in your disaster recovery planning, because that's what will have to happen after the breach responders have performed the cleanup and given both halves of the hybrid AD a clean bill of health.

> **Note** Synchronized users and groups in Entra ID contain a lot of information about their on-premises counterparts – enough to allow for a barebones recreation of those objects should your team not be able to recover Active Directory after all. But beware – all this information is lost once you convert orphaned synchronized objects to cloud-only users and groups!

For dealing with hard-deleted objects and those that are not part of the synchronized identity but still maintain relationships to it, like enterprise applications, conditional access policies, or administrative units, you should consider implementing a dedicated disaster recovery solution for Entra ID. While these tools cannot give hard-deleted objects their Object ID back, they record all relationships an object had prior to its destruction and recreate them based on the new Object ID. Some of these tools tout the ability to perform recovery to a different Entra ID tenant. Before you let this capability influence a purchasing decision, visualize the limited value it is able to provide. Everything that is based on UPN cannot be recreated seamlessly in a new tenant until the domains the UPN suffixes belong to have been migrated to that tenant! And this is no small feat, even when you have control over everything. If you have lost administrative control over the tenant the domains are currently attached to, it is simply not possible. At the end of the day, the biggest value you can derive from the "recover to different tenant" feature is the ability to validate backup data by performing an actual restore – an important one to have but not one that will save the day if a disaster strikes!

Should you find yourself robbed of administrative control over your Entra ID tenant one day, your only solution is to call Microsoft and have them restore your administrative access. There is a documented procedure for this, but in order to facilitate it, you have to produce commercial documents proving your ownership of the tenant in question. Do yourself and your organization a favor; take the time to read through the requirements and have the commercial parts of your organization produce the required documentation. Keep it on a medium you can access without either AD or Entra ID being in a working state!

10.6 Functional Monitoring

Everyone running an IT infrastructure needs to monitor its operational health – CPU and RAM utilization, free disk space and I/O queue depth, services running and stopped, and so on. None of these parameters is per se security-related, hence "functional monitoring" to distinguish from watching the security posture and authentication behavior we will look at in the next section In the vast majority of cases, this kind of monitoring uses three sorts of sensors:

- A presence/absence value (host is pingable, port 443 is listening, service "ADWS" is running, and so on)
- A numerical value that is expected to stay within certain thresholds (disk queue below 1.0, RAM utilization below 90%, remaining certificate validity above 14 days, etc.)
- A presence of patterns in data (event logs, regex analysis of text logs or data dumps, SQL queries, and similar)

Sometimes custom sensors are deployed to the monitored systems, but they usually provide a threshold-bound value that the monitoring system knows how to process.

There are two aspects that have to be taken into account when including AD, PKI, Entra ID Connect, and other Tier 0 identity systems in functional monitoring: the definition of "health" to be monitored against and the placement of the central monitoring facilities in regard to their possible impact on identity systems.

10.6.1 Monitoring AD Health

Beside the health metrics that are monitored for every server (uptime, CPU, RAM, disk space, etc.), there are specific performance indicators to monitor for Tier 0 and specifically for Domain Controllers. The most important non-security item is the replication health for AD and SYSVOL. Both can be established by a custom sensor, e.g., a PowerShell script, but many enterprise-grade monitoring systems have ready-made sensors for this.

Monitor the time service on the PDC emulator – it must be in sync with the chosen external time source. All other computers must synchronize their time with the domain – an important parameter to monitor as well. In doing this, you need to be prepared for the PDCe role being moved to a different DC.

If performance of Domain Controller operations is a matter of concern, Windows offers a plethora of performance counters detailing all sorts of operations. Many of them can even be used for security monitoring like NTLM Binds per second or user object creation attempts per second. Most of the PerfMon counters offered by ADDS are really about performance and are especially valuable if monitored as a long-time trend rather than a snapshot value of the current state. If your chosen monitoring product not only has the ability to display trend graphs but can also detect anomalies in time series, analyzing various "operations per second" counters can help you catch problems in AD itself, malfunctions in the systems consuming AD services, and maybe even some malicious activity.

If monitoring the internal PKI also falls under the AD team's purview, don't forget to monitor the CRLs' freshness, not just their availability. This is less trivial when using OCSP so might warrant a custom scripted sensor running on the OCSP host.

10.6.2 Designing Tier 0 Monitoring

More often than not, monitoring systems work with agents. There is only so much data that can be gleaned remotely, and for remote monitoring, firewall ports must be open and the monitoring system must be in possession of very high-privileged credentials. Since it's not feasible to store local monitoring user separately for each monitored host (and even less feasible to roll their passwords on a regular basis), remote-first monitoring leads to God-mode accounts opening the door for lateral movement and escalation attacks. Agents take care of authentication by running in the SYSTEM context of the monitored host, and in rare cases they also take care of inbound firewall ports by maintaining an outbound connection to the monitoring system instead of the latter polling the agents remotely. Monitoring agents, however, are updated on a regular basis, creating a strong incentive to automate this process. If the agents are able to self-update, the monitoring system becomes one with the ability to deploy executable code to the monitored hosts, and the code is executed in SYSTEM context. Replace "monitored hosts" by "Tier 0 systems," and you are looking at a love child of Solorigate and NotPetya if someone decides to attack your environment using the monitoring as their base of operations!

The popular SNMP protocol is a special kind of agent-based monitoring. Here the "agent" is usually delivered as a part of the operating system itself, and Windows is no exception. SNMP can (and should) be authenticated, but in most implementations SNMP authentication is not tied to Windows authentication and offers far less abuse potential than remote monitoring. Before jumping on the SNMP train, however, you should be aware that Microsoft stopped actively developing the SNMP subsystem in the late 2000s. There are alternatives on the market, but they are rarely worth implementing since most enterprise-grade monitoring products have highly optimized agents of their own.

CHAPTER 10   OPERATING A MODERN AD

Computer systems running agents in the SYSTEM context of Domain Controllers are not unheard of – any security software, backup solutions, or even virtualization platforms do that. However, those systems are classified as Tier 0, hardened and protected accordingly. Monitoring in a larger IT environment is explicitly designed to span the entire server fleet in order to maintain dependencies of services on each other and other kinds of advanced business logic. Monitoring administrators (i.e., the very persons who check new agent versions in for automatic distribution or handle remote monitoring credentials) often come from infrastructure rather than security or identity. This creates a challenge of monitoring Tier 0 potentially from a Tier 1 system.

There are four solution approaches to this challenge, and your IT organization must commit to the selected approach because changing the monitoring architecture after the fact does not usually work very well:

1. Declare all functional monitoring of servers a Tier 0 activity. This requires limiting administrative access to the monitoring system to specialized Tier 0 accounts and ideally to Tier 0 PAWs and jumphosts. This also requires administrator training and a very stringent patching and configuration management regime as befits Tier 0. Since monitoring systems usually do not use their computer account to connect remotely to monitoring hosts (many of them cannot be joined to AD at all), there is no danger of leaving traces of Tier 0 credentials on Tier 1 machines. If the chosen monitoring product does use remote credentialed access, the credentials used for Tier 0 must be different from those for Tier 1.

2. Evaluate the interactive features currently in use. The author has encountered multiple IT teams during his career who knew very well what was

CHAPTER 10   OPERATING A MODERN AD

"normal" in their respective environments and what trends to watch out for. It allowed them to forgo the built-in dashboarding and reporting of the monitoring product and simply have the monitoring server use SMTP or APIs to notify about dangerous trends, deviations from the "known normal," or other singular events by sending an email or opening a trouble ticket. Since notifications are traditionally an outbound activity, a Tier 0 monitoring system can provide them in a secure manner without having to maintain a separate mail server or ticket system for Tier 0.

3. Some monitoring systems support distributed monitoring but maintain separate protocols for consolidated dashboarding and consolidated administration. If your chosen monitoring product has that capability, you can consolidate dashboarding, notifications, and business logic on the front-end monitoring server while maintaining separate back-end servers for Tier 0 and Tier 1. This concept is doable even with Microsoft SCOM but requires three management groups (MG) – the front-end and the two "tiered" back-ends, resulting in a rather convoluted and hard-to-maintain architecture. If you have good SCOM skills in your IT team, this solution can work very well if done right.

4. A rare approach (but one the author encountered in the field) is to include the Tier 0 monitoring system *as a monitored host* in Tier 1 monitoring but to provide sensors for all the different Tier 0

systems and services. This way, the front-end (Tier 1) monitoring would not show "CPU utilization on host DC0107" but rather the "service status of DC0107_CPU_Utilization on host T0MON." The Tier 0 monitoring system must have very good APIs for this to work properly.

Distributed monitoring using the same product in Tier 0 and Tier 1 (approach #2 and #3) has the distinct advantage of using Tier 1 as a staging/testing area for new agent versions and infrastructure-specific sensors. When working with a Tier 0 system without staging, use the test environment to preflight agent updates and disable automatic self-updating of agents.

10.7 Security Monitoring

In an organization that takes IT security seriously, analysts investigating possible incidents in the SOC should not be involved with operating the systems they are protecting. As their investigations progress and turn into containment and mitigation, they most probably involve the teams responsible for running the systems in question – and Active Directory is almost always on that list. This is not to say that AD teams should not do security monitoring of their own and put their know-how, automation, and tooling to good use. There are multiple approaches to monitoring Active Directory for security vulnerabilities and ongoing threats, and not all of them require a full-blown SIEM and a SOC consuming the signals from it.

10.7.1 Attack Surface Monitoring

The better your processes are in preventing and mitigating configuration drift, the less immediate value a classic attack surface scan, i.e., a check for known misconfigurations in Tier 0 systems that enable certain attack techniques, will yield. It is still worth the while to incorporate a regular scan of your environment into your AD management regime. There are multiple tools on the market, the main difference between free and commercial ones being that the former have to be run manually on demand while the latter run continuously and warn you if or when a vulnerability pops up that hadn't been found before. This can be either because a new attack vector has been found (assuming that the tool you use has the ability and the permission to update itself) or because the configuration of your environment has changed in an undesired manner. In any case, any finding on the attack surface is a call for action – even if the action to take may be trivial.

10.7.2 Attack Path Analysis

A different and arguably more valuable kind of configuration monitoring that is complementary to the attack surface monitoring is attack path investigation. As early as 2015, John Lambert of Microsoft shared a piece that was titled

> Defenders think in lists. Attackers think in graphs.
> As long as this is true, attackers win.

Attack path analysis aims to help "list-minded" defenders assume the attacker's mindset and view the IT environment they know like the back of their hands, not in terms of systems, groups, permissions, policies, and firewall rules but as a series of hops leading from the perimeter towards the heart of the infrastructure – the Tier 0, the identity systems where the keys to the kingdom are.

There are a few tools, both free and commercial, to facilitate this kind of analysis. Probably the best-known of them is "BloodHound" that exists in several editions and is able to consume a variety of sources by means of collector applications populating the central graph database. "Forest Druid" follows a different approach, providing a more monolithic application but also capable of ingesting a variety of systems, some of them not exactly identity-related (e.g., backup solutions) but capable of both protecting identity and exposing it to risk at the same time.

10.7.3 Using Functional Monitoring for Security Monitoring

A number of tools available for both attack surface and attack path analysis can be easily automated or provide an API to consume the results of their analysis programmatically. That makes using the functional monitoring facilities for dashboarding and notifications in lieu of confronting security personnel with yet another set of new dashboards a very appealing proposition. The biggest challenge with adapting security monitoring to the functional monitoring mindset is that most monitoring systems in operation today are host-centric. Even those products whose business logic allows for the definition of "applications" still tend to view an "application" as an aggregation of hosts. AD is a distributed application, so a misconfiguration of an object or an overly generous ACL does not belong to any single Domain Controller. Some of the best implementations of this approach the author has seen or assisted in creating just provision an aptly named Windows host per forest and present the security monitoring results as "services" or "performance counters" of that host.

10.7.4 Tapping into Your SOC's Behavior-Based Monitoring

If your organization already operates a SIEM system collecting logon, Kerberos, replication, and change events, it's a very good idea to familiarize yourself with that product, its search capabilities (that will probably include an SQL-like language like Kusto), and the retention policies the SOC team has defined for different event sources or classes. It will come in handy when investigating account lockout, suspicious activity, or a misbehaving service.

Do not try to roll your own event-based monitoring from first principles. Try to leverage the existing SIEM for your operational purposes. If there is no SIEM consuming Active Directory event logs yet, you can set up one of the free or open-source products available. But be prepared to tear it down in the future once your organization decides to implement a central log collection facility because different log collection agents may not play well alongside each other, and in any case, they will put double the load on your Domain Controllers.

10.8 Summary

In this chapter, we revisited several operational aspects of the modern AD. We looked at day-to-day operations, challenges of onboarding new technology, backup, restore, and monitoring. We also covered disaster recovery that some IT admins would not normally consider an operational discipline. There are challenges specific to every one of these activities, and we highlighted solution approaches for them.

AD is an extremely resilient technology and will often continue running smoothly under less-than-optimal conditions. However, a well-thought-out and rigorously automated administration combined with configuration drift monitoring, constant vigilance in functional monitoring, regular security checks, and preparedness for all sorts of disasters are necessary to ensure successful AD operations for the decades to come.

CHAPTER 11

Transitioning to a Modern AD

It is certainly a very rare occurrence these days that an Active Directory organization of significant size and complexity is being built in a vacuum, without years' worth of infrastructure, data, and processes to take into account. While new companies, non-profits, and public institutions are created every day, they often start off as "cloud first," or are embedded in an existing framework of systems, processes, and policies, or – especially in research and education – are basing their new infrastructure on Unix or Linux and make use of authentication and configuration providers available in that ecosystem. The only cases an AD is built without a pre-existing AD are

- The previous AD infrastructure has been damaged beyond all hope of repair (usually due to a cyber incident), and recovery is either not possible or not economically feasible. In such cases, the overarching requirement is not to rebuild the AD organization as close to the previous state as possible but rather to build the new directory service up to modern security standards to prevent a repetition of the disaster.

CHAPTER 11   TRANSITIONING TO A MODERN AD

- The organization has decided to move lookup, authentication, and authorization to Active Directory from a different technology. The reasons for this are mostly consolidation to the Microsoft technology stack, or implementation of specific components of that stack like Microsoft Exchange, or – the author has been part of at least tree such engagements – loss of previous platform know-how due to people retiring, leaving the organization, or, in one case, even dying.

If a "modern AD" is commissioned to be built, the goal is usually to transition to it from an existing AD infrastructure that is in active operation. The reasons for that are even more diverse than for replacing the core technology stack and often include:

- A security incident that did not cause total destruction but created awareness at the management level

- Changes in the organization's naming, ownership, or affiliation that make the current domain and account naming undesired

- Cyber insurance providers or new company owners require adherence to certain design, implementation, or operation principles

- A rare but perfectly possible case where the current namespace design prevents successful coexistence with a new owner, subsidiary, or partner organization

In this chapter, we will look at possible motivators for transition and investigate the methods, processes, and design principles you can use to facilitate a painless and timely transition.

11.1 In Situ Modernization vs. Migration

A full-scale migration is never friction-free. Even if technically everything works flawlessly, some applications will tolerate namespace changes and SID translation worse than others, and in the end, humans will suffer. Many IT teams fear AD migrations, especially those who have experienced one that did not end up working flawlessly. But even if everybody knows what they're doing, a migration is invasive and should be avoided if the alternative is acceptable.

Consider the four motivators for transition listed above. Two of them, a rebuild post-cyber incident and a rebuild for compliance purposes, imply that there are things in the current AD that

- Either cannot be changed in an existing domain/forest but must be taken care of nonetheless

- Or are so hard to find and difficult to clean up that a rebuild appears politically attractive and economically feasible

An example of the former would be the knowledge (from the previous cyber incident) that the malicious actor is in possession of an older DC backup. DPAPI is so pervasive and foundational in Windows that simply nothing can be done to prevent this attack vector from being reused – except rebuilding the domain.

The latter, on the other hand, reflects the myth of a "polluted AD object" that is so popular that it even prevented a number of technically feasible AD migrations in the past – the fear of polluting the new AD forest with artifacts from the old one prompted some decision-makers to go "full disaster" and recreate everything from scratch (or from the HR database, but it does not hold passwords, permissions, or user profiles). There *are* things in AD that may be non-trivial to find (we talked about hidden malicious administrators in Chapter 4), but the engineer's way is to know what's the intended state and detect deviations from that state, even if they are well-hidden. There are specialized consultancies out there that will find everything an attacker would, especially if they are granted enough privileges to both read and replicate!

From the end users' perspective, an in situ transformation is always preferable to a migration. This is why, if a migration – for whatever reasons – is inevitable, you should invest time, effort, and money in making the experience as non-invasive for the users as possible.

11.1.1 Coexistence Is the Real Challenge

Bear in mind that not the actual migration (i.e., creation of AD objects, rejoining of member systems to new domains, translation of permissions, and so on) is the painful part, but the necessary coexistence. A "big bang" migration (starting in the new environment on Monday after a weekend's worth of downtime) used to be possible even in decent-sized organizations because all devices, clients and servers alike, were wired and office-bound. With good preparation (provisioning target identities, adding new permissions ahead of the switch, creating and testing scripts or checklists for application server, etc.), enough personnel, and a working coffee machine, an entire enterprise or a largish public agency could be switched to a new Active Directory forest over a long weekend.

Today, bringing all devices in for migration is not realistic in almost any organization. Applications have grown, servers have spread, and protocols they communicate with each other on have become more diverse than they used to be in Active Directory's early days. This calls for what some migration experts call "rich coexistence" – connecting old and new infrastructure in a way that allows every user, regardless of their migration status, seamless access to files, data, and applications in both environments, i.e., also regardless of *their* migration status. This looks extremely good on paper, but in reality, at least one of the access scenarios will not work, or will not work in all applications, thus causing even more confusion on the end users' part.

CHAPTER 11 TRANSITIONING TO A MODERN AD

The traditional approach to rich coexistence involves

- Creating a forest trust, the idea being of the source forest trusting the target one but not vice versa, because the Source is assumed to be potentially compromised
- Synchronizing the users' passwords to enable a seamless logon experience
- Populating sidHistory in the Target by SIDs from the Source and disabling sidHistory quarantine on the trust

This creates several challenges:

- A trust means that Source and Target cannot have overlapping UPN suffixes (or identical domain names, for that matter).
- SidHistory blows up the access token in the Target, regardless of whether the access is within the target forest or cross-forest.
- Non-migrated users cannot access resources in the target forest, which often leads to the trust being expanded to bi-directional.
- Permissions for Source SIDs cannot be removed from migrated resources until the last user has been migrated.
- SidHistory cannot be removed from Target users and groups until the last resource has been repermissioned to include Target SIDs in the ACLs.
- While sidHistory works for permissions (at least in applications that use the Windows authorization model) it does not help with user mapping to profiles within applications.

To illustrate the last item, consider a Windows user profile on a workstation. If you rejoin the workstation to the target forest, the user's account in Target has sidHistory populated, and you either manage to create the user account in the target forest using the GUID from Source (the 11th character of **dsHeuristics** allows specifying GUID on object creation, but of course the desired GUID must be available) or add a profile mapping to the target SID to the registry, and the user will be able to log on and load their user profile seamlessly. The GUID is evaluated before the SID in profile mapping; the user has permissions granted by sidHistory, so the profile will load. However, any application that saved something in the registry, in configuration files, or in its own database using the SID – or the UPN, for that matter – will fail.

11.1.2 What Is "Migrated"?

To plan an AD migration the engineer's way, you must agree on some definitions up front. You will talk about "migrated users," "migrated servers," "migrated applications," and other "migrated" artifacts for weeks or months to come, and different people have different expectations of what that qualifier really means. The layman's idea of an identity migration is that it is magically "transferred" to a different (Target) forest and disappears from the previous (Source) forest – identity, after all, is supposed to exist only once, isn't it?

Technically, of course, it's only true for an intraforest migration where an object is *moved* between domains. But in all cross-forest migration scenarios, objects, including identities, are created in the Target while still active in the Source. Therefore, it makes sense to define the "migrated" state. The following is but one definition and not a universally accepted terminology; it just illustrates the kind of conditions you may want to include in the definitions:

Object type	In coexistence	Migrated	Cleaned up
User	Target account is active; the user knows the password and logs on to their primary workstation using the Target account, which allows them to access the majority of applications. Source account is still active and can be used to access certain applications and data.	Source account is inactive or deleted.	sidHistory and memberships in Source groups are removed from Target account.
Group	Target group is populated by members from Target and, in some scenarios, Source.	Source group is not assigned permissions in any Target system.	SidHistory and Source members are removed from Target group.
Computer	Permissions or profile mappings from Target are present on the machine.	Machine is joined to Target.	No permissions or SIDs from Source are present on the machine.
Application	Application accepts user connections from both Source and Target.	All servers and service accounts that constitute the application are from Target.	No Source artifacts, except in logs and historical transactions, are present in the application or its data.

Your definitions may look differently, and you may call the three migration stages differently, too, but it is extremely important that everybody involved speaks the same language. When presenting the migration plan or the progress thereof to Management, keep in mind that they are probably not familiar with, nor interested in, this terminology. But if presenting in layman's terms, alert your team members about it in advance to avoid confusion on their part if you suddenly start using agreed-upon terminology differently in a meeting.

11.1.3 User First or Application First?

If your team is new to the migration business and you are confronted with the requirement to evaluate an AD migration, one of the most important questions you will have to ponder is that of the migration strategy. Migration old-timers often refer to it as the "user-first vs. server-first" question, although in reality the question is and always has been about the applications running on servers rather than the servers themselves.

In the "user first" scenario as shown in Figure 11-1, the coexistence phase from a particular users' point of view starts with logging on to their workstation (which can be migrated simultaneously with the user or at a later point in time) with user credentials from the target forest.

CHAPTER 11 TRANSITIONING TO A MODERN AD

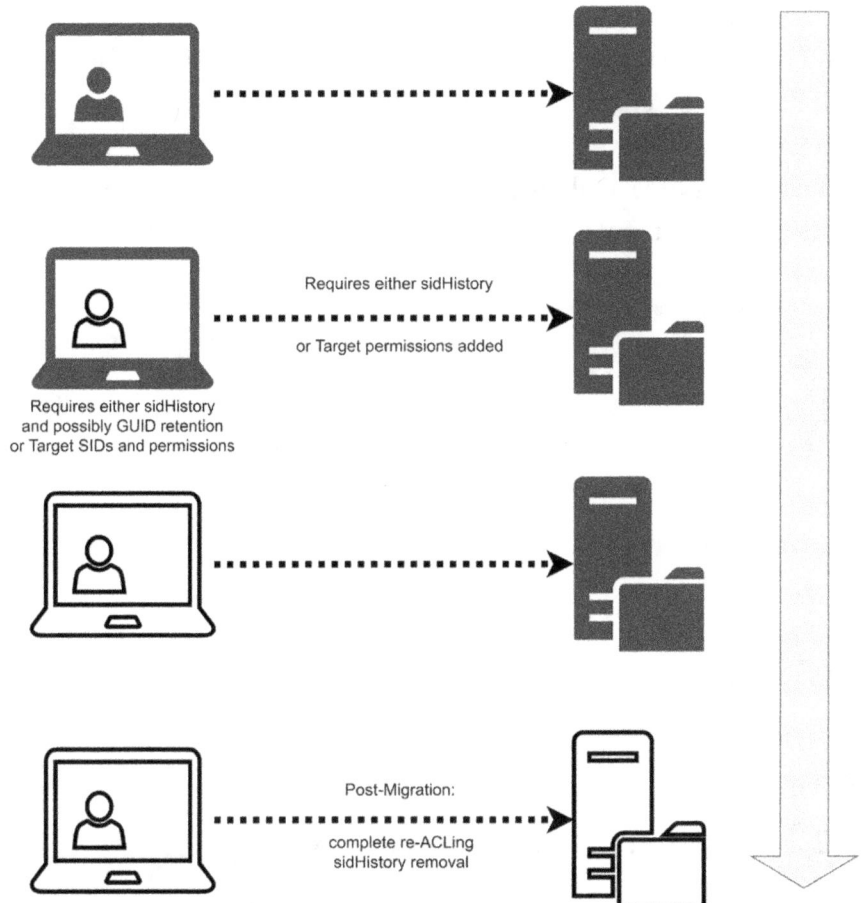

Figure 11-1. *User-first migration depends heavily on sidHistory*

From this moment onwards, they access the applications in the Source using their Target identity, which in most cases requires sidHistory to provide seamless authorization to resources that are using Source for authorization.

After all users (and their client devices, in case they are AD-joined) have been migrated, applications and servers running them are migrated on their own time, followed by breaking the trust, translating all permissions and profile mapping to those from the Target and removing sidHistory from all objects.

CHAPTER 11 TRANSITIONING TO A MODERN AD

"Application first" or "server first" migration, as illustrated by Figure 11-2, can be made to work without sidHistory if you have facilities at your disposal to reliably translate the ACLs and profile mappings during the coexistence. However, this migration scenario requires the trust to be from Target to Source, making it much less attractive in situations where the Source environment is believed to be (or has been) compromised.

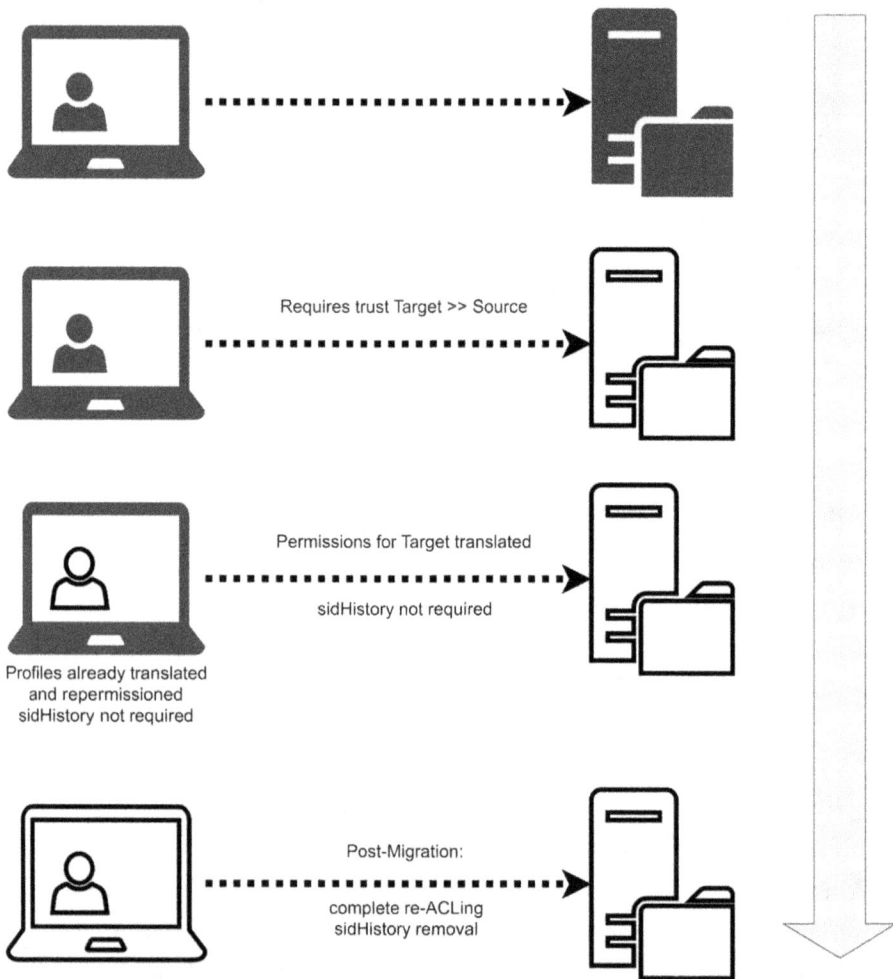

Figure 11-2. *Application-first migration can introduce undesired security dependencies*

We mentioned sidHistory several times throughout the book as something that is a bad thing to have in your AD organization. The reason for it is threefold. Firstly, sidHistory blows up the logon token size. Secondly, there are multiple attack techniques that make use of sidHistory and knowing that **no object should have** sidHistory populated makes detecting them much easier. Last but not least, there is an operational component to it: it is very easy, access rights permitting, to remove sidHistory values from an object, but there is no supported way to "simply write it back," at least once the source of that SID is gone. If your organization has implemented a tool that is able to revert sidHistory changes, it can help, but otherwise just be careful and do whatever is needed to get rid of sidHistory as quickly as possible.

11.1.4 Application Is King

In the previous paragraphs, we were being deliberately vague about what a "resource" is that is being accessed from one environment or migrated to another. This is because applications that make use of Active Directory services do it in a vastly different manner:

- If the "resource" in question is just a file server, i.e., the client application uses Windows to perform authentication, authorization, and data transfer, then lookup and authorization are all that "rich coexistence" must provide. Cross-forest group nesting, additional ACEs or sidHistory, plus cross-forest DNS resolution will get you the required functionality easily, albeit maybe not "quickly" if permissions must be reapplied to large folder structures.

CHAPTER 11   TRANSITIONING TO A MODERN AD

- If the "resource" is an application that makes use of the accessing user's SID for internal user management (rather than just having Windows evaluate the access token for access authorization), then the application must become aware of the new SIDs being mapped to existing user profiles within the application.

An example of the second behavior is the user profile mechanism in Windows – traditionally, the profile was mapped by the SID in the registry and the access to it authorized by the access token – sidHistory would provide access to the profile folder and registry, but for Windows to actually find it, a new SID mapping must be added or the existing one changed to incorporate the new SID. In order to support moving objects between domains within the same forest, which changes the SID but retains the GUID, the GUID mapping was added to the profile location mechanism. It is checked first, even before the SID mapping, allowing a moved user to reuse their profile. That works really well, but an application that stores the SID internally in its own registry branch or in its own settings file cannot find the migrated user's settings because the SID has changed.

Before the final decision about the migration method is made, collect information about the most important applications your organization is running and visualize their behavior if

- A user's SID and potentially GUID changes
- A user's UPN and potentially sAMAccountName changes
- A user's workstation changes its domain membership
- An application server changes its domain membership and potentially FQDN

Write these "partial migration scenarios" down and mark the applications that will present problems along the way. For these, exceptional workarounds will have to be found in cooperation with the application owner, vendor, and the infrastructure team.

Applications that integrate especially tightly with AD, like Microsoft Exchange, Skype for Business, or SharePoint, do not make coexistence any easier to set up and maintain. A low-friction migration of a complex IT environment is practically impossible without using third-party migration technology. This is why we will look at in situ modernization first.

11.2 In Situ Modernization

If the reason for the AD modernization initiative does not require the current environment to be destroyed, you will usually achieve better results with less user aggravation by transitioning to a modern AD "in situ," e.g., by editing existing objects, their permissions, and attributes, than through a full-scale migration. The main advantage of the in situ modernization is that you forgo any coexistence requirements completely because there is no Source and Target domain or forest but simply a "current" and "desired" state!

You can perform most of the provisioning tasks for your "modern AD" framework without even touching production objects:

- Create new privileged groups and users

- Provision all required OU structures, including custom "New Objects" containers, and limit their visibility to hide them from unprivileged users and preexisting administrative identities

- Provision the Red Forest, create and harden the PIM trust, Shadow Principals and other required objects and structures

- Provision new PKI in the Red Forest
- Provision PAWs for Tier 0 administration in the Red Forest
- Provision automation facilities in the Red Forest
- Enable List Object mode, disable addition of computers by unprivileged users, and remove unused Full Access and Replication rights from the domain
- Provision new baseline and exception GPOs, limiting their visibility until they are ready to be rolled out

This allows you to start implementing all new management processes the same way you would have done it on a green field. Once that is ready, start testing and preflighting the transition of users, servers, and clients into the new structure. Always create new service accounts for applications being transitioned and attach appropriate Authentication Policies to them. Remember that a functional test of a system is not complete until it has been rebooted at least twice! Schedule this with application owners accordingly.

After every object being used in production has been moved into the new structure and all necessary exceptions from the baseline have been deployed, there are two cleanup tasks to complete:

- Have an external security professional (or at least one external to the migration project) analyze the security posture of the transformed environment, specifically telling them to ignore ACLs of OUs that are (a) empty and (b) outside the new structure.
- Have server or application owners remove excessive permissions added to AD users and groups in the systems under their purview.

If you have Recycle Bin enabled, remove permissions from the old OUs and roll passwords of old admin accounts prior to deleting them.

11.2.1 The Case of Intraforest Restructuring

The "modern AD" framework favors single-domain forests over the multi-domain topology. If the current forest is of the latter variety and the reasons for multiple domains have become obsolete (e.g., WAN topology) or never really existed in the first place (e.g., "separation of concern" by granting domain admin privileges in a subdomain), you may be compelled to simplify the forest topology by removing all domains but one. You do not, however, get to choose which domain will be left standing – you cannot remove the root domain from the forest.

The "user-first" approach lends itself slightly better to these "simplification migrations" than "server-first," but if you were thorough in identifying applications that make explicit use of the SID, an intraforest migration is usually very straightforward and low-friction.

You will want to pay special attention to DNS, especially if you run it AD integrated. Set your subdomain-specific DNS zones to be replicated forest-wide, lest they get removed when you demote the last Domain Controller from "their" domain. You will want to keep FQDNs and SPNs of servers and services unchanged to reduce friction on the users' part, but have the application owners agree to switch to the root namespace when they upgrade their systems.

Do keep in mind that you still must plan for cleaning up sidHistory because it blows up the token size.

11.3 "Rejuvenation Migration"

A "rejuvenation migration" is a process of building a new AD forest that, for all intents and purposes, looks and feels exactly like the old one and ideally has the same domain name both for NetBIOS (prepopulated for user logon on Windows clients) and DNS (the basis for SPN suffixes and computer FQDNs). A "rejuvenation migration" mostly also includes a hardware and OS version refresh. Reasons for a "rejuvenation migration" are very often security related, where the security people want all SIDs, GUIDs, and cryptographic secrets changed while the internal communications people advocate for as little friction on the users' part as possible.

It is clear that a "rich coexistence" in this case is not realistically achievable – even if some tools available on the market will manage to inject sidHistory into the target objects by "hacky" methods, a trust between two domains with identical names is simply not possible.

Depending on the size of the environment and the tools you have at your disposal, a "rejuvenation migration" can sometimes be achieved by two consecutive "big bangs" into a placeholder forest with a different namespace and then into the designated target forest. Still, SIDs change and GUIDs mostly change, too, so that applications will have to be processed under pressure. Having the clients joined to Entra ID exclusively helps with this part of the migration, but you have to reconnect your "rejuvenated" users to the cloud and reenable Cloud Kerberos with the new virtual RODC.

A special case of a "rejuvenation migration" is migrating one domain out of a multi-domain forest. We will look at it in the next section.

CHAPTER 11   TRANSITIONING TO A MODERN AD

11.4 Mergers and Acquisitions – Migrating into Existing Infrastructure

In the last 25 years, there probably have been more Active Directory migrations happening due to political, legal, and commercial reasons than technical or security-related ones. Companies split, merge, acquire each other, and go their separate ways again. Not every one of these transactions results in an immediate transition of identity – if an entire company changes its affiliation, it is often allowed to continue operating its IT, including identity, the way it was operated prior to the legal change.

But if two entities have decided to merge permanently, there will come a day when a common identity infrastructure becomes vital to leveraging the synergy effects the merger was supposed to bring about. This is the perfect moment to introduce the "modern AD" tenets into the infrastructure in case it has been operated in a legacy way until then.

11.4.1 Anatomy of an (AD) Merger

There is no "one size fits all AD migration for a merger" because there will be at least as many political reasons influencing the decision-making as technical ones. Usually, one of the following three scenarios will be chosen for the identity consolidation:

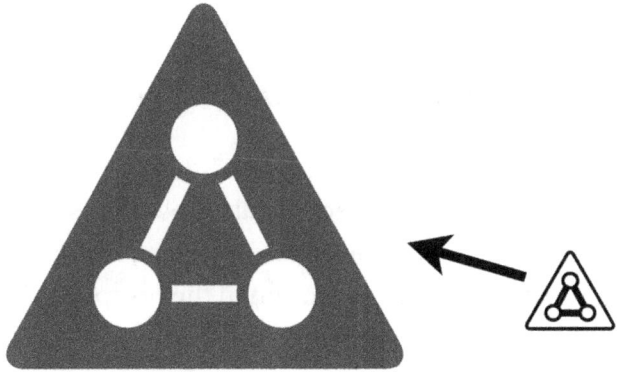

Figure 11-3. *An "integration" is typical if the partners are not equal*

An "integration," as illustrated in Figure 11-3, is a very probable scenario if the receiving entity is larger, better equipped, or has more seats on the board of the new combined entity. This sometimes happens as a result of a "hostile takeover," where the IT department of the organization being taken over is not interested in being swallowed up by the other entity. The author encountered several such transformations in which the IT team had already left.

If the receiving Active Directory is a well-designed and well-managed one, such a migration can be a chance for the organization being incorporated to move towards better security and usability without reinventing the wheel.

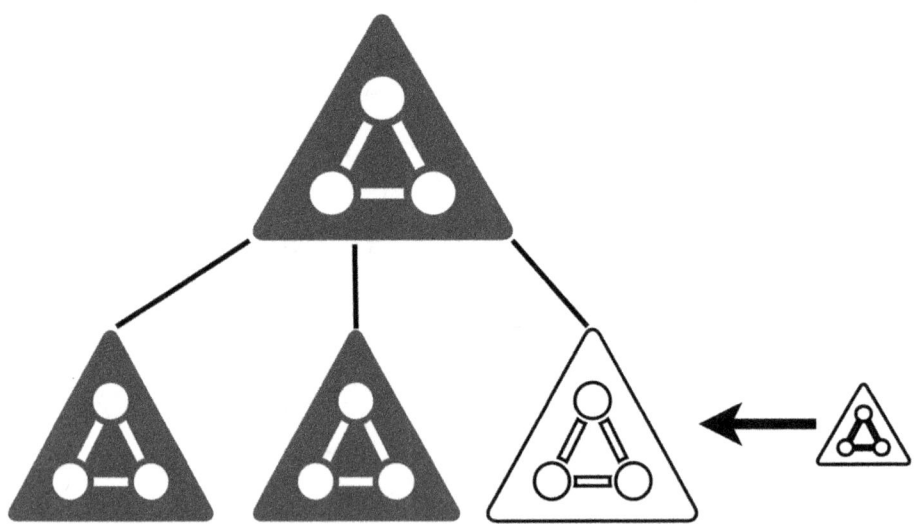

Figure 11-4. *Migration into a subdomain can be a huge step back for a modern IT team*

The "least modern" scenario, technically speaking, is the one depicted in Figure 11-4 – one forest is dissolved and migrated into a subdomain of another forest. Whatever led to this design in the first place, if you are part of the organization being dissolved and you have managed to run your directory successfully using a single-domain topology, you should put up at least some – well-justified – resistance and explain to the combined management the disadvantages of the chosen approach.

This is especially true if the new subdomain will be the **first** child domain in the receiving organization's forest, thus transforming it from a "modern" topology towards a "legacy" one – a lose/lose situation!

You can expect the most harmony and the least friction in scenarios where all parts of the combined entity (Figure 11-5 shows two, but there may be many more parties involved) create a new modern infrastructure and migrate their identity, applications, and privileged management into it without political pressure getting in the way of engineering. This scenario is also potentially easier to implement because the new entity introduces new namespaces for email and DNS so that IT doesn't have to deal with overlapping suffixes and DNS zones.

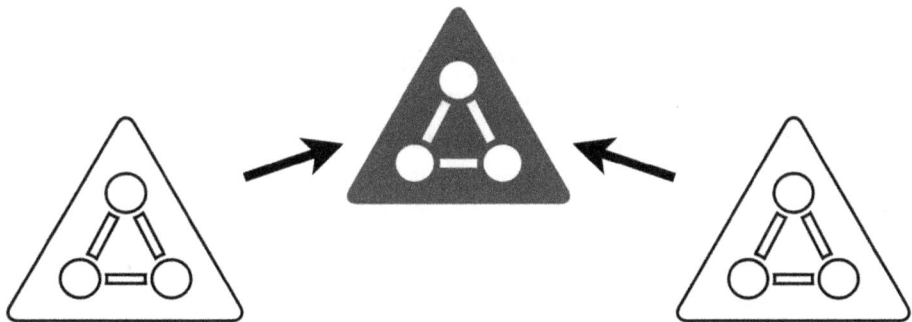

Figure 11-5. *Consolidation into a new forest allows everybody to make the right choices in their own time*

In this or similar migration scenarios, some core systems are often consolidated earlier, well prior to the identity consolidation. Typically, those include HR, Payroll, email, and groupware. This is usually possible with very few issues if security considerations allow for the new target infrastructure to trust the source forests. If parts of the consolidated infrastructure are cloud applications like Teams or Exchange Online, synchronization to Entra ID becomes an interesting challenge. This requirement, however, is solvable by out-of-box tooling even at the time of writing. Entra ID Connect allows synchronizing the anchored identity (the one performing SSO in both directions) from one forest and various application-specific attributes from another forest.

11.4.2 Divestment from the Previous Owners' Point of View

A fairly typical scenario in M&A is a company acquiring not a whole other company but a single business unit. We looked at the challenges that the moving and receiving entities have to contend with earlier in this chapter; however, there are also concerns specific to the divesting part of the organization, i.e., the previous owner. Depending on what business the organization is in, the conditions of the deal, and the specifics of the receiving organization, identity systems may be part of the inventory being handed over – or not. From an AD security operations perspective, the second choice is the ideal one; unfortunately, IT security seldom gets a say in the matter. That may change in the future as many countries pass legislation requiring businesses to adhere to the highest standard of IT security. But at the time of writing, instructions on what the buyer will be taking with them are usually handed down from the boardroom.

A part of what makes this scenario problematic from the AD security perspective is that a formal handover often does not mean a physical cutover – no matter what measures the IT team puts in place to enforce a separation of concerns, the servers remain in the datacenter, and the clients and shopfloor machinery stay in place so that there is a significant physical and logical exposure for the remaining part of the organization. More often than not, the migration of identity systems will occur in place, with the receiving organization extending its network to the joint datacenter. But even if the leaving part of the organization leaves the premises physically, the remaining administrators still have reasons to be concerned.

By handing over parts of their AD organization, they give away secrets that must be changed as soon as possible, secrets that cannot be changed, but also information that an attacker can use against the previously integrated parts of the directory. From the remaining AD's point of view, there are the following scenarios to consider:

1. The leaving part of the organization is implemented as a separate "golden" forest (or multiple forests).

2. The leaving part can be mapped to one or multiple domains of a multi-domain "golden" forest.

3. The leaving part is carved out of a homogenous structure, possibly in the form of OUs.

The first scenario is ideal both from the security standpoint and in regard to the amount of effort required for separation. On the leaving side, some cleanup should be conducted prior to handover:

- Remove sites and subnets not used by the leaving entity
- Remove administrator accounts created for remaining IT personnel
- Remove all cross-forest group memberships from domain local groups
- Remove conditional forwarders to remaining forests in DNS
- Break trusts to other forests, specifically to the Red Forest

- Uninstall agents from Domain Controllers if the respective backend is not part of the leaving infrastructure

- Remove or rename GPOs that point to objects in other forests

- Remove CA certificates belonging to the remaining organization from the trust stores and GPOs

- Create new generic administrative identities for the receiving organization

On the remaining side, the cleanup would concern primarily Shadow Principals, groups, and SCAMA EKUs created specifically for the privileged administration of the leaving forest, DNS forwarders, sites, and subnets (if a complete site is being separated), and cross-forest group memberships in resource forests, if any.

Carving domains out of a forest (scenario #2) involves all the steps listed above plus cleaning out the metadata of the domains that remain from the leaving organization's database. It is, however, much trickier and more dangerous in that the forest root domain must leave (as a clone) along with the relevant child domains. Depending on what objects are present in the root domain, the cleanup may require deleting a substantial number of objects. If the forest root domain was empty, the exposure due to the DPAPI backup key being handed over is fairly limited.

Note If you delete privileged identities in a forest where AD Recycle Bin is enabled, make sure to assign them an FGPP with password history disabled and change the password three times prior to deleting them. Alternatively, set the Deleted Objects Lifetime to 1 day and let deleted objects become tombstones or just delete them permanently using PowerShell or other low-level tooling.

The third scenario should be avoided at all costs because you give away the KDS Root Keys, DPAPI backup keys, actual Domain Controllers, albeit as clones, and an authority to create SIDs from your production domain. In this case, you may want to offer the receiving side (and your own organization, after you made the risks involved with this sort of migration clear to Management) a "rejuvenation migration." This approach can also present a possible solution for Scenario 2 that would remove the requirement of giving away the forest root domain. If a "rejuvenation migration" is not desired or not feasible, at least clone the production forest and replace the one or two Domain Controllers you would be giving away by new ones, invalidating the previous DC's machine identity.

11.5 Migrating People and Processes Along with Systems

Every transformation involves communication. A transformation of an identity system will require you to spend a lot of time talking to application owners, security officers, management, or your counterparts from other organizations if an acquisition or a divestment are the reasons for the transformation. You will also have to organize communication to the affected end users, be it to reconcile migration windows for their endpoints or to prompt them to log on with their new account (or to let them know that they are getting a new account in the first place).

A migration is a great opportunity to question not only systems put into operation years ago but also processes established to manage them. "Established" often does not mean that someone thoroughly engineered a management process but that people had to make do to get through their day, and then procedures became "accepted practice" within the organization. If you encounter procedures that are not a good fit for the "modern AD" framework, use the communication channels the migration has opened for you to facilitate change here as well.

CHAPTER 11   TRANSITIONING TO A MODERN AD

Unless the transition to a modern AD involves handing every user a Yubikey instead of the password, a well-engineered migration will subject administrators to change way more than it does end users. Prepare for it – use whatever communication capabilities you are offered to convey the "modern AD" message. Run a webinar and a town hall for Tier 1 administrators during the migration (but be prepared to be asked for it to continue even after the migration is formally over). Involve Tier 0 admins in application migrations to remind them of the crude tooling some colleagues in Tier 1 have to work with every day. Speak to application owners about automation, not necessarily implementing it during an AD migration but embracing it as a concept – you can use your "modern AD" as an example.

We started this book with the acknowledgment that Active Directory's bad reputation is as much due to Microsoft's design decisions as it is due to the implementing teams' poor judgment, a lack of understanding, and shoddy processes. None of us can do much about the former, but in transitioning to a modern AD, we can take care of the latter, both on the infrastructure and on the management side.

11.6 Summary

In this chapter, we analyzed the possible reasons for transforming existing Active Directory structures into new, or at least different ones. Some of these transformations are security-related; some stem from a misunderstood potential threat that is not actually there; and some are of a purely political nature, like in the case of mergers, acquisitions, or divestments.

An in situ modernization has the lowest impact on the end users and application owners, but it's not possible in every scenario. Other migration scenarios, like a "classic" cross-forest or a "rejuvenation" migration that

CHAPTER 11 TRANSITIONING TO A MODERN AD

leaves the namespace intact but changes everything else, all come with specific challenges, especially if a "big bang" switchover is not feasible and rich coexistence is required for a prolonged period of time.

The most important success factor in any Active Directory transformation is knowing the applications that consume the services provided by the identity system: Lookup, Authentication, Authorization, and Configuration.

CHAPTER 12

Conclusion

A "modern AD," secure and resilient enough to support your business-critical applications for decades to come, is possible. It takes a lot of work, both on IT systems and on humans using and managing them, to get there, and the result will always fall short of 100% of what you envisioned. But after reading this book, you cannot claim ignorance anymore – it's time to roll up your sleeves and get to work.

Start with gathering requirements. And if you are managing an existing AD infrastructure, you can start simply by critically assessing it and writing down things that you know should have been done differently. Every one of them falls into one of two categories. Either it's a "because we have always done it this way" artifact, then it can be changed right now, or in the next maintenance window, or with the next platform refresh. Or it is due to a requirement by "the business," and the first question to ask is whether this requirement is still valid! Sometimes that piece of machinery that required NTLM, unsigned LDAP, and SMB1 breaks beyond any hope of repair, and the shopfloor just forgets to tell IT (true story)! If you are designing a new AD for an organization, you are often not expected to present a vision, just to "build the damn thing." Present a vision nonetheless, tell them horror stories, and get them to listen. But remember what Thomas Edison once said: vision without execution is hallucination, so have answers to "how" and "when" ready along with the "whys."

This book reflects, in a way, a typical Active Directory architecture or transformation engagement as I experienced it more times in my career

CHAPTER 12   CONCLUSION

than I care to remember. A roller-coaster ride from reviewing an enterprise security architecture and presenting to C-Level in an oak-paneled boardroom to hashing out details of Kerberos encryption and replication latency with overworked admin teams. From devising a disaster recovery strategy, imagining unspeakable evils that might befall the customer, to fielding a third-level support call from a livid user who is not going to meet their deadline after a seemingly unrelated change in group policies.

The fascinating thing about Active Directory in particular and identity systems in general is that they are at the core of everything. For this very reason, each day spent working with AD opens a whole field full of rabbit holes, and it's easy to lose yourself in the intricacies of identity, security, and enterprise authorization. Everyone who ever completed a large-scale AD migration knows more about the peculiarities of line-of-business applications, idiosyncrasies of users, out-of-policy devices, and even about that secret network breakout in the Gents' (true story) than any single other person in the organization. If you are that person, the scars you got along the way are marks of a warrior. Wear them with pride.

Do not take shortcuts, but do not take well-trodden paths either simply because those methods worked in the past. I have two items on my desk to remind me every day what this identity business is all about. One of them is a "hooded hacker" figurine someone gave me at a conference years ago. Always design, create, and manage identity systems knowing that the proverbial hooded figure is not far away, lurking in the shadows, waiting for you to make the one mistake that lets them take your system down. The other item is a BULLSHIT button – a big red button that cries "Bullshit!" if you hit it. I do not recommend using it in a change advisory board meeting. But I like having it at hand every time I intend to propose a solution that I know is not ideal but has worked well enough in the past. Never agree to a good approach without at least mentioning the perfect one.

CHAPTER 12 CONCLUSION

This book was never intended as a deep dive into the inner workings of Active Directory, and I intentionally left a number of useful features out. They solve specific problems that you may or may not have to contend with in a particular implementation. If you encounter a new requirement not mentioned here, you can safely assume that your organization is not the first to struggle with it and that AD has something to offer that covers it. Just keep in mind that a partial solution you're about to offer must fit in with the overarching "modern AD" framework.

I sincerely hope that this book will help you steer your team – or your customers, if you are a consultant – in the right direction when deciding on the future of their identity infrastructure. Not everyone can put their identity in the cloud today, or even tomorrow. Nor is cloud identity inherently more secure than well-engineered and well-maintained on-premises identity. It is true that the protocols used in the cloud (mostly HTTPS dialects of some sort) allow continuous access evaluation and other zero-trust techniques that SMB, LDAP, or DCOM lack. It is also true that many business-critical applications powering the world today require these protocols and will continue doing so for the foreseeable future. But the good old Active Directory still has some aces up its sleeve. If you embrace Kerberos armoring, restrict visibility of privileged objects, and keep administration out of production forests, your team can sleep much better at night. Protect even unprivileged credentials by VBS or at least LSASS protection, require MFA for all cloud apps, do not allow direct LDAP access from the edge, and you will finally have time and peace of mind for strategizing the next phase in the endless story of your organization's most prized IT asset – identity.

APPENDIX A

Glossary

The IT industry is known for its love of acronyms. Since there are only 17,576 possible three-letter words and a mere 456,976 four-letter ones, collisions and ambiguities are inevitable in different areas of IT, leading to the same abbreviation having different meanings, depending on the topic. If in doubt, the explanation given below is the one used in this book.

Item	Explanation
ACE	**Access Control Entry**. An element of an ACL describing permissions granted or denied to a specific principal and their propagation to child objects of the object the ACL belongs to. Complex permission structures may lead to an ACL containing several ACEs for the same principal.
ACL	**Access Control List**. A representation of an object's security descriptor.
Active Directory	A suite of 5 Microsoft technologies related to identity and security. All of them are Windows Server roles.
AD	See **Active Directory**. In the context of this book, "AD" is using synonymously with "ADDS."
ADAC	**Active Directory Administrative Center**. A Server Manager-based GUI tool shipped with Windows that provides graphical management of objects in domain partitions, AD Recycle Bin, Fine-Grained Password Policies, Authentication Policies and Silos, and Dynamic Access Control.

(*continued*)

APPENDIX A   GLOSSARY

Item	Explanation
ADAM	**Active Directory Application Mode**, see also "ADLDS." ADAM was a separate download until it became a Windows Server role in 2008.
ADCS	**Active Directory Certificate Services.** This is Microsoft's implementation of an enterprise PKI, comprised of a Certification Authority, Validation Authority (CDP and OCSP), and several enrollment services.
ADDS	**Active Directory Directory Services.** An LDAP compliant directory service combined with Kerberos KDC, multimaster distributed database, and a replicated share for Group Policy distribution. This technology is the primary topic of this book.
ADFS	**Active Directory Federation Services.** A SAML and openID compliant federated authentication provider.
ADLDS	**Active Directory Lightweight Directory Services.** An LDAP-compliant distributed directory based on the same replication mechanisms as ADDS but not offering Kerberos authentication or Group Policy.
ADMX	In Group Policy editing, administrative template files that allow the editor to display the policy in a human-editable manner. ADMX technology added multi-language support and other enhancements to the previously used (and still technically supported) ADM files.
ADRMS	**Active Directory Rights Management Services.** An encryption-based document rights enforcement engine.
ADSI	**Active Directory Service Interfaces.** A set of COM interfaces used to access the features of directory services from different network providers.
ADUC	**Active Directory Users and Computers.** A MMC snap-in (dsa.msc) which is the primary tool for managing objects in domain partitions for a great majority of AD administrators.

(continued)

APPENDIX A GLOSSARY

Item	Explanation
ADWS	**Active Directory Web Services.** A SOAP wrapper for ADSI, installed by default alongside Active Directory Domain Services and used by the Active Directory PowerShell module.
AGDLP	**Account-Global-Domain Local-Permissions.** A widely accepted standard for implementing RBAC using Active Directory security groups.
AGPM	**Advanced Group Policy Management.** A Group Policy management, delegation, and versioning tool offered by Microsoft as part of the Desktop Optimization Pack (MDOP).
AMA	**Authentication Mechanism Assurance.** A feature of Kerberos in Windows that inserts SIDs of universal groups into a TGT obtained via a smart card logon in case certain OIDs are part of the logon certificate.
AppLocker	A Windows technology for application execution control. Can be used for application whitelisting to a certain extent.
API	**Application Programming Interface.** A way for computer systems and applications to communicate with each other.
APT	**Advanced Persistent Threat.** A stealthy threat actor which gains unauthorized access to a computer network and remains undetected for an extended period.
ASR	**Attack Surface Reduction.** A set of hardening techniques provided as part of "Microsoft Defender for Endpoint."
ATT&CK	A framework for classification of offensive techniques maintained by MITRE.
CA	**Certification Authority.** In a PKI, the instance that signs certificate requests with a private key whose corresponding public key is trusted by the intended users of the certificate.

(*continued*)

APPENDIX A   GLOSSARY

Item	Explanation
CDP	**CRL Distribution Point.** A facility enabling a system looking to validate a certificate to access the CRL. The usual protocols to achieve this are LDAP or HTTP (not to be confused with OCSP).
CIFS	**Common Internet File System.** A Microsoft-developed file access protocol adopted by many vendors to emulate Windows behavior. CIFS is sometimes considered identical to SMB 1.0.
CIM	**Common Information Model.** A management abstraction for IT devices and applications developed and maintained by the Distributed Management Task Force. See also WMI.
CIO	**Chief Information Officer.**
CIS	**Center for Internet Security.** A US-based non-profit organization formed in 2000 to "help people, businesses, and governments protect themselves against pervasive cyber threats." It publishes hardening benchmarks for a variety of IT systems that have become an accepted standard in the industry.
CISO	**Chief Information Security Officer.**
CRL	**Certificate Revocation List.** In PKI, a list of certificates that have been revoked by a CA, signed by the CA certificate of that CA. CRL and OCSP are two ways to verify whether a certificate has been revoked.
CSE	**Client-Side Extension.** In Group Policy operation, the facility on the machine governed by Group Policy that performs local actions based on the content of the policy, like setting a registry key, running a logon script, or mapping a network drive.
D3FEND	A framework for classification of defensive techniques maintained by MITRE.

(*continued*)

APPENDIX A GLOSSARY

Item	Explanation
DAC	**Dynamic Access Control.** A claims-based authorization mechanism, providing central policies to govern access to files according to the properties of the accessing user, the computer the access is being attempted from, and the content of the files themselves, reflected in form of classification.
DC	**Domain Controller.** In ADDS and in Windows NT domains, a computer holding a replica of the directory database and offering lookup and authentication services. In a more general IT discourse, "DC" is often used to describe a "DataCenter." This convention has not been used anywhere in this book.
DCOM	**Distributed Component Object Model**, originally called "Network Object Linking and Embedding" is a Microsoft protocol for facilitating secure inter-process communications between networked computers. It is based on RPC.
DCShadow	A Mimikatz scenario based on emulating a Domain Controller and replicating information of the attacker's choice into the directory. This technique can be used for injecting sidHistory, setting the Primary Group ID to a group the user is not a member in, and a variety of other attacks.
DCSync	A Mimikatz scenario based on abusing replication permissions and replicating attributes out of the directory that would not be readable by standard protocols like LDAP.
DDCP	**Default Domain Controllers Policy.** A Group Policy with the well-known ID of {6AC1786C-016F-11D2-945F-00C04fB984F9} which is applied to the "Domain Controllers" OU. The classic Audit Policy, if set by AUDITPOL.EXE, is reflected back into DDCP.

(continued)

APPENDIX A   GLOSSARY

Item	Explanation
DDI	**DNS, DHCP, IP**. Usually a commercial term for products providing or managing these services (or both) in a unified manner.
DDP	**Default Domain Policy**. A Group Policy with the well-known ID of {31B2F340-016D-11D2-945F-00C04FB984F9} that is applied to the domain head. Only from this policy the Account Policies are copied to AD – and even reflected back into the policy if modified on the domain head.
DFL	**Domain Functional Level**. A parameter of a domain that enables certain functionality or changes default behaviors. Cannot be higher than the Forest Functional Level of the forest the domain belongs to.
DHCP	**Dynamic Host Configuration Protocol**. A network protocol for automatically assigning an IP configuration and other configuration settings to a computer.
DMZ	**DeMilitarized Zone**. A "perimeter network" or a "screened subnet," a DMZ, is open to the Internet on certain protocols and ports but isolated from the internal LAN by firewalls. The usual agreement in threat modeling is to treat any system in a DMZ as potentially compromised and lateral movement within the DMZ as technically possible.
DN	**Distinguished Name**. A name that uniquely identifies an entry in a directory. It contains the path, including the root of the directory, which makes the DN not immutable.
DNS	**Domain Name System**. A distributed, hierarchical name service for computers on IP networks.
DNSSEC	**DNS Security**. A suite of security enhancements to DNS, mostly concentrated around signing DNS replies by a certificate published in DNS.

(*continued*)

APPENDIX A   GLOSSARY

Item	Explanation
DoH	**DNS over HTTPS**. A protocol, proposed by browser manufacturers, for performing DNS name resolution over HTTPS connections.
DPAPI	**Data Protection API**. In Windows, the encrypted storage facility for secret information like stored passwords or private keys of certificates. The encryption is tied to the current password; on regular password change, all previously encrypted secrets are re-encrypted using the new password. To prevent losing the protected information on password reset, a second universal decryption key is stored in AD. Since there is no supported procedure for rotating that key, every Domain Controller backup since the creation of a domain contains a key to decrypt DPAPI-protected secrets of all users and computers from that domain – even those not yet created at the time of backup!
DR	**Disaster Recovery**. The process of reestablishing first vital services and subsequently all required services following a catastrophic event. Disaster Recovery in IT is often viewed as a separate discipline from recovering other business-critical facilities such as factory buildings, road access, electricity, water, or cash flow, but in reality, it cannot be separated from the other components. Note: "DR" in "ITDR" does *not* mean "Disaster Recovery."
DSC	**Desired State Configuration**. A facility to keep a system or systems configured in a certain way, regardless of the initial state or configuration changes introduced by other means after the desired state has been reached.
DSRM	**Directory Service Restore Mode**. A special startup mode for Domain Controller machines similar to Safe Mode, in which authoritative restore operations are allowed.

(*continued*)

APPENDIX A   GLOSSARY

Item	Explanation
EDR	**Endpoint Detection and Response.** A set of technologies for continuously monitoring processes and changes on an endpoint device (client, server, or a mobile device) to detect malicious activity, alert about it, and take corrective action, including isolation or factory reset of the offending device. Evolved from traditional antimalware.
EKU	**Extended Key Usage**, in Microsoft documentation and products mostly "Enhanced Key Usage." In PKI, a policy, represented by an OID, that prescribes what cryptographic processes and protocols the certificate is allowed to be used for.
Entra ID	A suite of cloud services operated by Microsoft dedicated to modern authentication, zero trust, and secure access. Initially it was named "Azure Active Directory," which led to some confusion, since the cloud directory has little in common, technologically, with AD.
ESAE	**Enhanced Security Admin Environment.** A secure privileged administration framework including Red Forest and Administrative Tiering as the two main security-enhancing features. At the time of writing, ESAE is still being used by Microsoft internally, despite being deprecated for general use.
FAST	**Flexible Authentication via Secure Tunneling.** A Kerberos substandard describing authentication flows where all Kerberos communication on behalf of the user is encrypted by keys derived from the client's Kerberos authentication exchange. This adds the client identification to Kerberos ticket requests, allowing the KDC to decide upon ticket issuance depending not only on the user's but also on the client's identity.

(*continued*)

APPENDIX A GLOSSARY

Item	Explanation
FFL	**Forest Functional Level.** A parameter of a forest that enables certain functionality or changes default behaviors. Cannot be lower than the lowest value of the Domain Functional Level of any domain in the forest.
FGPP	**Fine-Grained Password Policy.** A special object in AD containing all the settings that can be specified in the domain-wide password and account lockout policy. FGPPs can be linked to users or **global security** groups, and a preference order mechanism determines which one will be in effect for a particular user. FGPPs can be used to both relax and restrict the domain's password policy.
FIDO	**Fast IDentity Online.** An open industry association with the declared goal of promoting authentication standards that "help reduce the world's over-reliance on passwords."
FSMO	**Flexible Single Master Operations.** A feature of Active Directory that prevents conflicting changes to the directory configuration made possible by its multi-master database design. Every AD forest has two FSMO roles: "Domain Naming Master" and "Schema Master." Every AD domain has three FSMO roles: "PDC Emulator," "RID Master," and "Infrastructure Master." Every role can be only held by one Domain Controller at a time, hence "Single Master," but this assignment can be moved, hence "Flexible."
FSRM	**File Server Resource Manager.** A Windows Server feature related to the File Services role that enables file system quota and content-based classification on Windows file servers.

(*continued*)

APPENDIX A   GLOSSARY

Item	Explanation
FT	**Fault tolerance**. The ability of a system, not necessarily in IT, to withstand failures in its components without degradation or downtime. FT is an essential capability for providing HA but should not be confused with it.
dMSA	**Delegated Managed Service Account**. In Server 2025 and later, a special type of service account that does not actually hold its password but, once used by a specifically entitled computer, can request and acquire TGS to any services known to Kerberos.
gMSA	**Group Managed Service Account**. In Server 2012 and later, a special type of service account (derived from the computer object class) that is subject to automated password changes performed by Active Directory. Authorized computers are able to retrieve and decrypt the password from AD to be used with services and scheduled tasks.
GPMC	**Group Policy Management Console**. An MMC-based tool shipped with Windows Server as a feature and with Windows client OSs as part of RSAT for managing group policy objects, their filtering, and linking. It also offers group policy modeling and remote generation of RSoP.
GPO	**Group Policy Object**. A configuration container that consists of an object in AD that holds information about functionality, filtering, and delegation, and a folder in SYSVOL holding the actual configuration payload. GPOs provide a structured configuration delivery model that is sometimes confused with "configuration management."
GPP	**Group Policy Preferences**. A part of a group policy object managing configurations not initially included in the GPO framework like drive maps, printers, registry, files and folders, scheduled tasks, ODBC data sources, and many more. A very important feature of GPP is item-level targeting (ILT).

(continued)

APPENDIX A GLOSSARY

Item	Explanation
GUID	**Globally Unique IDentifier.** A different name for UUID, more specific to Microsoft products.
HA	**High Availability.** A characteristic of an IT service that ensures an agreed level of uptime and sometimes also of performance in case of a partial failure. The distinguishing factor of HA is that scheduled downtime is taken into account in the same way as unscheduled one. HA has been confused with FT more times than the author cares to count.
HTTP	**HyperText Transfer Protocol.** A stateless object-oriented application-level protocol designed for use with distributed, collaborative hypermedia systems. HTTP is used for all World Wide Web traffic and serves as the basis for many modern data transfer protocols, especially for those used on the public Internet.
HTTPS	**HyperText Transfer Protocol over SSL.** An enhancement to HTTP to provide Transport Layer Security integration. Early versions of TLS were called SSL, hence the "S."
IAM	**Identity and Access Management.** A framework of policies and technologies that aim to ensure that identities for correct users are provisioned in all applications the users need access to and granted the appropriate access to resources there.
IANA	**Internet Assigned Numbers Authority.** A standards organization that oversees global IP address allocation, autonomous system number allocation, root zone management in DNS, media types, and other Internet-related numbers. Among others, IANA is responsible for assigning Private Enterprise Numbers (PEN).

(continued)

APPENDIX A　GLOSSARY

Item	Explanation
IDM	**Identity Management.** A framework of policies and technologies that aim to ensure a strict lifecycle for all identities in all applications and identity stores. Often part of an overarching IAM implementation.
IFM	**Install from Media.** In Active Directory, a mode of promoting a server to a Domain Controller using a directory export previously created on a different DC of the same domain and operating system level, thus avoiding replication of the whole dataset over the wire.
IPAM	**IP Address Management.** A framework of policies and data, implemented in software, for planning and managing IP addresses throughout the organization. IPAM products often evolve into full-scale DDI management.
ILT	**Item-Level Targeting.** In GPP, the ability to apply (or not) individual preference items based on a variety of queries about the computer and user in question, ranging from CPU and RAM to OU placement to WMI queries.
ITSM	**IT Service Management.** The entirety of activities performed by an organization in order to plan, build, deliver, and control IT services offered and delivered to customers, internal and external alike. There are several formal frameworks describing ITSM, the British ITIL being the most popular one at the time of writing. The abundance of regulation around ITSM has made the term rather unpopular among administrators because some implementations did end in more clunky tools and box-ticking than actual work. The author prefers to think of ITSM as the entirety of things being done in IT rather than the regulatory frameworks around them.

(*continued*)

APPENDIX A GLOSSARY

Item	Explanation
JEA	**Just Enough Administration**. A feature in PowerShell in conjunction with WinRM remoting that enables delegation of privileged tasks to less-privileged users. JEA configurations specify which cmdlets a certain less-privileged principal is allowed to run, which arguments they are allowed to use, and which values may be assigned to each parameter. Once these conditions have been satisfied, the cmdlet in question is then run in the context of a high-privileged virtual account or of an AD account.
JIT	**Just-In-Time Administration**. Usually describes the time-based group membership feature introduced in Server 2016 as part of the AD optional feature "Privileged Access Management."
JSON	**JavaScript Object Notation**. A text-based data interchange format for exchanging structured data from a basic selection of object types. Not as powerful as XML but much more compact and mostly human-readable.
ITDR	**Identity Threat Detection and Response**. A security discipline consisting of cyber threat intelligence, behavior analysis, tools, and structured processes to enhance identity infrastructure security and accelerate the remediation of identity-centric attacks.
KCC	**Knowledge Consistency Checker**. In ADDS, a built-in process that runs on all Domain Controllers generates replication topology for the Active Directory forest.
KDC	**Key Distribution Center**. In Kerberos, a process containing the Authentication Service (AS) and the Ticket Granting Service (TGS). It uses AD as its account database and the Global Catalog for directing referrals to KDCs from other domains.

(*continued*)

APPENDIX A   GLOSSARY

Item	Explanation
Keytab	**Key Table.** A binary file containing User Principal Names and Kerberos key material for different encryption types. Keytab files can be used in lieu of cleartext passwords for requesting a TGT or validating a TGS. On Windows, Keytab files are usually created using the KTPASS command.
LAN	**Local Area Network.** A computer network that interconnects systems within a limited geographical area, mostly within a building or a campus. A LAN is expected to have very high bandwidth, very low latency, and to be 100% available.
LAPS	**Local Administrator Password Solution.** A group policy CSE rotating the password of a local account on a member computer and writing it back to the computer object in AD. The first version, developed by Microsoft Consulting Services and distributed as a separate download without support guarantee, would write the password back in cleartext. It is now called "Microsoft LAPS." In 2023, Microsoft integrated "Windows LAPS" into Server and Client OSs. Windows LAPS uses its own policies and its own schema attributes, independent from Microsoft LAPS. Passwords can be stored encrypted or sent to Entra ID instead of AD. A very welcome addition are post-logoff-actions that will rotate the password every time it has been used and even log off the session if the administrator neglected to do it. Server 2025 enhances the functionality yet again by providing not only password management for existing accounts but also account creation using randomized names.
LDAP	**Lightweight Directory Access Protocol.** A network protocol for retrieving and manipulating data stored in a directory service.
LLMNR	**Link-Local Multicast Name Resolution.** A name resolution protocol that uses DNS packet format over multicast, allowing for local name resolution if no DNS servers are available.

(continued)

APPENDIX A   GLOSSARY

Item	Explanation
LOB	**Line of Business** (application). A term used to distinguish an application needed by a certain business unit or process from a. infrastructure and b. business applications required by everybody in the organization. Among IT security, deployment, and infrastructure specialists, "LOB application" often refers to going against accepted security standards and deployment practices.
LSA	**Local Security Authority**. A subsystem of Windows that is responsible for authentication, authorization, and cryptography.
MDM	**Mobile Device Management**. A process, supported by an IT system, for managing devices that are not necessarily deskbound. It started out as enterprise smartphone management in the 2000s but quickly pivoted to managing configurations on laptops of different operating system families.
MDOP	**Microsoft Desktop Optimization Pack**. A suite of technologies offered to Software Assurance customers. It consists of "Advanced Group Policy Management," "App-V," "User Experience Virtualization (UE-V)," "BitLocker Administration and Monitoring (MBAM)," and "Diagnostics and Recovery Toolkit (DaRT)."
MDT	**Microsoft Deployment Toolkit**. An enhancement product to Windows Deployment Services which allows installing and configuring computers with Task Sequences rather than by pushing preinstalled images to them.
MECM	**Microsoft Endpoint Configuration Manager**, see SCCM.
MITRE	A non-profit corporation based out of the Massachusetts Institute of Technology that provides guidance, among others, on cybersecurity matters.

(*continued*)

APPENDIX A GLOSSARY

Item	Explanation
MMC	**Microsoft Management Console.** A component of Windows that provides a uniform management experience by using COM components for various management scenarios as snap-ins. It has been an integral part of Windows since 2000 but was available as a separate download for Windows NT as early as 1998. The version used at the time of writing is 3.0, introduced with Windows Vista/Server 2008.
NIST	**National Institute of Standards and Technology.** The successor to the National Bureau of Standards, an agency of the U.S. Department of Commerce. NIST regularly evaluates cryptographic algorithms and recommends their deprecation when they become too weak for the increased computing power.
NTFS	**NT File System.** The proprietary journal-based file system introduced with Windows NT 3.1 and used in Windows to this day.
NTLM	**NT LanManager.** Challenge-handshake authentication protocol introduced in Windows NT as the successor to notoriously insecure LAN Manager.
NTP	**Network Time Protocol.** A standard protocol for synchronizing clocks between computer systems defined by RFC5905.
OCSP	**Online Certificate Status Protocol.** A HTTP-based protocol allowing a system trying to establish the validity of a certificate to check whether it has been revoked and, optionally, whether it has been issued by the CA in the first place. The information is assumed to be more current than a CRL; however, in some implementations, OCSP is based on CRL so has roughly the same degree of freshness. OCSP has been known to be abused for data exfiltration.

(*continued*)

APPENDIX A GLOSSARY

Item	Explanation
OID	**Object ID**. An object identifier format used in Simple Network Management Protocol (SNMP) and X.509 cryptography. It is standardized by the International Telecommunication Union (ITU) and ISO/IEC for naming any object, concept, or "thing" with a globally unambiguous persistent name.
OS	**Operating System**. System software that manages computer hardware resources and provides abstracted resources and services to computer programs running on top of it.
PAC	**Privileged Attribute Certificate**. A part of a Kerberos ticket data structure that holds information about the user principal and its privileges.
PAW	**Privileged Access Workstation**. A hardened computer which administrators use to connect to critical systems in order to perform privileged administration tasks on them. A PAW's mission is to protect both the access to the target systems and the administrator credentials being used.
PDC	**Primary Domain Controller**. In Windows NT security domains, the PDC held the only writable copy of the domain database. Changes made to the domain data by the PDC were then replicated to Backup Domain Controllers (BDC) for read-only access and authentication. This architecture is the reason that, to this day, a password change made against a DC is pushed to the PDC Emulator by default, independently of replication.

(*continued*)

APPENDIX A   GLOSSARY

Item	Explanation
PDCe	**PDC Emulator**. Due to the PDC's exclusive write ability, lots of applications and components have been developed for Windows that insist on locating the PDC specifically and expect a certain behavior from that system. To accommodate these applications, Active Directory presents a "PDC Emulator" FSMO role, offering PDC-specific behaviors to legacy applications.
PEN	**Private Enterprise Number**. A universally unique integer number assigned by IANA, allowing organizations and even individuals to maintain a universally unique OID namespace for SNMP or PKI. The author's PEN, e.g., is 50161, while IBM holds the number 2.
PHS	**Password Hash Sync**. A technique by replicating on-premises users' passwords to Entra ID. It involves salting the original hash twice and putting the result through a modern hash function over a thousand times. Once the hash has been transferred, cloud authentication has no dependency on the on-premises directory. See also PTA.
PKI	**Public Key Infrastructure**. A set of policies, systems and procedures needed to create, manage, distribute, use, store, and revoke digital certificates and manage public-key encryption. The main components of a PKI are the Certification Authority (CA), Registration Authority (RA), and Validation Authority (VA).
PKINIT	**Public Key Cryptography for Initial Authentication**. In Kerberos, a subprotocol that enables the use of public key cryptography in the initial authentication exchange in lieu of password.

(*continued*)

Item	Explanation
PTA	**Pass-Through Authentication.** An authentication method in Entra ID that involves sending authentication requests over a secure connection to an agent that will attempt authentication against on-premises AD and communicate the result back. This is the worst possible hybrid authentication scenario supported in Entra ID at the time of writing.
RADIUS	**Remote Authentication Dial-In User Service.** A networking protocol that provides centralized Authentication, Authorization, and Accounting (AAA) for users who connect remotely to a network service.
RCG	**Remote Credential Guard.** A technology for protecting credentials and still allowing for second-hop authentication in RDP sessions. Requires Kerberos SSO; cannot be used with NTLM or saved credentials.
RBCD	**Resource-Based Constrained Delegation.** A variation of Kerberos constrained delegation introduced in Server 2012. In RBCD, the backend service administrator is responsible for allowing specific frontend services to delegate *to* it instead of the other way around.
RFC	**Request for Comment.** The standard for publications of the Internet's standard-developing bodies, most prominently the Internet Engineering Task Force. RFCs were invented in 1969 by Steve Crocker to document the development of ARPANET.
RFID	**Radio Frequency IDentification.** A technique for identification of physical objects by using a passive (i.e., energized by the scanning device) transponder in the radio wave frequency range attached to them.
RDP	**Remote Desktop Protocol.** A protocol for establishing a desktop session and transferring keyboard, mouse, and display information over a network. Initially developed by Citrix for Microsoft in the 1990s.

(continued)

APPENDIX A   GLOSSARY

Item	Explanation
RID	**Relative Identifier**. The last portion of a SID that describes an object as relative to the identifier authority, e.g., AD domain.
RODC	**Read-Only Domain Controller**. An AD feature introduced with Server 2008R2 to allow Domain Controllers to be placed in locations with poor physical security without risking the compromise of high-privileged credentials like administrators or **krbtgt**. It is able to conduct authentication during site isolation by caching a specified subset of user passwords.
RPC	**Remote Procedure Call**. Mechanism to allow a program to execute a subroutine in a different address space, usually on another computer, without the developer having to explicitly program a remote interaction.
RPO	**Recovery Point Objective**. In backup and restore, the maximum loss of production data, measured as the time in which that data has been created, in case of a restore event. Webshops and financial institutions aim to provide (and may be legally bound to maintain) an RPO of zero for transaction data.
RSAT	**Remote Server Administration Tools**. A set of consoles, commandline tools, and PowerShell modules delivered as a feature in both client and server versions of Windows for remote management of Windows Server OS, roles, and features.
RSoP	**Resultant Set of Policy**. The resulting overlay of all applicable GPO settings for a user or a computer. A MMC-based graphical tool of the same name is part of Windows even at the time of writing, but it does not provide precise results since Windows Vista SP1 and should not be used.

(*continued*)

APPENDIX A GLOSSARY

Item	Explanation
RTO	**Recovery Time Objective.** In backup and restore, the maximum time it takes to restore production data from a complete loss to the state detailed by the RPO. Data restoration does not mean service restoration, so when using backup for DR, the time needed to restore the service from a workable data set must be added on top of the RTO.
SAML	**Security Assertion Markup Language.** An XML-based markup language for exchanging authentication and authorization information between an identity provider (IdP) and a service provider (SP).
SCAMA	See "AMA."
SCCM	**System Center Configuration Manager.** Previously "Systems Management Server," later "Endpoint Configuration Manager," a Microsoft server product for deploying operating systems, software packages, updates, and managing the configuration of Windows systems throughout the organization.
SCOM	**System Center Operations Manager.** Previously "Microsoft Operations Manager," a multiplatform distributed monitoring application from the System Center suite.
SCT	**Security Compliance Toolkit.** A set of documents, GPO templates, and tools provided by Microsoft to facilitate baseline-assisted systems hardening.
SDPROP	**Security Descriptor PROPagation.** A recurring internal process in AD that replaces the security descriptor of users, groups, and computers that chain up to one of the privileged groups by that of the AdminSDHolder container, disabling inheritance unless it was erroneously or maliciously enabled on that container. Paired with the SDHolder process that assigns the value of 1 to the **adminCount** attribute of those objects.

(*continued*)

APPENDIX A GLOSSARY

Item	Explanation
SID	**Security Identifier.** Binary structures used to uniquely identify security principals such as users, computers, groups, or service accounts.
SIEM	**Security Information and Event Management.** A system that provides long-term storage and real-time analysis of security-related structured data (usually log events) from a multitude of systems, allowing security analysts to conduct environment-wide analyses of authentication, configuration changes, and other activities.
SLA	**Service-Level Agreement.** A document (or an unwritten agreement if it's between parts of the same organization) detailing at least the service being provided by one entity to another and the availability of the service. In the context of this book, SLA mostly pertains to backup and restore, where the important parameters are RPO and RTO.
SMB	**Server Message Block.** Microsoft's protocol for accessing shared files and printers. The file subprotocol of SMB is compatible with CIFS.
S/MIME	**Secure Multipurpose Internet Mail Extensions.** A standard protocol for encryption and signing of email data to ensure authenticity, integrity, privacy, and non-repudiation, based on public key cryptography.
SMTP	**Simple Mail Transfer Protocol.** The established standard for sending Internet email. At the time of writing, SMTP is described by RFC5321.
SNMP	**Simple Network Management Protocol.** A systems monitoring and management protocol governed by RFC3411-3418 and RFC6353. While SNMP is an established standard for monitoring network devices like switches, routers, telco equipment, or printers, monitoring modern operating systems via SNMP is far less common.
SOAP	**Simple Object Access Protocol.** The first widely used protocol for web service access in a service-oriented architecture.

(continued)

APPENDIX A GLOSSARY

Item	Explanation
SOC	**Security Operations Center.** A facility, internal to an organization or commissioned externally, that performs round-the-clock security monitoring and reacts to possible security incidents by triage, classification, investigation, and mitigation (or dismissal).
SPN	**Service Principal Name.** In Kerberos, a globally unique identifier for a service being authenticated against.
SQL	**Structured Query Language.** A de facto standard for querying and manipulating relational databases and other structured data sources.
SRP	**Software Restriction Policies.** An early application black-/whitelisting technology in Windows. Although still supported at the time of writing, it has been largely superseded by AppLocker and Windows Defender Application Control (WDAC).
SSH	**Secure SHell.** A cryptographic network protocol for operating network services over an insecure connection. Initially developed for Unix in 1995, it has been ported to Windows several times and finally adopted as a fully supported open source project maintained by Microsoft's PowerShell team.
SSL	**Secure Sockets Layer.** A precursor to more generalized TLS, it was developed by Netscape in the 1990s specifically for HTTP. SSL underwent several revisions until the final version 3.0 was deprecated in June 2015 by RFC7568.

(continued)

APPENDIX A   GLOSSARY

Item	Explanation
SSO	**Single Sign-On.** A facility to reuse authentication tokens issued by one identity provider with a system using a different identity provider for authentication and authorization. Not to be confused with "Same Sign-On," which simply means the same username and password are valid for authentication against multiple disparate systems without the account owner explicitly setting the password in all those systems to the same value.
TGS	**Ticket Granting Service.** In Kerberos, the facility that grants and encrypts TGTs and service tickets (session keys). While technically incorrect, "TGS" is often used interchangeably with "Service Ticket," and this book is no exception.
TGT	**Ticket Granting Ticket.** A data structure, encrypted by the KDC, that proves that a user authenticated successfully within the lifetime of the TGT. A TGT can be submitted to a Domain Controller to request a service ticket.
TLD	**Top-Level Domain.** In DNS, the rightmost part of a domain name, behind the final dot. In public DNS, every TLD has an assignment authority handing out second-level domains to customers according to its own policy.
TLS	**Transport Layer Security.** A cryptographic protocol to provide communication security over insecure networks. It was first defined in 1999 by RFC2246 and underwent several revisions since. At the time of writing, TLS 1.0 and TLS 1.1 have been deprecated for several years, TLS 1.2 is the mainstream, and TLS 1.3 is being rolled out.
TPM	**Trusted Platform Module.** A secure cryptoprocessor compliant with the standard specification maintained by the Trusted Computing Group. Its primary function is to ensure the integrity of the hardware platform, regardless of the operating system being booted.

(continued)

APPENDIX A   GLOSSARY

Item	Explanation
TTL	**Time to Live**. In computing, usually an interval after which certain objects are removed automatically. In the context of this book, TTL applies to dynamically registered DNS records and to time-based group memberships.
TTP	**Tactics, Techniques and Practices**. Patterns of behavior specific to malicious actors. The concept is well known in anti-terrorism and military intelligence.
UAC	**User Account Control**. An access control enforcement feature first introduced in Windows Vista and Server 2008. It is based on providing an unprivileged access token to privileged users in a local logon session and requiring additional confirmation before making the privileged token available to the session if and inasmuch as a certain operation requires it.
UNC	**Uniform Naming Convention** or **Universal Naming Convention**. An addressing scheme in Windows to describe access to filesystem resources, both local and remote. `\\Server.domain.com\Share\Folder\file.doc` is an example of UNC.
UPN	**User Principal Name**. In Kerberos, the UPN identifies the principal performing the authentication.
UUID	**Universally Unique IDentifier**. A 128-bit long identifier without a centralized administration authority. It is covered by RFC9562 and usually known in Microsoft products as GUID.
VBA	**VisualBasic for Applications**. A VisualBasic dialect provided as a part of Microsoft Office and a select third-party applications to offer a rich macro programmability.

(continued)

APPENDIX A   GLOSSARY

Item	Explanation
VBS	**VisualBasic Script**. An object-oriented scripting language that has been part of Windows since Windows NT. Not to be confused with Virtualization-Based Security (below).
VBS	**Virtualization-Based Security**. In Windows, a suite of security features that make use of process and memory isolation techniques initially developed for Hyper-V. The Hyper-V role as such is not necessary for the activation of VBS; however, the technical requirements are similar.
VDI	**Virtual Desktop Infrastructure**. A software solution to provision, host, and broker remote access to virtualized operating system instances in lieu of physical desktop OSes.
VPN	**Virtual Private Network**. A network architecture for extending a private network over public, i.e., potentially hostile, network segments. The most widely used underlying technologies are TLS ("SSL-VPN") and IPSec.
WAC	**Windows Admin Center**. A browser-based, server-centric, extensible systems management experience introduced by Microsoft in 2017 as "Project Honolulu" and released to the general public in 2018. A WAC downloader/installer has been added to Windows Server 2025 as a preinstalled feature. For managing Windows server roles, WAC relies heavily on PowerShell remoting and WMI.
WAN	**Wide Area Network**. As opposed to LAN, a computer network spanning long geographic distances and often crossing borders of cities, states, or even continents. In the context of AD topology engineering, a WAN is expected to exhibit significant latency, limited bandwidth (although multi-Gigabit WAN links are becoming fairly common at the time of writing), and be not 100% available.

(continued)

APPENDIX A   GLOSSARY

Item	Explanation
WDAC	**Windows Defender Application Control** A native application whitelisting technology in Windows starting with Windows 10/Server 2016, initially called "Code Integrity," which is why a WDAC policy is often named "CIPolicy." It is implemented at a very low level and allows whitelisting of boot-time drivers.
WINS	**Windows Name Service**. A legacy name resolution service proprietary to Windows. It implements NetBIOS Name Service (NBNS) defined in RFC1001 and RFC1002.
WLAN	**Wireless LAN**. A network physical layer technology based on radio transmissions and governed by the IEEE 802.11 family of standards.
WMI	**Windows Management Instrumentation**. A Microsoft implementation of CIM for Windows and other Microsoft technologies.
WSB	**Windows Server Backup**. A Windows Server feature that implements a very simple backup/restore solution for the local Windows server based on VSS. Popular belief has it that you should have at least one WSB-created backup handy if you want Microsoft to work with you on disaster recovery.
XDR	**eXtended Detection and Response**. A term coined by Palo Alto in 2018 for cybersecurity technologies aimed at detecting and mitigating cyber security threats. Usually considered to be an improvement over EDR.
XML	**eXtensible Markup Language**. A structured text-based data file format that supports schema descriptions and data transformations. XML is the de facto standard for passing rich data structures.

APPENDIX B

Ten Immutable Laws of Security

Published in 2000 by Microsoft. At the time of writing, the original text under https://learn.microsoft.com/en-us/previous-versions//cc722487(v=technet.10) was available online.

Law #1: If a bad guy can persuade you to run his program on your computer, it's not your computer anymore

Law #2: If a bad guy can alter the operating system on your computer, it's not your computer anymore

Law #3: If a bad guy has unrestricted physical access to your computer, it's not your computer anymore

Law #4: If you allow a bad guy to upload programs to your website, it's not your website any more

Law #5: Weak passwords trump strong security

Law #6: A computer is only as secure as the administrator is trustworthy

Law #7: Encrypted data is only as secure as the decryption key

Law #8: An out-of-date virus scanner is only marginally better than no virus scanner at all

Law #9: Absolute anonymity isn't practical, in real life or on the Web

Law #10: Technology is not a panacea

APPENDIX C

Ten Immutable Laws of Security Administration

Published in 2000 by Microsoft. At the time of writing, the original text under `https://learn.microsoft.com/en-us/previous-versions//cc722488(v=technet.10)` was available online.

Law #1: Nobody believes anything bad can happen to them, until it does
Law #2: Security only works if the secure way also happens to be the easy way
Law #3: If you don't keep up with security fixes, your network won't be yours for long
Law #4: It doesn't do much good to install security fixes on a computer that was never secured to begin with
Law #5: Eternal vigilance is the price of security
Law #6: There really is someone out there trying to guess your passwords
Law #7: The most secure network is a well-administered one
Law #8: The difficulty of defending a network is directly proportional to its complexity
Law #9: Security isn't about risk avoidance; it's about risk management
Law #10: Technology is not a panacea

APPENDIX D

Internet Sources

Here are some of the sources of knowledge available online that have been used by the author in his long consulting career. They are not referenced directly in the text, except for the RFCs. Since the Internet does forget, and at an alarming pace at that, the selected sources are mostly Microsoft documentation and RFCs. Some information is found exclusively in third-party blogs, so we included the links here at the peril of them not being available one day. This has been known to happen to original Microsoft documentation as well. We hope that, if all else fails, the Wayback Machine will provide the desired content: https://web.archive.org.

D.1 Introduction

SpecterOps: What Is Tier Zero: https://posts.specterops.io/what-is-tier-zero-part-1-e0da9b7cdfca

10 Immutable Laws of Security: https://learn.microsoft.com/en-us/previous-versions//cc722487(v=technet.10)

10 Immutable Laws of Security Administration: https://learn.microsoft.com/en-us/previous-versions//cc722488(v=technet.10)

APPENDIX D   INTERNET SOURCES

D.2 Engineering Topology

FSMO placement and optimization on Active Directory domain controllers: https://learn.microsoft.com/en-us/troubleshoot/windows-server/active-directory/fsmo-placement-and-optimization-on-ad-dcs

D.3 Engineering Lookup

Property Sets: https://learn.microsoft.com/en-us/windows/win32/adschema/property-sets

D.4 Engineering Authentication

RFC6150: https://datatracker.ietf.org/doc/html/rfc6150
RFC6649: https://datatracker.ietf.org/doc/html/rfc6649
Credential Guard: https://learn.microsoft.com/en-us/windows/security/identity-protection/credential-guard/
RFC6113: https://datatracker.ietf.org/doc/html/rfc6113
RFC4556: https://datatracker.ietf.org/doc/html/rfc4556
PKINIT in AD: https://learn.microsoft.com/en-us/openspecs/windows_protocols/ms-pkca/d0cf1763-3541-4008-a75f-a577fa5e8c5b
Wagging the Dog by Elad Shamir: https://shenanigenslabs.io/2019/01/28/Wagging-the-Dog.html
KDC Proxy for Remote Access by Steve Syfuhs: https://syfuhs.net/kdc-proxy-for-remote-access

D.5 Engineering Authorization

Dynamic Access Control overview: https://learn.microsoft.com/en-us/windows-server/identity/solution-guides/dynamic-access-control-scenario-overview

Kerberos token size: https://learn.microsoft.com/en-us/troubleshoot/windows-server/windows-security/kerberos-authentication-problems-if-user-belongs-to-groups

LSA Authorization token size: https://learn.microsoft.com/en-us/troubleshoot/windows-server/windows-security/logging-on-user-account-fails

D.6 Engineering Configuration

AGPM: https://learn.microsoft.com/en-us/microsoft-desktop-optimization-pack/agpm/technical-overview-of-agpm

Capacity Planning for ADDS: https://learn.microsoft.com/en-us/windows-server/administration/performance-tuning/role/active-directory-server/capacity-planning-for-active-directory-domain-services

Managing RID Issuance: https://learn.microsoft.com/en-us/windows-server/identity/ad-ds/manage/managing-rid-issuance

Windows Firewall for domains and trusts: https://learn.microsoft.com/de-de/troubleshoot/windows-server/active-directory/config-firewall-for-ad-domains-and-trusts

Additional LSA Protection: https://learn.microsoft.com/en-us/windows-server/security/credentials-protection-and-management/configuring-additional-lsa-protection

APPENDIX D   INTERNET SOURCES

D.7 Engineering Administration

Remote Credential Guard: https://learn.microsoft.com/en-us/windows/security/identity-protection/remote-credential-guard

Application Control for Windows: https://learn.microsoft.com/en-us/windows/security/application-security/application-control/windows-defender-application-control/wdac

Delegation Wizard task examples: https://learn.microsoft.com/en-us/previous-versions/windows/it-pro/windows-server-2003/cc772784(v=ws.10)

AD Management Framework: https://admf.one/

Protect-CMSMessage: https://learn.microsoft.com/de-de/powershell/module/microsoft.powershell.security/protect-cmsmessage

SCAMA, local resource access and "Always wait for network on logon": https://support.microsoft.com/en-us/topic/description-of-ama-usage-in-interactive-logon-scenarios-in-windows-a61e0931-f11a-73ad-6221-e117ed6e913f

Index

A

Access Control Entry (ACE), 104, 228, 423
Access Control List (ACL), 104, 106, 319, 321, 323, 417
ACE, *see* Access control entries (ACE)
ACL, *see* Access control list (ACL)
Active Directory (AD), 1, 401
    and access management, 11, 12
    administration (*see* Administration)
    anti-patterns, 16
    application partitions, 74–76
    and configuration management, 12, 13, 251–254
    defaults, 6–9
    demand for flexibility (misunderstood), 14, 15, 351
    domain controller, 3, 6, 13, 18
    domain controller distribution, 71, 72
    enterprise address book, 13, 97, 98
    functionality offered, 10, 33, 34, 93, 251
    Global Catalog placement, 72–74
    hardcoded behaviors, 6
    and identity management, 4, 5, 11
    infrastructure, 413
    issued ticket tracking, 5
    managed by principals from AD itself, 3, 4
    modern (*see* Modern AD)
    partitions, 385, 386
    patterns, 15–18
    permissions, 107, 108
    problems, 2
    replication, 349
        SMTP-based, 60
    transitioning (*see* Transitioning to modern AD)
Active Directory Certificate Services (ADCS), 362
Active Directory Management Framework (ADMF), 333
Active Directory Rights Management Services (ADRMS), 226, 250
Active Directory Web Services (ADWS), 301
AD, *see* Active directory (AD)

INDEX

AD administration
   ADSIEdit, 318
   tier one operations, 318
   tier zero management, 317
   tier zero operations, 317
ADCS, *see* Active Directory Certificate Services (ADCS)
ADMF, *see* Active Directory Management Framework (ADMF)
AD management, 294
Administration
   AD infrastructure management, 317
   administrative privileges, 314–324
   automation, 325–332
   ESAE, 293, 294
   Helpdesk role, 318
   privileged access, 295–314
Administrative privileges
   AD administration, 317–319
   certificate issuance, 323, 324
   DNS administration, 322, 323
   GPO administration, 319–322
   granular permissions, 315–317
   PKI administration, 323, 324
   Red Forest, 315–317
   task recurrence, 315–317
AdminSDHolder, 134, 319, 323
AD security, 432
ADRMS, *see* Active Directory Rights Management Services (ADRMS)

Advanced Group Policy Management (AGPM), 260
AGDLP, 247
   AGUDLP, 240
   and AUDLP, 240
   authorization groups, 237
   deployment, 238
   domain local groups, 237
   permissions, 238
   process-based resources, 239
   project-based resources, 238
   role groups, 237
   swap folders, 239
AGPM, *see* Advanced Group Policy Management (AGPM)
AGUDLP, 240
Application whitelisting, 152, 312
   See also Windows Defender Application Control (WDAC)
ASA, *see* Alternate Service Account (ASA)
AUDLP, 240, 247
Authentication, 33, 34, 41, 42, 51, 55, 57, 59, 62, 71, 82, 93, 124, 140
   certificate-based, 207–209
   credential, 141, 142
   credential harvesting protection, 161, 162
   engineering, 152–155
   Kerberos, 151–153, 179, 362

LDAP bind, 248
NTLM, 144-147, 341
in perimeter networks (*see* Perimeter networks)
reconnaissance, 143
risk management strategy, 143
service ticket abuse, 162-165
Tier 0 admins, 157-161
Authentication Mechanism Assurance (AMA), 209, 445
Authentication Policy, 225, 307
Authentication Policy Silo, 154
Authorization, 33, 34, 82, 92, 110, 115, 136, 225
ADRMS, 226
automatic classification, 225
DAC (*see* Dynamic access control (DAC))
delegating administrative tasks, 241-247
modern defaults
administrative tasks, 249
bind account, 248
file servers, 248, 249
nested group memberships, 248
RBAC, 247, 248
token, 248
permissions, 227
RBAC, 235-241
SIDs, 225
using authentication policies, 225
Automatic classification, 225

Automation
DSC, 332, 333
on schedule vs. on demand, 325-327
script code signing, 332
sprawl, 331
storing and retrieving credentials, 328-330

B

Backup/restore
AD, 390
anti-patterns, 382-385
archive, 384
DCs, 388, 390-392
GPO, 388
group policies, 388, 389
NTDS.DIT database, 387
replication, 383
restore operation in AD, 385-387
sandbox restore, 390
temporary location, 389
vendors' marketing, 382
VSS BACKUP, 390
WSB, 359, 392, 393
Big Bang (migration), 416
BitLocker, 281, 282, 318, 348
Network Unlock, 282
BlackBerry, 22
BloodHound, 409
Break-glass account, 160, 306, 307, 357

INDEX

C

Center for Internet Security (CIS), 261, 279
Certificate-based authentication
    next-level privileged access, 209–211
Change Advisory Board (CAB), 353
CIS, *see* Center for Internet Security (CIS)
Claims, 154
Cleartext passwords, 142
Client-side extensions (CSEs), 257, 261, 262, 269, 270
Cloud Kerberos, 206
Cloud PAWs, 309, 313, 314
Cloud Sync, 400
Computer accounts
    ADUC, 196
    anti-pattern, 197
    anti-patterns, 196
    authentication, 197
Configuration, 33, 34
    DCs, 270–282
    default containers, 290–292
    domain controllers, 126
    domain join, 282–289
    security principals, 117
Configuration management
    deliver configurations
        behavior-defining attribute, 254
        dial-in attributes, 254
        hardcoded behavior, 252, 253
        information stored in AD objects, 252
        information stored in group policy, 253
        offline files, 254
        operating system, 253
        pre-logon VPN, 254
        roaming profiles, 254
    features, 251
    impact estimation, 251
    lifecycle tracking, 252
    versioning, 252
Constrained delegation, 170
    See also Kerberos
Continental domains, 47
Convergence time, 63, 64
COVID-19, 22, 205
Credentialed vulnerability scan, 380
Credential harvesting, 155–157
CredSSP, 162
Cryptographic Message Syntax (CMS), 329, 330
CSEs, *see* Client-side extensions (CSEs)
Cyber attack, 32, 141
Cyber insurance, 414

D

DAC, *see* Dynamic access control (DAC)
Data Protection API (DPAPI), 347, 415, 434
    backup key, 142, 330, 415

INDEX

Day-to-day operations, 369–374
   configuration drift, 370–373
   IT environments, 370
   sneakernet, 370
   task list, 369
   topology, 373, 374
DCLocator, 59, 69
DCs, *see* Domain controllers (DCs)
DCShadow attack, 116
DDCP, *see* Default Domain
   Controllers Policy (DDCP)
DDI, 70
DDP, *see* Default Domain
   Policy (DDP)
Default behavior, 198–200
Default containers, 290–292
Default Domain Controllers Policy
   (DDCP), 199, 258, 282
Default Domain Policy (DDP), 256,
   258, 264
Delegated Managed Service
   Accounts (dMSA), 16
Delegating administrative tasks
   certificate template, 241
   client administration, 246, 247
   DNS administration, 245
   group policies, 244, 245
   lower tiers, 244
   overpermissioned methods, 242
   permissions/memberships, 242
   server administration, 246
   tier 0 administration, 243
Desired State Configuration (DSC),
   332, 333, 370

Digital workplace strategy, 260
Directory security, 24–26
Directory Service Restore Mode
   (DSRM), 189, 307, 325, 328
Disaster recovery (DR), 281, 282,
   348, 356
   anti-patterns, 396–398
   global effort, 398, 399
   in hybrid AD, 399–403
   operational/organizational, 393
   typology 101, 394–396
Disasters
   cyber breaches, 356
   design options, 356, 358
   DR, 356
   god-mode account, 358
   natural disasters, 356
   tools, 358
Distribution groups, 240, 241
DJOIN command, 203
dMSA, *see* Delegated Managed
   Service Accounts (dMSA)
DMZ, 350
DNS, *see* Domain Name
   System (DNS)
DNS administration, 245, 322, 323
dnsHostName, 103
Document Encryption, 330
   backup, 391
   configuration, 271
   distribution, 71, 72
   foreign functionality, 270
   interactive administration, 299
   PDCe, 64, 273

483

INDEX

Document Encryption (*cont.*)
  RODC, 278
  sizing, 272
Domain controllers (DCs), 3, 31,
    33, 39, 48, 52, 62, 67, 70, 93,
    105, 119, 126, 174, 181, 270
  authentication, 362
  backup, 388, 390–392
  configuration, 271
  deploying, 363
  DFS-N, 270
  distribution, 71, 72
  environment, 296
  foreign functionality, 270
  functions, 271
  hosting, 395
  IFM, 363
  interactive administration, 299
  networking, 272, 273
  NTDS database, 270
  operations, 404
  PDCe, 64, 273–275
  read-write/read-only, 373
  RID pool, 277, 278
  RODC, 278
  RODC, 337, 347
  securing, 278–282
  sizing, 271, 272
  temporary, 361
  writeable, 275–278
  WSB backup, 349
Domain join
  administrator entering
    credentials, 284–286
  monitoring and cleanup, 288
  msDS-MachineAccountQuota, 282
  provisioning scenarios, 283, 284
  removal of default group
    nestings, 289
  restrict access, 286
  types, 284
  VM by third-party system, 286
  workflow, 287
Domain-joined task server, 328
Domain join process, 202–204
Domain members (DCs), 175
Domain Names
  externally resolvable, 58
  namespaces, 55–59
Domain Name System (DNS),
    121, 139
  and abuse, 126, 127
  access restriction, 138, 139
  AD-related records, 128
  bulk access, 125, 126
  in edge networks, 131, 132
  LDAP querying, 132, 133
  and reconnaissance, 123–125
  record creation, 127–129
  security enhancements, 130
  Service record (SRV), 124
  target system, 121
DPAPI, *see* Data Protection
    API (DPAPI)
DR, *see* Disaster recovery (DR)
DSC, *see* Desired State
    Configuration (DSC)

INDEX

Dynamic access control (DAC), 225, 226, 231–233, 235, 249, 250

E

Edge networks, 131, 132
Enhanced Security Admin Environment (ESAE), 39, 157, 293, 294
Enterprise Administrators, 314
Enterprise Domain controller, 114
Enterprise runbook automation, 326
Entra ID, 400–403, 432
Ephemeral jumphosts, 310
ESAE, *see* Enhanced Security Admin Environment (ESAE)

F

Facebook logon, 55
FAST, *see* Flexible Authentication over Secure Tunneling (FAST)
Fast-tracking design
  application, 338
  design proposal, 339, 340
  email domains, 336
  geography and topology, 337
  infrastructure team, 338
  Office programs, 337
  RODC, 337
  security, 340

UPNs, 337
VDI, 338
File Server Resource Manager (FSRM), 235
File servers, 248, 249
Fine-Grained Password Policy (FGPP), 286, 343, 365, 434
Firewalls, 91, 102, 126
Flexible Authentication over Secure Tunneling (FAST), 154
Forest and domain structure
  multi-domain anti-pattern, 46–50
  multi-domain forest, 45, 46
FSMO roles, 45, 357, 392
  distribution, 76–79
Full disaster, 415
Full Volume Encryption (FVE), 281
Function account, 187
Functional monitoring
  AD health, 404, 405
FVE, *see* Full Volume Encryption (FVE)

G

Get-GPOReport, 373
Global Catalog, 45, 46, 53, 72–74, 76, 93, 96, 121
Global DR effort, 398, 399
Globally Unique IDentifiers (GUIDs), 418, 424, 428
gMSA, *see* Group Managed Service Account (gMSA)

485

INDEX

God-like privileges, 116
God-mode account, 299, 358
Golden forest, 317, 344
GPMC, *see* Group Policy Management Console (GPMC)
GPPs, *see* Group policy preferences (GPPs)
GPO administration, 319–322
GPO caching, 269, 270
GPO framework
 baseline, 261–263
 DDP, 264
 enforcement, 264
 individual, 261, 263, 265
 naming convention, 265
 OU structure, 262
 Shopfloor automation, 264
 Trusted Roots, 264
 unintended effect of close linking, 263
Granular permissions, 315–317
Green field, 335
Group Managed Service Account (gMSA), 16, 325, 328–330
Group memberships
 msds-memberOfTransitive, 233, 234
 msds-tokenGroupNames, 234
 msds-tokenGroupNamesGlobalAndUniversal, 234
 msds-tokenGroupNamesNoGCAcceptable, 234

sidHistory, 235
tokenGroups, 234
tokenGroupsGlobalAndUniversal, 234
tokenGroupsNoGCAcceptable, 234
Group Policy, 137, 203, 255
 ADMX, 266
 attack vectors, 259
 CSE, 257
 CSEs, 257
 DDP and DDCP, 258
 for features or applications, 255
 framework, 255
 groupPolicyContainer objects, 256
 Group Policy Management Console, 260, 261
 loopback, 268
  disabled, 268, 269
  merge mode, 268, 269
  replace mode, 268
 object (*see* Group policy objects (GPOs))
 password policy, 258
 performance, 255
 Policy Analyzer, 261
 "Read" rights, 256
 RSoP, 256
 security, 260
 software installation, 257
 Starter GPOs, 267
 SYSVOL permissions, 260

INDEX

wait for network, 270
WMI filter, 255–257, 264, 319
groupPolicyContainer, 320
Group Policy Editor, 245
Group Policy Management
    Console (GPMC), 245,
    260, 261
Group policy
    objects (GPOs), 49
  in AD, 260
  Backup-GPO, 261
  backups, 388
  caching, 269, 270
  central store, 266
  cleartext passwords, 259
  cross-domain/cross-forest
    application, 257
  DCGPOFIX command, 258
  DDP to domain head, 258
  elevation and persistence, 259
  framework, 261–266
  guidelines, 258
  Link GPO, 265
  linking, 267, 268
  local GPO, 257
  loopback policy, 268, 269
  plaintext files, 260
  in SYSVOL, 260
Group policy preferences (GPPs)
  DCs, 292
  FGPP, 286
  ILT, 257
  with ILT, 277
  item-level targeting, 269
  local users and groups, 259
  targeting sites, 275
Groups, 226–235
  Account Operators, 290
  Administrators, 289, 299, 307
  Authenticated Users, 107, 119,
    128, 134, 135, 322
  cross-forest nested, 239
  distribution groups, 241
  DnsAdmins, 128, 245, 323
  Domain Admins, 103, 110, 202,
    204, 246, 289, 321
  Domain Computers, 107
  Domain Guests, 102
  domain local, 45
  Domain Users, 107
  Enterprise Administrators, 314
  Enterprise Admins, 45
  Everyone, 106
  global, 46
  Guests, 102
  memberships, 233–235
  nested, 239
  nested groups *vs.* propagated
    permissions, 227–230
  Pre-Windows 2000 Compatible
    Access, 9, 106, 113–115
  Print Operators, 134
  Protected Users, 6, 159, 171,
    172, 177, 184, 300
  Schema Admins, 314, 316
  Server Operators, 299
  universal, 45
  Users, 289

Groups and object hierarchies
    admins, 227
    folder tree, 226
    NTFS, 226
    permissions, 227
GUIDs, *see* Globally Unique IDentifiers (GUIDs)

H

HVCI, *see* HyperVisor-assisted Code Integrity (HVCI)
Hybrid AD, 399–403
Hybrid identity, 34
Hyper-V clusters, 346
HyperVisor-assisted Code Integrity (HVCI), 280

I

Identity management (IDM) system, 365, 366
IFM, *see* Install From Media (IFM)
ILT, *see* Item-level targeting (ILT)
Immutable laws
    of security, 471
    of security administration, 473
Information Disclosure, 94, 95
In situ modernization
    advantage, 425
    applications, 423–425
    cleanup tasks, 426
    coexistence, 416–418
    compliance purposes, 415

intraforest migration, 427
    schedule, 426
    SID translation, 415
    testing and preflighting, 426
    vs. migration, 418–420
Install From Media (IFM), 363
Interactive administration, 296–301
    hardening administrator sessions, 171, 172
Internet, 40, 58
Internet sources
    engineering administration, 478
    engineering authentication, 476
    engineering authorization, 477
    engineering configuration, 477
    engineering lookup, 476
    engineering topology, 476
    RFCs, 475
Intraforest migration, 427
Invisible privileged identities, 115–119
iPhone, 22
Item-level targeting (ILT)
    filters, 265
    GPPs, 257, 277

J

JEA, *see* Just Enough Administration (JEA)
JIT, *see* Just-In-Time Administration (JIT)

Just Enough Administration
  (JEA), 301
Just-In-Time Administration
  (JIT), 316

K

KDC, *see* Key Distribution
  Center (KDC)
KDC Authentication, 362
KDS Root Keys, 435
Kerberoasting, 142, 163, 165, 195
Kerberos, 147–150, 328
  Alternate Service Account
    (ASA), 179
  armoring, 154
  cloud, 36
  encryption, 166–169, 243, 440
  Keytab file, 179
  preauthentication, 150
  Service for User (S4U), 170
  token, 231, 232
Key Distribution Center (KDC), 149
Knowledge Consistency
  Checker, 66

L

LAPS, 152, 198, 247, 249, 297, 318
LDAP, *see* Lightweight Directory
  Access Protocol (LDAP)
Lightweight Directory Access
  Protocol (LDAP), 94, 350,
  354, 355

Link Local Multicast Name
  Resolution (LLMNR),
  121, 122
List Object mode, 112, 113, 135,
  136, 426
LLMNR, *see* Link Local Multicast
  Name Resolution (LLMNR)
Location attribute, 69, 91
LSA protection, 280

M

Malicious actor, 415
Management jumphost, 360
Management Summary, 339
MaxTokenSize, 231
Mergers and acquisitions
  anatomy of, 429–432
  divestment, 432–435
  identity infrastructure, 429
Microsoft Defender for Identity, 35
MicrosoftDNS container, 322
Microsoft Identity Manager
  (MIM), 12
Migration, 418–420
  AD, 415
  application, 419
  applications, 423–425
  big bang (*see* Big Bang
    (migration))
  computer, 419
  definition, 420
  definitions, 418
  due to domain rename, 56

INDEX

Migration (*cont.*)
    group, 419
    intraforest, 418, 427
    low-friction, 425
    mergers and
        acquisitions, 429–435
    partial scenarios, 425
    people and processes, 435, 436
    post-cyber incident, 415
    rejuvenation, 428
    rich coexistence, 416
    status, 416
    user, 419
    user first/application
        first, 420–423
    user-first approach, 427
MIM, *see* Microsoft Identity
    Manager (MIM)
Modern AD, 94, 439, 441
    application developers, 353, 355
    automation, 27, 28
    change, 30
    changes in requirements *vs.*
        changes in infrastructure,
        352, 353
    cloud first, 413
    cloud integration, 34–37
    DCs, 363
    deploying applications, 363
    deployment, 359
    design defaults, 82, 83
    directory security, 24–26
    disaster, 31, 356–359
    exceptions, 29
    fast-tracking design, 336–340
    functional monitoring, 403–408
        sensors, 403
        tier 0, 405–408
    green field, 335
    greenfield, 366
    IT organization, 23
    onboarding
        applications, 364, 365
        users, 365, 366
    operations (*see* Operations,
        modern AD)
    PKI, 361, 362
    policies, 28, 29
    prerequisites, 345–351
    production objects, 425
    proof of concept, 355
    Red Forest, 361, 362
    remote seeding cells, 360, 361
    requirements, 21
    risky sites, 88
    SaaS, 355
    security, 27
        deal with insecure
            applications, 341, 342
        domain local groups, 343
        golden forest, 344
        GPOs, 344
        operational paradigm, 342
        Red Forest, 345
        Shadow Principals, 343
    security monitoring, 408–411
        behavior-based, 410, 411
    seeding cell, 359

site topology, 83–86
tenets, 26
test environment, 347
well-engineered framework, 353
work requirements, 22–24
Modern defaults
  computers, 136, 137
  DNS access restriction, 138, 139
  Kerberos defaults, 220
  non-privileged users, 135, 136
  password policy
    defaults, 219–221
  privileged access defaults, 221
  read permissions restrictions, 134, 135
  SELF permissions, 137
  service account, 221
  session protection, 221
Multi-domain forest, 395, 427
  anatomy, 45, 46
  anti-pattern, 46–50
  challenges, 53–55
  extreme anti-patterns, 50–52
  motivation, 52, 53
Murphy's Law, 397

N

NAC, *see* Network Access Control (NAC)
Naming convention, 59, 192
Nested groups *vs.* propagated permissions
  explicit assignment, 228

  on multiple levels, 229
  with nested
    memberships, 229
  high-privileged users, 230
  lowest-level folders, 230
  management models, 227, 228
  permissions inheritance, 230
NetBIOS, 47, 121, 122, 344, 428
Network Access Control (NAC), 41
Network Time Protocol (NTP), 351
NOKIA Communicator, 22
Non-privileged users, 109, 135, 136, 164
NotPetya malware, 357
NTAuth container, 324
NTDS database, 386
NTDSUTIL, 394
NTLM, 144–147, 341, 439
  applications, 178
  authentication flow, 180, 181
  Domain Controllers, 181
  getting rid of, 173, 177
  knowledge, 182
  logging, 181
  SMB, 183
  SYSTEM process, 183
  usage, 184

O

OpenSSH, 302
Operations, modern AD
  DR, 393–403
  end of lifecycle, 378, 379

INDEX

Operations, modern AD (*cont.*)
 exceptional
  requirements, 375–378
 platform components, 374, 375
 security operations, 379–381
Organizational unit (OU), 98
 AD administrators, 103
 as LDAP BaseDN, 99, 101
 structure, 99–103
OUs, *see* Organizational unit (OUs)

P, Q

Password Hash Sync (PHS), 357
Password policy, 258
PAW, *see* Privileged access
  workstation (PAW)
PDCe, *see* PDC emulator (PDCe)
PDC emulator (PDCe), 64, 65,
  273–275, 351, 404
PEN, *see* Private Enterprise
  Number (PEN)
Penetration Test, 380, 381
Perimeter networks, 131
 logon, 216, 217
 user access, 217, 218
Permissions
 granularity, 103–105
 installation-level, 364
 replication rights, 105
 write, 237
PHS, *see* Password Hash
  Sync (PHS)
Platform backup, 348

Policy Analyzer, 261
PowerShell, 183, 300, 301, 332
Prerequisites
 global WAN, 345
 permanent and temporary
  networks, 349, 350
 storage and backup, 347–349
 test environment, 346
 time source, 350
Private Enterprise Number
  (PEN), 210
Privileged access
 break-glass account, 306, 307
 concept, 295
 interactive
  administration, 296–301
 jumphosts, 309, 310
 network access, 295
 PAW, 307–314
 remote administration
  protocol, 301–303
 remote-interactive, 303–306
 security, 295
 service tickets, 295
Privileged Access Management,
  117, 185
Privileged access workstation
  (PAW), 294
 AlwaysOn VPN, 311
 BIOS, 311
 Cloud PAWs, 309, 313, 314
 deployment, 312, 313
 deployment options, 307
 direct administration, 308

492

INDEX

hardware, 312
Internet, 311
keylogger, 311
management, 313
patterns and anti-patterns, 307
RDP, 310
RunAs, 309, 310
SCAMA, 308
third-party EDR/XDR, 313
Protect-CMSMessage, 330
Public Key Infrastructure (PKI), 130, 361, 362
administration, 323, 324
autoenrollment, 324
CDP, 133, 323, 362
configuration, 389
CRL, 133
infrastructure, 324
modern defaults, 222
OCSP, 133, 164, 323, 362, 389, 404
deterministic revocation checking, 323

R

Ransomware attack, 395
RBAC, *see* Role-based access control (RBAC) models)
RCE, *see* Remote code execution (RCE)
RCG, *see* Remote credential guard (RCG)
RDP, *see* Remote Desktop Protocol (RDP)
Read-Only Domain Controller (RODC), 18, 72, 79–81, 84, 278, 337, 347
Reconnaissance, 40, 94, 95, 123
Recycle Bin, 385–387, 427, 434
Red Forest, 81, 82, 315–317, 322, 339, 345, 361, 362
Rejuvenation migration, 428
Remote administration
benefits, 296
protocol, 301–303
Remote code execution (RCE), 152
Remote credential guard (RCG), 303–305
Remote Desktop Protocol (RDP), 303–305, 309, 310
Remote-interactive
administration mode, 304
RCG, 303–305
RDP, 303–305
restricted admin, 303, 304
Remote procedure call (RPC), 300
Remote seeding cells, 360, 361
Remote Server Administration Toolkit (RSAT), 1
Resource-based constrained delegation (RBCD), 170
Resultant Set of Policy (RSoP), 256, 257, 262, 268, 270
caching, 269
RFC, 475
Rich coexistence, 428
RID Master, 63, 88, 277

INDEX

RODC, see Read-Only Domain Controller (RODC)
Role-based access control (RBAC) models, 247, 248
    AGDLP, 237–240
    AGUDLP, 240
    AUDLP, 240
    distribution groups, 240, 241
    multiple roles, 236
    resources, 235
RSAT, see Remote Server Administration Toolkit (RSAT)
RSoP, see Resultant Set of Policy (RSoP)

S

SaaS, see Software as a Service (SaaS)
sAMAccountName, 424
SAML, 1
SCAMA, 209, 295, 308, 323, 343, 371, 434
Schema permissions, 119, 120
SDHolder, 300, 323
SDPROP, 128, 241, 273, 300
SecureBoot, 280
Secure SHell (SSH), 302
Securing DCs
    BitLocker, 282
    hardening, 278
    LSA protection, 280
    RPC, 278
    SYSVOL share hardening, 279

Security, 27, 39, 40, 44, 49, 55, 73
    enhancements, 130
    object classes, 119
    permissions, 103
    principal, 107
Security Compliance Toolkit (SCT), 261
Security identifiers (SIDs), 225, 231, 232, 234, 241, 248, 250, 417, 424, 428, 435
Security monitoring
    attack path analysis, 409, 410
    attack surface monitoring, 408, 409
    using functional monitoring, 410
Security operations
    backup and restore, 382–393
    penetration test, 380
    penetration tests, 381
    scans, 380, 381
    system hardening, 380
Segal's law, 351
Server Core, 296
Service and task accounts, 184
    administrator, 188
    documentation, 189
    gMSA, 191
    identification, 193–195
    naming convention, 192
    password, 189
    remote automation, 188
    rotating accounts, 191
    service principal, 187
    SPNs, 190

INDEX

task account, 186
typology, 185–187, 190
Windows service account, 186
Service Principal Name (SPN), 103, 151, 164
Service tickets, 169–171
Shadow Principals, 308, 343, 434
sidHistory, 417, 418, 421, 423, 424
SIDs, *see* Security identifiers (SIDs)
Simple Network Management Protocol (SNMP), 405
Single-domain forest, 44, 395, 431
Single Sign-On (SSO), 156
Sites, 60–62, 83–86, 96
    autonomy, 40–43
    guiding principles, 66–68
    links, 89–91
    multi-forest organization, 69–71
    name and location attribute, 68, 69
    satellite, 62, 88
    spoke, 62
Smart Card Authentication, 362, 389
SMB, 301
SNMP, *see* Simple Network Management Protocol (SNMP)
SOC's behavior-based monitoring, 410, 411
Software as a Service (SaaS), 355
SPN, *see* Service Principal Name (SPN)
Spoke-hub connectivity, 86–88

SSO, *see* Single Sign-On (SSO)
Starter GPOs, 267
Subnet, 60–62
    guiding principles, 66–68
    multi-forest organization, 69–71
    name and location attribute, 68, 69
Swap folders, 239
SYSVOL
    GPO, 260, 269
    share hardening, 279

T

Tabletop gameplay, 397
Task recurrence, 315–317
Task Scheduler, 325, 327
Test environment, 346, 347, 380
TGT, *see* Ticket Granting Ticket (TGT)
Ticket Granting Ticket (TGT), 148, 149, 152
Tier 0
    administrators, 157–161
Time-to-live (TTL), 118
Token bloat, 231
    data structures, 231
    delegation model and granularity, 233
    groups limit, 241
    Kerberos token, 231, 232
    LSA token, 231–233
    MaxTokenSize, 231
    SID compression, 232

Token bloat (*cont.*)
  sidHistory, 231
  sidHistory, 232
  size and restrictions, 231
tokenGroups, 248
Tombstone Lifetime, 385
Topology, 96, 373, 374, 431
  AD organization, 39
  AD partitions, 42
  defaults, 65, 66
  ERP application, 41, 42
  hub site, 62
  information, 96
  remote domains, 360
  single-domain forest, 44 (*see also* Single-domain forest)
  site, 96
  site autonomy, 40–43
  site-local forests, 43
  spoke site, 62
  WAN, 39, 352, 353
TPM, *see* Trusted Platform Module (TPM)
Transitioning to modern AD
  authentication and configuration, 413
  cyber insurance, 414
  rejuvenation migration, 428
  security incident, 414
  in situ modernization, 415–427
Trust, 45, 81, 211, 231, 362
  anti-patterns, 214, 215
  authentication, 212
  defaults, 222
  direction, 212, 213
  hardening, 53, 119, 214
  one-way, 53, 119, 294
  PIM, 117, 362
  shortcut, 51
  SID History, 212
  transitivity, 213
Trusted Platform Module (TPM), 161, 221, 281, 312, 348, 359, 375
TTL, *see* Time-to-live (TTL)

U

UAC, *see* User account control (UAC)
UEFI, 280
Universal Group Membership Caching, 73, 275, 276
Unprotect-CMSMessage, 330
UPN, *see* User Principal Name (UPN)
User account control (UAC), 296, 299
User Principal Name (UPN), 47, 53, 55, 179, 337, 339, 402, 417, 424
  suffix routing, 53

V

VBS, *see* Virtualization-Based Security (VBS)
Virtualization-Based Security (VBS), 161, 280, 303, 375

Virtual machine (VM), 162, 310
VM, *see* Virtual machines (VM)
VMware, 29, 187, 283, 351

W, X, Y

WAN, 17, 40–43, 65, 71, 77, 337, 345, 391
   bandwidth, 71
WDAC, *see* Windows Defender Application Control (WDAC)
Windows 95, 255
Windows Defender Application Control (WDAC), 312
Windows NT, 30, 103, 106, 143, 153, 255
   domain, 3, 64, 109, 113, 150

Windows Server Backup (WSB), 348, 359
   backups, 392, 393
   restored machine, 348
WinRM, 300, 301
WMI, 123, 128, 193, 300
   filter, 96, 99, 244, 255, 264, 319, 321
WSB, *see* Windows Server Backup (WSB)

Z

Zero-touch attack, 23
Zero Trust
   access, 35, 40
   techniques, 441

GPSR Compliance

The European Union's (EU) General Product Safety Regulation (GPSR) is a set of rules that requires consumer products to be safe and our obligations to ensure this.

If you have any concerns about our products, you can contact us on

ProductSafety@springernature.com

In case Publisher is established outside the EU, the EU authorized representative is:

Springer Nature Customer Service Center GmbH
Europaplatz 3
69115 Heidelberg, Germany

www.ingramcontent.com/pod-product-compliance
Lightning Source LLC
LaVergne TN
LVHW010332260326
834688LV00036B/672